Continuities in Cultural Evolution

D0221772

Continuities in Cultural Evolution

Margaret Mead

with a new introduction by
Stephen Toulmin

Transaction Publishers
New Brunswick (U.S.A.) and London (U.K.)

Library of Congress Catalog Number: 99-17824
ISBN: 0-7658-0604-5
Printed in the United States of America

Library of Congress Cataloging-in-Publication Data

Mead, Margaret, 1901–1978.
  Continuities in cultural evolution / Margaret Mead ; with a new introduction by Stephen Toulmin.
      p. cm.
  Originally published: New Haven, Conn. : Yale University Press, 1964. With new introd., in series: Terry lectures
  Includes bibliographical references and index.
  ISBN 0-7658-0604-5 (pbk.)
  1. Social change. I. Title.
HM101.M37   1999
303.4—dc21   99-17824
                                                                    CIP

For Nora Barlow and her children
—my living links with Darwin

Contents

List of Illustrations

Introduction to the Transaction Edition

CALLING Margaret Mead an anthropologist is like calling Abraham Lincoln a lawyer: a crucial half-truth. At a time when scholars were narrowing their focus of attention, and defining the scope of their subjects in terms that cut them off from all others, she was more interested in exploring the intellectual territories adjoining her own field of study than in shutting herself up inside a "pure" discipline. The profession of law led Abraham Lincoln out of the Midwest, into national politics and the presidency, and his legal principles finally convinced him about the justice and political necessity of emancipation. If Margaret Mead's legacy is relevant and absorbing for us today, it is because she never sought to fence off anthropology, to protect it from adulteration by (say) biology or psychology. Least of all did her robust good sense allow her to believe that the human sciences must remain *value free*, to avoid being contaminated by ethical or political preferences. (We cannot allow such methodological arguments to override truths we all feel on our pulses.)

What was the point of studying the lives of peoples in other countries, unless these studies could teach us something about the ways we ourselves live? Whether in Bali or Sudan, Montenegro, Samoa or British Columbia, we come to understand things about other human lives that can influence the ways in which we direct our own lives, shape our arts, or organize our societies. Taking care to understand the variety to be found in other peoples' ideas and practices, indeed, will only improve our ways of dealing with ethical, cultural, and political issues in our own situations.

Morally serious anthropologists, then, do not look at other peoples *de haut en bas*, from the standpoint of superior persons. Margaret Mead did not regard the people of Samoa as "primitive" and wholly different from us: we learn about our own practices by reflecting on their likenesses with, and differences from, those of other peoples. Nor need anthropologists maintain the detached objectivity of the ornithologist who watches birds from a hide: recording the habits of other tribes without their noticing. Instead, she set out to decipher the significance of the customs she studied by sharing the lives of the people she studied: pioneering what we call *participant observation*.

For Immanuel Kant, the term *anthropology* embraced all the human sciences, and laid the foundation of familiar knowledge we need, to build solidly grounded ideas about the moral and political demands of human life. Margaret Mead saw mid-twentieth-century anthropology as engaged in a project no less ambitious than Kant's own, and her Terry Lectures on *Continuities in Cultural Evolution* provide an excellent point to enter into her reflections.

She gave the Lectures at Yale University in 1957, though they were not published until 1964, after extensive reworking. The time she spent on the revision is evidence of the importance she attached to their topic: the need to develop a truly *evolutionary* vision of human culture and society. This was desirable, in her eyes, both in order to reinforce the historical dimension in our ideas about human culture, and to keep in the front of our mind the relevance of historical and cultural diversity to social, economic and political action. Re-reading her lectures today, in the light of our own intellectual or political situation, it is hard to think of any work in the human sciences dating from the twenty years after World War II whose republication is more timely. Given the present state of academic and public discourse alike, Margaret Mead's Terry Lectures speak to us in a language we badly need to recover.

* * * * *

If Mead did not fully accept the value-neutrality of the social sciences, neither did she fully conform to other widely accepted procedures of anthropological research. From Malinowski on, this research focussed on the internal relations within a culture at a particular time: the standard method of analysis—as the saying went—was to be "synchronic" not "diachronic." So, anthropologists tended to make a single field trip to a chosen locale, to study the ways in which the elements in a people's customs and beliefs hung together and threw light on one another. At the same time, they hoped those relations might illuminate, also, the synchronic relations within other people's lives and cultures. So began the theoretical tradition that culminated, in the 1970s, in Clifford Geertz's program for analyzing "cultural systems."

Conversely, few anthropologists in the 1950s paid attention to "diachronic" issues: the ways that cultures change from year to year, or decade to decade. This choice of method was in some respects patronizing. At first, many anthropologists also served as officers of the colonial powers, and they naturally assumed that historical change was a feature of the developed countries of Europe and America— what we now call *the North*. By contrast, primitive peoples presumably lived conservative lives, with customs that had immemorial beginnings. As a starting point for research, these may be legitimate assumptions, but they conceal some important questions. Could a tribe, e.g., survive for any length of time in the state of conflict Turnbull reported in the Ik? Or were the Ik undergoing violent historical changes in the years when Turnbull was anthropologizing them? Such "diachronic" questions were at any rate worth asking.

Margaret Mead's curiosity and imagination were too broad and free to ignore such issues. Her collaboration with Gregory Bateson put her in touch with the most lively and original circles of evolutionary biologists and psycholinguists in her time; and, as time went on, she showed a remarkable ability to assemble scholars and scientists from many disciplines, and catalyze discussions of child development, crosscultural interaction or a dozen other interdisciplinary topics. Gregory Bateson's father William, furthermore, was himself a major biologist: one of the founders of twentieth-century genetics. So, Margaret could not ignore the problems raised by Darwin, nor was she tempted to do so. The sixteen chapters of this book testify to that. They give a good picture of the issues about the "evolution" of human cultures that were being actively considered forty years ago: the questions they pose are as urgent for us now as then, even though our present intellectual and practical situation is different.

* * * * *

At this point, a warning is in order. As an umbrella word, "evolution" covers a wide range of different issues which had been topics of vigorous, contentious debate throughout the nineteenth century. All these issues had to do with the links between corresponding "units" in Nature or Society at different historical times: beyond that, they were very varied.

Some of them focused on the *direction* of historical change. Johann Gottfried Herder, for instance, transformed "the Great Chain of Being" from being a timeless vision of *co-existing* complexities in Nature—ranging from lifeless objects, by way of vegetables and animals, up to rational humans—into an historical account of *successive* phases or cultures. His own vision of "the Chain of Cultures" was to dominate nineteenth-century social philosophy, *via* Hegel and Marx, to Durkheim and Weber. Even today sociologists and historians, writing about *social and cultural evolution* with the experience of Europe in mind, still think of History as tracing out a standard sequence—ancient, medieval, early modern, modern, and contemporary—in turn. But Herder's historical vision at once raised questions about Progress: Are the later phases in this sequence *improvements* on earlier ones? By what standards can Modernity (say) be considered *better than* Antiquity? In posing questions of this kind, Auguste Comte in France and Herbert Spencer in England launched academic sociology on a "progressivist" research program.

Other questions about "evolution" are neutral as between the merits and defects of successive phases. Charles Darwin was keen to find the processes by which distinct organic species emerge from the successive generations of their ancestors' offspring. He wrote about the *Origin of Species* (that is) as the outcome of variation and natural selection *in particular habitats*: what we call "speciation." Being human himself, he understood that special skills and capacities mark humans off from their ancestors— e.g., those associated with language, and the use of tools— but nothing in his theory of speciation assumed that later species had to be "improvements on" their ancestors. Many evolutionary processes in fact show the opposite: processes in which variation and natural selection result in the *loss* of previously functional organs and activities. (Species of fish that live in subterranean waterways have rudimentary eyes, though these are no longer operative.) In the vision of Nature we call Darwinism, however, one particular feature stands out. Distinct species "evolve" only in habitats where the variant populations are so completely separated from their ancestors that they will no longer interbreed in the wild. So long as such cross-breeding continues, by contrast, what we observe is not the evolution of new Darwinian "species," but the appearance of new "races" of humans, "breeds" of dogs, or "varieties" of plants.

When anthropologists speak of *cultures* as "evolving" (then) two preparatory questions need to be clarified:

1. Are they, like Herder, theorizing in *progressivist* terms? Or are they, like Darwin, discussing the *origin* of novel cultural forms by variation, isolation and differentiation in specialized habitats? Or again: are they analyzing their subjects in ways that combine these two methods of approach?

2. In each case, what do they take as the *units* of evolutionary change?

Here Margaret Mead's discussion is very helpful, notably as regards question (2): see, e.g., chapter 8 on the units of cultural micro-evolution. For historical reasons, however, her discussion of question (1) is a bit dated: evolutionary biology has come a long way since 1960. She gave the Terry Lectures at a time when all of the natural sciences were about to face the emergence of *molecular* biology, which has affected our ideas about organic evolution quite as deeply as it has done the rest of biology. How, we may ask, would this have changed Mead's Terry Lectures?

Elsewhere, the Lectures show that she was well aware of the other problems that face the anthropologist in pursuing evolutionary lines of thought. When talking about cultural evolution, for instance, we cannot treat cultures as evolving from each other in just the way that "species" evolve from each other. It is not that the terms *evolve* and *evolution* are downright ambiguous: speaking of species or cultures as *evolving* is not just a play upon words. On the contrary, both sets of issues concern the ways in which the bodily structures of organic species, or the historically changing patterns of human activity, are "adaptive" to the demands of a given habitat. At one extreme, they may be *adaptive* as an outcome of purely genetic changes, at the other for purely historical reasons, but many intermediate features can involve both culturally acquired habits and genetically transmitted structures.

By the 1990s, we can see how hard it can be to tell genetically transmitted features from cultural features. Identical twins born in Ecuador may end up flat- chested if they are raised at sea level, pigeon-chested if they are raised on the plateau of the *Altiplano*: conversely, many East Asians lose a taste for milk after infancy through a genetically based lactose intolerance. Romance languages, too, evolved from Latin, and each other, when the *patois* current in neighboring regions were no longer intelligible to people across (say) a mountain range: once this happened, they separated from each other for the same reason as variant species living in distinct habitats.

So, pragmatically minded anthropologists keep a variety of intellectual methods in their quivers: organic and cultural evolution are not as different as we have tended to think. Indeed, the question is even raised today, whether the young Charles Darwin was not led to think about "adaptation and natural selection" as much on account of his cultural studies of human populations in Tierra del Fuego as by his subsequent zoological observations of finches and tortoises in the Galapagos.

* * * * *

None of this would have been a surprise to Margaret Mead. She did not work on cultural anthropology for the sake of developing a theoretically "neat" science alone. Her interests were always practical: directed toward a comprehensive, broadly based understanding of human life, which found room for all its varied dimensions, and so gave us the ground we need to guide our lives, our arts, and our societies. When she set out to define the "units" of cultural micro-evolution, for instance, these *units* were not just abstract theoretical notions: they were meant to make sound practical sense of her experience in the field as an observer of, and participant in, the lives of a people.

She did not seek to develop a systematic classification of all cultural groups, or set out—like Balzac—to be the "Linnaeus" of Society or Culture. On the contrary, she knew that the bonds which unite members of any social "unit" have a political as well as a taxonomic point. Cultural and social groups are defined in terms of their shared ideals or ambitions: to accept this definition is implicitly to endorse their ambitions. Consider the parties of schoolchildren who daily troop through the National Museum of Anthropology in Mexico City: they enter as unself-conscious Toltecs or Zapotecs, but they leave as self-conscious Mexicans.

This does not make nations or tribes or clans or sects any less effective as foci of loyalty and organization. Theological ideas unite the Wahabi of Saudi Arabia and the Taliban of Afghanistan, but religious commitments differ in kind from genealogical bonds like those of the Campbells or the MacGregors, or the intellectual interests of high-energy physicists. Any part of the globe, any period in human history, and any professional activity, develops its own criteria of *unity*: the units of cultural evolution are thus redefined as our attention shifts from the Tuareg of the Sahara or the Marsh Arabs of the Euphrates Delta, to either the Aborigines of Australia or the members of the United Mineworkers Union.

In our own time, we see fresh "cultures" emerging, united by ideals of kinds that Margaret Mead would surely welcome. In the 1990s the system of Nation States that has defined our politics and diplomacy for three centuries is falling apart at the seams. National loyalty threatens international destruction: famine, disease, or environmental degradation ignores State frontiers. For many people today, the humanitarian need to help the starving and the diseased everywhere and the moral imperative to condemn torture or insist on human rights in all lands, quite as much as demands to respect the global environment, provide foci of loyalty that are as demanding as, and may even outweigh, the claims of Nationalism and State Sovereignty.

Nongovernmental organizations (NGOs) like the International Committee of the Red Cross, Amnesty, and Greenpeace work transnationally. They recruit subscribers and field workers from a pool of like-minded people, regardless of their nationality or citizenship. Their activities are not submitted to governmental control or censorship: they insist on challenging the activities of nation states or business corporations alike. They, too, form a new Culture. So, at this point, the study of cultural evolution leads us through yet another door, into the field traditionally known as "political" theory.

* * * * *

Margaret Mead (I said earlier) spoke a language that we badly need to recover in the present state of academic and public discourse. For her, anthropology was always (so to speak) a *clinical* science. Her aim was not to create a narrowly theoretical field, with its own abstract terminology or battery of "value-free" issues: rather, it was to refine her insights into the lives of the people she lived among, and whose way of life she came to understand through living with them. So in her case it is harder than it is with many scholars or scientists to distinguish her academic and scholarly views from her moral and political ones. By reflecting on all she taught us on this level of clinical understanding, we may thus see more clearly how much we lost by way of *phronesis*—or practical wisdom—in the course of the last thirty years.

I recall Margaret Mead as standing, politically, for New Deal attitudes of kinds that have lost ground to the conservatism of the 1980s and 1990s. (At times, I find it hard to disentangle my recollections of her from my memories about Eleanor Roosevelt.) If she were with us, she would play a leading part in the debates about welfare reform or gun control, as well as the current epidemic of prison building. She would rightly remind us of all the evidence about the wastefulness and inefficiency—above all, the inhumanity—of incarceration: can we not learn this much at any rate from the history of punishment, and the experience of other countries? Working in the government in World War II, again, she did all that she could to keep American social policy shaped by an understanding of all the peoples with whom this country was engaged: in Asia and the Pacific as well as in Europe. (This understanding reached deeply into foreign policy, too: looking back from the 1990s to J. William Fulbright and the other giants of mid-century America, we cannot help being a bit envious.)

For ten or fifteen years after 1945, these liberal attitudes continued to play a part, but, by the mid-1970s, cold war pressures were having an effect: laying a basis for the neoconservative reaction against the counterculture of the 1960s and the Vietnam protests. Taking slogans from Leo Strauss, a generation of polemicists arose (e.g., Allan Bloom) who denounced history and anthropology as Pied Pipers that distract the electorate from the Eternal Truths of political philosophy, and lead them into the quagmires of historicism and relativism. As the cold war reached its climax, these writers saw no other way to fight the doctrinal rigidity of the Soviet Union than to make Western thought an equally rigid doctrinal system. In their view, wise policy was based not on sympathetic understanding of the full diversity of cultures, societies or peoples, but on a political demand that other peoples acknowledge that America's leadership is indispensable, and its economic and cultural theories uniquely correct.

In the 1990s, as the mid-twentieth-century Soviet Empire fades into memory, the limits of neoconservatism are beginning to show themselves. The events of 1989 have freed us to meditate on the wisdom of Margaret Mead's feeling for the relevance of cultural diversity to all aspects of human life. Meanwhile, the unhappy effects of economic reform, based on universal economic principles, are encouraging the World Bank—if not, so far, the International Monetary Fund—to broaden their analysis in ways that make room for the cultural diversity Margaret Mead so well understood.

*   *   *   *   *

Reviving an evolutionary approach to the human sciences, as Margaret Mead here proposes, does not merely free us from the political constraints of neoconservatism: it also frees our scientific ways of thinking about human life and mental activity from the formalism into which they sank in the 1970s.

Theories of Mind and Society have for long swung between two extremes. At one pole, social organization and mental activity are explained as outcomes of our bodily make up: we act as we do because we are made as we are. At the other pole, they are explained as outcomes of the influence of external agents, beginning with the family: we act as we do because all these agencies cause us to do so. (This contrast is often referred to using the phrase, *Nature vs. Nurture*.) Neither approach has much to say about *spontaneous* action. Both find *causes* to explain our activities: in the one case, internal, physiological causes; in the other, external, social, or psychological causes—control by family members, or the seductions of advertisers.

The former account—"Nature"—leaves no room for cultural variation: our brains and bodies are as they are because of our inherited make-up, and Culture does little to affect them. The other account—"Nurture"—allots Culture a larger role: we act as we learn to act, at home or at school, or in the world of social, cultural, and economic exchanges and transactions. In this intellectual pendulum swing, the years either side of World War II gave special weight to Nurture or Culture. This is true of American ideas of child rearing or conditioning, as developed by B.F. Skinner, of the German tradition of *Volkspsychologie* (or crosscultural psychology) inherited from Wilhelm Wundt, and also of the ideas of concept formation and language devised in Russia by Pavlov, Vygotsky, and Luria. America's own home-grown tradition in psychology is the most *nurture-*oriented of all these: Wundt's work on sensory discrimination took its roots from the physiology of Müller and Helmholtz, while Pavlov and Luria both paid just as much attention to neuroanatomy as they did to conditioning.

The shift of emphasis since 1970, by which linguistic, social, and cultural activity came to be seen as expressions of anatomical structures and neurological processes—downplaying Nurture, in favor of Nature—was thus a major change of academic perspective. On the one side, Noam Chomsky suggested that the rules of "deep" grammar are embodied in inherited mechanisms, and dismissed Darwin as irrelevant to the problems about language and culture: "Anyone who asks about 'evolutionary precursors' of language [as he insisted] does not understand what Language is." On the other, the neurophysiologist Jean-

Pierre Changeux writes a best-selling book called *L'homme neuronale* (*Neuronal man*). In his eyes, all the problems of cultural life are scientifically intelligible, only if they exemplify neurophysiological processes that we understand. Meanwhile, the dominant school in American economic theory argues that all economic agents share the same preferences, tastes or *utilities*: if we find economic transactions differing from culture to culture, that indicates only that we do not yet understand how such transactions serve our universal preferences.

* * * * *

It is time for the tide to turn. In scientific theory, as in practical life, we need to recover the courage of our convictions and insist on the reality of cultural diversity. To assume that our institutions have a common structure in all countries and epochs, so that the experience of one people can be transplanted to all other peoples, just as it stands—as the current fad for "the market economy" assumes—will cause us a lot more trouble before we are through.

Far from being Pied Pipers, history and anthropology are in fact indispensable. Just how a *market* operates in Bangladesh or Mongolia, Bolivia or Burundi, depends on the cultural, social, or political histories of the four countries. It was the genius of Muhammad Yunus that led him to rethink the economics he had learned at Vanderbilt University, in the light of the real life transactions he found going on in the markets at Chittagong: this alone made possible the cultural innovations of the Grameen Bank. If Dr. Yunus can now provide credit even to the poorest of the poor, it is not because he introduced new methods of bookkeeping: it is because his Bank is an institution of a novel kind, which operates in a way that hardly any bank had done before. He created it as he did, because he saw that the economic theory of finance and banking, and the assumptions it embodied about the nature of "the market," took for granted historical facts about economic exchange as it had evolved down the centuries, from Augsburg to London, Milan and New York. It took *anthropological* imagination for him to put flesh on the abstract theories he had been taught in America, and so make them relevant to the situation in Bangladesh. He was a successful banker *in practice*– in other words—because he had *also* learned to think like a cultural anthropologist. (It is a story Margaret Mead would have relished.)

Similar lessons can be learned about the Family or the State, Power or Religion, Festivals or Authority. None of these are usefully discussed in Platonist terms, as though they exist in one and only one form at any place or time. Recall the opening words of Leo Tolstoy's *Anna Karenina*, "All happy families are alike, every unhappy family is unhappy in its own way": to this, experience might have led Tolstoy to add, "and there are no *totally* happy families, either." If we wish to understand culture and society, abstract theories alone will never be enough. Anthropological studies of a wide range of particular cases will also be indispensable; and we can hardly do better than start by re-reading the writings of Margaret Mead.

Stephen Toulmin

Preface

MY INTEREST in evolution was reawakened in 1948, when I was asked to review *Touchstone for Ethics*[1] and, while I was doing so, also took time to reread *The Origin of Species*.[2] This reading in turn reawakened memories of discussions, in the mid-1930s, about science and ethics with C. H. Waddington[3] and Gregory Bateson.[4] Renewed interest in the study of animal behavior, an interest which I owe originally to Kingsley Noble[5] and Ray Carpenter,[6] was stimulated by contacts with Konrad Lorenz in the World Health Organization Study Group on the Psycho-biological Development of the Child,[7] and later by work with both American and European students of comparative animal behavior in the Macy Conferences on Group Processes.[8]

Two pieces of writing—*Male and Female*,[9] written in 1948, and "Cultural Determinants of Sexual Behavior," first written in 1950 for the compendium, *Sex and Internal Secretions*[10]—which I was able to discuss extensively with Evelyn Hutchinson, focused my attention on the need to integrate more specifically our knowledge of man's species-characteristic behavior, the peculiarities introduced by domestication, and our knowledge of cultural evolution. An invitation to participate in the second of two Symposia on Behavior and Evolution, organized by Anne Roe and George Simpson in 1955,[11] created the necessary focus. I found then that I had to go back over the whole question of appropriate units for the study of cultural evolution to the inquiries begun in organizing *Cooperation and Com-*

petition among Primitive Peoples,[12] to *Naven,*[13] and to
discussions with Gregory Bateson, Lawrence K. Frank, and
J. H. Woodger in the summer of 1939, and to the attempt
to define a unit for the study of cultural patterning of
nutrition in the "Manual for the Study of Food Habits," [14]
in 1945. I found that the preparation of my paper for the
Symposium on Behavior and Evolution, "Cultural Determinants of Behavior," [15] which in its published form is
essentially the ground plan for this book, also involved a
re-examination of the field methodology I had used from
the beginning of my field work in 1925, when, without
any full recognition of why it was necessary, I had begun
to specify every individual member of the culture I was
studying individually, contextually, and socially.[16] In preparing the papers of Ruth Benedict for publication,[17] I
went back to my notes on Franz Boas' lectures, and I found
that in these lectures, so many of which were devoted to
clearing away the stupid underbrush of nineteenth-century
arguments based on ethnocentric superiority or insistence
on identifying evolution as a particular form of progress,
a sufficient ground plan had been worked out for taking
up the discussion of cultural evolution.[18]

The invitation to give the Terry Lectures at Yale University in the autumn of 1957 gave me an opportunity to
expand on the point of view developed for the Behavior
and Evolution Symposium. The lectures had to be given
six months earlier than had originally been planned. Consequently, their preparation for publication has taken far
longer than either the Yale University Press or I had
hoped. In fact, preparation extended throughout the period of the Darwin Centenary, during which a vast body
of literature on every aspect of evolution was organized.
Many points which, before the Centenary, it would have
been necessary to document extensively, at least in bibliographical form, can now be taken for granted—or the

reader can be referred to the volumes of the University of Chicago symposium and to other symposia and discussions of evolution which have appeared recently.[19] While the volume was still in manuscript form, I was given an opportunity to read *Evolution and Culture,* edited by Sahlins and Service.[20]

Controversies over man's intervention in the evolutionary process have also been sharpened by the steps which were taken to isolate the New Guinea tribe suffering from *kuru,*[21] by renewed discussion of the use of oral contraceptives, and by the possibilities of transplanting embryos into female hosts.[22] While I was working on this manuscript, I had the privilege of reading the manuscript of C. H. Waddington's *The Ethical Animal.*[23] And before I undertook the final revision, the American Academy of Arts and Sciences organized a series of conferences on evolution, in the course of which an impassioned discussion took place between those who advocated the improvement of the human gene pool by the mildest methods—but phrased in words that were scientifically unacceptable to the anthropologist—and those who, while advocating cultural rather than biological intervention, were still profoundly deterministic and pessimistic about man's ability to make such interventions in time.[24] New cross-disciplinary lines were established in the Symposium on the Expression of the Emotions in Man, at the 127th Annual Meeting of the American Association for the Advancement of Science in 1960.[25] At an even more recent conference, the Workshop on Approaches to Instinctive Behavior, held at the Menninger Foundation in January 1961, traditional psychoanalytic thinking on the life and death instincts was brought into sharp engagement with biochemical, ethological, and anthropological theories.

In such a ferment of ideas, a book on the same subject, long overdue, leads a strange existence and, like the Old

Man of the Sea, changes shape beneath the firmest hands. It is quite impossible to assay accurately the effect of an evening in the spring of 1960, when L. S. B. Leakey painstakingly demonstrated to my students his most recent findings in Kenya,[26] or a snatched conversation with Loren Eiseley[27] about Boskop Man while we were at a Board meeting of the *American Scholar,* or a suggestion made by Evelyn Hutchinson that it was the variation in the thickness of the hymen which gave it evolutionary significance,[28] or a comment by Gregory Bateson that evolution had us in a double-bind, or moments of wondering about Nora Barlow's matching of the present and the past, or a telephone call to George Simpson to ask him what he had done about Darwin's *Expression of the Emotions in Man and Animals,*[29] or long arguments with C. H. Waddington about the value of making analogies from units rather than from process, or the joint preparation of a paper with Theodore Schwartz, the originally assigned title of which was "Non-Evolutionary Typologies." [30]

Nor is it possible to assay accurately the parallel growth in my own theoretical structure, which was not directly related to this particular enterprise but which fed on it and into it. Most of the active discussion about and actual preparation of this book was done in 1959 and 1960, while I was Sloan Visiting Professor in the Menninger School of Psychiatry, and during shorter visits to the School of Psychiatry of the University of Cincinnati College of Medicine. From these contacts, with all their diversity and wealth of criticism, inspiration, and material, I have gained new insights into those aspects of the evolutionary process with which Freud struggled with great imagination and very poor anthropological material in writing *Totem and Taboo.*[31] These insights are the beginning of a new area of research and are as yet too little explored to include formally within these pages, but they must be acknowledged.[32] A request to speak at the Annual Meeting of the Menninger Foundation,[33] just as I was writing the concluding chapters on the appropriate institutional structure for evolutionary innovation, caught me (like Kafka when he was asked to describe the perfect institution in which a writer could write) describing the very place where I was, in fact, writing. But my description of such a structure also reflects my indebtedness to many of the new institutions within which I have been privileged to work: the Macy Conferences,[34] the conferences held under the auspices of the World Federation for Mental Health,[35] and the World Health Organization,[36] the Merrill–Palmer Institute of Detroit,[37] The New York Academy of Sciences,[38] the American Association for the Advancement of Science,[39] the Menninger School of Psychiatry, the Cincinnati School of Psychiatry,[40] the University Seminars of Columbia University,[41] and the Conference on Science, Philosophy and Religion.[42] It includes also the institution within whose halls I have for thirty-five years been free to follow the dictates of both scientific curiosity and scientific responsibility, The American Museum of Natural History.

For advice and help on the content of this manuscript I am indebted to Gregory Bateson, Ray L. Birdwhistell, Ruth Bunzel, Lawrence K. Frank, Geoffrey Gorer, G. Evelyn Hutchinson, Peter Klopfer, Rhoda Metraux, Theodore Schwartz, and C. H. Waddington. For painstaking work in preparing it for press I am most grateful to Caroline Cohen, Joan Gordan, Bridget Merle, Barbara Price, and Dorothy Sellars.

With this book I pay tribute to Barnard College on the occasion of its 75th anniversary.

M. M.

New York
June 5, 1963

Introduction

IN THIS BOOK I am concerned with certain kinds of communication: communication between parents and children, between associates of the same status, between members of different societies and, through the mediation of various kinds of coding—tools, art, script, formulas, film—between cultures distant from each other in time and place. I shall be concerned to show that we must deal not only with evolutionary sequences, in which our ability to articulate and codify parts of the culture enormously increases our ability to intervene in the cultural process, but also with the coexistence at any period of history of earlier forms of communication side by side with later ones.

In Part One, a consideration of these continuities, I shall draw on my own field work to illuminate, but not in any sense exhaust, the dimensions which must be considered in any such discussion. I shall emphasize most those aspects of the problem on which I have the fullest cultural materials, and I shall necessarily neglect important problems on which we do not yet have adequate data. The most immediate lack is on pattern or gestalt learning, which is exceedingly important but not yet documented by the order of field work on which I am drawing here. In *Balinese Character*[1] and in *Growth and Culture*[2] we have, it is true, presented visual documentation of a culture pattern of the kind that is visible to the child and the stranger, but the steps by which the child apprehends this pattern have not been worked upon in sufficient detail for the level of analysis I am making here.

In Part One I discuss various kinds of communication, the role of the recognition of cultural forms, such as language, the ways in which the processes of imitation, identification, and empathy shape learning, the borderline between teaching and learning, and the artifact as an early form of codification.

In Part Two I discuss the evolutionary importance of the cluster—the intercommunicating group of human beings who stand at some crucial point of divergence in a process of culture change. I argue that among the conditions which make it possible for a man of exceptional ability—that type of exceptional ability which we call genius —to make a contribution to cultural change is the special composition of the cluster of individuals with whom he interacts and through whom he interacts also with others. The extent to which the state of knowledge and the existing sociocultural forms determine the contribution an individual can make has been rather fully argued.[3] But I believe that the importance of the small group of identified individuals—identified in the most precise ways sociologically, phenotypically, experientially—who surround the leader or the innovator has not been so fully explored. The interacting individuals in a cluster, who stand in a crucial position in a cult, a new political movement, or a new science, relate themselves to one another in all the different modalities and at all the levels of codification that have been discussed in Part One. To such a group the man who is stupid or intractable, the unbeliever, the fanatic, the man who cannot "see" what the gifted leader is talking about, the man who "hears" the leader's voice as the voice of God, all make specific and identifiable contributions. The relationship between the very gifted individual, his period, his society, and his culture is one which emerges from an exceedingly complex process with many fortuitous elements. A first step in acquiring any measure of control over this process, if the process is to be understood, is a recognition that such clusters are worth studying and that this unit can be defined. This I have attempted to point out in Part Two. I conclude this part with a brief account of one evolutionary cluster—Paliau and his group of local leaders in the Admiralty Islands—which has been very thoroughly documented by field work.[4]

In Part Three I turn to the question of the conscious creation of conditions within which clusters of evolutionary significance may appear. We have at present no way of producing geniuses or even of spotting them when they occur. I argue, therefore, that our constructive imagination must be focused upon creating the conditions within which clusters containing highly gifted people are likely to form and, if they do, will make it possible for them to function well.

In the contemporary world we face a crisis which man must surmount if he is to survive. On every hand there are loud cries that solutions to our present dilemma should be sought consciously and energetically. Many of those who make such demands have little understanding of the ways in which the search for solutions can be undertaken, and they fail to recognize that innovations in the field of human behavior require conditions which are different from those necessary for innovations in the natural sciences or in technology.

In Part Three I suggest the conditions that will make possible the recurrence of clusters of human scientists who, confronted with problems of major human significance and communicating with one another simultaneously at many levels and within different sensory modalities, will be able to make the inventions necessary for massive evolutionary change. We are accustomed to speak retrospectively about "the man of the hour." The task of conscious intervention in the process of cultural evolution and human survival is the creation of the setting for the hour which will find such men—and women—and bring their gifts into play.

Binding the three parts of this book together are certain premises about the nature of communication and creativity, and also the belief that new ideas are born in the simultaneous play of different kinds of imagery, different kinds of information, both within the individual human mind and between human minds. Such creativity is, I believe, most likely to appear under conditions of conscious urgency —an urgency that is embodied in living human beings who must be fed or taught, cured or converted with immediacy. I do not argue that this is the only way in which cultural innovation can occur. The lonely figure in the British Museum, the solitary scientist sitting at his desk with only a slide rule—each of these is surely another and a vital part of the process. But although ideas may be conceived and nourished in loneliness, their impact on human life is a function of groups of human beings, and the idea or its originator himself must find a place in such a cluster. These clusters we can construct, if we will.

No man is an island, entire of itself; every man is a piece of the continent, a part of the main; if a clod be washed away by the sea, Europe is the less, as well as if a promontory were, as well as if a manor of thy friend's or of thine own were; any man's death diminishes me, because I am involved in mankind; and therefore never send to know for whom the bell tolls; it tolls for thee.

JOHN DONNE
DEVOTIONS, XVII

PART I

1. The Climate of Opinion and the Study of Evolution

IN THIS BOOK I shall be concerned with one kind of contribution that anthropology, particularly field studies of living primitive peoples, can make to our constructive understanding of the processes of evolution. I stress the word *constructive* because I shall be concerned with what we know as it bears or may be brought to bear on what we do. I shall be concerned with some aspects of the evolutionary process as it is found in *Homo sapiens,* which, when it is understood, can be modified by conscious effort based on scientific knowledge. We—mankind —stand at the center of an evolutionary crisis, with a new evolutionary device—our consciousness of the crisis—as our unique contribution. This book will deal with some new ways in which we may participate in evolution.

Although our understanding of evolution must be set within an enormous time span, to which we have access only through fossilized fragments of the past, I shall draw primarily on experience with groups of living creatures— whether these be flocks of geese, herds of deer, troops of monkeys, or groups of living and identified human beings. Our interventions must be made within such living groups, and it is on our understanding of their properties that we are necessarily most dependent.

The choice of problem in science is never entirely free from influences from the wider world of public opinion. As science becomes more a recognized part of life and less a separate compartment for the private and special inquiries of those who are mysteriously dedicated to their esoteric endeavors, the connection between scientific direction and society will become greater. This is especially the case in the human sciences, where the scientifically unsophisticated are almost automatically alerted to the interest they have in the conclusions of the scientist who ventures to think about human beings. When we lower the barriers between what is called "pure science"—those scientific inquiries that are pursued primarily out of intellectual curiosity and a commitment to problems internal to some scientific disciplines—and what is called "applied science"—those inquiries that have a known and an immediate application to the affairs of men—the participation of the public in the choice of problems to be explored becomes explicit and inevitable. This is inconvenient for the scientist who wishes to force his point of view or the reforms he advocates on a public defined, in his own mind, as "the ignorant masses"; but public participation is supportive and valuable to the scientist who feels that any gap between the scientist and other members of a society is a defect to be overcome as quickly as possible.[1]

Choice of problem in turn dictates both our choice of classification and our point of view—our intellectual stance. Interest in evolution has waxed and waned with the changing climate of opinion in the Western world, as thinking men in general have been caught up in an awareness of an expanding or a shrinking world and as men's ties with the universe have seemed to require a strengthening or a loosening of the ties between human beings and the rest of the living world. The time span within which Western men have seen themselves as actors has undergone a similar widening and narrowing. At times men have looked neither very far ahead nor very far back. The philosophical needs of the society ended with a knowledge of Biblical times or, for the skeptical, their substitute, Grecian times. The astonishing widening of the contemporary world, which came with European explorations beginning in the fifteenth century, and the deepening of man's biological past into unknown aeons of time, which came with discoveries about the age of the earth and with the formulation of the theory of evolution, could both be comfortably domesticated by the peculiar application of evolutionary theory to the recently discovered savages who peopled the still little-explored continents and the far-flung islands.[2]

The closer we came, in fact, to an understanding of man as one manifestation of life on a planet in one solar system in one of many galaxies, the more violently we shied away from the attempt to absorb man into a universe of such wide extent. In the late nineteenth century of clipped hedges and rounded corners for nursery tables,[3] the need for a concrete and immediate dignity led men to distort the ideas of evolution by inventing myths of Nordic superiority[4] and equally mythological views of the evolution of human society from primitive collectivism through the growth of the institution of private property to an ultimate collective utopianism,[5] or from primitive group marriage and matriarchy to an ultimate patriarchal capitalistic monogamy.[6]

The vicissitudes of including the history of human cultures within the framework of evolutionary theory have been as significantly related to current political ideas. Early American thought, developing among European-originated Utopias, preoccupied with the relationship of the emerging American culture to its parent cultures in Europe, and still hopeful that the "new nation brought forth on this continent" would reach a moral stature greater than that of the parent nations, found thoroughly congenial the postulation of an evolutionary sequence that reached its climax in a contemporary Western culture, which, in turn, might bring forth Utopia.[7] So we contributed to contemporary social thinking Lewis Morgan's ideas of an orderly sequence of social forms; through *Ancient Society or Researches in the Lines of Human Progress from Savages, through Barbarism to Civilization*,[8] these ideas caught the attention of Friedrich Engels, and so became part of the intellectual apparatus of Marxism.

Franz Boas, who immigrated to the United States as a young adult, dominated the next period of American anthropological thought, at the time when we were beginning to feel our identity as a separate civilization—a civilization to which Indians and Africans and Asians, as well as Europeans, had contributed.[9] Working within this stridently independent, isolationist climate of opinion, anthropologists occupied themselves with efforts to document the independent development of the high civilizations of the New World. The plausibility of their viewpoint was increased by the absence from these civilizations of the wheel, Old World domesticated animals, Old World forms of writing, and certain other diagnostic traits.[10] At no point did Boas challenge the general propositions of evolution or question the theory that human cultures had evolved from initially simpler forms. In fact, he was at pains to specify that the choice of a point at which we might speak of man as "man" was an arbitrary one, made for purposes of convenience and usefulness.[11] But his whole interest was directed toward combating the postulation of a smooth, one-way development, with our Euro-American civilization at the peak, since he regarded such a view as artificially simplified and unreal. Without ever challenging the greater simplicity of earlier social forms, he meticulously documented the disproof of any given small, inevitable short-term sequence that any evolutionist attempted to introduce into the argument.[12]

Among well-documented anthropological polemics, perhaps the best known is Boas' opposition to Haddon's theory of evolution in art. Haddon[13] tried to demonstrate the existence of one-way sequences from the realistic to the geometric, and Boas wrote his paper on Eskimo needle cases[14] to show that it was equally possible for art to develop from the geometric to the realistic and representational. Essentially, Boas took the position that evolution on a planetary scale does, of course, occur, but that the application of evolutionary concepts to the temporal sequences of a few centuries is misleading, since change can go in any direction—toward simplification or toward complexity.

This is a position with which most modern evolutionists would be wholly in agreement. But to American anthropologists of the early part of this century, working within the framework of American isolationism, only short time sequences were of real interest.[15] Cultural evolutionism became identified with the viewpoint that within any given society there is an inevitable progression of invention and change, uninfluenced by borrowing of any sort. As adequate field work on primitive cultures and (within one area) knowledge of adjacent cultures plainly showed this viewpoint to be erroneous and nonsensical, the study of cultural evolution became arid and as unfashionable as was the study of Old World origins of New World traits, by way of Asia. Yet at the very time when the heresy of advocating Old World (Asian) origins for the high civilizations of the Maya and the Inca—or even for aspects of less complex cultures—disqualified a student from academic patronage,[16] the search for Old World (European) and Old World (African) origins of *contemporary* American Indian and Negro American culture traits began to flower in the work of Elsie Clews Parsons[17] and Melville Herskovits.[18] So, at one and the same time, we asserted that traits from outside the two Americas had penetrated American Indian cultures and had survived in American Negro culture to a greater degree than had been expected, and vigilantly maintained the independent origins of the high civilizations of the Andes and Mexico and the less elaborated cultures, for example, of the Northwest Coast.

Meanwhile, with the spectacular advances in technology, a new direction was given to the relationship between the lines of inquiry and the developing climate of opinion. Boas had systematically separated man's increasing and cumulative technical control over nature from man's social inventions, such as forms of marriage or forms of art. In analyses of art forms, one form was shown to replace another without a definite progression or any demonstrable superiority of a particular form.[19] There was as yet very little recognition of the possibility that the human sciences might introduce a progression into man's control over himself and the social institutions in which he lived. The Marxist viewpoint, then usually spoken of as "the economic interpretation of history," [20] permitted human beings a role in altering the *rate* of change but not its *direction*.[21] Other institutions were regarded as dependent on the state of technology, which in turn was determined by the different forms of organization and distribution, rather than by the level of energy use—as in the viewpoint that later came to dominate the thinking of other determinists (for example, Leslie White[22]).

A sense of the inevitability of technical change likewise pervaded non-Marxist thinking. In *Social Change with Respect to Culture and Original Nature*,[23] a work which reflected the Boasian view that technical change is cumulative and essentially irreversible, Ogburn set forth the idea that many social institutions were attempts to adapt to the discrepancies that occurred as a result of technical change. Man's social dilemmas were brought about, he suggested, by something called "lag." Whereas the Marxists advanced confidently toward a world in which social institutions would be congruent with the stage of economic development, American sociologists and anthropologists emphasized the inevitability of technical complication, but characterized social development as capricious, poorly controlled, and unprogressive.

Other intellectual currents also influenced the contemporary view of man and, consequently, the stance that anthropologists took toward evolution. Psychoanalysis, while it reaffirmed man's animal nature, set civilization and that very nature in opposition, as civilization was interpreted as a neurosis, the by-product of man's fight against himself.[24] To the extent that a more optimistic view of man's potentialities entered the picture, it came by way of educational permissiveness.[25] Excesses in permissiveness were caricatured in the story of the child who moved from a permissive to a nonpermissive school and, after a few days, said with a sigh of relief, "If you want to be good, you can, and if you don't want to fight, you don't have to!" To the extent that man as an animal was recognized, this recognition was tinged with a dread of unconscious impulse and the unsavory origins of what had once been regarded as man's higher nature. In popular interpretations of Freud, man's greatest work was now represented as merely a sublimation. In the 1920s, one of the most influential books (now almost forgotten) was Robinson's *The Mind in the Making*,[26] which shaped the thinking of those who believed they were following the rigorous dictates of scientific research. The word *rationalization,* as a gloss on man's lower impulses, competed with *rationalism,* a word that had described the glories of man in the eighteenth-century Age of Reason.

Parallel to psychoanalysis were the various American interpretations of Pavlov's theories of conditioning. In its peculiarly American form, behaviorism eliminated any recognition of differences between individuals in temperamental propensities, and relied on the effect of environmental influences operating on an extremely narrow repertoire of instinctual responses. This viewpoint was expressed in an exceedingly popular work, *Why We Behave Like Human Beings,* by George Dorsey,[27] a rather obscure and an otherwise conventional ethnologist. Inevitably, behaviorism was treated hospitably by an anthropology that regarded all men, irrespective of the level of civilization of any people at any given time, as equally members of the species *Homo sapiens* and that stressed the idea that culture is learned and that race, language, and culture vary independently of each other.[28]

Both the school of thought in which man's "animal nature" is regarded as intractable and civilization is defined as an imperfect perennial attempt to deal with these intractabilities and the school of thought in which the human being is regarded as a *tabula rasa* at birth, conditioned by his environment, continue to the present day to influence the positions taken by contemporary anthropologists toward theories of cultural evolution. One school of thought has come to rely more and more on naturalistic observation and on the experimental use of naturalistic situations in work on living creatures of all sorts, but there has been a shift away from a primary interest in apes and monkeys as subjects toward an acceptance of observation and experimentation with creatures as remote from *Homo sapiens* as tortoises and spiders and cockroaches. The other school of thought bases its models on experiments in controlled situations with laboratory animals, pre-eminently rats, and relies on the learning capacities of these animals in situations in which man is the master of the maze-running experiment.

These two approaches to man—one of which sees man

as a creature with species-characteristic instinctual patterns that play a continuing part in the forms that civilizations take, and the other which views man as lacking species-characteristic behavior patterns and as capable of being conditioned to almost any kind of system that takes into account survival needs—cross and recross each other. The optimism of the Watsonian position in the 1920s has been tempered by the experience of the following three decades, during which "techniques" of conditioning were used in the service of absolute or irresponsible power. It is not accidental that B. F. Skinner is preoccupied with problems of the bureaucratic control of human beings and is, at the same time, an advocate of programmed learning with learning machines in the teaching of mathematics and languages.[29] A related complication can be found in the work of Eliot D. Chapple, in which he combines a strict behavioristic approach to human behavior, as conditioned by culture, with a respect equal to Pavlov's own for innate invariances of temperamental response.[30] So, too, W. Grey Walter combines a preference for behavioristic explanations with an interest in intractable temperamental factors in behavior.[31]

A secondary argument about the presence or absence of intractabilities in human nature (different from and beyond the simple needs for food, water, and rest, which human beings share with all other organic creatures) has centered on the problem of the primacy of early childhood experience. Here ethological studies, such as those made by Lorenz[32] and by Tinbergen,[33] have provided one kind of model in which early childhood experience is regarded as definitive. The behaviorists in human psychology have opposed the Freudian model, and the behaviorists who prefer laboratory experiments to observation in natural conditions have opposed the ethological model.[34]

As a result, we are faced with a curious paradox. On the

one hand, those who expect to find that there are innate temperamental differences among individuals of the same species are suspected of harboring racist ideas.[35] On the other hand, both among those who are sympathetic to and among those who are fearful of the possible dominance of communistic totalitarianism, one finds individuals who insist on the almost infinite modifiability of the human being, the relative unimportance of qualititative individual differences, and the lack of priority of early experiences over later experiences—whether these are expressed in ethological, psychoanalytic, or anthropological terms.

These curious crossings and interweavings of ideas, characteristic of different positions, illustrate vividly the extent to which a climate of opinion, of which explicit political and religious ideologies are only components, provides the atmosphere in which the scientists of a period make the very choices which they regard as dictated rigorously by the contemporary state of their particular discipline.[36]

Meanwhile, in response to our rapidly increasing technological control—as evidenced by the development of aviation, communications, electronic automation, and the release of nuclear power—the discussion of cultural evolution shifted from a consideration of technology and the inevitability of invention to the problem of levels of energy utilization. Ogburn, who had been trained in economics and who responded to anthropological data, was a proponent of the first position. Leslie White, who was originally trained in physics and later became an anthropologist, has emphasized the second. The central importance of energy utilization was also a basic tenet of the technocracy movement.[37]

As a measure of cultural evolution, the use of the amount of energy available to any human group at a given period in human cultural development provides a convenient macrocosmic framework for the discussion of political and technological evolution. These two streams sometimes flow together, sometimes at different rates. A society that is able to muster the services of thousands of slaves to grind corn may have the same amount of energy available as has a group that relies on windmills. The technological development of the second group may be greater than that of the first, but its political organization may be less developed.[38] However, considerations of this kind need not obscure the argument, provided that all of planetary civilization is taken into consideration and that long time intervals are used as units.

In the 1930s and 1940s, the work done by Leslie White,[39] in the United States, and by V. Gordon Childe,[40] in England, roused little interest or enthusiasm, except among students who worked closely with them on these problems. We were, in the 1930s, in the grip of a worldwide depression, and the problems facing mankind were defined as political rather than technical. In a situation in which unsalable food was burned in one country while people starved in another, it is small wonder that short-time political solutions and correspondingly short-time scientific problems attracted the attention of research workers. In the United States, isolationism had fostered an interest in a time span short enough to give place of honor to the parallel development of high civilizations in the Americas. The time span of current preoccupations was even further foreshortened: How to reduce the frustrations that were believed to result in aggression,[41] how to encourage local initiative and improve the situation of minority groups,[42] and so on.

With the rise of Nazism, the focus on group contacts was sharpened and, with the outbreak of World War II, the interest in short-time change became even more widespread. Consideration was given to such problems as the ways in which outside intervention could bring about changes in institutional forms (especially in Germany and Japan) that would be reflected in changes in the character structure of a people, in alterations of their political behavior, and, indirectly, in increased world stability.[43] A second short-time goal, related to the first, involved studies of cultural process made for purposes of psychological warfare in Germany and Japan and for other wartime purposes.[44] After 1948, further work on cultural process, initiated during the war, was carried out in studies of the East European bloc and the Far East.[45]

Even the enunciation of the Four Freedoms and the immediate postwar upsurge of hope, based on the knowledge that it was now technically possible to feed the population of the world, did not turn the attention of students to the longer-term problems in which Childe and White were interested. Julian Steward, who since 1936 had been actively interested in the study of long-term parallel trends that occur under similar economic conditions,[46] temporarily abandoned this interest to direct the Puerto Rican study with its short-term, immediate, and ameliorative emphasis on "the development of distinctive and rural subcultures in Puerto Rico." [47]

The same pervasive interest in short-term, rapid change may be seen in many different anthropological approaches, all part of the postwar optimistic belief in the possibility of rapidly bringing the underdeveloped countries into the modern world.[48] However much they differed from one another in their several approaches, Arensberg,[49] Bateson,[50] Birdwhistell,[51] Chapple,[52] Fried,[53] Gorer,[54] Keesing,[55] Mead,[56] Steward,[57] and Wagley[58] all focused in their work on problems of change within one generation. The underdeveloped countries were to catch up. People who moved from rural to urban settings were to find ways of adjusting their lives to their changed situation. Racial tensions were to be solved by increased understanding and enabling legislation. Children born in countries that had been authoritarian in their structure were to be reared to find free institutions congenial. Mental illness was to be reduced by changing the social institutions that produced ill health or by creating a new atmosphere in the institutions in which the mentally ill were treated.[59] Whether the emphasis was on crop diversification, on removing real estate restrictions that hindered the free movement of minority groups, on legislation for the reduction of racial tensions, or on the felicitous results of student exchange programs, productivity teams, or programs of cultural exchange, the prevailing belief was that we could bring about "better things in our time," and that an increased knowledge of the processes of change could make a substantial contribution to the attainment of these goals.

Yet, although the time span was a short one, the general approach was still predominantly macroscopic, for up to this time only a few investigators had grasped the fact that new mechanical methods of recording for later analysis would make possible great refinement of research.

While these studies of short-time change were being carried out, there was a growing realization of the threat posed by the possibility of a nuclear catastrophe, and an increasing awareness that vast changes must be faced in order to prevent the possibility from becoming a reality. The first attempts to come to grips with the problem were made by the atomic physicists and those few anthropologists, psychologists, and sociologists who recognized the danger to the future, of which the explosions at Los Alamos and Hiroshima were only the prelude.[60] A more widespread recognition that mankind now had the power to destroy itself as a species came only slowly. Earlier responses included a boom in real estate at some "safe distance" from a major city like New York and discussions of the best type of Peruvian valley in which to tuck away civilization's record. But with the first applications of atomic reactors to industrial uses and the apparent imminence of space exploration, a new climate of opinion began to develop.

Interest in the far future and in interstellar space grew simultaneously, counterpointed by a sense of immediate danger and a growing awareness that there might be no future of any kind. Discussions of mutations, cumulative only through generations, were balanced by panics over the presence of strontium-90 in milk which might "injure my child now." Americans, who had never looked very far into the future, had greeted the news of the atomic bombing at Hiroshima almost as a preferred form of "quick and painless death," in which "you'd never know what hit you." [61] This first response only began to shift when John Hersey's *Hiroshima* was published in 1946,[62] and the idea of hours or days "without a doctor" began to penetrate public consciousness.

In 1955, the National Academy of Sciences appointed six committees to study the effects of high-energy radiation on living things.[63] In *The Biological Effects of Atomic Radiation,* the first public report in which technical findings and recommendations were published, the Report of the Committee on Genetic Effects clearly posed the question of time span:[64]

> A discussion of genetic damage necessarily involves, on the one hand, certain tangible and imminent dangers, certain tragedies which might occur to our own children and grandchildren; and on the other hand certain more remote trouble that may be experienced by very large numbers of persons in the far distant future.
>
> No two persons are likely to weigh exactly alike these two sorts of danger. How does one compare the

present fact of a seriously handicapped child with the possibility that large numbers of persons may experience much more minor handicaps, a hundred or more generations from now?

Humanitarians waxed indignant over the possibility of "a seriously handicapped child" in the present. In their thinking they confused the question of taking a chance (a chance far smaller than that taken by our endorsement of a motorized civilization) with the ethical problem posed by Dostoyevsky when he raised the question of whether a new order of society could be founded on the death of a single child.[65]

The new attention given to problems of biological mutation gave rise to another double position. On the one hand, there were fears of what the ultimate consequences of a higher rate of mutation might be; on the other hand, there was a new interest, variously expressed, in the development of different kinds of human beings. There was, for example, an increased, although largely subterranean, interest in extrasensory perception. There was some recognition that modern medicine could save individuals who, because of some physical defect, had been doomed to perish in the past. There were demands that the gene pool should be selectively protected. Fantasies of extreme tampering with genetic processes were built up around ideas of incest or the possibility of preserving regenerative tissues of great men[66] in order to make available to each generation a supply of "Churchills" or other recognized great men. As counterpoints to these optimistic fantasies, there were the gloomy fears that man may be deteriorating, that men are becoming "soft," and that the "unfit" are being reproduced and preserved in such large proportions as to overwhelm the "fit," and so on.[67] Each position, however extreme, could be logically argued.

But beneath the rational arguments were the irrational fears—fears that the "white race" would be overwhelmed by the "yellow race" or the "black race"; fears lest a rise of political racism in Africa or Asia should spell the doom of the Western world. Responses to the population explosion, as they expressed the feeling of being overwhelmed or inundated, repeated in a different form the contemporary dread of being caught in a universal catastrophe.[68]

As the far future and the far distant in space began to shape contemporary hopes and fears, a complementary interest developed around ideas of the far past[69] and the depths of the sea.[70] The deprived children of our cities, who are fed on television and comics and who represent with heartbreaking accuracy the current state of the national consciousness, tired of spacemen soon after *Explorer* went up and turned, instead, to frogmen.[71] And the interest in history—which for the general reader still tends to stop with the abridged edition of Toynbee[72] and with the question, "Will our civilization fall as Rome's civilization fell?"—has begun to shift to an interest in man's evolution through thousands or millions of years.

In fact, our model for thinking about the processes of man in nature must draw on a knowledge of long-term change. The pessimists—those who view man's existence in terms of a series of ultimately self-defeating cycles, each perhaps more complex than the last but without evolutionary significance—invoke the short-time perspectives of recorded history to herald the doom of Europe, the decadence of America, and the rise of other centers of civilization with comparably short life expectancies. In contrast, those who are concerned with evolution that is directional and emergent not only include a far longer retrospective look at mankind, but also have a much greater awareness that man's present condition differs from anything in his past.[73]

Finally, as a counterpoint to our current preoccupation with the infinitely vast—with aeons of time, with multiple galaxies—there is our preoccupation with the infinitely small—with the single individual, with the single gene. Just when Harlow Shapley said that man is, for the fourth time, being cut down to size in galactic terms,[74] George Beadle, in his comparison of the complexity of gene structure and the complexity of the universe, was building man up.[75] Not long ago scientists spoke derisively about the "so-called Great Man theory of history" and a whole school of literary biography was built around the idea of exploding the myth of the great man.[76] Today, with the shift in attitude, there is a renewed interest in the contribution of the individual.

When the world had less than half a billion inhabitants and the decision-making groups in the nation-states sometimes could be counted in the hundreds, there was a great willingness to speak about the inevitable processes of history and to cite the repetition of inventions (even the invention of the idea of evolution itself) as an inevitability.[77] For example, there was a school of thought that contended that, with or without Hitler, the renaissance of nationalism in Germany would have taken the same course. And in April 1941, when Theodore Abel presented a paper on the theme that wars are made by individual men who make individual decisions,[78] his ideas were rejected out of hand. Today, in contrast, there is a hypertrophied interest in particular individuals, in members of native elites, in the psychological processes of leaders, in prophets and cults centering around individual visions, and so on. The Fifth Macy Conference on Problems of Consciousness ended with a plea for the study of the individual;[79] Gardner Murphy has proposed the felicitous phrase, "a science of uniqueness";[80] and Edith Cobb's work, with its conception of individuality as "speciation," is at last reaching publication.[81] A more receptive climate of opinion now makes possible serious consideration of the limitations of the perception of the self, such as were raised by Brickner's paper on telencephalization[82] and his film records of a two-headed turtle.[83] And, in 1959, it did not take the announcement by the Department of Defense that, after exhaustive tests, the choice of the first American to be launched into space had been narrowed to seven men, to heighten the sense of the significance of individual life as the interlocking world of men and nature grows vaster, more complicated, more interconnected, and more potentially dangerous.

Moreover, the development of new kinds of machines which extend man's higher faculties (whereas earlier machines for the most part extended his less developed and less distinctively human faculties) has contributed to the change in the climate of opinion. Men's first tools, rough stones, hardly differed from the objects with which a horde of monkeys pelt an intruder. Early forms of shelter were less complex than the nests made by some species of bird. The first great step occurred when man made a creative tool, a tool that was not merely an extension of his physical ability to push or pull, lift or throw, parry or deliver a blow, but instead was an extension of his ability to *make something*. As man's ability to make tool-making tools increased and his power over the natural world increased, the question of how these tools should be regarded— crudely, as animate or inanimate, or, stated with more sophistication, as in some way related to the life process— was a recurrently preoccupying one. Many primitive peoples endowed tools and weapons with a life of their own (technically called *mana*, from the Melanesian word [84]), and this response is a perennial one, made over and over again by those whose perceptions have not been rationally disciplined—children, primitives, the uneducated, poets, and artists—who refer to a ship, a train, an automobile, an airplane as something which is somehow alive.

It is important to realize that, in a sense, this is a problem which does not alter. The underlying conception of the "liveness" of things—objects—is one that has shaped the thinking of men in extraordinarily different cultures: the Manus Islander, who thought that his Sir Ghost (the spirit of a recently deceased male member of his household) could take away the "soul" of his fishing apparatus, just as he could take away the soul of a human being;[85] the bards and minstrels who described the personalized sword of the hero (Roland's Durandel, Siegfried's Balmung, Arthur's Excalibur, Angantyr's Tyrfing[86]); the men who ascribed good and evil repute to a ship; those whose first poetic perceptions of machines with engines endowed them with a kind of life; and those who, today, envisage a future in which "computers" will replace men as the designers and engineers of new machines, a future in which a computer can "have another little computer" or in which we finally discover that "this whole life we lead is really being run by a great computer somewhere." [87] The puzzle of man's relationship to the extensions of his creativity has not lessened, and today this puzzle can be phrased as Life–Man–Machine by one of our most gifted specialists in the human factor in design.[88] One aspect of these poetic visions is the conflict in the minds of those who wish to invoke what man has made as a model for man and yet fear that some obscure reductionism will result from the attempt to do so.

Another development, which began much later in history, was man's technical extension of his sensory relationship to the outer world. With the invention of the telescope and the microscope[89] man began the intoxicating extension of his powers of perception, which today has led to the development of the electron microscope, to the bombardment of a single chromosome, and to such projects as turning the surface of the moon into a giant reflector. The first excitement attending the discoveries of the infinitely large and the infinitely small—which set off a whole series of fantasy voyages into space and play with changes in scale[90] —was a prefiguration of one of our current preoccupations.

But while these earlier inventions enormously extended man's capacity to see the very distant and the very small, all that was seen through the lenses still depended for duration on drawings made by human hands. Even when a single instant of observation could be caught by the newly invented camera, the links connecting one picture with another had to be supplied in other ways. Then, with the invention of the motion picture camera and methods of recording sound and, still later, with the invention of automatic synchronization of the visual image and the auditory record and, very recently, with the invention of methods of slowing down performance so that the records of movement could be studied in detail, microanalysis became possible. For example, methods have now been developed for making films of plant growth, for recording experimentally controlled interaction between fish or animals or birds, and, most recently, for recording the complexities of unique events occurring in groups of human beings.

Parallel to these developments have been the new precision methods for the control of long time spans by the analysis of tree rings, by carbon-14 dating, and by various other techniques of geochronology.[91] Similarly, a new and refined method of handling time–space relations has been developed through the techniques of air archaeology.[92]

So the rhythmic relationship has continued, creating a climate of opinion in which a threefold approach to human evolution can now flourish: studies of evolution that deal with very long time periods and with the enormous changes that accompanied man's cultural development after the appearance of *Homo sapiens;* studies of comparable evolutionary sequences, in which human groups, starting with a common stock of ideas, have worked them out in roughly similar ways (Steward's multilinear evolution); and studies of the actual processes of change as they occur in one generation or between adjacent generations.

Interest in these three approaches to evolution goes across the board as generations of drosophila, with due allowance for the experience of each generation, are studied by Waddington,[93] as the behavior of individual, identified Greylag geese is studied by Lorenz,[94] as the vocalization patterns of birds, reared under different conditions, have been studied by Thorpe and others,[95] and as detailed studies are made of small human societies in process of change.

As we make studies of such small human groups, we find ourselves able to consider the contribution made by the particular individual, not only as a carrier of "good" genes or as a mutant with reproductive possibilities but also as a contributor to the culture in which man, as he is and as he may become, must live. So it is no longer meaningful to insist, as Dobzhansky and Birdsell have insisted,[96] that the only point of evolutionary significance is the *biological* contribution made by the individual to succeeding generations; and one must regard as untenable Leslie White's contention that the individual, as such, is of no importance.[97]

Today we can study in appropriate detail the contribution of the individual to cultural evolution, and we can also make clearer statements about the possibilities of studying divergent as well as convergent phenomena.[98]

2. Stress on Continuity

IN THIS INQUIRY I have been guided by Julian Huxley's definition of evolution as framed in the statement that "the whole of phenomenal reality is a single process, which properly may be called evolution" and that "evolution is a self-sustaining, self-transforming, and self-transcending process, directional in time and therefore irreversible, which in its course generates ever fresh novelty, greater variety, more complex organization, higher levels of awareness, and increasingly conscious mental activity." [1] But Sir Julian, after presenting this unitary definition for the use of anthropologists, follows current usage in anthropology in stressing the discontinuity between man as a culture-building animal and all other living creatures. That is, he treats culture as *sui generis* by accepting the idea that "what evolves in the psycho-social sphere," characteristic of human evolution, is "a new supra-organic entity demanding an appellation of its own." In his definition, culture has "characteristics not simply explicable or directly deducible from a knowledge of the general psychological or physiological properties of human individuals," and "differences between cultures are no more explicable or deducible from a knowledge of their material basis than from that of their psychological basis in the minds of individuals." [2] After this tilt with reductionism, with the latter part of which anthropologists would agree, he goes on to declare the independence of a culture from "the intrinsic (genetic) psycho-physical properties of the human population of a society, and the intrinsic peculiarities of single individuals within it, [which] can and do to some extent condition the form and development of the culture, but do not determine it." [3]

At some periods in the history of anthropology it has been important to stress the discontinuity between man as a culture-building animal and all other living creatures. It has also been important to stress the point that man is a mammal with certain types of behavior appropriate to mammals and to identify these behaviors which can be recognized as related between apes and man or between monkeys, apes, and man. [4]

The choice of points of discontinuity within the process of evolution may be determined either objectively as "quantum leaps," on the basis of an analysis of known phenomena, or by the state of the particular science and the tools and problems with which it is concerned. At a time when the climate of opinion was dominated by a common belief in the intrinsic superiority of European "races," which led to a spurious identification of "cultural" and "racial" progress and to the creation of artificially defined sequences of "progress" whose end points were identified by current Western practices, it was most important for scientists to dissociate "race" or the biologically transmitted characteristics of human racial groups, such as skin color or hair form, from the "cultural" practices of these racial groups, by pointing out that at different periods in the historical transmission of human culture, populations with different racial characteristics had occupied different positions on the innovative or borrowing or merely maintenance scale, and that members of any racial group could learn the cultural behavior which had been elaborated by some other racial group. It even seemed necessary to treat language as separate from culture and to discuss "race, language, and culture" as three independently varying systems.[5] These distinctions were designed to do double duty in breaking down racist thinking and in creating a climate of thought in which the psychic unity of mankind, as a species, could be assumed as a background for research on man's learned behavior. As long as it was assumed that members of human "races" differed—as groups—in their ability to learn what other "races" had invented or learned, comparative research was impossible. If the behavior of remote primitive peoples was to provide us with data on species-wide human potentialities, stress on the discontinuity between their racially specific biological inheritance and their cultural inheritance was necessary. Singling out language as a separately varying system, gross as such a selection was, helped to dramatize the fact that men of every physical stock and coming from societies of every level of technological and political development could "learn" the "same" language. As long as the term "learning" was used in a very generalized and formal way and little attention was given to usage as opposed to grammar, this formulation served very well in establishing a basis for modern anthropological research.

Today, with the greater refinement of linguistic analysis, it is necessary to specify much more exactly what is meant by the independent variation of culture and language. It is true that a language can be "borrowed" and learned by an entire population who differ in race from the present carriers of the language; or the type of culture of the borrowing group may be different, as when a nomadic people adopts the language of an agricultural people; or the borrowers may belong to a different culture area, as when an African population learns a European language or a Micronesian population learns Japanese. But the language so borrowed will be systematically modified by its new speakers in ways that reflect their own cultural background as well as their own subcultural variations in religion, socioeconomic status, and ecological setting.

Today we would emphasize first that all natural languages that survive are sufficiently redundant that they can be learned by the members of any *Homo sapiens* group. Then, rather than speaking of the independence of language and culture, we would say that any language developed by a human society can be learned by the members of another human society, and that this borrowing is possible both because of the redundancy, which provides for a wide range of individual differences in sensory modalities, memory, and intelligence, and because language has been conceptualized the world over as a part of culture that can be learned by members of different cultures.

When it is said that culture varies independently of race and that the members of any racial group can learn, maintain, and develop any cultural form, this must be understood as a statement of our present knowledge of the relationship between the range of individual differences and a cultural whole. That is, it is a statement about group competence in situations in which the learning group is sufficiently numerous to provide for a wide range. It includes the recognition that there is no information about systematic differences in the range of identifiable abilities among racial groups that are relevant to the ability of any one group to learn the culture of another group and to produce succeeding generations who are able to develop within the adopted culture.

When, however, the independence of the "racial" factor is carried over to the independence of a cultural form not only from the physical stock of the group who happen to be its carriers at a given time, but also from the individual gifts of identifiable individuals who occupy strategic positions of cultural leverage at a point of possible change, this formulation becomes not enabling but obfuscating. The same arguments may be advanced when "language" is treated as somehow separate from "culture," instead of as one cultural subsystem—like the subsystem of technology —which can be transmitted somewhat independently from other subsystems of a particular identifiable culture. A tremendous advance was made in the study of linguistics by the temporary isolation of language from the study of the rest of culture.[6] However, it will be unfortunate if pride in the advances of linguistic analysis, which are majorly related to the physiological substructure of the linguistic system of culture, prevents the recognition that what was assumed to be independent variation from the rest of culture is not confined to language but is equally true of technology, and for the same reasons: The formal structure of a technology, like the formal structure of language, can be separately transmitted from one group of users to another as a system of behavior, because it has been separately conceptualized and because of its internal coherence.

It was also historically valuable to distinguish between those levels of behavior sometimes called *subhuman* and *human* behavior as characterized by the use of tools and language. This emphasis served two purposes: It was a defense not only against the reductionism that treated man as "only an animal," but also against the materialism of an approach like that of Haeckel,[7] and it focused attention on the uniqueness of cultural behavior. It will no doubt be necessary periodically to reaffirm the tremendous significance of the break between man and ape, not only with experiments like those carried out by the Kelloggs[8] and by Hayes,[9] but also as one gambit in a possibly re-emerging battle between systems of ethics as the relevant questions change. The ultimate ethic on this subject which the Judeo–Christian world has been able to produce is re-

flected in discussions of capital punishment [10] and in taboos
on man exploiting man and needlessly punishing animals.[11]
But the question of how the boundaries between man and
the animal world are to be respected will recur as nation-
states with many other religious tenets become influential
in determining the world climate of opinion on such matters as meat consumption, vivisection, and experimental
attempts to produce human–anthropoid hybrids.[12]

The development of new attitudes toward child training, in the 1920s and 1930s, in which the mammalian inheritance of the human child was taken systematically into
account (as in the child development movement in which
L. K. Frank participated and which he did so much to
shape[13]), suggests that if the "mammalian nature" of the
child is treated with love and respect, then "mammals"
themselves become more dignified.[14]

However, in the 1920s and 1930s, the attempt to identify
our mammalian inheritance, which was given impetus
both from the field of child development and from that of
psychoanalytic thinking, temporarily blocked any recognition of the usefulness of looking at human behavior in
terms of our knowledge of any class other than the Mam-
malia.[15] The key use of the insects in anthropological
teaching became the ants trapped in Baltic amber, which
had not changed for many millions of years, and comparisons based on such matters as the division of labor in
the insect world were treated as analogies, and sterile
analogies at that. It was not until the late 1940s that an
orderly cross-comparison could be made between observations on birds and findings on human beings, when it was
recognized that birds are creatures that are two-legged,
erect, dependent on vision and auditory signaling—with
little dependence on the olfactory senses—in pair formation, and need artificial parental protection and feeding
during infancy.[16]

Meanwhile, with increased contact between the students of animal, bird, fish, and insect behavior—partly because of the use of improved observational tools—there was a progressive application to these studies of methods developed in the study of human beings.[17] This provides for greater communicability but it also introduces new pitfalls, for the possibility of anthropomorphizing birds is at least as great as that of a zoomorphizing man.

It will be the contention of this book that at this moment in history it is useful to consider man and man's learned behavior within the entire context of the living world, without emphasizing the discontinuities between the different orders of living beings, between subhuman and human, preliterate and literate, primitive and civilized man. In treating living behavior as a continuum and in treating as comparable the behavior of different biological orders or men of different levels of technical development in different parts of the world, I follow Huxley in advocating the use of a "new, revolutionary classification, which would combine the advance and ancestry principles. We would then have *groups* of common ancestry—Classes, Orders, and other familiar designations, and *grades* of advance (advance sometimes independently achieved, sometimes in common), for which new designations would have to be coined." [18] As an illustration he suggests that "Birds and Mammals, as separate ancestry groups, would continue to rank as two Classes, but would both be included in a single grade, which might be called *Homotherma,* since temperature-regulation is their diagnostic improvement." [19]

The student of culture is concerned with a characteristic which man displays more markedly than any other known creature—the ability to transmit what he has learned. In following the procedure I suggest, the learning of *Homo sapiens* would be treated as a further specialization of the concept of grades, with the recognition that in some species

—possibly even in some orders—the ability to learn may represent not only an improvement, in an evolutionary sense, but also an increase in vulnerability. Man's unique, high ability to learn, coupled as it is with a small amount of built-in behavior, represents such a vulnerability. It is a vulnerability at many levels—at the level of the single individual whose survival depends on cultural, not biologically given knowledge, of the small group which has no built-in selective factor that will assure its means of making a viable choice in a crisis situation (such as war-making or migration), and of the entire species, when the capacity to transmit and to cumulate experience leads to inventions like our present thermonuclear weapons.

By regarding the ability to learn and the ability to direct learning as potentialities of organic creatures that have appeared in particular species or subspecies of many classes, we place man's singular ability in a context that need not be treated as a total discontinuity. The further steps in man's ability to transmit what he has learned by storing information in verbal symbol systems, outside his own body and at a distance in time as well as in space, then will be seen as unique only in the way in which other evolutionary developments are unique—in the bird's evolutionary mastery of life in the air, or that of the fish in the sea.

Cultural systems will be treated as extensions of the power to learn, store, and transmit information, and the evolution of culture as dependent upon the biological development of these abilities and the cultural developments that actualize them. Man's increasing mastery over the natural world, with its increments of available energy use, can be seen from this point of view as one consequence of his capacity to learn, invent, borrow, store, and transmit the necessary technological and political inventions for the changes of scale involved in increasing utilization of energy. Instead of focusing attention on discontinuities—the invention of tool-making tools, the invention of agriculture, the invention of writing, and the invention of invention as a conscious pursuit—this discussion will focus on the continuities involved and on the extent to which older forms of communication, energy use, and social organization also undergo transformation in the course of cultural evolution.

I must reiterate that I am advancing this approach not as better than, or even alternative to, those approaches which have focused on discontinuities, but simply as a way of looking at the material which seems more appropriate to the kinds of problems I wish to discuss. It also seems that an emphasis on discontinuities within culture or among living organic forms lends itself to what I do believe to be a distortion—namely the insistence that biological evolution ceases with the appearance of *Homo sapiens* and that innovation can no longer be regarded as deriving from the actions of biologically specified individuals but as a superorganic form of evolution, independent of particular individuals and hence of both the constitution of identified individuals and the gene pool of any given human stock.

Cultural evolution depends, ultimately, on small crucial innovations that occur at points of divergence in history. Although each attained grade of development contains within it the possibility of a series of further grades, the potential advances toward the next grade actually are taken by groups of particular individuals. Changes in the functional interrelationships within a culture, which may be identified so as to place any given culture as a "culture type" in Steward's sense,[20] are at some point set in motion by the innovation or borrowing of some particular group. If we focus on very long periods of history or very striking changes—such as the development of stone tools or the recent spread of industrialization—we ignore the choice points in the original change that made it possible for parallel sequences—multilineal evolution—or special evolution in Sahlins' and Service's sense,[21] to occur. This book is an attempt to provide a framework within which the actual phenotypic constitution of individuals and their unique experience, as well as the level of cultural development which they represent, may be implicated. Only by bringing about a nexus between particular individuals and particular cultural forms can we provide a basis for discussing cultural evolution as still a part of biological evolution, instead of insisting, as both Kroeber[22] and Huxley[23] do, that genetic evolution has ceased to be significant.

As Julian Steward has pointed out,[24] the preoccupation of those who wish to view cultural evolution as a species-wide, worldwide phenomenon is with a sequence of forms which occurs anywhere in human culture. Which society, which form of culture reaches the next grade is of less significance in this overall view than that the next grade, from seed-gathering to agriculture, from hunting to herding, from herding to ploughing, and so on, is in fact reached. A remark once made by Kroeber about Leslie White, namely that his evolutionary scheme does not involve his own field work, is actually only a statement about different levels of attention. As an evolutionist, White is only passingly concerned with which culture happens to reach the next grade. He treats the appearance of innovations with favorable survival chances as a biologist might treat the appearance of favorable mutations if he is interested in speciation but not in the ecological specifics which made the mutations viable or in the details of the gene pool within which the mutations occurred.

Julian Steward's approach is comparable to that of the ecologist who specializes in analyzing constellations within which comparable evolutionary developments take place. In Steward's approach, the stage of culture at a given moment of time is taken as given and as a precondition of the possibility of attaining the next stage; the ecological circumstances then are examined and causality is attributed to a constellation of features.

Once one such change has occurred, it provides the base for the next change, and the phenomena of the system at a given moment in history, in relation to surrounding systems, provide the conditions for survival of the new form. The limitations of each advance are examined in survival terms which include self-limiting features. Characteristically, students using Steward's approach turn for biological analogues to such concepts as the ecological niche and radiation of particular biological forms.[25]

A finer level of analysis, which still ignores the individual participants in change, is that of Murdock, who combines a survey of what appears to have occurred historically in such matters as change from patrilineal to matrilineal systems, or vice versa, with intensive structural analysis of the consequences and the difficulties of change from one form to another.[26] A large number of analyses that stress structure are being made. They involve such matters as shifts from bilateral to unilateral descent reckoning; from matriliny to patriliny; from complete nonliteracy to universal literacy; from an economy without any form of money—as contrasted with a primitive "money economy" employing a diversity of objects, some of them divisible, interchangeable, and portable, and some less so—to a modern form of currency; from a culture with little division of labor—as contrasted with a highly diversified trading economy with a low level of political organization—to a modern form of social and political organization.[27] Such studies are comparable to those investigations in biology which relate mutation to anatomical structure and the viability of a mutation to the structure of an organ and the limitations and direction provided by the form which that organ has already taken.

Ruth Benedict's study of the forms taken by cultural borrowing in cultures with different configurations,[28] although expressed in terms of preferences for one kind of behavior over another—Dionysian as opposed to Apollonian—which then provide a basis for the acceptance or rejection of alcohol, peyote, or other methods of inducing extreme states of feeling, was essentially of the same sort. She analyzed the preference found in the practices—or the individual personalities studied for regularities—of the members of a society, for its potential receptivity to available new forms of behavior. In this kind of analysis the actual individuals are of no more significance than they are in the kind of analysis of social organization done by Murdock. In Ruth Benedict's analyses, organized feeling or ethos is a cultural given which, though it is more difficult to express in analytical terms, can be abstracted from behavior,[29] just as a kinship form like unilateral descent can be abstracted from behavior.

In addition, it is necessary to discuss the contrasting focus on divergent or convergent development, which Steward thinks is one of the great differences in interest between those whom he classifies as "cultural relativists," i.e. those who are interested in the uniqueness of each culture and so stress divergence, and those who are interested, as he is, in regularities among many cultures, and so stress convergence.[30] Huxley has also emphasized the importance of convergence as unique to human evolution. Stated in biological rather than cultural terminology, this is a way of saying that one of man's achievements in the field of communications has been the ability to transmit and to borrow—and, in part at least, this ability is a function of *Homo sapiens'* continuity as one species.

3. Conditions of Early Forms of Cultural Transmission

CULTURE may be seen as a process through which man creates his living environment and is able to improve it progressively by retaining and modifying advances made by previous generations, teaching the whole to subsequent generations, borrowing innovations made by other groups, and making innovations which are capable of perpetuation. When the word *culture* is used, it will be used in this general sense to describe the process of man's species-wide culture-building behavior. *A culture*—the culture of the Sioux, the Balinese, the Bushmen, or of fifteenth-century Scotland—will be used to designate the historically unique learned behavior of a particular society. The term *society* will be used to describe the largest unit of political autonomy recognized at a given cultural grade. So, among a food-gathering people, a society might be those who claimed ownership of a particular territory but who did not use organized warfare to defend it; among a slash-and-burn horticultural people, the definition of a society might include definite conceptions of membership which might be used to distinguish between killings that were murder and those that were warfare; in the modern world, a nation is such a society. Within a society differences in the culture characteristic of subgroups, geographical regions, classes, and occupational or religious groups will be designated as *versions* of the culture of that society.[1]

Culture in the sense of man's species-characteristic method of meeting problems of maintenance, transformation, and transcendence of the past is an abstraction from our observations on particular cultures, which in turn can only be obtained by observation of particular acts performed by particular individuals, identified as members of such particular cultures or by artifacts in which results of previous acts have been preserved. The confusion between culture as an abstraction and a culture as a "shareable body of material," for which nonanthropologists often chide the cultural anthropologist, comes only from a failure to make this distinction clear.[2] The shareable bodies of materials can then be classified in ways appropriate to the problem at hand. Huxley finds useful Bidney's terms, *artifacts, sociofacts,* and *mentifacts,*[3] and it is certain that we need more formal and abstract categories than the traditional ones of "social organization," "religion," or "material culture," which were the rough boxes in which earlier ethnographers ordered their concrete data. But the point at which the categories are introduced is always significant. The kinship system of Culture A is a reality in the behavior of the members of Society A, in whichever way the scientific observer may choose to abstract it from the observed behavior of members of Society A. If this is kept clear, we need not have the kind of discussion found in Buettner-Janusch's recent paper on Boas' controversy (in 1887) with Otis T. Mason and J. Wesley Powell, in which Boas insisted on the importance of retaining the empirical data.[4]

Cultural behavior means behavior that has been learned and can be transmitted. It is—to use a computer analogy —read into, not built into, the human organism. (But this is, of course, too passive an analogy, as the living organism participates in the learning.) We have been accustomed to use such terms as *biologically given* to designate the kinds of behavior that are species-characteristic, and *learned* for behavior that is peculiar to members of particular cultures, but this usage leads us into certain difficulties in a discussion like this one. It is customary to say that man is a culture-building animal. In this statement, the ability to build a culture—which can be spelled out to mean the ability to build a system of communication, to make and use tools, and so on—is treated as if it were a species-characteristic piece of genotypic behavior that is in some way independent of learning. It might be more useful to say that *Homo sapiens* is a species which can only survive in a man-made environment, using man's dependence on culture as the species-characteristic statement. Such a statement combines the biologically given conditions of a prolonged infancy with complete dependence on adults, for whom no environmental substitute is adequate, and the genotypic capacities of brain, eye, hand, and so on that make it possible to learn a culture and to act within it, to maintain, transform, and in some instances, transcend it. Man may then be said to be a *culture-living* creature. But because of the peculiarities of his dependence at birth on the learned behavior of other, older human beings—a dependence which contrasts in complexity with the dependence on maternal succoring and group protection of other organic creatures—man's biologically given capacities are *learning* capacities alone, while man's *teaching* capacities are embodied in cultural forms rather than in any species-characteristic behavior as yet identified.

The term *cultural transmission* covers a series of activities, all essential to culture, which it is useful to subdivide into the capacity to learn, the capacity to teach, and the capacity to embody knowledge in forms which make it transmissible at a distance in time or space. The simplest human cultures of which we have any records, such as the cultures of the Australian desert tribes, the Bushmen, the

Andaman Islanders, and the Eskimo[5]—peoples without agriculture, wholly dependent on hunting and food-gathering, and organized into small groups, the size of which was consonant with the amount of territory needed to support life—already possessed the rudiments of all these processes. They could learn. Children learned from their elders the techniques of subsistence, the forms of social activities, the myths, and the visual and plastic forms of dance and design. Furthermore, from members of other cultures, the adults could learn a new design, a new weapon form, and so on. They could teach. An adult could intentionally and consciously explain or demonstrate a process, enunciate a prohibition, repeat a verbal routine, or demonstrate a dance pattern in such a way that it could be learned by others.

They also had simple forms within which cultural knowledge could be encoded: tools that could be recognized as tools, weapons, houses (Eskimo), designs made in paint and fur or carved on bone. These might be found, recognized, and copied by other groups. The very simplest of them possessed a machine tool—a hammer to shape other tools. The aboriginal Australians were capable of conceptualizing and coding into an abstract form certain aspects of their cultural behavior, i.e. their rules of marriage and descent. In the classic instance of the Kariera, there were four marriage "classes" which regulated both marriage and descent, so related as to form a cycle. The rules of marriage and descent among the Kariera, as described by Radcliffe-Brown,[6] are shown in this table:

FATHER	MOTHER	CHILD
Banaka	Burung	Palyeri
Burung	Banaka	Karimera
Palyeri	Karimera	Banaka
Karimera	Palyeri	Burung

When the members of two different Australian tribes met, they were able to work out ways in which the marriage classes of one group could be regarded as equivalent to the marriage classes of the other.

The most primitive peoples who have survived to be studied at the present time had already evolved all the essential elements for culture as a communicating system, although, when they were first encountered by Europeans, they had not invented or incorporated or borrowed such practices as agriculture, herding, navigation, wheel transportation, the use of metals, and so on. It is the formal completeness of the communication systems of these very simple peoples that tempted some anthropologists to feel that there was something essentially noncumulative about what used to be called—revealing a bias—"the nonmaterial culture." It was very easy for anthropologists to experience primitive people as whole men, to insist that anything that could be said in any language could be said in their language—with enough patience and circumlocution and inventiveness on the part of the communicators—and to feel that if the essentials of human culture were present in groups so far removed from us in energy use, no evolution took place in the nontechnical sectors of culture, but that a system of communication and social organization temporarily effloresced, only to be replaced by another system, which might be temporarily stronger but was essentially like the first—another episode in human history in which there is really no progress, only cyclic change. However, this view has been altered by a recognition of the way in which evolutionary change in the scientific sector of culture has resulted in change in the symbolic structure.[7]

If we attempt to go back of the evidence of contemporary primitive peoples and use, on the one hand, archaeological evidence and, on the other, the behavior of other primates, it is possible to hypothesize various precursor states, in which there were organic creatures—erect, with hands capable of manipulating materials—who could, for example, use a stone or a stick as a tool, but who were not able to embody any information in the manufacture of the object which would designate it as a tool in the absence of a user. It is also possible to hypothesize a period in which most of the repertoire of sounds was still under genetically determined morphological restraints, but the organic creatures were able to learn to recognize other sound systems made by other creatures with a genetically given repertoire or by organic creatures who already had a cultural repertoire.

In such a hypothetical setting, it is important to allow for the presence of groups of other creatures, some with fewer capabilities than the members of the group under discussion and others with more. A neighboring group, open to inspection, might chance upon a practice, using lower levels of communication than the group we are considering, and might then copy the behavior but use a more elaborated mechanism for doing so.

Recent studies of the behavior of the Japanese monkey (*Macaca fuscata*)—especially the studies of the formation of new food habits—present a good illustration of such a possibility.[8] These monkeys learned to eat potatoes. They then made the innovation of washing the potatoes—a trait which was first the behavior of a single individual and then spread among a whole group. Later still, among a group by the sea, the modification was made of washing the potatoes in salt water—and now some monkeys do this. Here a self-selective food discrimination ability, at least in the initiating monkey, may have been the trigger for the washing in salt water, which was then spread by imitation. A group of hominidae with more efficient methods of communication could have watched these monkeys washing their potatoes in salt water and could have returned either to demonstrate or, with the help of language, to describe the practice to others of their own kind, and the practice might then have become part of the repertoire of learned behavior of the superior group.[9]

Comparably, the ability to learn, to broaden a learned repertoire, to utilize species-characteristic capacities which have not hitherto been used can also be radically changed by the presence in the environment of a species on a higher level of learned behavior. Thus the highly patterned behavior of the pariah dogs of Oriental towns, which Boas used to cite as an example of culture among animals,[10] is a good illustration. The streets, the division into "blocks," the relationships among the dogs' owners, were all cultural phenomena. Within this man-made environment, the dogs were able to differentiate their behavior on a group basis and to transmit to other dogs—on the spot but presumably not away from it—this humanly patterned behavior.[11]

Examination of cases of this kind helps to clarify the differential development in other species of one or another of the behavior components characteristic of cultural transmission. The chaffinch (*Fringilla coelebs*) provides a particularly interesting example of learning song within a community under different conditions, since, in this bird species, the basic pattern of the true song appears to be innate and its development is unaffected by the presence of birds of *other* species. However, the chaffinch may incorporate alien notes in the subsong (which apparently fulfills some practice function for the true song). The full elaboration of the normal song depends on the presence of experienced chaffinches—a characteristic which bird fanciers have long made use of in training young birds in "competition" with specially selected adults. In contrast, when human experimenters have isolated chaffinch nestlings from adult birds from September to May, the young birds reproduce the true song phrasing pattern (apparently learned very early), but the details vary, approximating a community pattern. In further experiments with hand-reared chaffinches, isolated from other birds but not from one another, each community of isolated birds developed a highly uniform community pattern peculiar to itself.[12]

Equally striking is the ability of rats and other species studied by Richter to make discriminating use of modern man's capacity to extract and synthesize biochemical substances which have been known to men only in the last quarter century.[13] Inspection of the behavior of both domesticated laboratory and wild but partially parasitic creatures of other species points up the complex character of what is involved in "cultural transmission." There are many kinds of creatures whose ability to learn has far outrun their ability to transmit what they have learned. A new field of investigation of the ability to learn and to communicate within the species has now been opened up by the material on dolphins from Lilly's laboratory.[14]

It is worthwhile to keep in mind not only the consequences of the changing surface of the earth as man and man-initiated sequences of events, like fires, have changed the contours of the land, the stands of wood, the nature of grasses, the presence of plant and animal species, but also the fact that man, as an indirect consequence of these activities, has accommodated himself to a changing environment, in which some of the changes in insect and fish life may also be traced back to man's own activities.[15] In this long-interdependent sequence man has been able to learn from every segment of the living world. For instance, observation of the swimming behavior of fish has been a guide in submarine construction, and the flight of birds in plane construction; in turn, plane and submarine research have reflected back on the study of birds and fish. Sometimes man's efforts to domesticate and train animals have provided him with new experiences in teaching as well as with models of learning, which have been extended to human children. The lessons of the dog trainer, the horse trainer, the lion trainer have been fed back into ideas of "breaking a child's will" or making a child "housebroken." Such observations and experiences with teaching animals may also be used to raise the level of human teaching, as when Gertrude Hendrix carried over her experience of schooling horses, through her increased recognition of nonverbal awareness, to the teaching of higher mathematics to human children.[16]

Returning to the question of cultural transmission, it is necessary to recognize not only that man's ability to learn is no more than one component in this process, but also that there are many kinds of learning, each of which is itself dependent on styles of teaching. We may hypothesize that the ability to learn is older—as it is also more widespread—than is the ability to teach. Learning can proceed on the basis of sheer imitation, with the teacher merely performing acts already learned without conscious involvement in any teaching activity. Indeed, this is the simple formula which early anthropologists adopted in their thinking about cultures. It was thought that through time, by innovation and borrowing, new items were added to the cultural store, and the young learned by imitation. Much of this learning became, as Boas called it, "automatic,"[17] a concept that in a rough way coincides descriptively with the psychoanalytic "preconscious" and that refers to types of behavior which are not in the focus of consciousness but which owe their peripheral position merely to the fact that they were never brought into consciousness in the course of learning—not to repression or splitting of the psyche.

Even though a culture were to be examined from the standpoint of automatic learning without giving attention to other modes, it would be necessary to discriminate for each culture those areas which are left to "simple" imitation and those in which a conscious recognition of the process is made verbally or demonstrably. Such matters as ways of walking, sitting, and standing, distinctive for each culture, may be transmitted simply by imitation. In a culture where men's and women's postures are nearly identical, there may be very little teaching of posture, and so very little conscious learning of posture. But whenever differences are introduced—between the postures appropriate for ceremonial occasions and for everyday activities or between the appropriate modes of sitting for males and females—some consciousness is involved. It is possible to identify crucial elements. For example, in one culture the correct seated posture for a woman may be with her legs drawn under her and to one side, and the correct seated posture for a man may be cross-legged. Little boys and girls will be corrected, tactilely or verbally, but the bulk of the corrections may be merely denotative in this phrasing: "Girls don't sit like that!" or "Sit like a man!" As the critic may not even have a vocabulary to describe these differences, the presence of the living models —men and women sitting "correctly"—is essential to the communication. The ability to disapprove may have been one of the first teaching abilities to emerge during man's early struggle to build a transmissible culture. Further refinements would come with the ability to name a culturally correct posture—with words for squat, kneel, bow, stand erect, and so on—combined with pointing to specific forms of correct and incorrect behavior.

As the human body has systematic properties related to its anatomical structure, its physiological state, and the ability to perceive movement, the recognition by members of a society of a few elements of a posture–gesture system serves to specify, without words, the rest of the pattern. The English verbal admonition, "Stand up straight!" includes a set of values which are exemplified also in the construction of railway stations without benches and in a large number of other postural and moral imperatives. In contrast, Americans say, "Take the load off your feet." But from an English point of view, the relaxed postures of American soldiers, leaning against the walls of English station waiting rooms—treating the walls as substitutes for chairs or benches—were an exhibition of a type of behavior which could only be regarded as "sloppy" and "slack."

Recent analyses made by Birdwhistell and his associates demonstrate that behavior may be very highly patterned and completely predictable, even though it is neither verbalized nor consciously taught and may not even be recognized as "behavior." [18] Today, with the ability to make fine linguistic–kinesic analyses, it has become possible to indicate in detail what goes into, for example, a three second episode of an interview with a mother and child. (See Plate 14.)

We may think of early man as depending very heavily on imitation without instruction, and on such minimal instruction as is involved either in demonstrating the right behavior or in pointing with disapproval at the wrong behavior. Any further forms of reward and punishment may well have developed together with the domestication of animals, either through the incorporation of animal models, models from animal training, or counter-models, in which human beings, as distinct from animals, had to learn in a "human way," either by gentle manipulation, or verbally, or by the use of "reason."

All recorded cultures use both unintentional imitation, in which neither parents nor children are consciously engaged in the process, and intentional imitation, as when children fashion play models of some adult activity or adults fashion toys representative of adult activity or point to living models. An examination of toys in different cultures illuminates these contrasting usages.[19] Among the Indians of the North American Plains, parents construct child-size paraphernalia—small tepees, cradle boards, weapons—and give them to the children to "play with." [20] In other cultures children, unassisted by parents, may pass on to one another a play world in which certain aspects of adult life are acted out with crude, child-made versions of the adult cultural material. This learning by children may be said to include a conscious effort to mimic the adult role, but the adults may be doing no "teaching" at all. Or the child may be given a small working replica of the adult's tool or weapon—a small girl may have a small-sized carrying bag placed on her head or a little boy may be given a small-sized bow and arrow. Then, as part of everyday life, following along after the adult, the child may use the bag or bow and arrow, not in a playful way in which no end purpose is involved, but to carry food or to kill small game. Or children may be given as toys things which are used only by children—kites, tops, pinwheels, and so on. The adult or older child demonstrates how to "play" with the object, and the child plays with it. Or children may be left to their own devices.

In this type of communication, which appears in many societies, a distinction is not yet made between what it is necessary to teach *children* because they do not *know* it and the establishment of a child-oriented body of behaviors, play villages, miniatures with which the children learn special skills—small canoes, ponies, spears. It precedes these forms as it also precedes the school in which the conscious need to teach has become dominant over the felt need to learn.[21]

We may assume a period in human history when adults were already conscious of some need to teach and had worked out a variety of implicit devices for teaching the next generation—holding the child's hand while it learned to walk, dipping it into the water among swimming people while it learned to swim, even fashioning learning toys or miniatures—but when they had little consciousness of learning not patterned on the adult-to-child or adult sponsor-to-initiate model; teaching situations then of necessity included individuals who knew and individuals who did not know how to do a particular thing.

Another component of cultural transmission almost as important and universal as the practices of teaching and learning across a generation is the ability to borrow from the cultural repertoire of a group which is separated by boundaries from one's own group. In this the appreciation of a difference between *we*—who do things this way—and *they*—who do things another way—is the necessary condition for bringing parts of culture into consciousness so they can be manipulated. The perception that another group of people speaks in a different and unintelligible way may serve only to classify them as "not like us," or on the contrary it may lead to the recognition that there are cultural systems of verbal communication called "language," and that this other group has a different language. The perception that a language is learned by children from parents and is not an inseparable aspect of one's differentiating physique probably could arise only under the stimulus of perceiving that a neighboring people spoke a different language and some experience of learning at least a few foreign utterances. Captured women may have provided some of these early experiences, which made possible the recognition not only that there is *speech,* which adults have mastered and young children have not, but also that there are *languages* which differ systematically from each other and can be learned. This perception is still imperfectly articulate in the average naive member of a society like the United States. Many Americans assume that the languages of primitive peoples have no grammar, or they are surprised to find that in France *little* children speak *good* French.

In New Guinea, a very large number of mutually unintelligible languages are spoken by peoples who are not separated by clearly defined borders. Between clusters of villages whose members clearly speak one language or another, there may be villages where the linguistic status is unclear, where people, as is said in Neo-Melanesian, "all i turn em talk," and people "hear" the languages of neighboring groups even though they cannot speak them. Here again the ability to learn precedes the ability to teach. In contrast, in present-day America, theories of language teaching are more articulate and better organized than is the culturally patterned ability to learn a foreign language. We have, in fact, reached a state in our handling of languages, in which awareness of systematic differences—once a step forward in facilitating learning —has become, in the hands of the grammarians, a block to learning.

Paradoxes of this sort occur throughout the development of means of cultural transmission. Without some degree of abstraction, through the separation of a behavior form from identifiable human actors, the behavior cannot be consciously transmitted. One cannot believe that a skill that appears to be an inalienable aspect of father—and of no other human being—can be acquired by anyone else. This is equally true of behavior which is assigned to a sex or a group, as a "sense of rhythm" is sometimes assigned to Americans of African ancestry. As long as the house form, the method of fighting, the dances, or the ceremonies of the next tribe are thought of as part of their physical being, no diffusion will occur. True, a captured woman may learn the language of her captors, learn to make their kind of mat and dance their dance step, but she has *become one of them.* The next step, in which People A borrows some item of behavior from People B, requires the implicit recognition that this behavior has been learned by those who display it now and so can be learned by others.

The recognition that an item of behavior is learned can be part of the cultural consciousness of either one of the two peoples involved in the diffusion of an item which, considered from this point of view, we call a *trait.* A trait is a unit of culture—making a fire, shaping a tool, plaiting a basket, performing a ritual act—which can be diffused from one culture to another independently of the complex of behavior in which it has been embedded. Occasionally ethnographers describe a culture primarily as an aggregation of traits.[22]

Such a description, when it is combined with a map of the distribution of each trait, gives the impression that each culture is simply an array of items, selected from a larger inventory of available items, but the distribution of these traits also reflects with fair accuracy the state of cultural consciousness within the area, in which these traits are all available, of what can and what cannot be diffused, either by being taught or 'sold' *to* other people, or learned, bought, or stolen *by* other people. It is significant that the routine technical term for diffusion is "borrowing," as if the ethnographer were uncertain of the exact status of the trait, which, as it is possible to buy it, if taken without payment is presumably only borrowed. In the same way the technical linguistic term for words diffused from one language to another is "loanword," reflecting again a feeling that items of vocabulary *belong* to one language and can only be *borrowed* by another.[23]

Cultures differ greatly in the facility with which their members conceptualize their own system as learned and teachable and are receptive to traits from other cultures. In situations of contact between cultures of very different technological levels, it may appear perfectly clear to the members of the higher culture that their methods of preparing the ground, planting seed and harvesting crops, or irrigating, are traits, technical items which men have invented and other men can learn, while to the members of the lower technological level, this may not be self-evident. When it was pointed out to the people of Dobu that missionaries grew yams without the magic which the Dobuans insisted was essential for the growth of a garden, the Dobuans simply denied that the missionaries' crops were any good.[24] This lack of comprehension of the extent to which a technical trait can be diffused is also found in the behavior of the New Guinea native who asks the European to "teach" him to make paper or glass. The European has great difficulty in explaining that although he uses paper and glass—although he in fact claims possession of the higher technological culture in which people know how to make paper or glass—he himself is totally unable to carry out and so to teach the processes.

Our present materials suggest that for every type of culture—and this may require a multidimensional typology which has not yet been developed but which machine computation now makes a possibility—there may be an optimum conceptualization of the kinds of traits that can be advantageously diffused and those that cannot. A people who regard their entire culture, from the seeds that proceed from a sacred store provided by a mythical ancestor, to their own methods of producing children, by spiritual rather than direct biological means, as peculiar to themselves and part of their cultural identity obviously are not able to take advantage of the innovations of their neighbors. Furthermore, if such a people comes in contact with a people who have a much more complex technology, to which they cannot respond by adaptive learning of selected portions, they not only are unlikely to make positive progress, but also are likely to make progressively worse adaptations as they invent ways of *not learning* from the other culture.[25] This maladaptation may take the form of flight from the area that has been invaded by members of the higher culture, as in the case of the Siriono of Eastern Bolivia[26] and other forest-dwelling peoples of South America. Or it may take the form of deprecation, as when Americans regard a foreign language as something spoken only by immigrants, who also demonstrate their inferiority by speaking "broken English" and who cannot, therefore, be regarded as suitable models for Americans. Maladaptation may also be a function of self-deprecation, as when a people, technologically inferior or politically subordinate to another people, accept the estimate of the superior culture and regard themselves as "unable to learn" what "the Europeans," or "the White Men," or "the Japanese" learn.[27]

New Guinea may be described as an area in which the conceptualization of culture as learned behavior has developed with very little idea of a differential ability to learn on the part of one tribe as compared with another, and with an indiscriminate lack of appreciation of ways in which a trait like pottery-*using* differs from pottery-*making* and both differ from a custom like marriage with a father's sister's daughter. In the Sepik Aitape district, any item of culture can be bought and sold. Those who have acquired a culture trait are interested partly in using and adapting it, and partly in selling it to other people who do not happen to have the particular articles, or technical processes, or cultural institutions at that moment in history.[28]

The ability to conceptualize a part of cultural behavior in a form which makes it suitable for teaching, as well as for inarticulate learning, and suitable for purposeful, conscious cross-cultural borrowing or conscious diffusion has to be seen as a dimension of every known culture from the most simple to the most complex. It is manifested today in attitudes toward the transmissibility of political systems like Communism or representative democracy, or religious systems like Christianity or Islam—in contrast to religious systems like Tibetan Buddhism, with its institution of the Dalai Lama, and Judaism, with its emphasis on the ritual conditions in which the fully orthodox Jew must be conceived. It is found in confusions between the usefulness of a manual for a new type of computer and the belief that only by bringing the man who is to use the computer into a computer version of the culture can he learn to use it. Similar confusion exists in the different levels of abstraction at which the improvement of the living habits of other peoples are advocated, for example, whether infants in other countries must be fed some form of milk—as ours are—or whether other nutritionally equivalent substances are acceptable.

A polar contrast to the abstraction and fragmentation and teaching or borrowing of parts of culture can be found in those individuals who have lived at different periods of their lives in two or more cultures, and who, under appropriate conditions, can behave in ways appropriate to culture A or culture B, can think about a subject in one language or in another, but who are quite unable to abstract, isolate, or teach the elements in the styles themselves. These are sophisticated 20th-century counterparts of the captured women of primitive times who learned to speak like their captors.

4. Evolutionary Implications of Learning by Empathy, Imitation, and Identification

IT IS POSSIBLE to construct a conceptual scheme of the many kinds of learning of which man is capable by a variety of methods: running rats in experiments which will yield a cluster of learning patterns; studying individuals in great detail to delineate the small differences in their learning; exploring the species-characteristic learning capacities of many different types of species; analyzing the types of learning which have been institutionalized in different cultures.[1] Each method has its virtues, and only by a lively interchange among those who are using the several different approaches can we be assured of making rapid progress. Oversimplified Pavlovian models have been retained far beyond their usefulness.[2] Since Tarde's original publication,[3] the idea of imitation has been worked to the bone. Experiments on rats have been vitiated by a failure to take into account species-characteristic rat behavior.[4]

In every human society and among many nonhuman creatures,[5] the young learn from the adults and the newcomers to the group learn from the older members in a way which is conveyed by a rather loose use of the word *empathy,* or *Einfühlung,* a German psychological term which was originally used to describe an overall response to the form of a situation, as when an individual experienced discomfort if a picture hung askew on the wall.

Empathy is a far simpler and more global concept than either imitation or identification, both of which are involved in much inexplicit, nonverbal, nonformalized learning.

The difference may be illustrated by a consideration of the Manus children's responses, in 1928. When I showed these children a pencil with a human, rather protuberant bust—which I had taken along just as a miscellaneous item that might amuse them—they immediately threw out their own chests in the posture of the bust. They could not be said to be *imitating* the pencil head as a whole, nor could they be said to be *identifying* with it. Rather, they were acting out the feeling of having one's chest stick out, which was conveyed to them visually by the humorous little pencil top.

But when a Manus child learns from an adult or older child how to say a word, for example the phrase for "I don't want to," *pa pwen,* the teacher sets up an imitative singsong: the child says *pa pwen,* the adult says *pa pwen,* the child says *pa pwen,* and this may go on, especially if the teacher is only slightly older or rather dull mentally, as many as sixty times. Here the learning can be said to proceed by *imitation* of a specific act—in this case a verbal utterance. The teaching elder is imitated by the child, and the imitation is facilitated by the elder then imitating the child's performance. These sequences are characteristically initiated in Manus by the child; the cultural statement is that the elder repeats the child's word or sentence. Imitation of this sort begins a few seconds after birth, when one of the officiating midwives whose duty it is to care for the child—characteristically a representative of the father's lineage—imitates the birth cry of the newborn child. So the first experience of the child, as conceived of and experienced by the adult, is to *hear* a part of the environment around him get in step with him through a purposeful imitative act. This initial welcoming cry is transformed later into a lullaby, which, to Western ears that lack the initial clue, sounds like an appalling screech, rising in steady crescendo to drown out the cries of the child. I verbally recorded this lullaby style in 1928,[6] but at that time I was not allowed to witness a birth—since I myself had not borne a child—and so I lacked the clue of the imitated birth cry, first observed in 1953, which placed the whole behavior in sequence.[7] Seen from the Manus point of view, the nurture of children includes imitation by adults of the human behavior of the child, at the time of birth and later when the child makes its first attempts at coherent speech. This is even carried over to learning another language, as older boys tirelessly echo a smaller boy's first attempt to master the lingua franca—Neo-Melanesian.

In Manus group behavior, empathy and imitation sometimes can be seen to merge. For example, a number of people are standing on opposite sides of a house, supporting themselves by holding onto rafters above their heads; as those on one side initially raise their hands to the rafters, the group facing them will also shift and grasp the rafters—empathetically—and if someone shifts from right hand to left hand, this act will be mirrored by the group on the opposite side.[8]

Among the Manus one can also recognize *identification* behavior in the way in which a little boy reproduces the exact stance, walk, and tone of voice of his father. So, in 1928, it was possible to estimate the entrepreneurial status of the father by the posture and tone of his six-year-old, own or adopted son. It is necessary to invoke the concept of identification to explain the likeness in behavior. The child was not imitating a single act; instead he was acting as if he were the same as—or like—the parent as an individual.

Making this distinction throws into relief another form of Manus modeling behavior, exemplified by a bit of play by a three-year-old boy who climbed on a chair, got himself a piece of paper and a pencil, and *acted like a white man*.[9] The boy was not acting like a particular white man; he did not say he was being the anthropologist. Rather, he was using the anthropologist as a model for the behavior of white men in general. (See Plate 7.)

A further and somewhat different form of empathy can be seen in the behavior of peers. Among the Manus, boys and girls are treated very much alike until they reach the age of betrothal, at about ten years. Up to this time, the emphasis is on those forms of behavior which later will be more exclusively male—handling canoes, swimming, active movement of all sorts. Little girls move and stand like boys, and from a distance the girls' diminutive grass aprons, which are often omitted in play, are the only indication that the girls are, in fact, girls. But among the Iatmul of New Guinea, boys are classed with women and girls until such time as the boys are initiated. Up to the period of initiation boys spend more time with women than they do with men and engage in types of play which are female-modeled, mimicking those parts of family life which are visible to them as uninitiated boys. Among the Iatmul,[10] the stance and posture of ten- and eleven-year-old boys are feminine. Seen from a distance, without articles of clothing to identify them because of water play and so on, mixed groups of boys and girls all look like girls. Among the Manus and the Iatmul, this adjustment in stance and posture differs from such explicit matters as the proper clothing and ornaments for boys and girls, or among the Iatmul, the use of a feminine *thou* which is explicitly taught. The learning of posture may be regarded as empathetic learning that takes place when others put one in the context rather than when one makes the identification oneself. In sharp contrast, in our society, is the little tomboy who consciously identifies herself with boys—modeling herself on them and wishing to be included among them.

In Manus, in 1953, also, observation of the formation of children's groups revealed another extension of mixed empathy–imitativeness, namely, general rather than specific identification behavior. On the beach where a father is working on a canoe, a group will form which includes perhaps his teen-age daughter carrying a baby, a ten-year-old son, and a five-year-old daughter. The small boy may be watching or helping, the five-year-old playing in the sand, the daughter standing by with the baby. Then, depending on the accident of who passes next along that bit of beach, a new individual, who corresponds in age and sex to one of the children, may attach himself to the group. So we now have, for example, two ten-year-old boys in the group. Within a matter of minutes five or six little boys, all of about the same size, may be playing together, and the group may then break away from the canoe-making central figure and wander off on its own. This attraction to individuals of the same size and sex and the magnification of the pull, as more of these individuals become involved, are found in many societies where rigid restrictions do not interfere. But this sequence was more sharply accentuated among the Manus in 1953, I believe, because these people, who had just moved onto land after generations of living on the water, displayed more active following and seeking behavior than is often seen in societies where adults have age-old habits of interfering with the free movement of children.[11]

A further manifestation of Manus empathetic-imitative learning behavior was found in the style of children's imitative play in 1928 and again in 1953. In 1928, adults were caught up in a pattern of grueling economic competition, in which men fished and traded and planned and maneuvered ceaselessly to keep up their end of the continuous interchanges of the perishable and imperishable valuables on which the economic system depended. These interchanges were fully visible to the children; they were dramatic and colorful, and both men and women bedizened themselves for the occasion. Men taking part in one side of the exchange advanced on the village in war paint, with feathers in their hair and feather charms on their backs, wearing phallic coverings of ovalis shells, for the dance with which they would express their aggressive acceptance of the large amount of property which was to be given to them and for which they were to accept the responsibility of repayment. Long strings of dogs' teeth and shell money were festooned from house to house, from canoe to canoe, and from strings stretched between trees on the little artificial island which was the dancing ground. Standing high in the air on narrow carved wooden dancing platforms, the men would dance, flinging their shell-capped phalluses about in a rapid athletic scorning dance.[12]

One might anticipate that this spectacle would appeal strongly to children who had highly developed imitative and identificatory behavior. The little boys did learn the phallic dance with pleasure, practicing assiduously among themselves and sometimes before the proud eyes of their mothers.[13] They also still practiced throwing spears and dodging them as they would once have had to do in wartime, but now did in play—almost as if they were throwing darts.[14] But the financial aspects of the transaction— the great displays of shell money and dogs' teeth, the bridal wealth of aprons made of money, the piles of sago, and the pots of oil—had no counterpart in the children's play.

Samoan children, imitating ceremonial exchanges among

their elders would give a *lafo,* a ceremonial present, to the
one who acted as a talking chief to the chief child dancer,
but the Manus children ignored the whole conspicuous
complex of ceremonial finance which was the chief preoccupation of their elders.

When I recorded the children's behavior in Manus in
1928, I was at a loss to explain why such imitative children
should ignore the principal, conspicuous concerns of their
elders—these exchanges and likewise the spiritualistic
seances in which Manus adults conversed with the ghosts
through dead male-child controls. But in comparing the
behavior of children in 1928 and 1953, I found the clue.
Manus adult life, as it was lived in 1928, was one into
which young men and young girls entered with loathing,
with a sense that life was filled with heavy restrictions
and hard work, exploitation by financial entrepreneurs or
heavy, unending economic responsibility as entrepreneurs
themselves. With shame as a sanction, the adult role lay
heavily on the newly married and on the older adults
also. Warfare and long sea voyages, which provided some
surcease from the steady, exhausting work, had both been
forbidden by the government. What the Manus children
were doing, in 1928, was indeed empathetic and identificatory with the adult's deep *rejection* of the adult role.

In 1953 the culture had been redesigned to eliminate
the grueling exchanges and the tie-in between illness and
economic failure, which had been the principal explanation of illness and misfortune in 1928, and the adults were
enjoying their activities as housebuilders, canoe builders,
and participants in endless council meetings. And now the
children, as imitative as ever, were happily playing at all
of these adult activities; instead of ducking away from
ceremonies as they had in 1928, they sat on the logs that
framed the meeting place like a row of swallows on a telephone line, quiet and absorbed in the unspectacular rou-

tines which their elders now found meaningful and engrossing.

Thus, in delineating the process of transmission through
the forms of behavior which may be described as empathetic, imitative, and identificatory, it is necessary to allow
for a whole series of levels, in which the children may
imitate the affect behind the activity or the meaning of
the action to the adult, rather than the activity itself.

In this context it is necessary to discuss the importance
of identification as a guide to activities which will be
attended to, imitated, avoided, or transformed by omission. In the simplest primitive societies, children are presented with two principal roles, those of men and women;
in addition, some form of religious specialization—a shaman, a sorcerer, a garden magician—may be included. As
the behavior of the two sexes is distinguished in a variety
of ways, self-identification as a boy or a girl comes early.
This identification may be a primary one, so that a baby
boy is treated as a miniature man, and a girl as a miniature
woman. Their shared age stage may be minimized or on
the contrary, the fact that they are both little children or
big children may be stressed. There are many possible
sources of emphasis: vocabulary, dress, the stance taken
by the adult in caring for the child, admonitions of mod-
esty or assignment of different small tasks, permission to
enter the men's quarters or the women's quarters which
may be limited to only one sex or may be granted to both
sexes, and so on. But the kind of learning that takes place
will depend on whether sex or age is the primary orientation. One may even see a change in stress from one village
or one part of the society to another. In Samoa, little girls
on Tutuila were addressed by a different term from that
used for little boys, but in Manu'a the term of address *sole*
was used for boys and girls alike. Analogously, an American teacher may address her fourth-grade class as "Boys

and girls," "Children," or "Class"; in each phrase the sex
identity, the age identity, and the merely situational identity is differently stressed.

In cultures where there is no group term of address for
boys, for girls, or for children, where names are used instead, where there are no differentiating pronouns, and
where many other usages are equally undifferentiated,
children have a greater sense of individual identity and a
more developed capacity to learn from a wider variety of
models. In primitive cultures, where there is always the
possibility that a woman alone may have to perform men's
work—as an Eskimo woman may have to build a snow
house[15] or an Ojibwa woman hunt game[16]—it is not un-
common for girls to learn passively what boys learn actively, so that in emergencies they are able to perform
activities which have only been rehearsed in thought. The
difference in the quality of performance between the snow-
cutting and block-fitting of a man, who has practiced the
necessary skills since he was a small boy, and that of a
woman, who constructs a snow house only in an emergency,
muttering the while a series of precautionary deprecations,
"This is only a woman putting a little bit of snow together," is, of course, conspicuous and perpetuates the idea
that women don't know how to build snow houses and the
idea that women in an emergency can build a snow house
that will do.[17] Among the Manus in 1928, only males were
supposed to speak Neo-Melanesian—the lingua franca
they had used or would grow up to use as work boys.
But women, in malarial delirium, spoke the lingua franca
perfectly adequately; girls, sitting beside their brothers
while they practiced, had learned the language also.

There may also be completely negative learning, as a
child learns not to sit like, talk like, walk like, members
of the opposite sex; learns not to fish or hunt, cook or
weave or make baskets, not to dance or sing in a certain

way, not to pray aloud or go into trance, not to make speeches. In a culture in which sex difference is the primary distinction made between human beings, negative learning is part of the repertoire which each child learns from the last generation, and an accurate statement of what is transmitted includes these negative pictures. So, one can say, a Samoan girl learns how an oven is made. She learns that this is a large-scale household activity carried out by the head of the household in which a pit of hot stones is specially prepared for cooking; she learns also that girls do not make ovens, and she differentiates the parts of the cooking preparations that are appropriate for her. So, too, a Samoan boy learns how a fine mat is made, and also that boys do not make fine mats. The process of negative learning may be analyzed into these three forms: Something I will not do because I am a . . . ; something I will never practice but may have to do although I am a . . . ; something that I must never do if I am to be a. . . . This differentiation already gives considerably greater depth to our understanding of the learning process. Where identifications are heavily value-laden, as in societies where women are regarded as very inferior to men, or in more complex societies, where differences in caste[18] or class or race are value-laden, learning of the third type becomes crippling, and its repercussions may be amplified through the generations, as when a widow attempts to bring up a male child with the statement, "Although you, who are a boy, have to learn X activity, I, who am a woman, cannot show you; I can only *tell* you what to do."

In this kind of learning the role that age plays also varies greatly. So we may ask: In a particular culture, what is the age at which a child is able to imitate an adult? In what ways? Does the child use a toy version of an adult tool or weapon, which introduces an element of play? Does it use as a toy a tool or weapon which is no longer used by the adult? Does it use a smaller but real version of the adult implement?

Among the Cheyenne Indians, a group of children would camp out together—with toy tepees, puppies for babies, and toy weapons—thinking of themselves as a small-scale society.[19] Plains Indian adults, in turn, told tales of how a group of such children had survived, when the entire adult population was wiped out by a war party, and years later were found living as adults, completely replicating the way of life of their parents. It is interesting that this style of learning occurred among the horse-riding, buffalo-hunting, plains-living Indians, whose culture was a very recent development—as a configuration—made possible by the mobility and striking power that came with the horse and the gun, separately introduced from Europe.[20] Here it was the *pattern of life* which the children were helped to replicate, rather than the specific skills of making lances, bows and arrows, or leather-working knives. Similar children's societies are found in South Africa.[21] I have found only one among the five tribes I have studied in New Guinea.[22] Among the Iatmul, where the boys were cut off from all but the external features of the men's ceremonial life, children used to make expeditions into the bush; there the boys hunted small game, the girls cooked it, and the group played out the full visible life of the adults. This included mourning, which the boys learned from women and later, as men, would not share, and shamanistic performance, which women could watch from a distance.

The use of obsolete adult weapons as part of childhood play and learning is found among primitive peoples, just as it is in modern societies. So Manus boys learn to shoot fish with toy bows and arrows, although in adulthood they will use spears.[23] The learning involved includes estimates for refraction as the fish move through the water, but the actual motor movements are different from those needed for spear fishing. Similarly, Manus children learn to handle small canoes, but the relationship between the size of the child and the size of the little canoe is very different from that of adult to full-size canoe. Children also learn to make miniature canoes. In the 1920s they made models of European schooners, which they sailed, wading in the shallows. At that time, adults gave them a chance to punt canoes five times as long as the children were tall, to be part of the serious business of going from place to place for important reasons. In such changes of scale, it is possible for the children to learn behavior that is independent of scale. In looking at photographs, they still respond as readily to an image an eighth of an inch square as to one eight inches square.

Manus children's training gave them a chance to play with things scaled to their own size. From this play they learned: This is something children do with adult approval and help, something just for children that is fitted to their size, strength, and skill. When they were given a chance to play with miniature parts of the adult world, the point of scale with which they were playing was not the ratio of an adult man to a full-sized canoe or schooner but the ratio between themselves and the adults, translated into a kind of omnipotent giant relationship to the models they themselves made. At the same time they were playing at a part of adult life, manfully using a punt that was much too long and heavy, propelling a canoe that was much too large. It is interesting that today, as adults, they feel that the unreal, omnipotent type of play with miniatures was obsessive. In 1953, Kilipak, a Manus man, reminisced about his childhood, twenty-five years earlier:[24]

> When I was little I thought about a little canoe, a
> very little one. I was little and so I could not think

of anything else. However, I also could think about
shooting fish. When I woke from sleep in the morning I had no mind for anything else except going to
get my little fish spear, my little arrows—you remember the bows and arrows that Pomat and I made and
some of those you bought and took away with you—
and then I would hurry out to fish with them. But
they weren't big fish, they were only little ones. Sometimes they could be eaten, sometimes they were too
small to eat. These were just thrown away. The day
would pass and it would be night. I would sleep with
my father and mother, in the morning my thought
would be on going out fishing again. Then I would
go and shoot fish again. I wouldn't think of anything
else. If it was bad weather I would stay at home with
my father and mother and other children would come
and we would talk of something that we wanted to
make. We used to talk about it first, talk about toy
canoes, about coconut shell [craft]. If the wind from
one direction was right, all of us would go there. All
of us would gather [in a crowd] and do it. When play
finished and it was night, our minds would not give up
thinking about them [the canoes]. At dawn, I would
get up and think of nothing but playing with these
little canoes. Later, I spent all of my time in the sea.
My mother would wait and wait but I would not
come home. The food cooked for me would harden.
It would be cold. My mother would wait and I would
not come. Finally she would shout for me. I would
go and eat but my thoughts would still be on the
games with the canoes. As soon as I had eaten, back
I would go. Now I would play again with my little
canoes. Each day it would be the same. My thoughts
never turned to anything else. Because after all I was
a young boy. Now my mind was set on play only.

Peoples who live in small family groups, moving often and with little opportunity for children of the same age to play together, are likely to equip the children with miniature replicas of reality, with which they can play individually, and with child-sized versions of real weapons and tools. So Arapesh boys have small bows and arrows with which they shoot small game, especially rats; and little Arapesh girls are given tiny carrying bags to wear on their heads, while they themselves are still small enough to be carried in their mothers' carrying bags. Children accompany their parents and participate in adult activities which involve little skill. No attempt is made to develop skill; the emphasis is rather on an easy, pleasant identification with the activities of adults.

In contrast, among the Eskimo, where the adults are highly skilled and where the possession of the necessary tools and equipment is a matter of life and death, children learn adult skills very young.[25] The toys with which children play are real-life miniatures or the discarded paraphernalia of an adult ceremony in which the children have participated. By the time an Eskimo child is five or six, it is beginning to master the major techniques of survival.[26]

Among the Balinese, children are encouraged to imitate the theatrical and artistic aspects of life. They play with adult-fashioned toys—little grotesques which are also used as kitchen gods, or small versions of part of a ceremony, as a bamboo clapper with which a two-year-old can imitate the sound made when the dragon mask clatters its wooden jaws. They also have miniature bamboo arenas in which crickets instead of cocks can be teased with little sticks into fighting each other. Children may also spontaneously develop child-scale ceremonials of their own, with a boy-sized dragon, witch, and orchestra; the adults then take part in the play, "ordering the dragon" and "feeding the orchestra." [27] As the Eskimo in the arduous Arctic environment depend for survival on their skills, so it may be said that the Balinese depend most on the artistic and theatrical aspects of their culture. The skills which insure subsistence in Bali—the skills needed for irrigation, rice-planting, transplanting, and harvesting—are routinized and subdivided into tasks appropriate to different skill levels, so that there no longer is any possibility of disaster for lack of skill in food-getting, house-building, pot-making, and so on. Droughts or earthquakes or breakdowns of social organization in wartime may bring about catastrophe in Bali; but catastrophe does not stem from failure to acquire essential skills in childhood. But the arts on which the Balinese depend for the perpetuation of their special type of social organization are as essential to them as are the dog sled and snow house to the Eskimo, and the nexus between child play and adult life is found in the arts.

Where there are toys or games or activities—such as modeling or sliding on the muddy banks of the river—which are regarded as appropriate only for children and other activities which are appropriate only for adults and are strictly forbidden to children of both sexes—such as entry into the men's ceremonial house in Iatmul, or entry into the tent of a medicine man among the Cheyenne, or entry into a ceremonial council among the Samoans—there is the possibility that ideas about appropriate rate of growth may be introduced either to reward the child who gives up play earlier or, as in Samoa, to punish the child who goes too far ahead of the others. The conditions are present, too, for small children to mock and jeer at still smaller ones, and for ideas of success and failure, defeat and shame to be included in the learning process. But where children of different ages perform with different degrees of skill acts which adults perform with more strength, using bigger tools or weapons, catching bigger game, the single sequence from child to adult—with the adult doing something best—keeps each child's attention focused on the model and decreases the likelihood of competitive and contemptuous treatment among children. Age grading of behavior, involving any skill, changes this situation; even among peoples who do not yet keep track of exact age because they have no calendar or have no skill in counting, a rough count can be kept of which children are the same age or just a little older or younger. When, in addition, there are adult skills which some adults achieve and others do not, then competitive modeling between peers may be complicated by competitive efforts to attain these specialized skills as hunter or orator, wood carver or warrior.

Passive learning is characteristic also of cultural arrangements in which the choice of a boy to fill an adult role depends on his attainment of some particular adult skill and in which, once the choice has been made, the boy's wife also becomes a participant. In Samoa, for example, male talking chiefs are selected by the kinship group for their ability to memorize and their talents as orators. In the women's village council which replicates the men's, the wives of men who have been chosen as talking chiefs —an honor that finally comes in middle age—speak with as great differential fluency as their husbands do.[28]

The kind of learning that takes place is affected also by the person who is primarily responsible for the care of the small child—a child nurse, a grandparent, a parent.[29] The slightly older child nurse interposes an interpretive screen between the adult activity and the little child: The handling is less sure, the infant may be carried when it can easily walk, may be fed when it can feed itself, may be hustled away instead of being disciplined or reasoned with. It also makes a difference for the child's learning whether or not the child nurse is invariably a girl; if the child nurse is a girl, the infant's appreciation of the female style of behavior is twice mediated, once by the mother and second by the child nurse. But if girls carry girl babies and boys carry boy babies, the boy's first experience of the male style of behavior comes not from a man, but from a boy whose first model has been a woman. Every shift of this sort introduces a layering of empathetic learning, a possibility of break in style and in identification, which may or may not be represented in adult life.[30] In Bali and in Iatmul, where little girls carry babies of both sexes, and little boys carry boy babies, ceremonials and theatricals provide for a variety of reversals of sex behavior—in Bali even for double reversals, as when the dancing style of the female servant of the principal female character is danced by a girl imitating a boy imitating a woman. Where play, theater, or ceremonial permits reversals in age-typed behavior also, a sufficient amount of identification and empathetic learning may be preserved.[31] In those cultures in which (in adult life) behaving like a child or like a member of the opposite sex is severely penalized, sometimes unilaterally for one sex, the breaks thus introduced into the learning process may persist throughout life as serious defects in learning; this is, for example, the case with girls learning mathematics or boys learning the arts in the United States.

Seen from an evolutionary point of view, in very simple societies, these various forms of child care, age and sex discriminations, and various degrees of permissiveness in moving freely from one identificatory pattern to another are factors in the survival potential of any given culture.

Another variation of evolutionary significance is the cultural phrasing of the appropriate age when a given skill can or may be learned. There may be rigid cutoff points; for example, a girl who shows no grace in dancing when she first joins the group of dancing young girls may be immediately jeered out of dancing, and so she has no opportunity to learn slowly. This means that different kinds of slow learning do not become embodied in the style of behavior. Undoubtedly, such cutoff points encourage greater specialization in any activity. Hunting that is done only by those who have demonstrated a specially good eye for game and good aim with bow and arrow is more specialized and skilled than it would be among a people all of whom must be hunters, those with a good eye and those with a poor eye also. Where a culture has elaborated methods of learning—and/or teaching—that are adequate for every member of the group and the possible precision and skill requirements have been so modified that all may take part in an activity, there is a danger that we will also find lowered skill, a cheerful acceptance of relative failure, social support of the inefficient and, correspondingly, a fairly low ability to change and incorporate either innovation or borrowing. If there is no fixed idea of the age at which a skill may be learned—as in Bali, where old men may begin to carve or paint, go into trance, write script and, equally, very small children who show special proficiency may be allowed to perform far beyond their years—the acts so engaged in may bear within their style the imprint of the deficiencies and the virtues of the different ages at which apprentices begin to practice them. This provides another dimension of depth and also a receptivity at any age to new learning from outside.

Where, however, there is very rigid age grading and the old have special functions and tasks permitted only to them, as among the Australian aborigines, this may contribute to the culture a sense of finality and completeness with very low receptivity to change.[32] Children grow up looking forward to performing activities in which they cannot yet engage, and the passively experienced image of the possible future may deter them from learning anything new which might interfere with the attainment of the completely glimpsed and completely unrealized goal. This effect seems to be produced most sharply when there are special, visible behaviors restricted to the grandparental generation and the grandparents also play an important part in the actual care and education of the young, so that the children empathize the motor–kinesthetic behavior of the grandparents and, as spectators, identify with the behavior of individual older people. Such learning makes for very great conservatism and a willingness to cherish an impoverished pattern of life long after it has ceased to be capable of growth or adaptation and is steadily declining in viability.[33] Where there is an expectation that children will learn from peers, from grandparents, or from specially appointed mentors, then again parents' statements to children that they cannot show them, because they themselves are no longer children, or they are not yet old, or they are not specialists in hunting or fishing, and so on, will also include this negative element and will introduce into the learning process a sense of lack or loss.

The use of the next tribe as a model in defining learning by negative identification is also very common among primitive peoples; this is the case when the next tribe is seen as a people who *"do* something *we don't do."* [34] If this activity is disapproved and unvalued, then the invocation of the other tribe's behavior, "You are sitting, eating, moving, like the X's," is a suppressive device. For even though the child gives up the behavior, the possibility will be carried along negatively, coupled with fear of punishment or ridicule if the behavior should recur, and will have a crippling effect on the freedom to learn new things. If the only experience of a group other than one's own has been with such a negative model, the ability to learn from foreigners may be completely lost.

On the other hand, if the group which is designated as an unsuitable model—men for girls, women for boys, the next tribe, a different caste—is also described as practicing behaviors which are highly admirable, another sort of crippling may take place, as whole areas of behavior, bravery, strength, skills, and knowledge of special kinds, by virtue of the definition, may become "something which I cannot learn because I am not. . . ." Where disapproved behavior may be carried as something one fears one may lapse into, the superior, and apparently innately superior, abilities of another group help to define the self as someone who is *not* able to be, do, or act in valued ways.

This definition of the self was characteristic of the Mountain Arapesh, both men and women. They defined both their neighbors toward the sea and their neighbors inland as superior to themselves in every respect. Those nearer the seacoast were more skilled, cleverer, richer, more fashionable, and those in the interior were stronger, more skilled, and possessed of much stronger magic. Other people made beautifully patterned string bags, but they themselves could only make bags without patterns; other people carved designs on spears and arrows, but they could only haft together unornamented points and shafts; other people made pots, other people invented beautiful songs and complex dances, other people possessed or made musical instruments. They themselves could only work to import other peoples' superior products. When they attempted to make copies, the copies were in fact poor, oversimplified, and inadequate, reinforcing their own opinion of their own capabilities.[35]

This continuum of empathetic, imitative, and identificatory learning may be used in analyzing any culture. Such an analysis takes into account the degree of dependence on this kind of learning, the sensory modalities that are involved, the type of imitation (imitation of the act or of the feeling about the act, inhibition of imitation of the act or inhibition of feelings about the act), the number of identificatory pathways that are used (a simple dichotomy between men and women, between older persons and younger ones, between men and women, on the one hand, and shamans, on the other, between persons of higher and of lower rank, each group subdivided by sex, order of birth, and so on). Each culturally perceived difference in identificatory pathways changes the possibilities of learning by making available new and complex positive learning, by defining more types of negative learning—more ways in which individuals *cannot* move, feel, act—and by so doing alters the extent to which individuals may, or may not, add to the available store of learned behavior in a society.

The Iatmul use myth and folktale to validate membership in divisions of the social organization and also ownership of land. Knowledge of the correct version of the myth is therefore interpreted as proof of a kin claim to the land as well as to some type of group membership. The Iatmul have developed a style of reference to validating myths in which the plot is fragmented. In a debate a public speaker refers to a specific myth in terms of exoteric clichés; in this way he demonstrates his membership in a group and at the same time keeps outsiders in the dark as to the esoteric matrix of the story. Gregory Bateson demonstrates this style of reference through a retelling of the Red Ridinghood story, which goes as follows:

> "The better to eat you," she said.
> She put in her basket two pats of butter. There was an egg.
> And it wasn't the grandmother, it was the wolf.

In a Iatmul village there is a great stock of this kind of lore. Every intelligent man can dictate texts for hours, sometimes more and sometimes less cryptically, in which the conventions of time and space and generation are scrambled. The scrambling has become a cultural style and has its representation in the sense of the self. So a fourteen-year-old boy, replying to questions about his life, will start, in what appears to be an orderly fashion, with his early childhood and a memory of a head-hunting raid; but as one takes down the text one suddenly hears him say, "And then I married a woman of Wompun, and she bore me a male child." One looks up with a start, but it is still an unmarried boy talking. The mythology which validates the claims of each clan and each moiety is endlessly repetitious, each story very much like another. A study of all the myths would yield little more understanding than study of a few of them can. In one village, for example, the members of both sides of one of the dual divisions claim the sun as one of their totemic possessions; but one side will declare to the others with great assurance, *"Your* sun is decayed" (*stink–finish*, in Neo-Melanesian). Under these circumstances each individual's capacity to deal with a time–space reality is impaired, and a broken, discontinuous sense of the self is perpetuated; in addition, this is a very poor situation into which to introduce new knowledge.

This is clearly demonstrated in Gregory Bateson's description, in *Naven*, of how these esoteric discussions proceed:[36]

> The problems which most exercise the Iatmul mind appear to us fundamentally unreal. There is, for example, a standing argument between the Sun moiety and the Mother moiety as to the nature of Night. While the Sun people claim Day as their totemic property, the Mother people claim Night and have developed an elaborate esoteric rigmarole about mountains meeting in the sky, and ducks, and the Milky Way to explain its existence. The Sun people are con-

temptuous of this and Night has become a bone of contention. The Mother people maintain that Night is a positive phenomenon due to the overlapping mountains, etc., while the Sun people maintain that Night is a mere nullity, a negation of Day, due to the absence of *their* totem, the Sun.

Again, within the Sun moiety itself there is matter for dispute about the Sun. One of his totemic names is Twat-mali,[1] but there are two clans in this moiety who lay claim to this name. Each clan has its own string of names linked with this. Thus clan *A* claims that the series runs: Twat-mali, Awai-mali; Ka-ruat-mali, Kisa-ruat-mali; etc. (nine pairs of names), while clan *B* claims that the series runs: Twat-mali, Awai-mali; Ndombwangga-ndo, Kambwak-mbwangga-ndo; etc. (eight pairs of names). At some time in the past a settlement of this argument has apparently been reached in a compromise: that there are two Twat-malis, one of whom is the sun who shines nowadays, while the other is the old sun, who lies as a decaying rock somewhere in the plains north of the Sepik River. But the settlement is only partial, because it has never been agreed which of the two Twat-malis is which, and nowadays each clan taunts the other by saying that their own Twat-mali is in the sky, while that of the opposition lies rotting in the plains.

Another subject which is matter for this character-istic intellectual enquiry is the nature of ripples and waves on the surface of water. It is said secretly that men, pigs, trees, grass—all the objects in the world—are only patterns of waves. Indeed there seems to be some agreement about this, although it perhaps con-

[1] Other clans of the Sun moiety have other names for the Sun—Ianggun-mali, Kala-ndimi, etc. The dispute here discussed is concerned merely with Twat-mali.

flicts with the theory of reincarnation, according to which the ghost of the dead is blown as mist by the East Wind up the river and into the womb of the deceased's son's wife. Be that as it may—there is still the question of how ripples and waves are caused. The clan which claims the East Wind as a totem is clear enough about this: the Wind with her mosquito fan causes the waves. But other clans have personified the waves and say that they are a person (Kontum-mali) independent of the wind. Other clans, again, have other theories. On one occasion I took some Iatmul natives down to the coast and found one of them sitting by himself gazing with rapt attention at the sea. It was a windless day, but a slow swell was breaking on the beach. Among the totemic ancestors of his clan he counted a personified slit gong who had floated down the river to the sea and who was believed to cause the waves. He was gazing at the waves which were heaving and breaking when no wind was blowing, demonstrating the truth of his clan myth.

On another occasion I invited one of my informants to witness the development of photographic plates. I first desensitised the plates and then developed them in an open dish in moderate light, so that my informant was able to see the gradual appearance of the images. He was much interested, and some days later made me promise never to show this process to members of other clans. Kontum-mali was one of his ancestors, and he saw in the process of photographic development the actual embodiment of ripples into images, and regarded this as a demonstration of the truth of the clan's secret.

This intellectual attitude towards the great natural phenomena crops up continually in conversations between the anthropologist and his informants, the latter striving to pump the anthropologist about the nature of the universe. I learned very soon that the correct attitude to adopt in such conversations was one of extreme discretion. I parted with information only after insisting upon secrecy and then shared the secret as a bond between my informant and myself. With such preliminaries, what I said was treated seriously, but without them it was generally assumed to be exoteric lies. One man came quietly, boasting to me that he knew the European secrets about day and night; that a white man had told him that by day the Sun travelled over the earth and then during the night he returned to the East, travelling back over the sky-world, so that the people in the sky have day while we on earth are having night and *vice versa*—a pretty re-phrasing of the Antipodes in Iatmul terms.

The Iatmul way of handling the results of the scientific inquiries of a more evolutionarily advanced people as part of the esoteric stock-in-trade of their own mythological system—that is, as just one more bit of material about which to engage in endless, self-gratifying debate—contrasts vividly with the way in which the Manus, a people without such an esoteric mythology, handled a comparable piece of Western-derived scientific knowledge.

One night in 1953 when I was out in a fishing canoe, Manuwai, an older fisherman, remarked meditatively, "When I was little I thought the sun and the moon were one, that the moon was the sun only cold. Then one day I saw them both in the sky together and then I thought, 'There must be two.'" Some months earlier, the group of men whom I had known in 1928 as small boys had gathered on the verandah of my house; as they stepped down to the plaza in the center of the village, we saw that there was an eclipse of the moon. One of them said, "You remember, when you were here before this happened. And you took a ball and a large fruit, and showed us, with the lamp, what had happened." Now, tonight, out fishing, Manuwai wondered out loud whether one could catch up with a falling star, and easily accepted my explanation of what a falling star was. For the Manus, alert to the real world, there is always the possibility of new knowledge that will demand a new response because it is more accurate than the old.

So the social structure of a society and the way learning is structured—the way it passes from mother to daughter, from father to son, from mother's brother to sister's son, from shaman to novice, from mythological specialist to aspirant specialist—determine far beyond the actual content of the learning both how individuals will learn to think and how the store of learning, the sum total of separate pieces of skill and knowledge which could be obtained by separately interviewing each member of the society, is shared and used.[37] Bateson estimates that many Iatmul natives know from ten to twenty thousand names, in a rough but not fixed order, and the associated bits of myth provide images, visual and kinesthetic, which trigger off another pair and another. This type of proliferation, in which the style but not the content is shared and in which the style provides a culturally gratifying way of handling new information, exemplifies the hypertrophy of an initially valuable cultural invention—the division of labor for purposes of memorizing material in the absence of methods of writing to record it.

And when one considers the Iatmul, concentrated on masses of proliferated totemic names, and the Manus, concentrated on a set of shared skills in learning to deal with the physical environment, there is a striking contrast in the relative readiness of each of the two peoples for the constructive absorption of those parts of Western culture that are based on science.

Still another effect of a division of labor in information storing in human memories can be found among the Arapesh, who share with the Iatmul and many other New Guinea peoples the idea of initiatory secrets but who lack the trained capacity to remember much material. In all New Guinea initiatory cultures, the initiates, typically adolescent boys, are told a certain set of secrets, namely that the noise-making instruments—bull-roarers, water drums, flutes, whistles, etc.—are not the voices of supernaturals, but are operated by men, their own fathers and uncles and older brothers, and they are taught the necessary procedures for keeping these secrets safe from women and children. Where, as among the Iatmul, the initiation is accompanied by greater access to an exceedingly rich and complex system, the central fact—the knowledge that the spectacles which they have observed at a distance are in fact all man-manipulated theatricals or, stated more simply, are hoaxes on the women and children—is not necessarily the central part of the experience. But among the Arapesh, where there is no elaborate content, young Arapesh boys, who have run away with their frightened mothers on hearing the sound of the approaching supernatural, learn simply that the one thing in their lives which might hold interest, complexity, and content is really only a very tiring obligation to deceive the women for the sake of the women's own safety.[38] The major learning is, "This is all there is. It is tiring and necessary, and for the rest of my life, whenever there is a ceremony, I'll have to sit and blow flutes no matter how hungry I get."

In many cultures, rank and the forms of behavior related to rank may have the same effect as learning that is rigorously specialized by sex. Members of each rank learn both what they can do and what they cannot do; for example, a low-ranking man learns what he can do if no man of higher rank is present, as compared with an absolute proscription against some form of behavior in terms of rank. So, said the Samoans of Manu'a, a man of low rank could not be brave; he would be killed if he went ahead of a man of high rank. They assumed that in battle the leaders would always be men of high rank and that men of low rank would never have an opportunity to display the type of behavior they described as "brave." Such a prohibition tended to limit the ambition of members of low-ranking families; they did not learn to be brave nor did they learn to be orators with all the knowledge of the past and of verbal style that oratory demanded.

In Bali, people of different castes all take part in the same theatrical performance, and the chief role will go not to a member of the highest caste but to the man with the skill to act the part. Yet the etiquette of caste will be maintained among the actors: When they sit down to chew betel nut, high-castes will sit higher than low-castes. But when the play begins, the low-caste actor may be the prince and the Brahman his servant. Within a shared pool of skills, each individual can perform as an individual. But in Samoa there are dances performed only by the individuals who hold such special titles as *taupou, manaia,* and high chief of a village; the dances are dull but well-executed. All dances are accessible to all children as models, and every child learns to dance. But the chief dance models are status bound and must be of a kind that can be taught to the girl or youth selected to fill a role because of kinship position in the family of a high chief.

Cultural arrangements which debar men of lower status from the behavior of men of higher status thus reduce the exercise of individual skills and potentialities. In contrast, cultural arrangements in which a large number of special skills (such as the ability to dance, carve, make speeches, learn masses of tradition, or debate) are divorced from any special limitations of sex, or age, or rank may reinforce the actualization of individual abilities; so girls are proud of being allowed to do what boys do and men of low caste enjoy situations where their performance exceeds that of high-caste men. A counter-situation occurs when it is believed that those of higher status can more easily learn some skill which is, however, also engaged in and excelled in by members of the lower group.[39] So in Bali, the demonstration of a new activity to a high-caste, by pointing to a low-caste who has learned the new skill (for example, driving a car, touch-typing, or dictating into a tape recorder), is a way of facilitating the learning by the high-caste, who finds it unthinkable that a Brahman cannot learn anything —anything that is not defined as defiling—more quickly and better than a low-caste.

Even in the very simplest cultures we find conditions which are favorable or unfavorable to evolution in the ways in which age, sex, and the manipulation of even very small amounts of esoteric knowledge are structured, so that the specially gifted are assured—or deprived—of a chance to exercise their gifts in any particular field.

5. Evolutionary Significance
of Transmission
# of Culture Through Artifacts

THE CONSCIOUS ACQUISITION and use of the kinds of behavior that are perceived as separable parts of the culture are facilitated to the extent that these behaviors are embodied in persistent objective forms, separable in space and time from their makers and users.

It is necessary here to return to the very simplest level of the use and manufacture of objects. Possibly the first object to be diffused from one tribe to another was fire, which no one as yet knew how to kindle but which could be found smouldering in another group's abandoned camp, or could be stolen from an enemy who had been put to flight, or, in a truce situation, could even be given to a neighboring group.

Most of what can be said about early diffusion is purely speculative. But we do have enough material on the use of simple tools and weapons to construct plausible stages of cross-tribal cultural transmission mediated by artifacts and man-made objects. If a group has the idea of a tool—something which has been shaped for a purpose and can be used by someone other than the maker—then, when one of them encounters an artifact that has been dropped, lost, or discarded by other human beings, he is in a position to categorize this object, which shows signs of human workmanship, as a "tool." He can experiment with its use and if this proves satisfactory he can try to reproduce it. But in order to attempt reproduction, those who have found the unfamiliar tool must be able to make a series of conceptualizations, often in condensed form, but still there: "This was made by man, intentionally, out of a known—or an unknown—material. It was made by a process known—or unknown—to me. It was made for a known—or an unknown—purpose. I might use it in the same way that our X is used. I might try to see if it is useful as a Y. I have no idea what they, the known—or unknown—makers used it for, but as somebody made it for some purpose, it must be valuable. Therefore I shall keep and cherish it, even though I do not know how to use it."

Comparisons of different "accidental discovery" situations help to clarify the steps involved. A people who made stone tools might find a flaked tool dropped on a path by an unknown people, who obviously must use a tool of some closely comparable type. Or after an ambush, they might find an arrowhead in the dead body of one of their own number, an object made by a known people who were their enemies and whose manufacturing procedures could only be inferred, not observed. Or they might find some small object left on a beach by the crew of a ship they never saw. Or they might discover a bullet embedded in a tree trunk and have no clue to the kind of weapon in which it was used.

However different the situations of discovery are, the message to any tool-making people carried by any tool is clear: "This was made by man for use." What the subsequent steps will be—assigning a use to the new artifact; considering and identifying the material, available and named but hitherto not used for such a purpose; attempting to use it; attempting to manufacture facsimiles; keeping it as a sacred and powerful object of unknown use—will depend not only on a people's technological level but also on the available natural resources and their knowledge of them, the number of technological practices they already have at their command, and their sense of their own abilities to imitate, experiment, and innovate. Making the same object, when the process of manufacture can only be guessed at, by using a well-known technique—for example, copying a pot by a different pottery-making process, since the actual method used cannot be analyzed and perceived—is in one sense an innovation, but it is an innovation based on an artifact representative of knowledge that is already in existence in some other culture.

Some theorists have wished to distinguish sharply between diffusion and innovation, but it seems more useful here to consider as innovative all acts that are new from the standpoint of the one who performs them. It is useful to make a differentiation—to classify an act as innovative only if it adds to the sum of known inventions as made by the whole species and to classify it as merely "borrowing" if an already-invented artifact is the stimulus—only when one is taking an overall view of evolution, a view which includes the assumption that any invention will in time diffuse. However, in a given culture, when we want to know something about the conditions under which learning from other cultures will take place and about the likelihood of innovation arising from the willingness to use the strange and to experiment with processes of manufacture, then it is more useful to work on a continuum. So we may think of an individual picking up a strange object and keeping it; later it may act as a stimulus to someone other than the original finder. Or we may think of an individual picking up a strange object and attempting to use it as a substitute for an existing type of tool, without attempting to copy any of its features. Here again, as the finder uses the object, other people have an opportunity to see it in use, and they may begin to speculate about how it is manufactured. From the experimental attempt to make it by some known method, it is only one step to the experimental attempt to develop a process that will have these results, or to use the tool with a conjectured purpose to initiate activities hitherto unperformed. For example, a people who had always drunk liquids from globular containers might come upon a spoon made of bone; the conjectured use—scooping up small amounts of liquid—then becomes the route by which spoon-using is incorporated into the culture. The act of inventing a spoon, rather than responding imaginatively to an unknown artifact and so coming on the idea of its use, involves many of the same processes, beginning with a willingness to think of something new—which involves both a new act and a new object.

Detailed analysis will make it possible to identify not only different kinds of ability to conceptualize any item of culture (a tool or a word) or any cultural system (a language), but also optimum degrees of receptivity for cultures at different technological levels and with different combinations of available resources.

Eskimo culture has been discussed as one which was conducive to many small innovations.[1] The Eskimo were able to see the usefulness of certain artifacts of European culture and willingly adopted these; when parts broke or were lost, they showed great ingenuity in "inventing" replacements. This capacity for small innovative procedures can be related to the Eskimo experience of living a semi-nomadic life in an area in which technical adjustment meant the difference between life and death.

Eskimo technology was very specific. That is, the Eskimo had a preference for tools with special uses, such as a probe to measure the homogeneity or depth of the layer of snow from which snow blocks were to be cut. Successful use of this technology depended on a most detailed knowledge of local areas—depth of water, shape of shoreline, direction of wind, and habits of the game animals and birds within a very local environment.[2] The Eskimo habit of visiting carried with it, of course, complex hospitality patterns, including specification of the behavior between host and guest, the amount of equipment a man had to bring with him to permit him to set up—possibly with a borrowed wife—a separate fire within the igloo, and so on. During the guest's stay, the guest was deeply dependent on his host's knowledge, and patterned methods of conveying this information in an immediate and useful form had been developed. Where in other cultures conveying ecological information is patterned in relations between old and young, here the communication was between contemporaries. It has been suggested [3] that this is one reason why the Eskimo could dispense with the presence of old people —with the institution of gerontocracy, which was so important among the Australian aborigines, who were also a nomadic hunting people deeply dependent upon localized ecological knowledge.

Where cultural conditions continually require making small adjustments, and also carrying along as part of one's repertoire a set of substitutions—how to make a knife of ice instead of bone, how to make runners of frozen hide instead of wood or bone—the ability to innovate may become routinized in such a way that larger-scale innovations when needed may not be made.

Ecological information of the kind necessary for survival among the Eskimo may be entirely dependent upon face-to-face contact; here men share with other creatures part of this orienting behavior. So, among the red deer described by Frazer Darling,[4] it is the old females who know the paths; the death of all the old females would alter, perhaps fatally, the migration patterns of the herd.

We may also enumerate a set of ways of storing information about space which are progressively more efficient and which, as they progress, become more independent of the presence of specific tutors and pupils. These ways of communicating information about direction and space should not be regarded as an evolutionary series in a narrow sense —that is, the steps do not necessarily follow in a given order. But they form an evolutionary series in the wider sense that human beings in different cultures have evolved more efficient transmission devices.

We may consider now a continuum, defined only in terms of the degree of dependence on, or independence of, the presence of another organic being who "knows." At one end of the continuum we can place the red deer, which can only lead the way. At the other end there are such things as our very complicated navigational maps, which might be lost but would still be useful, hundreds of years later, to those who learned to read them.[5] We may then designate some of the innovations that have occurred in the course of the evolution of culture. There is, for example, the naming of geographical features, so that one who knows can point to a mountain and say, "That is Suapoli," and on another day can tell the person to "go to Suapoli." This is already an advance on the statement, "Come with me and I will show you." There is the naming of directions, so that without pointing it is possible to say, "Go toward the rising sun." Later, technological refinement makes it possible to say, "Go northwest by north." And now it is possible to say, "Launch on the 3rd of March at 0630 zebra (Greenwich time) at latitude $45°30''$ and longitude $85°43''$ at an inclination of $69°$; then at 0715 zebra activate the ejector stage until a velocity of 25,000 nautical miles/hr is reached . . ."[6]

Then there are the various ways men have devised for designating and measuring distance. One way of measuring distance by time was to say, "Then you walk-walk-walk-

walk-walk," a descriptive statement, the meaning of which is dependent on the similar use of reduplication by speaker and hearer. Later, it becomes possible to say, "You will have to walk three days and sleep two nights." With the designation of space units, it becomes possible to say, "Ride 23 miles," and still later, emphasizing relative velocity, "It takes seven hours by car to Laconia, and seven hours by jet to Paris." And today very fast aircraft (in fact, most aircraft) have a Mach meter which measures the speed of the vehicle relative to the speed of sound.[7]

Once man was dependent on immediate demonstration. Today we have the means of projection, the means of measurement, and the vocabulary of instruction necessary for sending a man on a journey into outer space, where no human being has ever been. Throughout this evolution of our ability to orient others so that they can proceed in a given direction without the presence of a guide, the orientation has included, in addition to the refinement of concepts, vocabulary, and systematic knowledge, the use of more and more artifacts.

The artifacts also may be arranged on a continuum. A few Pacific islanders in the small Micronesian islands developed maps to help them navigate the broad seas between their tiny islands.[8] Other peoples of the Pacific steered only by the stars and winds. But as recently as the 1920s there was a newspaper report that a ship, equipped with modern navigational instruments, was unable to find Easter Island, a land mass of some 35,000 acres at longitude 109°26″ W and latitude 27°10″ S.

The making of crude maps, giving directions to some section of the tribe which had been left behind, recurs. In some parts of the world map making developed into an artistic and scientific ability to preserve, independently of the individuals who had explored a territory, a record of that territory. The introduction of scale features, such as mountain heights, occurs earlier in some cases than in others, and the extent to which any map, however intricate, can be used independently of its maker is not directly related to its elaboration. In Great Britain the art and science of map making and the art and science of making construction plans are both highly developed; but at the time of the blitz in World War II it was found that there was no complete map of the railroad and underground systems of the City of London.[9] The essential information for integrating the vast system of switches and transfers was carried by the aging and experienced employees who were responsible for the nexus points and who sometimes had only one apprentice or subordinate who also carried the crucial information.

When we arrange ways of storing information on a continuum, this helps clarify two things. First, even the simplest existing society known to man has a culture which provides for learning and teaching, for specialized learning through the division of labor between young and old, men and women, shamans or magicians and others, for the storage of information outside the body, and for the transcendence of the need for living models and continuous human guiding activities. And second, in spite of all the modern refinements and complications of these transmission skills—the complex methods of keeping records, making maps, and devising organizational charts, the manuals and the rules of procedure—the modern city, the modern army, the modern governmental bureaucracy still depends at many points on actual face-to-face learning and on the presence of one or two key individuals who can transmit the information of which they are the sole carriers.

So an evolutionary chart which shows the progression in the amount of information that can be stored outside the body through written records, maps, charts, tables of specifications, models, and so on, presents an accurate picture of evolution in one sector of transmission. But such a chart also obscures the extent to which we have preserved *all* methods of transmission and *all* degrees of dependence on face-to-face relationships, living models, and single custodians of crucial knowledge.

I have already discussed the extent to which material objects may provide a coding system for cultural transmission in the absence of the user and/or manufacturer of the object. Material objects enter in many other ways into the transmission of culture from one generation to another.

Experimental and naturalistic observations of other organic creatures demonstrate that the ability to recognize and use objects is far more widespread than is the ability to construct objects or to teach another member of the same species how to use them. Not only can objects themselves be recognized and recognition be stabilized by practice, but they can also be given an affective tone. For example, in Masserman's experiments antipathies were set up by putting an artificial snake in a spider monkey's food box; the monkey then avoided the food box and refused to eat.[10] The history of training domestic animals includes a record of minute discriminations of pattern associated with known objects and disturbance when some slight part of the pattern is altered.[11]

To appreciate fully the role of objects in human transmission of information it is necessary to recognize the capacities involved, for example, the capacity to make fine discriminations based on pattern differences or single signs, such as change of color, and the capacity to learn from association with punishing and rewarding situations and to make corresponding alterations in behavior. But it is also necessary to recognize that none of these capacities is exclusively human.

The manufacture of objects appropriate for use by a single generation, especially in its parental role, and the use of these objects as a part of the learning experience of the young, is found among other organic creatures.[12] Birds in particular show a capacity to make substitutions in the materials necessary for the construction of their nests.[13] Experiments have shown impairment in the nest-building behavior of adults where the infantile experience was incomplete.[14]

In man the purposeful use of existing objects—using a stick or a stone as an extension of the flailing movement of the forearm, crawling into some aperture like a cave to find shelter, using an object (a stone to toss up and down, a piece of limp material to suck or wave) to intensify affective experience—may have had some instinctive basis that has long since been overlaid by cultural situations. But as yet we do not know whether the fact that a given human activity has a species-characteristic basis places it in a different position in the transmission process. For example, autistic children who make no response to human beings use walls to bump their heads against, sticks and cloth to suck and wave; they tear meat apart with their hands and drink by lapping up water. Many commentaries have explained these behaviors, when they are displayed by wandering children, in terms of folk psychology, that is, that these children, having been reared by wolves or bears, have "learned to behave like animals." But we now have abundant material on autistic children in our own culture, who after severe infantile trauma, behave in the same way.[15] It seems unlikely that the adults among whom such children must try to eke out a noncommunicative and terrorized existence teach them to behave like animals; it seems more likely that these are fundamental, unlearned types of response, genetically provided ways of satisfying biological needs. If this is so, then further exploration of the repertoire of autistic children should increase our knowledge of the simplest forms in which the use of objects can be seen as extensions of human abilities to break, bend, hammer, and so on.

Cultural transmission involves both the selection and manufacture of such objects and the learning–teaching situation by which the knowledge is transmitted to the next generation. In this connection it is necessary to differentiate between learning to use something over which one has no manipulative power—a cave, a break in the reef, a tree, a bridge, or a building in a modern city[16]—and the whole sequence of alteration of the environment by digging in the soil, transporting and putting together small objects—sticks or stones to make a nest, gnawing and chewing materials into new consistencies, using internal secretions and exudations, appropriating manufactured objects made by others (as when a parasitical creature uses the cast-off shell of another, or birds learn to lift the lids of bottles to get at the cream[17]). Additionally, we have to consider such matters as disposal by neglect, destruction, and replacement, or careful transportation and imitation of an object. All these behaviors have a wider-than-human distribution; and they are also found in the most advanced contemporary cultures. Our understanding of culture will be increased when, for example, we are able to specify the ways in which the utilization of a cave for shelter involves unlearned available human behavior and when its use is derivative from culture—so that a cave is experienced as a "natural" house—when we know the extent to which all material cultural solutions embody not only the anatomical requirements of human use (or sometimes dog or ox or cat use, although made by men), but also species-characteristic forms.

Autistic and severely regressed patients will, like frightened animals, cower in corners. An extreme psychoanalytic interpretation of this behavior, taking its clue from the fetal position often assumed by such disturbed individuals, is that it represents a "return to the womb." Individuals can assume fetal positions of this sort independently of the presence of rooms, walls, and corners. This frequently occurred among the Balinese. Or the wall may be interpreted as a substitute for the mother. In the Liddell and Blauvelt experiments with pairs of kids, the kid that was separated from its mother cowered in a corner against the wall.[18] It is, however, still a question whether a "corner" in a cave or a manufactured shelter must not be seen both as a "womb" or as "mother's or mother surrogate's body," and also as evoking a shelter-seeking response. The hypothesis of a regressive return to the womb assumes the continued availability throughout life of a fetal adjustment; but it takes no account of the mediation by maternal care of a series of later elaborations of the womb—the cradling of the child close to the body, the proliferation of shawls, bags, baskets, cradles, cribs, and cradleboards by means of which the human mother creates an external womb or a continuation of the womb for the newborn.

We may consider that the behavior of the child or severely repressed adult combines what the mother can do with her hands to enfold the child or make a nest for it and the mother's behavior in seeking shelter under a tree or cliff or in a cave. Then we may see the continuation of the ideas of shelter-seeking and shelter-giving, both of which are available to both sexes, as implicit in all shelter-giving objects: lean-tos, tepees, earth lodges, tree houses, houses on stilts, cliff dwellings, mud houses, wooden cabins, snow houses, automobiles, submarines, spaceships, and so on. The possibility that such a continuum exists is reflected in the way in which disturbed children use a chance to draw a building, which may be either own body or the body of another within which the child is sheltered or within which it is given no shelter.[19] Such a hypothesis makes full allowance for the presence of infants, juveniles,

and adults of both sexes within the culture-building precursors of man, and the involvement of genetically given
appropriate behavior for both sexes at different ages, both
in seeking for something to satisfy their own needs and in
enabling them to meet the needs of other members of the
group.

An analysis of the behavior of the Adelie penguin of
Antarctica illustrates this in another species.[20] While the
parents are away seeking food, the chicks cluster around
unmated adults; apparently it is the seeking behavior of
the chicks, rather than the protective behavior of the
adults, that leads to this crèche formation in which the
chicks are protected from the predatory skuas.

Shelter-giving may be fortuitous, and shelter-seeking
may be genetically determined—as when these young
Adelie penguins gather around unmated adults and are
thus protected from predators. Among Wyoming moose,
the older bulls provide protection for the newly weaned
yearlings. In the spring the heavily pregnant moose cow
chases away her growing yearling, and after futile efforts
to rejoin their dams the juveniles—especially the males—
may enter into a "satellite attachment" with one or more
elder moose, usually older bulls.[21] Different species have
made different assignments of the kinds of seeking or sheltering behavior which, taken together, provide the determinants of a house.

Observations of the simplest forms of human societies
suggest that the need of human beings for shelter, beyond
that provided by the natural world in which they live and
in which they take refuge with their young, may have been
correlated with the presence of other inventions, such as
the use of fire, the preparation and storage of food, the care
of the old and the sick in a sedentary situation—rather
than as necessarily expendable when they could no longer
keep up with a nomadic existence—some kind of clothing,

which made it possible for a people to venture into a climate where shelter would also be necessary, equipment greater than would be carried by the members of the group on the march. In this connection, the cache—also found among other species, such as dogs, insects that establish stores, and so on—in which food is stored against a return visit—and various primitive forms of carrying—a basket, a drag, a sled, a raft—may, just as the house, be seen as extensions of the original interpersonal group pattern of survival through care extended by different members of the group to each other. When a whole group of men drag a large log fastened to vines through the forest, this is still a close parallel to the activities of beavers and ants and may be regarded as a perpetually available response—present to cultivated eyes, among men used to employing human resources; to primitive eyes, among men used to watching the behavior of living creatures, and implicit in the presence of at least two adults with tasks to perform.

It will also be clear that any manufactured object can be seen as an extension of the body. The female body provides the fuller imagery, with the womb as the precursor of large containers; the womb and the arms beneath the breast as the precursor of shelter; the breast as the precursor of food-making, food-storing, and food-dispensing objects; and the process of conception and gestation as the observable bodily prototype of creativity. The male body provides the prototype for the extension of the arm and hand equally with the female, and for the possibility of carrying and sheltering against the body. But, characteristically, at simple levels the female carries both objects and infants; the male enters the carrying picture when more than one person is needed to drag a log, erect a house beam, track an animal, surround a herd, and so on. Thus, a fair case can be made for considering that female behavior, or possibly female species-characteristic behavior, is more readily involved in all manufacture which is a simple supplementation of the capabilities of the body by manufactured objects, that is, containers and clothing, and by the preparation and dispensing of prepared food, and for considering that male behavior involves cooperation with outside objects, other human beings, animals (e.g. hunting dogs or draft animals), and material objects of wood or stone or metal, which can be brought in relation to and can be used in the human situation. Perception of the possibilities inherent in the surrounding world for alteration to transcend the limitations of the human body may be seen as more likely to arise from male models. This correlates with all we know at present about activity ratios between male and female: the male's greater strength, greater activity, superiority in handling spatial organization, and so on, and the female's use of her own body as a theater of action.[22]

However, just as it is important to recognize that such constancies as greater male size, strength, or locomotor ability, may be reversed in some species, it is also important to recognize that there may be many exchanges of models within a learned transmission and innovation system like human culture. A house may be primarily something which a man makes on a hunting trip or it may be a shelter which a woman makes for her children and her children's food, to which the hunter—who away from home takes refuge under a tree or a protruding cliff —returns. Then again, a house which is built by highly organized communal labor involving many men, for example, the great men's house among the Iatmul, after all the male work has been done—cutting huge trees, dragging the trees to the village, hewing and carving them into shape, setting the carved trunks up as house posts and beams—may be called "a womb," and may be used to act out a theatrical rebirth of the initiates to the men of the tribe.[23]

Lorenz has remarked that it is probably inappropriate to speak of certain sets of behavior patterns, which are more often found in the male (or the female), as specifically male (or female), since these sets may also appear, en bloc, in the opposite sex. In his opinion it would be more appropriate to think of such sets of behavior patterns as species-available.[24] We may then consider the economy of sex placement. Tanner has suggested that, as constitutional heterozygosity is desirable, endomorphy is carried by the female, since it is relatively less functional in the male.[25]

We may now look at the basic repertoire of early human inventions in these terms. Containers and carriers are appropriately used by females, but are made and used by both sexes. Tools, which are characteristically male, are made by men and are used more narrowly or domestically by women, as they are used in predatory and defensive behavior, hunting, and large-scale modifications of the environment by men.[26] And when we consider the amount of learning encoded in a house, it is evident that one important element in the way culture is transmitted through material objects is the extent to which the house is regarded as an extension of the female body, appropriately made, used, presided over, owned and disposed of by females and by males.

I would now like to analyze briefly the kinds of transmission which a house makes possible. I shall take as a model the Samoan house as it has been studied most extensively and beautifully by Sir Peter Buck.[27]

The form of a house, as I commented earlier in this chapter, is overdetermined. Therefore an analysis of shelter, in which the particular cultural type of shelter is unspecified, is arid. It is commonly said that "man is a shelter-building animal"; more accurately, man is a creature capable of building shelters and constructing ways of life through which the environment is so modified that he can inhabit it only with the help of his artificial productions. But it is the type of shelter that is built that becomes significant in any given culture.

THE SAMOAN HOUSE

In a Samoan village the growing child saw houses of four principal types. Fronting on the beach, in the place of honor, were two types of guest house, a long house with rounded ends, *fale afolau,* and a tall round domed house, *fale tele.* Set back of these were the dwelling houses, called *fale o'o,* each with its cook house, *fale umu,* which sheltered the earth oven, and some small simple lean-to sheds, mere thatched roofs on posts, behind it. Down near the water's edge, providing shelter for the canoes, were the long, more roughly built canoe sheds, called *afolau.*

The guest house was known also as *fale 'ulu,* the house built of the superior timber of the cultivated breadfruit tree (*'ulu*); in contrast, the ordinary dwelling house, built of any timber from the forest (*vao*), could be called *fale vao.* Stepped terraces of small stones led up to the guest houses; the one belonging to the chief of highest rank had the largest number of terraces—at least one more than any other in that village. The guest house built for a chief with the help of the whole village was known also as *fale tali malo,* the house to meet the stranger. Such a house served a dual purpose as the meeting place for the *fono,* the ceremonial gathering of the heads of households who held hereditary titles, and as the formal place for greeting visitors from other villages.

The guest house was essentially a circle of posts. Though each post was structurally like every other one, each served to specify a position in relation both to rank and to function. A post fixed the position of the highest ranking person present in any given context: at a *fono;* on the occasion of a visit; at the ceremony when the new house was completed, when the chief carpenter took precedence; at the *auamaga,* the meeting of the young men, when the *manaia,* the titled leader of the untitled young men, took the foremost place. At the same time, position in the circle denoted functional divisions between chiefs and talking chiefs, host and guest, and placed those who served the ceremonial drink, *kava,* those who distributed it, and so on. In this way the circle of posts, with its fixed form and number of seating places, provided a frame within which seating plans could be developed which bodied forth the formal arrangements of a gathering of any kind.

When young people were in the house, the head of the house might relinquish to the appropriate person his position as chief host. During a gathering the center of the house could be traversed only ceremonially by the youth or maiden who was serving *kava* or woven platters of food. If a messenger came to a house in which titled men were ceremonially seated, he squatted down outside the house by the post of the man to whom he wished to speak and delivered his message in a whisper. The level of the seated men was the level of courtesy. For anyone except the specified servers to stand would be an affront.

From his experience of the house and from the answers to his questions about particular posts, which were given to him in terms of rank and situation, the growing child could learn the principles of Samoan social organization, as he came to recognize the way in which positions were combined and recombined in space to express changing relationships, with the enclosing circle as the fixed ground plan.

From another viewpoint the structure of the chief's guest house expressed the relationship of each household in the village to the whole through the symmetrical assignment to each of some part of the materials of which the house was built: wood for one or two posts, wood for the rafters, the plaiting of coconut palm leaves for the Venetian blinds that hung between the posts, the provision of sugarcane leaves for a section of the thatch, the sewing of a section of thatch, or the provision of a supply of sennit, the coconut fiber cord with which the posts and rafters were lashed. In this way the house in its construction reasserted the essential symmetry of the whole system, within which those of higher rank—chiefs or talking chiefs— nevertheless operated within a circle of titled heads of households.

The Samoans, scattered on many islands, had a concept of a Great Fono, within the circular ground plan of which every high title on all the islands had its place. There is no record of a gathering of this Great Fono; essentially it represented a conceptual extrapolation of the basic house plan which could be adapted to accommodate all the members of an extended family, all the households of a small village, all the titles of a district, and ideally, every high title in the whole of Samoa.

A useful comparison might be made between the set of ideas communicated by this type of meeting house and the set of ideas inherent in the semicircular parliamentary building and meeting room, with its fixed "right" and "left," its fixed seats for individuals who hold different elective or appointive positions. Such a comparison would in itself highlight the extent to which building form can carry, maintain, and transmit a large number of very complicated political concepts.

All pieces of material culture carry a large number of messages about human behavior. The way in which a tool is hafted may carry, for those who use hafted tools, messages about the kind of stroke and the strength that must be used, the size of the user, the seriousness of the task, the value set on the task it is intended to perform. The continued use of like or related types of tools very probably explains the continuation of methods of manufacture in an area from which the original inhabitants have been displaced by another people with identifiably different ways of behavior—sufficiently different so that the archaeologist has no difficulty in placing in sequence the artifacts he excavates.[28]

The ornamentation of an object carries with it messages of the kind already discussed, i.e. this was made by a skilled —or an unskilled—craftsman; or, this is an object of high value. It may also carry quite another set of messages, encoded in the designs themselves. Comparative studies have shown that designs undergo alterations in various systematic ways—toward more or less elaboration, toward the disappearance, degeneration, or fragmentation of design forms.[29] If it is the custom to embody design in fragile or perishable materials, such as objects made of fur and feathers on the Australian desert, the artists, who make them once a year or perhaps once in five or ten years, must have a quite different order of memory from artists who in carving another house post, another canoe prow, or another arrowhead can take as a model an old one still in use. Freedom to change the design is quite different when the design lies before one; there is not the same danger of "being wrong" by accident because of a lapse of memory. When there is no way of keeping a record between ceremonies, the need for material forms probably plays an important part in making a culture rigid and in consolidating the position of the practitioners—whether old men or not—who are the only people who know how to make a ground painting *right*. Memorized sacred words or songs may have the same conservative effect; however, even between ceremonies, the practitioner repeats these over and over in his head. The aborigines of South Australia have cultivated a type of memory in which they have to walk through the terrain which is involved in a myth in order to be able to tell a long totemic myth correctly.[30] The stimuli which call the correct incidents to mind are outside themselves, in their territory. Under these circumstances, loss of territory has a very special meaning. Our modern equivalent is the individual who does not commit anything to memory and remembers only which book contains the information. Without books of logarithms or diagrams or formulas or poetry such an individual is unable to function at a high level.

Coupled with this relationship to the physical environment is a kind of *being in* rather than *seeing* the environment. There is a very moving instance of a group of Australian aboriginal children who were incarcerated in a reform school, far away from their own people.[31] One of the custodial staff, who had been a teacher, started the children in crafts and drawing. Suddenly, one day, a little boy shouted, "I see, I see! You don't draw it the way you *know* it is. You draw it the way it looks!" And the idea of perspective was born anew in his mind. The whole group then started to paint pictures so fresh that later they were given a special exhibit in London, and a special article in the London *Times* was devoted to their work.[32]

The conditions under which this event took place included the low level of arts and crafts characteristic of rural schools in the English-speaking world, probably at least one calendar with a cheaply conceived landscape, the unusual interest of an isolated teacher, and a group of children born into a culture thousands of years away from the style of the school in which they were imprisoned— their very delinquency a function of the disastrous culture contact between aborigines and English colonists. The boy's discovery exemplifies the complexity of the messages that can be carried partly in objects and partly in memories of objects, recombined to make something new and, in this case, quite unrepeatable.

In a fairly isolated society it is possible to find side by side many "stages" in the handling of the same design style, each stage carrying a different set of messages—a message about carelessness of form, about exquisite attention to detail, about slavish, exact copying, about free innovation. When, in addition, some forms are executed in stone, others in clay, others in wood, and still others in bark or leaves, where the design depends on the color contrasts of scraped and unscraped bark or of leaves picked yesterday and leaves picked today, the imagination of a people is, as it were, filtered through a set of time screens of different durations.

In Bali, for example, the new stone guardians of the temple gates are replicas of those made centuries ago, while the little kitchen gods, made of soft, frangible wood, allow for great freedom of design, and the long green palm leaf *lamaks*, which hang on each side of a house gate and are made to last only a couple of days, have different designs in every village. When one examines Balinese offerings, there are constructs made of objects of every degree of perishability: painted stands of heavy durable wood, which are periodically repainted with new and often different designs; water pots, which are mass-produced by hand on a potter's wheel, so that the form is extremely widespread and constant; elaborate constructs of palm leaves, in which an object that is used as a whisk contains within it a mass of smaller knots and folded bits that stand for different parts of the body;[33] beautiful cutouts of palm leaves; little umbrellas and lily-like flowers made of pigs' fat; pieces of folded cloth brought from India generations ago; small, blackened pieces of Chinese money; masks copied from other masks, set on bodies made of variously colored fresh fruit; pieces of cloth made in Japan or Manchester to be sold in Java.

The perception of the Balinese participants in a ceremony is fragmented and recomposed in ways that produce new congruences. Most of the objects have lost part of their earlier meanings, and one can recapture the whole meaning only by making a study of many different sets of offerings in different parts of Bali; then the piece of deerskin in one local set, the small carved deer with golden horns in another, and the tiny palm leaf model of a cage—with neither deer nor deerskin—in still another, taken together, speak of an image of deer once captured alive to use in a ceremony. The Balinese artist has available myriad fragments from which his own body images can be reconstituted, experienced kinesthetically, and reprojected in the ever new and fantastic forms, only a few from each artist but, placed together, presenting an astonishing and diverse array.[34]

Another kind of transmission occurs when people sit and weave wall panels from perishable materials or paint new designs on the rafters of a house which has posts of very hard wood, carved in traditional style. For example, in a Maori house, the light vine-like tracery on the rafters counterpoints the heavy carving. But it has been found that when two of these delicate designs are put together, one opposing the other, there emerge from this new arrangement "faces" that echo the faces in the wooden carvings.[35] If for some reason the carved wooden slabs disappeared but the rafter patterns were faithfully pre-

served, the image of the faces could be carried for many
generations, perhaps to a people far away in time and
space and culture.

Blazons, heraldic emblems, usually painted or carved
by men, provide another way of coding information about
one generation and making it part of the inheritance of
the next. But when the heraldic design is embodied in
perishable straw mats, as in the Marshall Islands where
men are the heralds but women weave the designs into
mats given as presents, the information about the past is
subject to greater vicissitudes, as changes occur in the behavior of one sex or the other.[36]

Still another way in which a pattern of relationships
may be coded and carried nonverbally to another generation is through the use of seals and signets, where the idea
of a signature may be combined with illiteracy on the part
of the "signer" or the "reader" of the sign, or both. The
Chinese, for example, for at least a thousand years, have
used seals denoting the power of office, and seals containing the characters for names cut upon stone, wood, bone,
ivory, crystal, china, glass, brass, and other substances have
been—and still are—used to establish the identity of particular individuals, artists, and businessmen.[37]

The range of examples presented indicates how very
abstract, nonverbalized relationships, involving the extension of man's mastery over the environment, may be
carried for any number of generations by objects. These
objects may be part of the transmission system of a culture. They may be traded across cultural boundaries. They
may carry coded information between peoples whose cultural levels may be very different. Objects provide a
method of storing information—a system comparable to,
but quite different from, storage by words.

6. Borderlines Between Learning and Teaching

ONE SIGNIFICANT ASPECT of cultural evolution is the extent to which a culture is learned without explicit teaching and the extent to which it is taught, complete with rule books, manuals, grammars, and the whole paraphernalia of formulated and coded statements. Either kind of learning, within a given setting, can be an advance or a retreat or it can inaugurate a new kind of communication process. At the present time we have a tremendous need to develop our existing capacities to handle intricate forms of coding (to program computers, for example), but we are no less in need of new facilities for presenting experience to children in forms that appear to be less coded because the coding occurs at a different level (in sound film and on television, for example). Formerly, children had the experience of learning to think about the unknown by reading about it with very little help from visual or auditory presentations. Today, on the contrary, long before children have learned to read—and so to handle symbols for which they themselves must supply the experience—they are presented with visual–auditory replications of experience.[1]

The lack of clarity about these two kinds of learning is made evident by the most casual inspection of contemporary discussions about teaching children to read or, alternatively, arguments between those linguists who consider only written languages as worthy of study and those who have studied languages that do not have a script. I propose, therefore, to discuss one aspect of the borderline between teaching—that is, the explicit handling of materials that have been encoded for transmission and the kind of learning in which the learning child or adult is on his own in organizing new experience. For this discussion I have selected small precise details from a simple and thoroughly studied culture, in the hope that a transient immersion in material that is not only detailed but also unfamiliar will convey better than any generalizations what I have to say.

Language learning is an area in which it is especially easy to discern the gap between what is taught and what is learned. We may consider, for example, what an Arapesh of New Guinea *knows* about the language he speaks.[2] He knows that there are languages. He knows also that the language spoken in his village is shared by the people of a number of named villages. He knows that there are correct and incorrect ways of speaking his language. But when he teaches small children, he concentrates his attention on the gender system.

Arapesh is a noun-class language with thirteen classes of nouns, in which accord involves identical phonemic segments for each of which there is a singular and a plural form to which pronouns, adjectives, and numerals correspond. As the verb is uninflected and is modified by particles, the noun classes carry a heavy burden of form.

For purposes of teaching, the Arapesh have a mechanism which depends on the presence in their language of an ambiguous noun class that deals with objects of unspecified gender (e.g. *child*) and also with imported nouns that do not fit phonetically into the system. In the plural for this class, a suffix is added to foreign nouns and also provides for combinations of objects of two or more noun classes in the pronominal and adjectival forms. For example, in this noun class, the third person plural pronoun, *se,* is used to refer to a combination such as a man and a woman; or a man, a pig, and a dog; or betel nuts, taro, and yams on one plate.

In teaching an Arapesh child to speak, every noun is given with the singular modifier, *one,* and with the plural modifier, *many,* in the form corresponding to the ambiguous noun class, but with the noun itself in its correct singular and plural form. For example, an adult sees a child looking at, pointing to, or touching a dog in a manner which, to the adult, indicates the child's readiness to learn the word for dog. The adult then gives the noun for dog in its correct singular form, *nubat,* and its correct plural form, *nubag,* but uses the numeral adjectives *atun* (one) and *minihisi* (many) in the forms appropriate to the ambiguous noun class, instead of *atut* and *minihigi,* the correct forms of modifiers of *nubat* and *nubag.*

This kind of learning may be compared to the use of two envelopes, one less correct than the other, but both correct. In this way the Arapesh learn that there is a way of saying *one* that can be used when you are not certain, have not yet learned, cannot place, or do not wish to specify linguistically the noun class of the object you are speaking about. They also learn that every word has a plural form which it is necessary to know. The teacher implies, "Once I have told you the singular and the plural in the envelopes of ambiguous modifiers, you will henceforth be expected to use the word correctly. Never again will you say *atun nubat, minihisi nubag,* but always *atut nubat, minihigi nubag.*"

For each new noun the child learns, this lesson is repeated, and the learning provides a substratum of consciousness which the anthropologist could then raise to a higher level by numbering the noun classes and introducing the word gender. Then two of our informants—

one who had a pliant and adjustable mind, and the other
a formal, classifying mind—were able to conduct an argument as to the place in the system of the English word
butter. The formal one claimed that as the word was pronounced *butah* (a pronunciation he had learned from an
English employer), it had no formal place in any noun
class and so belonged in the ambiguous noun class along
with other foreign words. The other, who had heard the
word pronounced with the terminal *r*, insisted that it
fitted into the noun class with the singular ending *r-l*,
plural *-igu*, in parallel fashion to the English word *nail*,
which in Arapesh became *něl* (singular), *nigu* (plural).

The people of the locality of Alitoa also consciously
recognized that the people of Liwo used an *r* where they
themselves used an *l*, and a *k* where they used a glottal
stop.[3] Without writing, without any other formal teaching, and without differences in prestige between Liwo
and Alitoa, this recognition of difference remained merely
an observation. People "heard" the Liwo pronunciation
without any conscious effort at making the transformations; however, whenever someone wanted to identify a
speaker who could not be seen at the moment of speaking,
he would make use of the recognized but usually dis-
counted systematic difference, and would say, "I heard a
voice in the night talking in the fashion of Liwo, saying . . . , so I know it was X (or) so I know it couldn't
be Y."

In Samoa, where written Samoan was introduced by the
missionaries, simple sound shifts had been institutionalized
between *t* and *k*, and *ng* and *n*. The Bible, *Tusi Sa*, was
written with *t*'s. Therefore all written communication
made use of the *t*-form; also in formal speeches, both
sacred and secular, words were pronounced with *t*'s. But
in 1925 the people of Ta'u used the *k-n* combination instead of the *t-ng* in their everyday speech. As I learned

the language partly by talking with the children,[4] I tended
to speak with the *k* and *n,* but this they would never permit me; they held me to a speech which they regarded
as appropriate for someone of my rank, and I had to use
the *t-ng* combinations in my everyday speech.

If Arapesh should now become a written language, it
probably would be affected by the curiously limited ideas
of Europeans about the correspondence of sound and
symbol, and the present ease with which the Arapesh allow
for the differences in speech between Alitoa and Liwo
would vanish. One form would become "correct," the
other "incorrect." Teaching would replace learning, and
the teaching situation, based as it would be on the conscious identification of a few aspects of a much wider system, would become limiting and rigid.

In contrast, we may consider the method by which the
Manus taught one another Neo-Melanesian in 1928.[5] No
attempt was made to state any sort of principle; the older
boys simply taught the younger ones to repeat phrases
after them: "You lookim whatname?" "Me lookim dog."
Later, the learner would encounter an articulate distinction between "talk whiteman"—pidgin spoken in a way
that was intelligible to the average European—and "talk
boy"—pidgin spoken in a way that was intelligible only
to another native. The principle behind this distinction
was not made articulate. But, in effect, the speaker learned
that in order to talk so that a "European" could understand, the words in pidgin that were derived from English
words (e.g. *bokis,* from *box*) and the words that had been
assimilated to English words (e.g. *soda-water,* originally a
native rendering of *salt water,* for the *sea*) must be pronounced more definitely like the English model or pseudo-
model. It was possible for a Manus to say, "This master
didn't understand you well because you talked 'boy' instead of 'whiteman'" (or "because you talked 'fashion be-

long bush' instead of 'fashion belong station' "), and these phrases made the distinction available for teaching. The teaching, however, proceeded horizontally between slightly more and less experienced peers, not yet having reached the level at which one person known as a "teacher" corrects another known as a "pupil."

Furthermore, when we look at these communications, we find that there are two pieces of coding that make articulate teaching possible: the word *talk,* which stands for "language as a system," and the phrases *fashion belong* (Neo-Melanesian) and *kaiye ala Usiai,* that is, "customary of Usiai" (Manus). Both pieces of coding are summary statements covering many million items of behavior which normally are perceived not as separate items but in larger units, such as *"our* burial customs" as distinct from *"their* burial customs" or *"their* speech-making style" as distinct from *"our* speech-making style." This kind of coding, which codes own behavior through the coding of the behavior of others, leaves the way open for the child, or the member of a third tribe, or the captured or married-in woman to ask, "What is the burial fashion of X tribe?" or "What is our own fashion?" The chances of being given an explicit answer are better for the customs of the outsiders, for it is easier to summarize the thousands of items which comprise a marriage ceremony of another people in such phrases as, "They pay for their women later, and a man can look at his mother-in-law," in which there is an enormous reduction in information. Within the group this coding leaves open a place for later perception and, on this basis, the child or inexperienced person may later ask about some way of arranging taro croquettes, or cutting up ripe coconut, or addressing the ghosts, or plaiting a croton leaf, or picking up food with a stick instead of one's fingers. The fact that one can phrase the question, "Is *this* our marriage fashion?" provides a principle both for organizing cultural experience within the tribe and for adding coded, reduced knowledge about the next culture, however faultily and meagerly, to the repertoire.

From an analysis of this kind of rudimentary coding of experience it is possible to see how "nonmaterial culture" becomes cumulative by means of the development of phrases or specific terms that summarize a large amount of known behavior, practiced in the past or at special rare intervals, so that most young people will hear about an event for years before they actually encounter it—for example, when there is a hurricane and they open the *masi* (breadfruit) pits, at intervals of about ten years, in Samoa; when they initiate whole groups of young boys together, at five- to ten-year intervals in many parts of New Guinea; or when a high chief dies; or when twins of opposite sex are born to a member of the Kesatrya caste in Bali. All such coding contains the double possibility of carrying information along in a form that makes it possible for an individual to ask about it, and so to learn more, and also of reducing complex behavior to partial formulas which, if the events referred to are never actually experienced, either artificially reduce the amount of information—as between a speaker who has experienced and a listener who has not and subsequently does not experience an event —or else provide pigeonholes, highly specified frames with an interior vagueness into which the listeners can pack a mass of idiosyncratic and fragmented images.[6]

Poetry is a particularly effective vehicle of such ambiguous references, as one can see in Stevenson's "Travel":[7]

> I should like to rise and go
> Where the golden apples grow;
> Where below another sky
> Parrot islands anchored lie,
> And, watched by cockatoos and goats,

Lonely Crusoes building boats;
Where in sunshine reaching out
Eastern cities, miles about,
Are with mosque and minaret
Among sandy gardens set,
And the rich goods from near and far
Hang for sale in the bazaar;
Where the Great Wall round China goes,
And on one side the desert blows,
And with bell and voice and drum,
Cities on the other hum;
Where are forests, hot as fire,
Wide as England, tall as a spire,
Full of apes and coco-nuts
And the negro hunters' huts;
Where the knotty crocodile
Lies and blinks in the Nile,
And the red flamingo flies
Hunting fish before his eyes;
Where in jungles, near and far,
Man-devouring tigers are,
Lying close and giving ear
Lest the hunt be drawing near,
Or a comer-by be seen
Swinging in a palanquin;
Where among the desert sands
Some deserted city stands,
All its children, sweep and prince,
Grown to manhood ages since,
Not a foot in street or house,
Not a stir of child or mouse,
And when kindly falls the night,
In all the town no spark of light.
There I'll come when I'm a man
With a camel caravan;

> Light a fire in the gloom
> Of some dusty dining-room;
> See the pictures on the walls,
> Heroes, fights, and festivals;
> And in a corner find the toys
> Of the old Egyptian boys.

Coding of this kind also makes it possible for the person who answers a question to endow the summary word with his own idiosyncratic experience. So he may briefly describe a type of ceremony given by the next tribe, "They pile up coconuts, and the mother's brother sings with a palm leaf rib on which are fastened all manner of things —a pig's skull *and lots of other things.*" Then he may add, "It is so cold in that place; the houses have bad roofs and the rain comes in. You cannot sleep for the cold, and the fires die down because of the leaks. Your eyes are red from the smoke, and your joints ache." For the listener the feast stands forever as a ceremony in which a "mother's brother" —a compound of his own mother's brother and the known costume of the next tribe—holds, in no clear position, a long coconut palm rib to which are fastened somehow a pig's bone and an undifferentiated series of objects, which one listener may fill in with a wholly inappropriate set and another may leave vague. The listener also includes in the picture the feeling of the cold, the wakefulness, the smarting eyes and aching joints, and this feeling perhaps will be decisive in his response to a proposal years later to adopt, by purchase, this "custom of the people of the next mountain, for a mother's brother to hold in his hand a wand." (See Plate 1.)

Within the tribe, the coding may take another form. A young Arapesh boy hears the word *balug,* and asks, "What is a *balug?*" He may be told, "Something that is done at initiation," and he files away the new word, without content, within the larger, equally vague frame. Or he may be told, "What the mother's brother brings to the sister's son before initiation," shifting the inquirer's attention to the kinship role involved. In this case, the answer is filed either with "initiation" or with "the behavior of mother's brothers to sister's sons." It is no clearer what a *balug* is. Or he may be told, "It comes before a *balagasi'*." This is the feast given by the sister's son's father to his brother-in-law, the initiate's mother's brother. But the questioner does not know what a *balagasi'* is. He may merely make a loose connection, *balug, balagasi'*, referring this to his unarticulated knowledge that these two clusters of sound resemble each other, not one of those things where the next step is one *balug*, many *baluki*, but some other sort of thing—unnamed, inarticulate, vague.

Or, instead, the questioner may see the object called a *balug* before he learns the name. In a fine flurry of coming and going, a tall man whom he has seen only a few times but who he believes comes from the inland direction, is dancing in the little open space before his cousin's house, holding in his hand a long coconut palm rib from which a lot of objects dangle—a bone or two, a couple of flowers, a lot of leaves, a piece of coconut shell, some feathers.[8] Too young to know the names of the leaves, flowers, or feathers, or to assign the bones to the proper animals, he forms an image, accurate in formal concrete detail, in which each object hanging from the rib now becomes a counter for a lot of possibilities called "leaves," "flowers," "bones," "feathers." His image will differ enormously from that of the questioner who was told "a pig's skull and *lots of other things* hanging from a coconut rib." But the opportunity to deviate later from a fixed form, while different, is perhaps greater, because he knows the classes of objects to which the "lots of other things" belong. Later, if he has to reconstruct this object, the *balug*, without help, he may decide either that the objects—leaves, flowers, feathers—were just *bilas* (flash, decoration, in Neo-Melanesian) or that they were "something that belonged to the ceremony." With these two categories at his disposal, he again has two possibilities. In the one case, he may construct a *balug* with a coconut palm rib from which hangs a miscellaneous collection of objects so that the arrangement looks like a *balug* but has lost all meaning. Alternatively, he may decide that the leaves and flowers and feathers were related to the ceremony, and say, "I don't know their names, so I can't make the ceremony." Then the ceremony may disappear entirely from the tribal repertoire.

There are also other possibilities. If the questioner asks someone who has a good memory, he may be given an exact description of the last *balug* the other person has seen. He may be told that it was constructed in this way:[9]

> A large, fresh young "palm" leaf is split down the midrib, so that it hangs in many strands. Beginning the enumeration with the end farthest from the stem, to these are fastened: a leaf of *peshuho,* a leaf of *minihil,* the small stem of *nyubut,* a small piece of a "young coconut" shell, the flower of the *alolo'u* tree, leaves of *binyaldi,* the bone of a "wallaby" (maybe phalanger or tree kangaroo), a "sago" leaf, a leaf of *wanumeku,* a small bare stem of "areca nut," a feather of a *nauwitep* bird, the leaf of the "yellow croton" *wenyal,* a leaf of "maize," a slit *monub* leaf, a *talalip* leaf (love magic type), a "cockatoo" feather, a slit *monub* leaf, a leaf of the *bagihas* type of "taro," a *wheibin* leaf, a "yellow croton" leaf, *wenyal,* the feather of a brown "pigeon," the stem of *nyubut,* a crescent-shaped piece of "coconut" shell, and a big *dilibo* leaf.

For the listener who has a concrete type of imagery, each item in the enumeration may set off a train of associations, as he thinks that the *wenyal* leaf is also used in yam magic and is put over the doorway of a man who is angry. If he has a more generalizing type of mind, an item like a wallaby bone may stand for a category and he will mentally fill in other bones that could be used instead—the bone of a phalanger or a tree kangaroo. He knows, perhaps, that some of the decorative items are crucial and others utterly meaningless, "put there for no purpose" or "put there as a decoration." He knows, too, that no one knows for certain which is which.

There is still another way in which the question, "What is a *balug?*" can be answered. Those Arapesh who have learned to speak Neo-Melanesian with its larger set of generalizing words, many of them lifted from some local language, may answer, "It is a *tangget* used by a boy's mother's brother to demand a feast." [10] There was in Arapesh no verbal equivalent of the word *tangget;* the intermediate language was necessary to gather together a set of Arapesh objects and practices under a classificatory word which means "a material object or set of material objects used to send messages, to make declarations, to warn trespassers, to remind a creditor or a debtor." The Arapesh have a series of such *tanggets,* for example, a long piece of rattan to record the size of a yam pile, a croton leaf tied in a knot to bind another man over to peaceful intent, leaves placed over the door as a sign that one will have nothing to do with some relative with whom he is quarreling, or, in more complicated form, a sign which is a declaration by a man that he will let his wife feed no more pigs. (See Plate 2.)

By borrowing from the wider area, through the use of Neo-Melanesian, the local group, who in their own language could describe concretely only each of the message-bearing objects, now have a term that classifies them together, and they can use this in passing on information. But although the word *tangget* places the *balug* in such a category, even more of the *balug's* actual composition is lost. If the questioner is content to know no more than that it is "a message composed of objects through which a mother's brother conveys a message to his brother-in-law," there is every possibility that later when he needs to make a *balug,* he will fabricate it anew and lose what concrete relationships there were in the original.

Finally, the man who knows how to do so may construct a *balug* to show the questioner how it should be done, but this involves a lot of work, and the tendency to replace significant herbs by nonsignificant ones which will stand for significant ones becomes accentuated. The object fabricated for demonstration becomes a sketch; the general idea of objects that stand for various kinds of food is preserved, but the rest is generalized.

So a culture of the Arapesh type presents an imprecise, loose, irregular screen through which information sifts, at different rates and in different ways. A corrective for such a screen can be found in the development of rote memory and in the insistence that individuals memorize exactly and repeat in the correct order a prescription for a ceremonial object. But the Arapesh did not institutionalize the use of rote memory.

For the acquisition of hunting skills, they recognized the wish to know and the need to learn; such wishes and needs were met by apprenticeship. The boy who wanted to be a hunter simply attached himself to the best hunter among his elder relatives, went with him into the bush, and learned from him. There was no formulation of practice in words or rules or demonstration. Very small boys were given small hunting weapons, especially bows and arrows, but these were not toys; they were simply weapons appropriately scaled to the child's size.

When it came to ritual knowledge, however, there were no specialists who were able to conserve pieces of ritual information. Instead, the Arapesh conceived of the one who knew as an individual who had been personally and recently involved in a situation. The woman who had just borne a child knew the proper ritual steps in childbirth as did the father of the new baby, who also had to follow ritual precautions. The general outlines of such ceremonies were preserved as blocks of narrative, which might or might not be inserted in a folktale, depending on the extent to which the narrator wanted to prolong the narration. In telling a folktale in which a strange girl comes to a village, where she is "held fast" by the inhabitants and later reaches menarche, the storyteller might include a condensed description of the ceremony for first menstruation,[11] preserving the rough outlines: the need for a ceremony, the principal appropriate participants, the affective tone which linked one kind of ceremony to another. But the details—which herbs, which grubs, which foods were eaten or tabooed—would not be included in such a narration. Instead, the individual in charge of a ceremony organized for himself, herself, or for a child, would call on the last person who had performed a similar ceremony. So the young mother was attended at her delivery by the last woman who had given birth, very possibly a girl younger than herself, who knew a minimum set of essential rituals. A further complication came from the custom of restricting herb collection to men, except for those herbs used in the specifically female activities that were regarded as "women's secret supernaturals"—childbirth, menstrual ceremonies, and dyeing women's aprons red. This meant that there were no specialists and also that the vague and diffuse knowledge was shared by only half the population. But an analysis of the ritual usage in such ceremonies shows that there was a certain clear consistency among the herbs used. The herbs in use in 1931 could be classified as follows:[12]

1. *Rite de passage herbs.* These may be divided into several small groups:—

a. Herbs used in ceremonies of release, particularly in the *dal amabis* ceremony which permits the tabooed person to eat meat again.

b. Herbs used for both men and women, either in the same ceremony, as after childbirth or making an *abullu* [yam ceremony], or in analogous parts of separate ceremonies, as for the girl at menarche and the novice at initiation.

c. Herbs of which different varieties are used for the two sexes in analogous parts of the same ceremonies, occurring either together, as in mourning, or separately, as in puberty segregation and initiation.

d. Herbs restricted to the ceremonials which involve one aspect of life to the exclusion of another, like *wanume'* which is used for ceremonial purification, after handling the sacred flutes, after making an *abullu,* and after handling the dead, or *mau'to'a* bark which is drunk by the father of a newborn child and by a yam harvesting magician, the first to purify himself after the childbirth, the second to purify himself before approaching the yams.

e. The crucial herb, specific to a given rite, such as the special nettles used at a girl's puberty ceremony or in mourning, is most likely to have some associations of sympathetic magic, while the general herbs which occur in many *rites de passage,* are more often spoken of as "herbs of purification," without any resort to explanations based on sympathetic magic.[1]

2. Ceremonial herbs. I use this term for herbs which are either general or specific in various social relationships other than *rites de passage* and which may be regarded as part of the rite, rather than as magical specifics, just as spoken words in the *rites de passage* may be regarded as part of the accompanying rites rather than as magic charms.

These ceremonial herbs include:—

a. Herbs which characterize the termination of relationships, such as those used in severing a *buanyan*ship.[2]

b. Herbs which characterize the intricacies of the blessing and cursing relationships between relatives.

c. Herbs which are used for special *tanggets,* such as the nettles and red and green dracaena used for sorcery *tanggets.*

3. Herbs used in magical procedures. These include:—

a. Generally potent magical herbs which occur in many recipes and are said to "merely watch."

b. Crucial specifics.

4. Herbs which are connected with ghosts and *marsalai* places. These include:—

---

[1] Here we note a point where the herbal usage for magic and *rites de passage* intersects, for in both there are general herbs regarded as appropriate for either one practice or the other, and crucial herbs which have a sympathetic magic content.

[2] Ceremonial exchange relationship between men.

a. Plants and trees which grow in *marsalai* places and are merely to be avoided with great care under fear of *marsalai* punishment.

b. Plants used in offerings to ghosts.

c. Herbs from *marsalai* places which are also used for other purposes, such as the *abo'* tree on which men let blood after an *abullu*.

d. Herbs specifically associated with ghosts and used in divination involving ghosts, divinatory dreaming, and in the divinatory oven. These ghost plants have deeply creased leaves which collect water from which ghosts can drink, or have red leaves, or are wild analogues of plants used by men, ghostly tobacco, ghostly pepper, etc.

5. Herbs connected with ritual blood letting of men and women. This blood letting occurs in the *rites de passage,* as well as at other times. These include the various nettles, the twigs which boys run up their urethras, special leaves upon which blood has to be let, etc.

6. Miscellaneous herbs to which various isolated superstitions attach: a long-leaved flower which if used by a boy to receive his blood insures that he will be tall; a plant with a penis-like flower which if eaten by a woman will insure the birth of a male child; an herb which if eaten by one cross-cousin will make another cross-cousin die, etc. Such beliefs have very little more status than isolated superstitions about the full moon, or spilling salt, or dropping a knife in our own culture. They may quite accurately be called superstitions, unintegrated bits of supernatural belief to which people subscribe with a shrug of the shoulder.

7. Foods with various magical properties, which must be avoided at certain times. This constitutes such a large part of Arapesh supernaturalistic practice, that it merits separate discussion, and I include it here merely for completeness.

The dependence of the Arapesh on recency of personal experience as the criterion for the selection of a suitable ceremonial sponsor was accompanied by considerable anxiety. What if, when one needed the protective formula for marrying a widow, there was no one alive who had married a widow? This anxiety served to focus a little more attention on the collection of herbs or the performance of a ceremony and, for the enterprising, provided a possible motive for collating information.

My best informant, a young man named Unabelin, had all the necessary anxiety, curiosity, and interest to start such a compilation.[13] He expressed this interest by giving me carefully prepared lectures. He would come from his distant village and announce, "I have thought about what you know. I think you do not know this. I will tell you. If I talk for two days will you give me a belt?" He would then proceed to give me a systematic lecture. Had Unabelin learned to read and write, he might very well have expressed this interest—which came into focus through the fortuitous presence of an anthropologist— by keeping records, by writing down long lists of ritual procedures, garnered whenever he could get anyone to take the time to give lists and prescriptions. A situation which until then had been fluid, capricious, nonconserving would suddenly have become solid—not in my monograph written ten thousand miles away and inaccessible to the Arapesh but within the culture. Although Unabelin ostensibly was "teaching" me, he actually was using the situation in order to learn from others. Had he been able to record as well as to learn, he might have used his records to teach and so, using the tools of an advanced literate culture, he might have set up a situation which other people, equally primitive but with different attitudes toward information storage, had set up without these means.

The Arapesh handling of teaching and learning is a concrete illustration taken from one specific culture. A necessary next step is to consider the problem in more general terms. It is possible, as Bateson has done,[14] to place the various forms of learning that have been identified by experimental psychologists, working with animal subjects, in relation to the expected forms of learning in particular cultures. For example, it is possible to differentiate between cultures that rely heavily on rote memory (in which a narrator, when he has been interrupted, has to return to the beginning in order to give a complete and accurate account of a ceremony, the details of which he has committed to memory), those cultures in which learning occurs through the experience of rewarding and/or punishing sequences (which may, or may not, be explicitly included by the teacher or model giver[15]), and those cultures in which learning occurs by instrumental avoidance and is never extinguished because it is never tested in reality.

Useful as it is to treat modern experimental work as a paradigm of culturally diverse teaching–learning possibilities, the formal typologies which are generated in this way must, in every case, be subjected to very close inspection. The difficulty is that it is all too easy to read into a partially described situation a learning–teaching constellation in which the behavioral consequences are, in fact, based on a very different set of species-characteristic responses (in animals) or conscious versions of behavior (in human beings).

The behavior of a group of female goats with suckling

young is a good example.[16] Within such a group, kids may be observed to wander away from their mothers. The other females butt them away, but their own mothers bleat, and eventually the kids find their way back to their own mothers. This could be viewed as a sequence in which certain female goats (not-mother, as it were) punish the wandering kids and send them back to their own mothers, who reward them by providing milk. Actually, the female goats are simply rejecting strange kids, and it is the structure of the group—with the simultaneous bleating of own mother and butting by other mothers—which permits each kid to find its own mother.

Much of the discussion of human learning seems to involve a similar kind of confusion. As one illustration, we may take a series of "learnings" by Balinese children.[17]

It is customary for the Balinese mother or child nurse to call the wandering child back to her, away from an area of danger or from something she does not want the child to touch or take, by uttering a sharp fright signal, *"Aroh!"* accompanied by some concrete threat, such as "Fire!" "Tiger!" "Snake!" "Scorpion!" "Police!" "Feces!" The child then runs back to the nurturing arms, much as small chicks are gathered in by the clucking of the mother hen. The mother then clasps the frightened child in her arms in a pantomime of rescue. The little drama which ends in this embrace may be said to be rewarding to the child, but there is no evidence that the mother sees it in this way. Fright, which she has herself instigated, is for her a game, a small drama, a situation in which fright can be played with. The lack of specific reality reference is accentuated by the indiscriminate use she makes of the concrete symbols; the child cannot learn to master the external world because likely and unlikely threats are mixed together— fire under the bed, a tiger in a friendly bush. The child learns to respond to the fear signal, *"Aroh!"* and learns that if it responds by flight back to the mother, there will be a gay little drama at the end of the scene. As the mother is playing with fear, so the child learns to play with fear.[18]

Or we may look at a more complex pattern in which a mother teases her own child, which is of the right age to be supplanted by a younger sibling, whether or not such a younger sibling actually exists, by borrowing babies with whom she flirts, to whom she gives the breast, or whom she even places upon her own child's head—a grievous insult. As her own child approaches a climax of rage and jealousy, the thread of the drama is broken; the mother may give the borrowed baby to her own child to hold, or she may pick up her own child and replace it in the baby sling, temporarily giving it the status of an infant. But then as her own child, reassured, seeks for some kind of climactic conclusion to this tantalizing interchange, she again breaks the sequence by laughing, looking away, talking to someone else.[19]

Looking at a scene like this from the outside, an observer may say that this treatment "teaches" children to expect broken climaxes and to expect that deeply affective situations will be dealt with theatrically. Where the real younger sibling is concerned, no such teasing and provocation as this takes place; the drama is played out with borrowed babies. It is more accurate to say that from these sequences, in which mothers repeat the games of which they were once the victims and which they have seen a thousand times, the children learn what the mothers already know; at no point is there any teaching or disciplining in which punishing or rewarding sequences are purposefully introduced.

In Samoa, children must learn to be quiet, courteous observers of etiquette. This is accomplished by holding the older child nurses responsible for the behavior of their younger charges. If a baby crawls where it does not belong, cries in the middle of a ceremony, or toddles out among its elders on a solemn occasion, the child nurse may be rebuked or cuffed, and this may be legitimately interpreted as punishment. The toddler, however, is either coddled and placated or is dragged, sometimes rather roughly, off the scene.[20]

Culture can be discussed in terms of the kinds of mechanisms available for the conscious transmission of culture within the society, between generations or between members of different parts of the society—for example, men and women, nobles and commoners, captors and slaves—or between one society and another. Furthermore, when we examine the behavior of the nonhuman world, we find that the ability to learn far exceeds the ability to teach. In fact, lacking the symbolism provided by language, animals can teach only through direct learning in which face-to-face contact is involved. To be effective, changes which do not involve such contact must become sufficiently part of the species-characteristic apparatus to operate without learning or teaching.

When we come to human beings, an examination of the most primitive cultures and also much more complicated ones shows that learning and teaching are forms of behavior which, once conceptualized as possibilities, can vary in a great number of ways. Learning in forms which, because they are unconceptualized, cannot be improved upon (as in model–mimic situations) may continue in some areas of life long after conceptualized learning–teaching has developed in others. In some sequences conceptualization can lead to real innovation; other sequences are less constructive. Teaching as a possibility may invade some area which is actually still taught mimetically, and it can lead to the development of complicated terminologies that convey absolutely nothing unless something else—a musical theme or a dance routine—has already been learned. Balinese music is one example of this kind of functionless pedantry; here such phrases as "White Horse" or "Toad climbs Papaya Tree" are used to refer to musical themes, or "Folded Flowers" is used to characterize a dance gesture.[21] The humming of three notes or a gesture which, in shortened form, recalled the dance routine would be more adequate mnemonic devices. As it is, the names simply add to the clutter of concrete detail with which a Balinese has to burden his memory, in addition to a language which is highly differentiated by status so that not one synonym, but two or three or more must be learned for every word that is used in everyday speech. What is true of music and the dance is equally true of the thousands of offerings. Many offerings have names, but these refer merely to a list; container, substantive elements (essential elements that are offered and later are consumed by the owner of the offering and elements that are left for the gods or spirits), and decorative alternatives. Each of these must then be specified in detail. Use of these names facilitates the interaction of experts among themselves. It has approximately the function that jargon has in an inexact and newly developing science; it speeds up in-group communication without adding anything to the transmissibility of the body of knowledge. Contemporary comment on this familiar situation is the well-known joke about the small in-group who had become so weary of each other's jokes that they referred to them by number, but refused to laugh when a newcomer attempted to use the same technique—because his "tone of voice" wasn't right.

An illusion of coding—where, in fact, the information can be transmitted only if the entire content of a sequence to which the "code" refers is restated—may serve merely to impede communication. When it is recognized that a nonverbal sequence of technical skill, dancing, or ritual behavior is something that must be demonstrated and experienced, because no words exist, appropriate procedures can be inaugurated in order to learn or to teach it. But where this recognition is obscured by a set of words that seem to imply coding, learning will be impeded.

Another kind of impediment can be introduced when an explicitly described behavior sequence is reduced to a code that appears to open a learning sequence to anyone but, in fact, does not do so. The vision behavior of the Omaha Indians is a case in point.[22] Among North American Indians, vision behavior was highly stylized. The youth who had not yet sought a vision usually was exposed to many accounts of other men's visions, accounts that described in detail the kind of experience that would be regarded as a "true vision" and the kind of special occurrence —an oddly shaped stone, a bird flying low on the wing, a feather dropping inexplicably from the air—that validated a supernatural encounter, and thereafter gave the visionary power to hunt, to lead a war party, and so on. Among the Omaha, however, folk tales gave no details of what visionaries had seen.[23] On closer examination it became clear that the vision had not been a mystical experience democratically open to any seeker but rather was a carefully guarded method of ensuring the inheritance within certain families of membership in a medicine society. Entrance to the society nominally was validated by a freely sought vision, but the dogma that a vision was an unspecified mystical experience that any young man could seek and find was balanced by a carefully guarded secret of what constituted a true vision. Young men who were eager to enter the powerful Mide society would go into the wilderness, fast, return and tell their visions to the old men, only to be informed—if they were not members of the elite families—that their vision was not authentic.

This may be contrasted with the experience of vision seekers in other Plains tribes, who were guided by the vision experiences in active circulation and by the advice of older men, to whose scrutiny a vision was submitted, and who helped the neophyte to get his vision "fixed up" to fill in the extra appropriate stylistic material necessary to make it into an acceptable vision.[24]

When the words used for transmitting information apply to specific parts of an object or a process, analyzed so that each part can be exactly demonstrated or verbally described, another step forward is taken in transmissibility. But each step toward articulateness also increases the possibility that the coding will have reference to teaching rather than to learning—will primarily carry messages to the teacher rather than the pupil. Each stage in such a procedure can be illustrated by the history of language teaching through the use of grammars, examples, mimetic pronunciation devices that rely on the pronunciation of known words in the languages of the learner, "trots" (in which an entire text is reproduced in both languages and the learning, conceived of as "cheating," includes the kind of block inarticulate learning for which there is no provision in the formal learning method), elaborate attempts at diacritical marks for cadence, and, finally, the introduction of a "canned model" on a tape or record.

But actually any area of a culture can be analyzed in terms of the types of coding involved. At one extreme one could analyze the manufacture of bull-roarers in a primitive Australian tribe, in which only the old men, in certain circumstances, at certain places, with certain rites, were able to fashion the little oval pieces of wood which, when whirred through the air, made sounds to bemuse and terrify the women and children. At the other extreme one could analyze the procedures demonstrating automatic programming at the installation of a new IBM or Univac computer. In all cultures we will find procedures that are not sufficiently rationalized so they can be "taught" rather than merely demonstrated and also procedures that can be sufficiently separated from experience so that with appropriate instructions they can be carried out from an instruction manual without face-to-face teaching.

However, the ability to code behavior in transmissible form is not necessarily valuable in itself. Such an ability may outrun the capacity of a society or a generation to absorb what can be taught or transmitted through the simple process of labeling an item, a set of items, or a part of a process as *transmissible*. It may well be that the kind of labeling found among the Balinese, in which a meaningless name is applied to a complex ritual offering, functions to alert the hearer to the nontransmissibility of the item in question. This would mean, in fact, that where a Balinese priest knows the names of the proper offerings—and knows he does *not* know the contents—the *toekan bantan* (offering expert) will know the contents but needs the guidance of the priest as to which offerings are needed for which part of the ceremony. Where the priest and the *toekan bantan* are both strangers in a village, other variables will be added as the local helpers say, "You need a *lis*. We make a *lis* this way." If the variation closely resembles what the *toekan bantan* has learned, and only involves, for example, some change in the cutout leaf decoration on the top or the substitution of one flower for another of the same color, he will raise no objection, but the possibility of including an unrelated variation will be increased. The more of such compartmentalization of processes there is and the less aware the officiants in the individual compartments are, the more variation can occur.

We can see such processes also going on at a high level of culture. Consider, for example, the thread of a screw. Seventy-five years ago, nuts and bolts to be used together had to be made in the same place and adjusted to each other, because there were no available devices for making one part in one place and one in another with sufficiently fine specifications that the two parts would fit. Today they can be made on opposite sides of the country or even in different countries. But this increased rationalization in the manufacture of machine parts does not mean that such rationalization is going on at a parallel rate in all aspects of contemporary manufacture. For example, design has been separated from manufacture and use to such an extent that most teapots and pitchers made today do not function fully as teapots and pitchers; that is, as containers for liquids out of which the liquids can also be efficiently poured. There is tremendous lag in the adjustment of use between articles which involve more steps in the fabrication and those which involve less. In fact, it is probable that one dimension in the capacity of a culture to maintain itself, to elaborate and innovate, has always been and may always be the extent to which the differential conceptualization for transmission by teaching or borrowing is even or uneven in various parts of that culture.

Nonfunctional rationalization may itself be either advantageous or disadvantageous. Very frequently, one society has borrowed from another an object or practice and in so doing has included details which are, in fact, irrelevant. For example, the Japanese reproduced the tiny cracks in certain worn forms of European pottery in such a way that this itself became a new, controlled form of pottery surface. From one point of view, such borrowing involves a failure to discriminate, insofar as the fracture in the pottery or the tuck in the sleeve of a mended model is regarded as part of the whole "good" object. But borrowing of this kind can proceed very rapidly. Copying the unessential as well as the essential, without any attempt to analyze and rationalize, is one very quick method of taking over the procedures of another culture. It is also, as Waddington has pointed out, a way of insuring a certain amount of continuous random variation within those elements which are not functionally necessary.[25]

For example, at the period when Stalin prizes were being given for the "invention" of equipment which was faithfully copied from Western models, Soviet manufacturers of electronic equipment copied patent numbers and other sorts of completely identifying data along with all the other features of a particular model.[26] As they drew on German, American, and English models, this initial "slavish" reproduction, while they were themselves deficient in production skills, meant that they were channeling into their own experience, in an inarticulate and unanalyzed form, the record of the manufacturing habits of the countries whose members still excelled them in just these respects. The West has treated with amused contempt the kind of copying that is a "slavish" imitation of a whole and shows no evidence of the atomization of process which we regard as the necessary precursor of the rationalization of industry. So far, this has proved to be a mistake; the country that first "slavishly" copied later was able to make important innovations.

At the extreme other end of the scale are the borrowing patterns of New Guinea tribes, who have carried the dissection of parts of culture into exportable items to a degree unreported for any other part of the world. On this second largest island in the world, it is estimated there are some 2.5 million inhabitants, who speak over 500 mutually unintelligible languages and dialects.[27] Groups speaking the same language vary in size from a few hundred people to groups as large as 15,000 to 20,000 (or perhaps more), but nowhere in the area has a society worked out a satisfactory means of completely integrating people into units (with warfare barred) of more than several hundred. Political boundaries are shifting. Even villages of a few hundred inhabitants are likely to fission, and parts of villages may form alliances with parts of other villages, or with other language groups. People speaking one language may spread and multiply in an unoccupied area or they may displace some other group, but there are no political devices adequate for constructing permanent large-scale groups. New Guinea peoples lack such political devices as the idea of permanent conquest, permanent alienation of territory, permanent alliances with all killing within the group forbidden, hierarchical leadership which could be extended over a wider and wider group. Furthermore, they have no conception of a body of custom which is peculiar to one group, and so is inaccessible to any other group.

I have suggested that the belief that some kind of behavior is an inextricable aspect of one sex, or a particular race, or some "other" people acts as a deterrent to learning. This impermeability to the ideas of others may well have been a condition of early man, especially if there were several relatively dissimilar groups of hominids whose differences from one another may have been as striking as the differences between themselves and less closely related primates. If this was the case, it would have made possible enormous varieties in behavior. But the peoples of New Guinea and the Melanesian peoples of the fringing islands, who with their canoes became part of the diffusion system, represent an extreme example of the opposite variation: *overwillingness to learn* from other people. In this area the idea of a "custom" is a giant list of unrelated traits, bits, pieces, methods, and beliefs—as variegated as the index to some anthropological monographs, in which circumcision and cross-cousin marriage and curvilinear design jostle each other in the classification system. Among New Guinea peoples any item of the "custom of the people of the Viper Road"—a word, a kinship term, a form of marriage, a piece of magic, a way of planting yams, an article of clothing, a ratio between articles of clothing, a method of subdividing the entire tribe for ceremonial purposes, a song, a design element, a secret, a taboo—can be included in the vast network of interchange by gift, exchange, barter, purchase, and indemnity, which is characteristic of the area. Not until different peoples, each with a long history, came together in public meeting places like the markets in Istanbul or in African cities has such diversity been available side by side. Significantly, the market in which one can today buy a hubblebubble pipe and a transistor radio, a veil which will completely cover a woman's body, and a pair of rubber baby pants closely approximates the situation in New Guinea cultures; the willingness to sell and to buy transcends any considerations of congruence or loyalty, and the special foods that one group eats at a feast, at which the group may also decide to massacre the eaters of other foods, are sold side by side with the foods of their enemies.

In the preceding chapters I have discussed cultural transmission in its varied forms, from the use of the mimic model through ever-improved ways of embodying some aspect of culture in an artifact, or of abstracting it in a form in which it can be taught to individuals who differ from the teacher in sex, or age, or class, or culture, and so on. In this discussion I have given less attention than is usual to increased control of the communication process through the development of coding first in symbolic speech, then in script, and then in special languages (e.g. for mathematical or musical notation), in analytical systems (e.g. for the analysis of kinship or economics), in diagrammatic representations (e.g. statistical tables or blueprints), in programming for different types of computers, and the completely new type of transmission in which a record of behavior can be preserved on sound film. Instead, I have stressed other, less usually discussed types of transmission as a way of highlighting the extent to which *all* forms of transmission of previous experience are to be found in the highest forms of human civilization today. Evolutionary advances in communication have not eliminated any one of the earlier forms. But one of the blocks in our ability to transform our present-day culture is our failure to recognize the extent to which different individuals, different occupations, classes, and cultures depend on implicit learning from artifacts, on empathetic, imitative, and identificatory learning, and on Gestalt learning—learning without the intervention of a teacher.

In my discussion I have given little specific attention to Gestalt learning in evolution. This is not because it may not be so important as, or even of greater importance than, certain other forms of implicit learning, but because we lack the precise material, on our own culture and on other cultures, which is needed for such a discussion. It is possible to speculate about the way in which the different types of learning discussed by Bateson in cross-cultural perspective[28] are cross-cut by the handling of Gestalts. One could contrast the way in which the Samoans can disassemble and reassemble units of social behavior at will,[29] while the Zuni who is interrupted in the recitation of some rote sequence must begin again at the beginning.[30] I can illustrate the precision with which the Manus handle time.[31] For example, in 1953, when I showed them a picture of a woman with a tiny child, each individual initially named the child as that one of the woman's five children whom he best remembered as an infant. But when I said, "I took that picture," each one immediately corrected himself, and said, "Then it must have been Sofia!" That is, each one now placed the baby correctly in the context of my visit twenty-five years earlier. In general it can be said that as our ability to deal with cognitive style increases, it will be increasingly possible to do detailed work with primitive and exotic cultures on Gestalt learning and to make systematic comparisons.

In this discussion I have dealt explicitly with two problems: the type and the degree of intervention in the transmission process by persons, objects, and symbolic notations. I was able to demonstrate the speed with which we have moved through new methods of encoding and manipulating knowledge based on past experience when, during the actual presentation of these lectures, I showed a film made in Bali, in 1937, depicting a dancing lesson being given to a small boy by the famous Balinese dancer, Mario.[32] Until the middle of the nineteenth century, we could have brought to an audience who had never been to Bali no more of a Balinese dance than was contained in the type of static record found on a Cretan mural. With the development of still photography, an observer still could record only a series of postures in the dance. The invention of the gramophone made it possible to record the music, music for which European notation is inadequate and which could not be performed with Western musical instruments. The dance itself could not have been preserved as information, still less could it be used as a model of style for non-Balinese peoples. But with the development of sound and film recording, it has become possible to record a kind of behavior which hitherto, throughout the history of man, has been dependent on face-to-face apprenticeship learning, and to preserve it in a form in which it can be used for learning. (See Plates 17–21.)

Expressed in this way, we can see in the sequence from the Balinese, who preserve their own dance and musical knowledge entirely by means of face-to-face transmission and a small nondenotative vocabulary and a caricature of musical notation, to our present means of recording both sound and movement in full context, the whole evolutionary development of our means of coding, storage, and transmission.

At the same time, another part of our worldwide communication system had evolved. Bali is now part of a free Indonesia, which has modeled itself on Western political systems, and now has a national language for the 90 million inhabitants of Indonesia's 3,000 islands. Mario and a troupe of his pupils, one of whom had appeared in our film made twenty years before, danced on Broadway in November 1957, half a world away from their small island. So the circle is complete. Side by side with our most evolved methods of preserving a complex form of behavior, we had the most simple—watching a member of another cultural group do something new and strange. Regarded as learned behavior, this was something that could be imitated. Were it to be regarded as a function of the "racial characteristics" of the Balinese, to whom incredible degrees of flexibility and subtlety could then be attributed, it was inimitable. Watching the dancers, the New York audience complained that their eyes hurt. In transplanting a group of Balinese to Broadway, one thing had gone unnoticed. In the United States, theatrical lights are set for gilt costumes, but the Balinese costumes were emblazoned in real gold.

In the films made in Bali in 1937, there is a sequence in which Mario tried to learn from and to teach a visiting dancer from Madras.[33] This sequence is a record of another important type of human learning—the learning that takes place between adults. In the film we see two interacting individuals, each of whom has already learned to live as a human being in one culture, trying unsuccessfully to learn the forms of another culture. When a dancer of one culture tries to teach—or learn—the dance of another culture, he relies to some extent on the model of the adult and the child, just as one does in trying to teach—or learn—a foreign language. In addition, in such a teaching exchange, each of the adults involved relies on his previous learning of a particular cultural form. As teacher or learner, he may see the previous learning as a barrier. If he does, habituation to one stylistic pattern may block the learning of another style, for this view of earlier learning implies that, because one has learned one style of dancing, speaking, eating, cooking, and so on, one can learn no other. So phrased, learning at all levels is a form of premature death, as the individual sees himself and his fellows sealed in little ethnocentric compartments, unable to grow because as adults they are unable to learn or teach across the lines of class or occupation or discipline or culture.

Learning by an adult can instead be seen as quite different from learning by a child, as the adult, to the extent that he has learned his own culture, is in a position to learn all cultures. If he has never learned to write his own language, then learning script will be an experience of a different order, somewhat resembling learning by a child. But experience in teaching writing to nonliterate peoples has demonstrated the great speed with which they can learn when their behavior does not have to wait on maturation, as a child's does; adults can use adult forms of grasping and applying a generalization.

There is one further requirement for transmission across lines, from adult to adult: as much as possible of the system being transmitted must be there—not only the written words, but also the sound of the words being spoken and the sight of native speakers talking to each other; not only the film of the finished dance, but also the sight and sound of the stages of learning; not only the finished pot or the graceful carving, but also the sight of the potter or the artist at work. Even in the simplest society, an adult can say, *"Because I have learned once, I can learn something of the same order again, and more quickly."* This is the necessary state of mind of the learning adult. The complementary position of the teacher requires the careful provision of experience of process as well as product, the inclusion not only of abstraction, symbolization, and patterned analysis, but also the more generalized experience of the uncoded and as yet uncodable elements through which the adult learner, like the child, can learn by empathy, imitation, and identification.

PART II

7. Directionality of Human Evolution

In PART ONE of this book I was concerned with outlining cultural processes of transmission which have themselves evolved and which, at each stage of their evolution, have permitted further evolution to occur. In my discussion I focused on some of those aspects of culture which are relevant to micro-evolutionary processes. In doing so I treated cultural macro-evolution as given, involving as it does progressive change in energy use in all its facets, adaptation to specific ecological settings, increasing exploitation of the environment, change in the sources of energy, change in forms of social organization in which human beings live, and change in the processes of information storage, information transmission, and the generation of new ideas. In fact, I treated as given the processes of worldwide general cultural evolution, as these have been discussed by Childe[1] and by White,[2] and also the shorter but still cultural macro-evolutionary sequences with which Steward,[3] Sahlins and Service,[4] and Lehman[5] are majorly concerned.

In cultural micro-evolutionary investigations, inquiry starts where these discussions stop. One way of clarifying the differences between micro-evolutionary and macro-evolutionary investigations is to ask the question: *What unit of cultural evolution is being used?*

The definition of the cultural unit may be handled in many ways. One way is to focus on the possibilities inherent in a single trait, a trait cluster, a functional complex, or a total culture. A second way is to focus on stages of complexity in energy use, that is, on the evolutionary possibilities of a food-gathering stage, a horticultural stage, a stage in which domestic animals are combined with horticulture or agriculture, and so on. A third way is to focus on types of social organization, from the simple band to the modern nation–state, in terms of energy utilization, size of population, possibilities for the division of labor and for increased stratification and cultural diversity, and so on.

Alternatively, it is possible to focus on the actual events of recorded history, as we now understand them, and to assay the evolutionary potentialities of known civilizations in terms of all these variables—ecological relations, stages of energy use, types of social organization, states of information transmission. This approach is perhaps best exemplified by Wittfogel's studies of hydraulic cultures.[6] Analyses of this kind may be refined in various ways. An analysis may, for example, include ideas of cultural flux, that is, ideas about periodic alterations of rhythm in which there is first an increase in complexity and then a decrease as possibilities are exhausted.[7] Or an analysis may emphasize the recurrent problems that human beings must solve.[8] But when such theories of periodicity of occurrence are combined with quasi-mystical theories, like those developed by Spengler,[9] directional evolution is replaced by some theory of repetitious self-defeat. And when, as in Ruth Benedict's configurational approach,[10] attention centers on the recurrence of cultural themes, the very idea of the directionality of cultural evolution may be lost sight of. Then, for example, modern forms of ritual murder, as carried out by the Nazis on Jews and Gypsies, may be regarded as differing only in scale from the forms of human sacrifice found in more primitive societies.

In all these approaches science itself has a somewhat

anomolous position. Science is seen by some historians as a characteristic of one cycle of human culture, which may in time exhaust itself. Mankind would then revert to simpler forms of relationship to the environment in which the world's peoples would be less interdependent. This viewpoint is well expressed in Kenneth Boulding's idea of political devolution into smaller governments,[11] or in Frank Tannenbaum's daydream of the Andean Indian, a thousand years from now, standing on a peak and saying, "The white man came. He did a lot of harm, and he went away." [12] Scientific development is also regarded by some social commentators as analogous to genotypic obsolescence; through science man may lose his viability as a species, and it may possibly play a disastrous role in the destruction of all other living creatures as well.[13]

Alternatively, we can regard science as the slow culmination of the capacity to order phenomena—a capacity which is manifested in the earliest cultures and in very young children—and, by ordering, to master the phenomena of the outer world. From still another viewpoint, science introduces a new dimension into evolution, so that from some arbitrarily chosen moment in time man is regarded as participating in the direction of his own fate—the date conventionally assigned to the beginning of the physical sciences or the first, or some future, flowering of the life sciences.[14] If one takes the viewpoint that science has made possible the human species' power of destruction and has not yet produced the knowledge necessary to curb and harness that organized destructiveness, two moments of high evolutionary significance are outstanding: The period of the beginning of the physical sciences and that of the beginning of man's understanding of an evolutionary process in which man, his mind in all its levels, and his organized relationships to his fellows and to the universe are included.

Every specific treatment of cultural macro-evolution must, at least implicitly, take some position on these questions. And in discussing these larger issues as background for a more detailed examination of the processes of cultural micro-evolution, it seems necessary for me to state, if only very schematically, the selection I have made from these various approaches.

I assume that the original impetus to the development of culture—as the predominant mode of human transmission, largely superseding genetic transmission—was given by the development of man's brain and the coordination of the body and the brain, especially of hand, eye, and vocalizing equipment. (Recent research on dolphins[15] brings into sharper relief the functional importance of man's physical configuration.) The actual development of human culture depended on the development of methods of transmitting information in other ways than through the use of simple mimetic behavior. But whether culture is described as a function of the complexity of the communication system, or communication is described as a function of culture, seems relatively unimportant.[16] From the time when any given group of human creatures had the ability, as a group, to vary their behavior and to use cultural means to transmit their forms of variation to the next generation, the possibility of one group borrowing from another was also present. Each complication in the relationship between transmission within the group, from one generation to another, and in transmission from one group to another resulted in greater evolutionary potentialities for change, including experimentation, preservation of the results of experimentation, and cumulation of cultural inventions.

The ecological setting, which in its widest sense includes not only the geographical and nonhuman living aspects of the environment but also all human groups within the area of communication, provided the conditions through which the course of cultural evolution was channeled in the direction of higher or, alternatively, lower social integration. The survival value of specific inventions in response to specific ecological conditions can be seen in the same general frame of reference as the survival value of various forms of biological mutation. In a given ecological setting some inventions (e.g. tailored clothing in the Arctic) have a higher survival value; others (e.g. buffalo hunting with bows and spears by a group in contact with another group having firearms) have a low survival value.

The elimination of practices with a low survival value is as essential to the directionality of human evolution as is the occurrence of the conditions for innovation of new elements with high survival value. For example, during the depression of the 1930s, the world demand for copra decreased. The inhabitants of some South Sea islands, who had come to depend on modern technology for light and cloth and other goods, could not pay for imports and so had to fall back on their abandoned practices of making bark cloth and burning candlenuts for light. These aboriginal practices had a high survival value for the groups of islanders whose contact with a higher culture was broken; at the same time their reinstitution was a symptom of a general retrogression in a global trade net which, during the worldwide depression, was losing its organizational integrity. Any condition in which a lower-level technique must be used because of a failure at a higher level highlights the conditions within which the higher-level techniques can survive and spread. A breakdown in transportation and communication, in the exchange of natural resources, in political integration (into smaller mutually hostile population units), or in political–ideological and economic inclusiveness may temporarily involve the use of an earlier and organizationally or technologically lower form of culture, but the local survival values of such lower forms must be viewed against the directionality of the whole of human culture and its potential availability to all members of the human species.

In any historical sequence—for example, the development of civilization in Mesoamerica[17]—it should be possible to discern smaller sequences and events which increase or decrease the evolutionary possibilities of that particular cultural sequence and to identify external events, natural and man-made, which have increased or decreased the evolutionary potential of this particular cultural segment. Sufficiently careful analyses and comparisons of such sequences should also make it possible to identify the evolutionary significance of the types of relationship internal to the system. For example, it would be possible to make analyses of the event sequences leading to the formation of the Mesoamerican and Peruvian civilizations, the event sequence through which the Spaniards came to the New World and, finally, the event sequence through which these several systems, each at one point in history external and unrelated to the others, came to form one interlocking system. From a comparative study of such analyses, one could develop higher orders of abstraction about evolutionary potentials, assay the consequences of various combinations of level of organization and type of environment, and work out the points at which certain environmental features, such as climate or local resources—for instance, coal or oil, gold or uranium—would be more or less crucial. Analyses of this kind would also illuminate the unique quality of cultural evolution, the interdependence of the state of natural resources, the physical configuration of the earth's surface, and the available cultural forms of social organization, technology, and ideology.[18]

An increased understanding of the directionality of the evolutionary process can be gained, first, by retrospective analyses of the place of particular civilizations in time and space in a total ecological frame; second, by inspection of the possibilities of near-contemporary events that bring about change; and, third, by inspection of possibilities as yet unexploited. This latter type of analysis is at present being used in an institution like the Air University at Maxwell Air Force Base, Alabama, as a means of exploring, through the development of *as-if* situations, of the possible repercussions of alternatives to political decisions made in the recent past. For example, an analysis of this as-if kind might be undertaken to consider what would have taken place, in 1932 and later, had United States air power been used to enforce a cessation of the Sino–Japanese "incident." The dissection of an event structure, combined with a thorough examination of alternatives that were *not* used, would go a long way toward demonstrating the precariousness of directionality in human culture and would focus attention on the points at which any given cultural invention has not yet been fully established.

The sense of inevitability which pervades White's work[19] results from his concentration on sets of events that did occur. Steward's work[20] is less deterministic insofar as he includes situations in which specific development might have occurred but did not, and to the extent that he sets these nonoccurrences over against a large set of sequences which are reassuring because they are multiple. But more detailed analysis of each recurrent and reassuring parallel sequence would reveal that in each of these there were also precarious elements. Such detailed analyses would in turn raise the question of just what the cultural conditions are that make it probable that a given set of sequences will recur with enough frequency to ensure directionality. This, however, remains a part of cultural macro-evolutionary analysis. (I shall return to the problem of insurance against the loss of cultural conditions of unidirectionality in Part Three of this book.)

Cultural macro-evolution may be defined as evolution that occurs in human cultures at a level at which the specification of individual actors is irrelevant. But a continuum might be constructed on which, at different points, we could distinguish various levels of specificity: a level at which the character of a particular society, but not any given individual within that society, is crucial; a level at which a group of individuals is crucial; and a level at which the single individual is crucial. This can be stated more technically in terms of networks. If the intersection of different networks is in an individual, and only in that individual, then the networks become disjoint without him.

Or a continuum might be constructed in which, at different points, we could distinguish various types of event sequence: at one end, events of the dimensions of an Ice Age; at some intermediate point, the type of event that involves a whole society in an enterprise (e.g. a war or a migration); and, finally, the type of event in which a single incident is crucial (e.g. the failure or the success of the engine of a particular airplane or the engine of a particular rocket carrying a particular individual). Directionality in evolution is assured only at those levels at which the primary specifications needed are: the size of the group of human beings, the level of culture, and the available types of proctection against events that could annihilate the group and/or destroy the culture altogether.

For this preliminary exploration of the problem, I shall arbitrarily define cultural micro-evolution as the level at which the particular individual, or a group of particular individuals, is significant. In contrast, cultural macro-evolution can operate with a population which is defined only as to type of organization, population size and sex and age ratio, and types of normal survival characteristics, such as freedom from a progressively lethal disease and the possession of a given state of human culture (language, social organization, tool use, etc.). So the propositions of cultural macro-evolution read: Given a population of X size, the existence of agriculture, literacy, form of state organization, then. . . . The arguments as to whether human beings should be treated as if they were subject to the gas laws still apply because cultural macro-evolutionary statements involve previous stages of organization which may be unrepeatable,[21] at least in extreme cases as, for example, when natural resources have been exhausted so that a lower level of technology cannot be initiated or restored.[22] But the very nature of human culture as an evolutionary mechanism allows for a very high degree of reversibility. The study of a culture like that of the Eskimo[23] or of the Polynesians[24] (either of which may very well be an adaptive simplification of a higher-level culture) or a culture like that of the Siriono[25] (which may be seen as a maladaptive reactive simplification) throws into high relief the extent to which statements of a statistical kind are possible. For example, it is possible to state that, given a large enough population, divided into groups, existing for a long enough period of time, with language, the probability that writing of some sort will be invented increases with the size of the population, the number of groups into which it is divided, and the length of time. Such a statement gives no indication of where, in which group, under what conditions, or when writing would be invented.

Here the study of cultural micro-evolution takes up the task in the attempt to specify the crucial significance of particular individuals in determining where, when and, ultimately, if any of the large-scale changes—changes which, retrospectively, will be seen as evolutionarily directional—will occur. This provides the point of juncture for cultural evolution and human genetics. The level of cultural macro-evolution and the level of biological evolution are matched, in the larger sense in which species-wide possibilities of mutation correspond to species-wide cultural inventions. To be significant at the cultural macro-evolutionary level, one would have to postulate a change of order of the kind one might find, for example, between *Zinjanthropus boisei* [26] and a next successor type.[27] At this level, once culture was established with a stable species as its carrier, the only mutations which would be of interest would be those which resulted in the development of another species. A speculation like that of Freud,[28] about the function of the break in man's maturation between early childhood and puberty (involving a leveling off of overt endocrine function), is a problem at the macro-evolutionary level, as are the problems of the significance of man's long dependency, the longer period of learning, and the conflict of generations, which have come about through the continuation of instinctive behavior appropriate to an earlier period of evolutionary development.

Problems relating to the gene pool and the characteristics of a particular gene pool are more likely to be significant at the level at which a whole society is the significant unit.[29] Characteristics affecting large populations, such as an immunity or a hereditary vulnerability to some disease, differential fertility–sex ratios and aging rates, might in time so differentiate one large population from another as to affect the course of cultural history.

So, at the cultural macro-evolutionary level, the smallest significant biological unit is the species. At the intermediate level, at which the part played by a whole civilization is relevant, the smallest significant biological unit is the gene pool of a particular population. Finally, at the cultural micro-evolutionary level, with which we are here concerned, the significant *biological* unit is the specific

genetic constitution of the members of each cluster of particular interacting individuals from particular family lines.
If we keep these distinctions in mind, we can avoid the
impassioned declarations for or against the importance of
the Great Man in History, and we need not insist on the
inevitability of cultural direction in which the individual
plays no part. We can avoid the slips of logic which occur
when "a little evolutionary significance" is attributed to
Leonardo da Vinci, or Einstein, or Napoleon, but none to
lesser figures.[30] For if at any point in human evolution any
one individual is of evolutionary significance, then a fine
enough analysis would reveal the potential evolutionary
role of every other human being, limited as this would be
to the period, the culture, and the society into which each
individual was born.

The significance of the individual, regarded simply as a
phenotypic representation of the genotype *Homo sapiens,*
can be discussed at all three evolutionary levels. At the
macro-evolutionary level, the individual who carries a
viable mutation and who survives to reproduce is crucial;
according to the definition of Dobzhansky and Birdsell,[31]
the only point of evolutionary interest is expressed in the
survival of the offspring. But even at this level, the issue
of mere survival, reproduction, and increase in numbers is
not all there is. Let us consider, for example, two possible
early groups of hominidae who live on terms of enmity
with each other and whose reproductive efficiency and
death rate are comparable. For both, the death rate is high
in part because of failures in food supply which come
about as a result of drought, on the one hand and, over a
longer time period, the lack of any means of preserving
information about ways of seeking and finding food when
there is a dearth, on the other.[32]

In the marginal areas of the world, the maintenance of
the life of a group depends on keeping alive the memory

of the exercise of some skill so seldom practiced that it might easily lapse altogether. Cultural conditions such as these may have continued for very long periods of human history. Estimates of the probable length of time in which Australian aborigines lived under approximately similar ecological and cultural conditions vary from about the middle of the seventh millennium B.C. to possibly the end of the Ice Age.[33] In the Arctic, the Eskimo, living under equally difficult conditions, have survived at least 2,000 years and perhaps much longer.[34]

Returning now to the two groups of early hominidae (groups whose language was inadequate to record directions without immediate human guidance), let us suppose that a mutation occurred in one of the two groups which, by extending the childhood period before conception was possible and by cutting short, through cessation of ovulation, the period of productivity, resulted in a shortened period of fertility in women. From the standpoint of the maintenance of population size alone, this mutation would lower the biological efficiency of the group, and this group would be at a competitive disadvantage with the other one. However, less exposed to the hazards of child bearing, the women of the former group would have a greater chance of surviving into later life and so of conserving for a longer time knowledge of the food resources of the physical environment. This, in turn, might increase the chances of survival of the children born into the group. So, even though such a mutation resulted in lower biological efficiency in terms of the offspring produced, it might become crucial in the establishment of a group of elders who could conserve more and more of the experience garnered in a lifetime, among a people who were as yet unable to transmit this information without demonstration, and so, indirectly, the mutation would alter the survival rate of the next generation.

In a small group of this kind, even assuming a gene pool in which the same mutation might be expected to recur, the life of the particular individual would be crucial and might affect the course of human evolution to an extraordinary degree. At present, the position one takes on the matter of evolutionary steps is open to choice. The position that decisive steps are likely to be lavishly over-provided for, the position taken by Beach and Lehrman, is the more popular one among Americans and is congruent with an economy of plenty and our traditional habit of overbuilding machinery for overstrain. (It should be noted, however, that this is disappearing.) The alternative view is that new adaptations depend on exceedingly finely calibrated genetic changes that fit together, in Lorenz' phrase, "like a lock and key." [35] Recent discussions of mutations that occur in the phenotypic lifetime suggest the extreme importance of the individual carrier of a mutation in a small population.[36] But reports on Mavis Gunther's research[37] in the United Kingdom, on the number of infants born whose mouths are too small for breast feeding, suggest the speed with which a genetic recombination that requires special conditions for viability (in this case bottle feeding) may spread even in a large population. In two socially competitive small populations, in which for some reason breast feeding was crucial either for the survival of infants with special needs or for a particular kind of character formation, a change of this kind could assume tremendous importance.

At the second level, where a whole society or civilization is the evolutionary unit, those genetic factors which affect whole populations in their essentially crude demographic characteristics become important. In a small Pacific island society, a shift in the sex ratio might have profound consequences for the survival of the group not only in terms of crude reproductive rates but also, if the shift persists through generations, in the group's response in terms of social organization. This, in turn, might determine how the group would respond to a local catastrophe or to new opportunities afforded by contact with peoples of other cultures.[38]

Differential extensions of life may also have a profound effect on the impact of the diseases of the third quarter of human life. For example, a critical examination of the observed low incidence of mental disease among the Hutterites showed that, in this group, it was associated with the extreme relative youthfulness of the population; this, in turn, was associated with a high reproductive rate.[39]

Where, among a hominid group without language, the preservation of older females through a menopausal cessation of fertility might be a tremendous evolutionary advantage, at a later stage of history, a large proportion of older people with chronic diseases and mental debilitation might constitute a heavy burden. The Eskimo, the Australian aborigines, and the Bushmen[40] were able to reconcile the good of the group and the absolute need for survival with the occasional sacrifice of old people who were not able to keep up with a moving group or contribute to the welfare of the next generation, but at higher levels of ethical development such a solution becomes untenable. So it may be said that any shift in the gene pool which alters the proportions of young, middle-aged, and old persons in a population may have evolutionary consequences. The effects of such shifts, brought about by other means, can be studied in those societies in which a large proportion of an age group has been withdrawn from the population—for example, as indentured labor in colonial countries or through death in war, as happened in Europe in World War I, in particular, but also in World War II.[41]

With existing tools of analysis, it is at present possible

to distinguish characteristics of the gene pools of large populations which are relevant to the cultural potentialities or the relative competitive positions of different societies only in terms of those which affect the proportions between different age groups, the sex ratio, or the relative immunity or vulnerability to disease of one group or another, and so on. It is, however, plausible that there may be an exaggeration of negative or positive traits in very small populations, especially where there is a high rate of inbreeding or where, through several generations, there is a systematic siphoning off of the most able members of a population while the least able remain in or return to remote villages, or where, in a very narrow hereditary elite group, there is a preference for endogamy which affects the inheritance of specific characteristics (e.g. hemophilia among the royal families of Europe[42]). If for some reason such a small group should become crucial to the continuation of a civilization, then its study would fall into the category of cultural microanalysis, in which the specific genetic qualities of particular individuals are relevant.

Broadly speaking, at the level of cultural macro-evolution, we rely for our knowledge of the history of human cultures on palaeontology and the study of the succession of early forms of man to provide the nexus of biological and cultural evolution. But when we are concerned with problems of cultural evolution which are associated only with *Homo sapiens,* it becomes useful to work with population statistics and to make use of such concepts as genetic drift, the characteristics of gene pools, the ecological niche, and so on.

At the next most particularizing level of analysis, the level at which the development of specific historical cultures is the subject of inquiry, it is a matter of choice whether one takes the position that the specification of individuals is unimportant, as Steward, Sahlins, Service, and others do, or whether one pursues the analysis further to explore those points in the evolution of cultures which were crucial in the inauguration of long-term, large-scale trends, and studies these retrospectively.

There is, moreover, an inherent difficulty in asking why one culture developed in a given way while another, exposed to like environmental influences, failed to develop in a similar way, retrogressed, or remained static. A question so phrased may lead to a reification of directionality and to an assumption that evolutionary development is to be expected, so that it is necessary to explain why, in any case, it does not occur. Yet Steward's[43] definition of multilinear evolution as a process which may, but need not, occur leaves one with the choice of stating why evolution did not occur, in cases where it did not, or of undertaking the kind of cultural micro-evolutionary analysis in which, in cases of equally favorable ecological conditions, the reasons for the development of each parallel trend are worked out in detail. That is, one would have to compare two societies, A and B, both of which at some point in time were potentially at the same cultural level and at the same general level of technical and social development, one of which developed from a band organization to a state while the other did not. It would then be necessary to specify in detail the conditions within which one society moved ahead and the other did not. A considerable variety of explanations can be invoked. Large-scale events, external to the two social systems, such as the impact of a volcanic eruption or an earthquake, conquest by an outside group, crop failure due to drought or flooding, or contact with another culture, may be invoked without specifying individuals. In many cases the specified events later seem adequate to explain the divergent courses taken by two related cultures. Once a clear developmental trend is discernible, the failure to develop in a given way can, it seems, be more readily referred to historical or cultural conditions than to the influence of individuals, singly or in groups.

But this is not the case if we look more closely at a society whose potential for change was in some way inhibited or diverted or, alternatively, at a society which did change, moving from a nomadic pastoral life to settled agriculture or from hunting and gathering to horticulture. Then we see that at some early point in the sequence, before any group in the area of communication had taken the first step toward change, certain decisions were in the hands of groups of individuals. Wherever we have adequate historical records, whether we are concerned with events in a small New Guinea village or in a great nation-state, it can be shown that particular individuals—as individuals and as members of particular groups responsible for making decisions and taking action—do make the decisions from which the events flow which later seem to have been "inevitable." And it is the sum total of these "inevitable" advances, combined with equally "inevitable" failures, which, as one looks back, constitute directional evolution.

Directionality, at any given period, is provided by the competitive status of cultural inventions of different types and the competitive status of the societies carrying them; the outcome of each such competition, as it involves irreversible change (for example, in the destruction of natural resources or an invention that makes obsolete an older invention), defines the directional path. The better the recording and the transmission systems are, the more irreversible elements can be included. And at any later time, looking back from $Time^5$ to $Time^4$, one can ignore the choice points that occurred at $Time^4$ and see, instead, the smooth working of inevitable, impersonal cultural evolution—horticulture following food gathering, settlement following nomadism, feudalism following conquest, and so on. In turn, this articulate categorization of events becomes one of the less reversible elements in the culture, shaping in men's minds certain firm expectations of what sequences ought to occur. From the ability to distinguish between good and evil,[44] celebrated in the story of the Garden of Eden, to the ability to make instruments capable of destroying the human species, these irreversibilities have defined the evolutionary course of human culture. But before the action, later celebrated in history, had gathered enough momentum to bring about directionality, there were crucial moments.

It is my assumption, therefore, that although evolution is directional, it is not ever completely predictable, except within very narrowly defined limits. At the present time, any prediction about man's future must include the possible totally destructive use of thermonuclear and other types of modern warfare; consequently, any statement about the future course of human evolution must be qualified by the possibility that the human species may destroy itself and in so doing destroy large portions or perhaps all of the living world. It does not seem necessary to equate directionality with predictability over a long time span, and the insistence on inevitability, crystal clear in retrospect, is in fact a recognition that at a given time a given activity was so well launched that its direction could be predicted, until or unless some major event, physical or social, deflected its course.

For purposes of illustration we can invoke the familiar case of water running over a smooth, sloping surface of known area, a surface not completely resistant to erosion. Initially the course taken by the water will be a condition of past conditions. But if there is some slight irregularity in the initial force of the water or in the surface, paths will be established that will become more determinate with every passing moment, and the deepening of these paths and the magnitude of the events necessary to shift the direction of the paths will be a function of time and of unpredictable events outside the system. But if the water continues to flow at the same rate and the surface remains tipped at the same angle, then it can be predicted with increasing certainty that the water will flow in the fixed pattern originally established by small irregularities within the system.

It is my argument that in human evolution one significant type of such functional irregularities is found in the actual, specifiable genetic constitution and postconception experience of specific individuals, whose presence or absence under given historical conditions is crucial. The significance of such idiosyncratic characteristics is greatest in those narrow areas where complete reversibility obtains. Later events—even though each event still will be mediated by individuals—will be more a function of the number of individuals involved and the degree of institutionalization of the change. (One form of institutionalization is embodiment in a record; a recorded element becomes transmissible and so recurrently innovative in the culture.)

Clearly, this set of assumptions is in conflict with some kinds of determinism, both the determinism that includes in its definition each event in the life of each human being, each broken paddle, and each torn sail that interrupts a voyage, and the determinism that defines a broad plan in which the main events are fixed but the speed and the location of events are not fixed. I look forward to an increasing ability on the part of the human sciences to identify potentially irreversible sequences of a more limited order and to work out ways of modifying such sequences.

The examination of the role of identified individuals and groups of identified individuals must always be conducted within specified, wider cultural contexts. It is these wider cultural contexts which, at a higher level of generalization, can be discussed without reference to individuals. For example, one may discuss the evolutionary significance of an invention like a phonetic script, in contrast to an ideographic script, without specifying the particular individuals who are the human carriers of the script at a given time.[45]

Similarly, in describing the relative vigor of two communities in a known cultural framework, which differ from each other in their capacities for maintenance and innovation, one can specify the available cultural equipment, literacy, knowledge of parliamentary and bureaucratic procedures, money stabilized against the currency of a major power, and so on, without in any way referring to the human actors. But let us suppose that the two communities have ancient and difficult scripts, so that if they are to become part of some larger, fully interacting cultural area they must adopt some more widely used system of writing. One community adopts a phonetic rendering of its language which accords with English; the other community decides to abandon its script for Arabic or Japanese. A very few, quite identifiable individuals, acting within a specifiable context, would in each case have made the choice; but the consequences of their choices might later show up as differential participation by the two communities in one of the sequences included in a Steward analysis.

Such points of divergence are occurring all over the world—in the battle over whether English will prevail in India, whether Tamil will become a strong second language in Ceylon, whether Macedonia, a tiny country, will have a language of its own or adopt, as its standard language, the language of one of its larger neighbors.[46] A generation after the battle for the adoption of a national language in Ireland, the choice has become a factor in the alienation of young citizens of Eire from their parents and their own soil and in the revival of folk music.[47] Centuries later, expressed in the smoothed-out statements of multilinear evolution, the role played by individuals in the decisions made at such choice points can be ignored for purposes of a different level of analysis. But it cannot for this reason be said that the role of individuals was *never* a crucial one in the choices that were made.

It should be noted that the order of statement made here is very different from one that might be derived from the sequence built up in the familiar jingle:

> For want of a nail the shoe was lost,
> For want of a shoe the horse was lost,
> For want of a horse the rider was lost,
> For want of a rider the message was lost,
> For want of a message the battle was lost,
> And all for the want of a horseshoe nail.

Another statement of this order would be: If Johann Sebastian Bach's grandfather had not lived to marry and beget children, there would have been no Johann Sebastian Bach. It is not with this order of antecedent events that I am concerned. The political leaders who make the choice between one script and another, one language and another, are part of a movement toward literacy which is already well under way. Their decisions are made within the ongoing situations in regard to language in India, Ceylon, Macedonia, and so on. Similarly, in New Guinea and the surrounding islands, the premature insistence on English, for which a few strategically placed individuals have been responsible, as against the other choices that were available, has meant a limitation on the natives' ability to absorb Western culture.[48]

A classic instance, within our own immediate history, of a significant choice is the rejection of the metric system by the United States and by Great Britain. In this case, a very few men swayed the legislators of their day to oppose a change that would have tremendously facilitated international communication in production as well as scientific and engineering interchange at many levels. Today, however, the costs of making a change of this kind have become prohibitively great, and both in the United Kingdom and in the United States the committees that have been working on the problem have all but given up the search for a solution.

It would be possible to say, at a Whitean level of analysis, that the rationalization of measurement is an "inevitable" step in evolutionary progress. The *Encyclopaedia Britannica* article, "Measures and Weights" and the accompanying "Table of Selected Weights and Measures, and of their Equivalents in U.S. Customary or in Metric Units" [49] (which fills seven columns!) vividly document the chaotic state of traditional systems of measurement and the incredible expenditure of human energy necessary to convert one system into another.

In this case, an examination of the recommendations *against* the adoption of the metric system contained in a report prepared by John Quincy Adams, dated February 22, 1821, and submitted to the House of Representatives, speaks for itself.[50] In this document, Adams reviewed the history of English weights and measures, which, as he pointed out, were based on "uniformity of proportion" rather than "identity," as in the metric system. Coinage followed the same system, but after King Edward I (1328) had debased the coinage, coins could no longer be used as weights. The loss of the idea of equivalency led to anomalies in the system of troy weights, and the system was further confused when foreign merchants introduced the use of avoirdupois weights.

After defining the metric system, adopted in France immediately after the Revolution, Adams stated his objections to the adoption of this new system in the United States. These were, in part:[51]

> But while decimal arithmetic thus, for the purposes of *computation,* shoots spontaneously from the nature of man and of things, it is not equally adapted to the numeration, the multiplication, or the division of material substances, either in his own person, or in external nature. The proportions of the human body, and of its members, are in other than decimal numbers. The first unit of measures, for the use of the hand, is the *cubit,* or extent from the tip of the elbow to the end of the middle finger; the motives for choosing which, are, that it presents more definite terminations at both ends than any of the other superior limbs, and gives a measure easily handled and carried about the person. By doubling this measure is given the ell, or arm, including the hand, and half the width of the body, to the middle of the breast; and, by doubling that, the fathom, or extent from the extremity of one middle finger to that of the other, with expanded arms, an exact equivalent to the stature of man, or extension from the crown of the head to the sole of the foot. For subdivisions and smaller measures, the span is found equal to half the cubit, the palm to one-third of the span, and the finger to one-fourth of the palm. The cubit is thus, for the mensuration of matter, naturally divided into 24 equal parts, with subdivisions of which 2, 3, and 4, are the factors; while, for the mensuration of distance, the

foot will be found at once equal to one-third of the pace, and one-sixth of the fathom.

Nor are the diversities of nature, in the organization of external matter, better suited to the exclusive use of decimal arithmetic. In the three modes of its extension, to which the same linear measure may be applied, length, breadth, and thickness, the proportions of surface and solidity are not the same with those of length: that which is decimal to the line, is centesimal to the surface, and millesimal to the cube. Geometrical progression forms the rule of numbers for the surface and the solid, and their adaptation to decimal numbers is among the profoundest mysteries of mathematical science, a mystery which had been impenetrable to Pythagoras, Archimedes, and Ptolemy; which remained unrevealed even to Copernicus, Galileo, and Kepler, and the discovery and exposition of which was reserved to immortalize the name of Napier. To the mensuration of the surface, and the solid, the number ten is of little more use than any other. The numbers of each of the two or three modes of extension must be multiplied together to yield the surface or the solid contents: and, unless the object to be measured is a perfect square or cube of equal dimensions at all its sides, decimal arithmetic is utterly incompetent to the purpose of their admeasurement.

Linear measure, to whatever modification of matter applied, extends in a straight line; but the modifications of matter, as produced by nature, are in forms innumerable, of which the defining outward line is almost invariably a curve. If decimal arithmetic is incompetent even to give the dimensions of those artificial forms, the square and the cube, still more incompetent is it to give the circumference, the area, and the contents, of the circle and the sphere . . .

Extension and *gravitation* neither have nor admit of one common standard. *Diversity* is the law of their nature, and the only *uniformity* which human ingenuity can establish between them is, an uniformity of proportion, and not an uniformity of identity.

Back of John Quincy Adams' argument lies an ideal conception of the proportions of the human body and of the relationship of man to the rest of the universe as well as, quite possibly, the practical consideration that men and women who were pioneering the expansion of the United States, far from cities, were in need of a measure which was "easily handled and carried about the person." It is significant that he could both be aware of the contributions of Pythagaros, Archimedes, Ptolemy, Copernicus, Galileo, Kepler, and Napier and not be aware of some implications for change inherent in their work.

At some time in the future a machine may be developed that will make less cumbersome the process of conversion from one system of measurement to another. Alternatively, the inhibition of the spread of the metric system, owing to the refusal of the United States and the United Kingdom to use it, may result in the development of a new and superior system.[52] This we cannot yet know. However, we need only consider the importance, today, of scientific communications, or the developing role of China in science and technology, or the effect of the Common Market on European interdependence, in order to realize that decisions of this kind, originally of interest to a very small group of men—men who were themselves differentially handicapped by the thinking of their times—may represent crucial points in the history of intercommunication systems of human culture.

8. The Unit of
Cultural Micro-Evolution

WE MAY NOW TURN to the question of the unit that is appropriate for the study of evolution when it is our intention to specify the nexus between the genetically and experientially given properties of particular individuals and their contributions to evolution as a whole.[1] To place cultural evolution in the overall picture of the evolution of life, it is only necessary to specify behavior peculiar to *Homo sapiens* and immediate precursor species. Similarly, in an examination of the contribution to a given historical period made by the population of a large area or by a nation-state, the properties of populations, such as sex ratio, age pyramid, rate of increase, and so on, in combination with the properties of specific ecological settings, may be significantly involved. In an examination of a large-scale sequence like the development of agriculture, with its specific adaptations to particular environments, we shift from a historical to an evolutionary frame of reference by centering the investigation on the contribution made by a specific civilization—for example, the contribution made by Sumer to the whole course of human culture. It is not the method of describing and analyzing cultural phenomena that makes a study relevant to evolution, but the relationship of the analysis to the next more general level of discussion.

It seems important to make this point, because one

of the arguments against the involvement of particular, identified groups in the evolutionary process is that this constitutes a form of reductionism similar to that involved in the reduction of biological processes to purely physical processes or social processes to purely psychological processes. For example, when the characteristics of a particular culture are specified in terms of the culturally determined character structure of its cultural carriers and a description is given of the means by which children in each generation acquire this character structure, it is sometimes inferred that the analyst has postulated that the child-rearing practices are the sole and sufficient determinants of a historical event.[2] Concretely, when discontinuities in the rigidity of infantile discipline of Japan are invoked as a partial explanation of Japanese behavior in historical situations, this is sometimes interpreted as meaning that Japanese methods of child rearing have *caused,* let us say, the Rape of Peking.[3]

This interpretation ignores the necessity of framing any evolutionary argument. It is possible to examine the details by which particular mutations or particular environmental changes have occurred in evolutionary lines of development, some of which have led to changes in grade, while others, involving the same processes, have not. If we are interested in delineating the steps by which the industrialization of Japan took place and the relationship of that process to the wars of the first half of the twentieth century, and if we are interested in working out the relationship between the development of nuclear energy and evolutionary change that is significant for the human species and (since man has become an important agent in directing the course of nonhuman evolution also) for all evolution on this planet and even beyond it, then not only the specification of the size of the Japanese population, the ratio of population to food supply, and so on, but also the specification of Japanese character structure enters into our understanding of the evolutionary process. Furthermore, to the extent that the timing of Japanese industrialization may be significant for the future of mankind as a species, small groups of identifiable individuals —for example, Commodore Perry and certain Japanese individuals—become significant also.

In all studies of human behavior, the units are human beings, members of one species. So in a discussion of a human population, if we shift from the specification of its multiple dimensions—the type of cultural organization by which it is characterized and its position in a part of the world and a period in history, and so on—to a specification of the gene pool only, this is a shift to a different level. Similarly, in a discussion of warfare, if we make the statement that warfare is brought about by aggression alone, whether we regard aggression in human beings as genetically determined, species-characteristic behavior or as a consequence of the necessary conditions of human child rearing, this also is a shift in level.

But as long as we take a group of human beings as our unit, even though groups may differ in size, in the length of time they have endured as a group, and in the spatial area they occupy, we may change our focus in order to investigate in greater detail the more finely specified properties of a group without thereby shifting the level of analysis. For here a change in focus does not involve the invocation of qualitatively different units. Had we the necessary records, the faceless nomads who pushed across the Bering Strait to people the New World would be specifiable in the same kind of detail as are the founding fathers of the United States in 1776, or the members of the Politburo in the Soviet Union in 1945.

Without the absolute assumption that Babylonians and Egyptians and Cretans were members of *Homo sapiens* and had the same species-characteristic properties as the modern investigator and the members of the society in which he lives, his speculations about and reconstructions of these past societies would not be apposite. All our understanding of the significance of social organization or level of technical development as a potential for change to a higher level of energy use is derived from our knowledge and detailed analyses of the uses which known human groups have made of technical devices or power sources. So, too, our understanding of human culture as a special evolutionary mechanism is derived from detailed studies of such problems as the ways in which culture traits can be diffused, the significance of learning and codification, and so on. Then, as we have achieved understanding of such processes as diffusion or character formation, it has become possible for us to include these in our analyses of a larger scheme of the evolution of life, and for us to re-examine behavior as an evolutionary mechanism which transcends the human species. In this wider framework, learning, for example, becomes a category that includes not only the primates but other orders as well, and we can examine and compare differences in the characteristic mechanisms of learning.

We may now consider the unit of cultural micro-evolutionary analysis which permits us to take account of the specific phenotypic characters peculiar to particular individuals. Like any other study of human beings, the study of human behavior can be pursued without any evolutionary reference. Where the purpose of an investigation is an analysis of the ways in which a culture provides the framework for the mobilization of human energies or for meeting crises, this inquiry may be pursued as an end in itself. For example, we may study the organization of trading fleets or war parties or reform committees and specify the position of each individual member. For the purposes of the inquiry which has been undertaken, the summative statement may then be: "In Manus culture, a group charged with carrying out a task will accomplish more—or less—work (specified units of the task) in proportion to the number of cross-cousin pairs—or pairs of brothers-in-law—who are participants." [4] This statement could have been made only on the basis of studies of actual trading fleets and a knowledge of each participating individual, which would include not only his kinship relations to the other members of a crew but also his idiosyncratic properties—whether genetic or experiential—such as gaiety, sense of humor, talkativeness, and so on. Without such a study it would not be possible to see that the superiority of a crew made up of pairs of cross-cousins and the inferiority of a crew made up of pairs of brothers-in-law is a function of the joking enjoined on cross-cousins and the reserved, constrained behavior enjoined on brothers-in-law. Only the knowledge that a given individual was temperamentally or characterologically gay and given to joking or, on the contrary, remote or sullen, would make it possible to distinguish between enjoined and idiosyncratic behavior, so that, in the end, one could arrive at a statement which excluded those individual properties that are attributable to constitution and life experience.

After making a study of this kind, the student of human social behavior can use his knowledge of the types of differentiations along kinship, class, or caste lines in a given culture in order to make a purely structural analysis —that is, an analysis at a different level of abstraction, from which the actual constitution–temperament and character of identified individuals is excluded. For example, one could use generalizations about the behavior of Italian immigrants toward their relatives and the contrasting behavior of Mexican immigrants toward their relatives as an explanatory feature in a description of the functioning of an identified social institution—a local trade union or a mutual aid society in the United States.

Earlier anthropologists reared constructs from the memories of a few survivors or the fragmentary reports of travelers and missionaries. Later, as anthropologists began to study living cultures, both those in which it was necessary to work largely with a series of selected individuals as informants on a culture undergoing change and those which could be observed as ongoing systems, the need for exact specification of individual members of the society about which generalizations were to be made became salient. So, in recording myths, Boas also recorded for each version of a myth the name of the person who told it.[5] In this system of specification, where the investigator worked with informants on the culture, it was necessary to know whether the teller of a tale was a man or a woman, young or old, glum or loquacious, intelligent or stupid, drunk or sober, and, if different clans knew or owned different myths, what clan the speaker belonged to. In fact it was necessary to make a whole series of specifications; some of these referred to heritable and some to experiential factors, some to the individual's position in the social system, and some were essentially situational.

As soon as it became possible to study groups of identifiable human beings who shared a common living culture and lived in an ongoing social group, it was clear that a new series of specifications must be included.[6] For in studies of this kind it is necessary to specify the relationships of all the members of the group to one another within the context of the total group. In a village of 300 or 400 people, if one is making a study of initiation and response, leadership and followership, and specialization of role—the formal role of the hereditary magician or the group-selected peace chief or the informal role of the self-selected shaman—it is necessary to ask not only whether a given individual is intelligent or stupid and what his life history has been, but also how much more intelligent or more stupid he is than the other members of the group, and where he is placed within the group. It is necessary to take into account both the special capabilities, genetic and experiential, of each man, his intelligence, bravery, strength, skill, and so on, and the formal position of each man with these properties. A stupid man who holds the position of a hereditary chief will play a different role from a stupid man with no claims to rank. So at all points it is necessary to analyze the formal structure, which prescribes whether descent, primogeniture, a physical property like strength, or a cultivable quality like oratorical ability will determine leadership positions, in relation to the actual constitution–temperament and character of the individuals who do or might fill each of these prescribed positions.

At this point, the anthropologist who is describing a level of cultural organization may drop out all discussion of such matters as the role of character structure or the importance of individual endowment, except possibly to mention in passing that a rigid practice of primogeniture in one group and a more flexible usage in another may have facilitated—or hindered—a society in the adoption or initiation of a change. The anthropologist who is studying change of energy utilization may note that a cultural practice, in which an essential craft such as iron-working is lodged in a hereditary group, may provide special limiting or facilitating conditions for the use of a new metal. The anthropologist who is studying the processes of character formation may note that differentiation of expected behavior among close relatives and affinals, such as cross-cousins and brothers-in-law, reduces the demand for expected gratification under all circumstances.

But the anthropologist who is interested in the problem of possible conscious participation in human evolution does something else. From small studies of the culture, the community, the processes of education, and the mode of functioning in given ecological settings, the student of cultural evolution must extract still another finding: the nature of the members of the group of identified individuals in a given community, culture, and period who foster or hinder change.

In Chapter 7 I discussed the significance of points of divergence in human history, some of which become of evolutionary significance. It is necessary to consider next the question of the relationship between the individuals who are historically placed to act at such a point and the course that is taken. The problem must, of course, be considered in the context of period, level of culture, the culture's ecological position with respect to natural resources, and its propinquity or accessibility to other cultures. These are matters that have been quite fully explored, and even the most enthusiastic apologist for culture change through improvements in the gene pool would hardly claim that an individual with the capacities of a Newton, an Einstein, or a Leonardo da Vinci would have made the kind of contribution that he did had he been born in a savage tribe, during the Palaeolithic Era, in a small city-state in 100 B.C., or on the Gold Coast in 1910. The dependence of innovation on the state of the culture has been well documented. Despite this, there is a tendency to overstate either the "inevitability of invention"[7] or, on the contrary, the peculiar qualities of the individual after whom an innovation is finally named, whether the man is a prophet, a scientist, or a philosopher.[8] So there is a polarization of discussion, centering, on the one hand, on the great man, an emphasis that is implicit in the search for gifted children,[9] some of whom may be the geniuses we need, and in longer-term attempts to increase the number of superior genes (or to decrease the number of inferior genes) in the gene pool[10] and, on the other hand, on the impersonal, superorganic sweep of human culture.[11]

One result of this polarization is that students have neglected to investigate the group of individuals *surrounding* the "culture hero," the "innovator," or the "genius" who is historically credited with a feat like the unification of a great area, the development of a code of laws, or the promulgation of the theory of evolution. Because of the general failure to treat a "great man" as a member of a group, all of whom are interacting with one another, providing checks and balances, facilitating or defeating definite courses of action, we have focused mainly on those points in culture at which change has occurred in dramatic relationship to evolutionary progress, whether the change comes about through the elimination of a civilization or through the next step ahead in energy use. While we name these leaps—these evolutionary successes—after individuals, we attribute the conspicuous failure of a social system not to the actions of individuals but to cultural processes, such as overbureaucratization, discrepancy between resources and methods of energy utilization, and so on; and sometimes we even refuse to involve individuals in the leaps ahead, claiming that these, too, are inevitable.

I believe it is more useful to assume that in all societies of whatever size, at any given moment in history, there are groups of individuals who are so placed that their decisions are crucial at certain points, all of which are points of divergence despite extreme differences in magnitude. The prime minister of Great Britain and his cabinet form a group the social consequences of whose acts, measured in terms of the number of those directly and indirectly affected, might seem of incomparably greater significance than the acts of the little group of scientists in the laboratory in which Klaus Fuchs worked—until Fuchs' betrayals became known. And both groups, because of the repercussions of their acts, seem incomparably more important than a group of elders in a Tibetan village, who are faced with the decision of whether or not to welcome the Chinese Communists, or a handful of primitive people on a South Sea island, who are trying to decide whether to adopt a modernization of their culture. But the fact that these groups have very different positions in a network of communication and innovation in the contemporary world and that there are vast differences in the scale of significance of their acts does not mean that the essential processes are different. In every case—even in the case of a prophet who returns for a time to a wilderness, an isolated laboratory, or an ivory tower—the ongoing course of events is channeled by face-to-face groups. What takes place depends on the ability and the willingness of individuals to listen to one another, to listen to the more and to the less particularly gifted, on their willingness to advance or to block a new solution, on their ability as a group to take a particular course of action.

The student of evolution can see any breeding population as continuously involved in evolution, whether it is maintaining its stability or is varying in different directions, which is a function of the stable factors and the mutants in the gene pool, expressed in identifiable phenotypes in each generation and their life span as determined by the presence of predators and the state of the food supply, and so on. So, too, the ongoing life of all the social groups which together make up mankind may be seen as containing evolutionary potentialities that are actualized by identified, strategically placed groups of living individuals. Whether the actions of such a group serve to maintain the stability of a society by supporting its ongoing style or by warding off threats to its existence, or bring about constructive innovations, or lead the society to absolute disaster, their actions have evolutionary significance. We can arrange the individual members of a group or a society at any given time, and the societies existing at a given period of time, and the periods of time comprising human history in terms of their apparent greater or lesser evolutionary significance in any given respect. But we can make this assessment only from a particular position; in ten years or in ten thousand years, other scholars in different positions will revise the order. For example, today marsupials appear to be a side line or a blind alley in vertebrate evolution; however, if a kind of warfare were to be invented that resulted in the extermination of all life on this planet except in Australia, the marsupials might have a very different position in the future evolution of life.

But changes in the significance of groups can also be seen on a very short time scale. For example, the present-day organization of the United Nations and world attitudes toward the rights of self-determination of all groups calling themselves nations provide a framework within which the great powers have made use of very small political units in their international political maneuvers, and groups which, a few years earlier, would have been disregarded or dismissed from the world scene now have genuine international significance and influence.[12] The legitimate monarchs of minute territories and the revolutionary leaders of small island societies suddenly assume world importance. But importance, in this context, is not a function of differences in stature among the particular individuals, for example, Franklin Roosevelt, Churchill, Lenin, Fidel Castro, and Paliau (the leader of the non-violent social revolution in Manus in the postwar period [13]). It is rather a function of the state of the whole interrelated network.

I believe it is useful to assume that the ability of any gifted individual to exert leverage within a society—remembering that this leverage may be exerted conservatively rather than progressively and that, consequently, there may be no record of his action in later annals of the tribe or nation—is partly a function of the exact composition of the group of those on whom he depends for day-to-day interaction and for the execution of his plans. At any given moment in history, it is theoretically possible to work out the position of an individual in any social system, whether it is a small peasant village or the United Nations Secretariat, in terms of his relative dispensability or indispensability. The least dispensable person, that is, the individual who would be most difficult to replace, may be perceived, contemporaneously or retrospectively, as the one responsible for a given set of acts, or inventions, or creations. Any group of any size may be analyzed into such a hierarchy of the more and the less replaceable individuals, and the replaceability of each will be a function not merely of his relative uniqueness as an individual but also of the relative uniqueness of his position within an intersecting network of the exact state of events. At a given moment the head of state is, by virtue of his office, less replaceable than is, let us say, a member of the legislature who may be his superior in every respect as a person. But the presence in the legislative body of several men of greater specific abilities than the head of state may alter the course of history and determine the direction of political history for many years. When the position of any individual is stated without reference to the lieutenants, producers, executants, opponents, rivals, and unconscious saboteurs who belong to his interacting group, the statement is incomplete.

The properties of individuals which are of potential evolutionary significance may then be defined as those properties which are most peculiar to a member (in the sense of being least replaceable) of those groups which possess the greatest leverage either for the perpetuation of the status quo or for innovation in a specified social unit of any size. The leverage group may be the tribal council of old men of an Australian tribe, the Central Committee of the Communist Party of the U.S.S.R., the executive board of a major industrial concern, or the leaders of a dissident group in a newly established African nation. Significant properties, in a given context, may be directly heritable qualities such as height, or physical appearance, or very special types of intelligence; they may be qualities of character acquired through experience, such as a particular type of education or a knowledge of another language, and therefore involve heritable qualities only secondarily; they may derive from a combination that involves both position and heritable qualities (for example, in a society with primogeniture, an individual who is both the eldest and the most intelligent or is the most emotionally stable and the most widely traveled). In those cases in which the particular properties, significant in the potential evolutionary role exercised by an individual, depend on special combinations of genetic qualities (rather than on experience, education, or situation), we are likely to use the term "genius" in describing the least replaceable person. For example, we speak of an "organizational genius" or a "mathematical genius," or we identify "genius" by referring somewhat indeterminately to the qualities of a great scientist or artist.

In fact, genius is the term we use for the individual who appears to be capable of carrying out—or who has carried out—some rare and difficult act because of some peculiar combination of genetic and experiential traits. The uniqueness of the particular combination is attested to by the failure of geniuses to replicate themselves. So students of hereditary ability must resort to a conception such as "stock" in discussing the group from which a number of variously gifted individuals have sprung, or "family line" in discussing a descent group with a family tradition which is peculiarly receptive to the appearance of certain kinds of gifts in the offspring and so provides an experiential base. For example, in families like the Darwins and the Huxleys, scientific ability will be nurtured, as musical ability was nurtured in the Bach family.[14] In discussions of the family settings of successive gifted individuals, the importance of the generation in which the most gifted individual is placed becomes transparently clear. Before Johann Sebastian Bach and Charles Darwin reached maturity, there was already a family tradition in which their particular gifts could flourish.[15] In turn, their achievements set up expectations for their descendants. In the Bach family the pressure for signs of musical talent and the denial of the possibility of lack of gift were so great that even Gottfried Heinrich Bach, Johann Sebastian's feeble-minded son, was described as "inclined towards music, especially clavier playing." [16] The fate of certain of the descendants suggests that what had been a positive fostering background for Bach himself and had supported some of his talented descendants became an impossible criterion of success which may actually have accentuated the conditions to which Bach's biographer is referring when he states that "physically and artistically the strength of the family was ebbing away." [17] The place of any given boy born into the family, considered now as one kind of interacting group, was radically affected, positively and negatively, by the genius which the group itself, both experientially and in terms of heritable qualities, had supported.

Family beliefs about the sources of the genius of its most conspicuously gifted member themselves create an

THE BACH FAMILY GENEALOGY

(Compiled from *The Bach Family*, by Karl Geiringer)

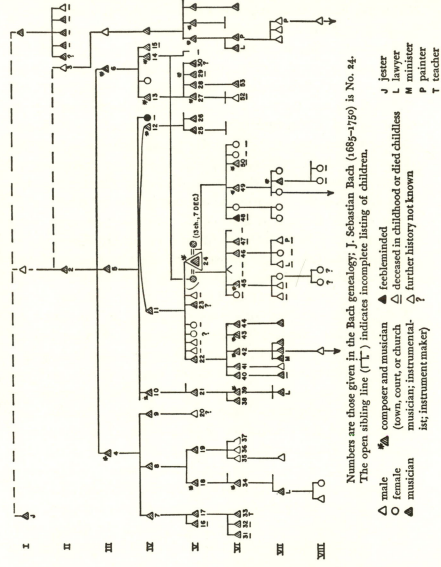

Numbers are those given in the Bach genealogy; J. Sebastian Bach (1685–1750) is No. 24.
The open sibling line (⌐⊤⌐) indicates incomplete listing of children.

△ male
○ female
▲ musician

✻▲ composer and musician (town, court, or church musician; instrumentalist; instrument maker)

▲ feebleminded
△ deceased in childhood or died childless
△ further history not known
?

J jester
L lawyer
M minister
P painter
T teacher

I
II
III
IV
V
VI
VII
VIII

atmosphere in which talent can actively flourish or may suffer special eclipse. In the Darwin family, the belief that Darwins are slow developers provides protection for Darwin descendants so that they are not pressured into premature school performances. The emphasis on the tremendous amount of hard work that Charles Darwin did has also provided an atmosphere within which choice of level of accomplishment is possible.[18]

When we turn from this kind of family line of several generations within which each individual is placed and against which much of his achievement is judged, cultivated, or rejected, to the groups of peers with whom an individual is educated, and with whom he conducts his political, scientific, religious, or artistic life, the interrelationship of the gifts and the characteristics of such groups becomes more striking because it is less complicated by the question of biological inheritance. The presence of two boys with very similar gifts within one small group may polarize their behavior throughout life. It may lead to one killing the other, taking his wife and rearing his son, who will in turn kill him—as may happen in some Eskimo groups.[19] It may contribute to the splitting up of a village, which previously had been barely strong enough to resist predatory neighbors, and thus to the disappearance of a culture, which either leader alone might have been able to save. Or two highly innovative and gifted scientists may settle down to a rivalry in which the gifts of one are expended in filling out the achievements of the other.[20] Or it may have far-reaching political consequences, as in the polarization of political strategy between Stalin and Trotsky and the terrible excesses of the 1930s in Russia.[21]

In a group in which there is only one outstandingly gifted individual, absence of anyone else of the same caliber may have equally important correlates. A stupid boy who is unchallenged in initiative may become an unchal-

lenged adult leader. A devoted and skillful follower may
enable a gifted individual to realize a potential that he
could never have realized alone. Where there is a strategically placed and delimited group whose members are
articulately concerned with some change—as, for example,
the twelve Apostles, the initiators of the American Revolution, or the original group around Lenin—the relationships of each to the other in each pair relationship may be
crucial.[22] Here, as in a family like the Bach family, self-
identification as a named group with a definite role in
history provides an atmosphere in which the interrelations
of the group's members all become more significant. So six
mountaineers who meet at an Alpine conference may idly
measure themselves against one another in terms of each
one's past feats, apparent skill and strength, or kind of
character. But should these same six men form a team with
a single unclimbed peak to scale, then, identified before
the audience of their peers, with a hoped-for place in history, the same qualities, the relative strength, skill, bravery,
or capacity for self-sacrifice of each in relation to the others
become very much more salient.[23] The ways in which these
abilities are combined in each individual climber and
among the climbers may determine both the fate of each
man and the success or failure of the whole expedition.
Where, previously, they were a group of men with a common interest and with rather unformalized peer relationships to one another, they become a recognized, articulate,
meaningful unit in history.

It seems probable that for the highly gifted individual,
the prophet or scientist or artist, the full sense of his own
genius, which seems such an inalienable part of the man
or woman who, in historical retrospect, is judged to have
made a great contribution, is partly dependent on the constellation of the group around him. If such a man is the
leader of a group which sees itself as a group, its members

will make more intensive use of their various talents and will attempt to compensate for—or even destroy—those whose weaknesses endanger the group. The simplest way to define such a group mission is to phrase it in terms of a single individual whose dream must be realized or whose power must be implemented. Thus, reflexively, the leader defines himself as indispensable in response to the group's identification of him. In the modern world, however, only very rarely will a man of high gifts willingly accept such an identification. Such identifications are most acceptable in the crises of revolution and war. More established societies are hampered in attempts to take another evolutionary step by the lack of a framework within which to define a leader as indispensable.

For the study of cultural micro-evolution, we need detailed records of the way in which a specific group of identified individuals has participated, in a given society, in cultural change. For full understanding of the process, we need accounts of innovation which show how the contributions of each of a group of individuals, each one fully specified, who together constitute the unit of sociocultural micro-evolution, are combined to produce the evolutionarily significant innovation. Turning to the past, there is no innovative situation of which we have a record that is full enough to be more than suggestive. Existing records of the ways in which the Founding Fathers worked on the Declaration of Independence, or Napoleon, as First Consul, worked with the *Conseil d'Etat* on the formulation of a uniform civil code for France,[24] or the early Bolsheviks developed their revolutionary strategy, or the members of the United States Manhattan Project in World War II built the atom bomb—all are lacking in enough specific details of individual interaction.[25] We know that something new came from each of these groups, but we have only the sketchiest ways of evaluating the interchange—

which person contributed which idea, whose question evoked what answer—even where we have the formal records of actual discussions, and where the participants or others were highly motivated to preserve records.

But in the not too distant future, we may hope to have such studies, where a group of individuals is set an innovative task and is isolated during the performance of the task from receiving any new messages from the outside. Laboratory simulations of important inquiries are, I believe, as unlikely to produce the necessary information as are laboratory experiments in other fields in which significance is sacrificed to control. The innovative task must be a significant one. For experimental purposes, the task must be one that requires isolation for its accomplishment. We cannot expect men who are trying to devise space ships or disarmament formulas voluntarily to isolate themselves from new information, however much such a group may isolate the rest of the world from its decisions. So a crucial experiment, an experiment in which a group of individuals, each of whom has been studied physiologically, psychologically, and experientially, is isolated and equipped to keep complete records of its transactions, must wait upon some occasion in which isolation, for example, in outer space or under the sea, is a necessary part of the task involved. It may be that we shall have to envisage the possibility of setting up such an experiment under various circumstances and then provide the equipment with the hope that in a few cases the necessary conditions of isolation will occur. Meanwhile, we could make great gains even with those imperfect experiments in which the information entering the system from outside was not controllable but in which the transactions taking place within the group were fully recorded. For we would begin to understand, as we do not now, how an evolutionary cluster works.

For obvious reasons, work of this kind cannot be undertaken in a primitive society. In an isolated society, its members have neither the scientific training nor the ability to record what takes place, and the introduction of an observer with the necessary scientific interest and training irrevocably alters the situation. There is, however, one situation of culture contact between a primitive and a complex culture in which the necessary conditions for such an experiment would exist and into which the observing anthropologist could reasonably come. This is the situation of constructive borrowing. The whole process of cultural evolution depends on borrowing of this kind as much as it does on the identifiable innovations. Furthermore, at present, our survival depends, perhaps in equal measure, on the success with which models from one type of culture can be borrowed and reworked in other cultures and the success achieved through innovation. Both borrowing and innovation are necessary aspects of the task of working out forms of global integration in which men, now able to destroy themselves, can protect themselves against destruction.

Consequently, it is of the utmost importance to form some estimate of the necessary conditions of such borrowing of foreign models under a variety of circumstances: where the borrowers are far removed in evolutionary grade from the culture from which they are borrowing; within a culture, where many grades are represented in fragmentary form; where the borrowers belong to one culture area or to one ideological bloc and the borrowed models come from another; where the borrowing takes place between cultures belonging to one ideological bloc; and so on. Studies of cases of constructive borrowing, where the borrowers were primitive cultures in the process of transforming themselves, would then fit into a larger series.[26]

For such studies as these, as for many other kinds of

research, primitive cultures are especially valuable because the societies are small, the store of knowledge is small (owing to the lack of any means of keeping written records), and the living members in small, prevailingly endogamous groups have, to a large extent, a common ancestry. Furthermore, the greater ease of observation, which is one of the rewards of studying a group far removed from the observer in culture and physical type, can be ample compensation for other losses resulting from work with a small primitive population—inability to apply statistical methods, dependence on events that occur only rarely, difficult social and physical field conditions, and so on.

Recent attempts by Europeans to study Europeans and by individuals to study small groups in which they are working participants or into which they have been introduced as observers amply demonstrate the difficulties of closeness and the corresponding advantages of distance in reducing self-consciousness and resentment. When the observer is working with a group of people who are very much like himself, whether the observer is a French-speaking anthropologist working in a Spanish village, a psychiatrist observing a World Health Assembly, a sociologist studying the organization of medical training in a particular hospital, or a sociologist who is also an Alpinist studying a bi-national team of six men who are attempting the ascent of a hitherto unclimbed mountain, a large number of tensions are engendered by the presence of the other person. The situation is quite different when an anthropologist has undertaken to study a native people whose previous encounters with outsiders have been with individuals seeking to change, coerce, convert, or improve them, and who now are responding to someone whose primary interest is to record the details of their ongoing behavior. Under these circumstances, the anthropologist's observations are more likely to be welcomed than resisted.

I wish, therefore, to recount rather briefly, partly as a model and partly for the sake of the actual content, the transformation of a small Pacific Island culture, which was first studied in 1928, when the society was in an early stage of contact with European culture, and then was restudied in 1953, after the culture had undergone profound change. The material on this culture permits us to specify the antecedent culture, the conditions at the time when change was undertaken, and the roles of particular individuals as they interacted to produce the change.

9. The Paliau Movement in the Admiralties

No LOCAL CHANGE, however significant it may be for the course of history, is fully meaningful without reference to the wider setting of place and time and the cultural tradition and human population within which it occurs. It is necessary, therefore, to discuss the Paliau movement at two levels, dealing first with macro-specific and then with micro-specific elements relevant to the development of the movement.

Beginning with the voyages of Captain Cook, the Pacific islands have been subjected to increasingly detailed and meticulous scientific scrutiny, as scientists have followed responsible naturalists into the area as observers.[1] The habit of making careful observations had already been well established when the exploratory expeditions were undertaken, and so in the Pacific islands we have had, since the eighteenth century, a social situation in which the conspicuous changes that have taken place in the island cultures have been well recorded. Long sequences of records —the earlier ones made by exploring expeditions, later ones by educated European residents, and the more recent ones by professional ethnologists—enable us to make studies of the acceptance of Euro-American models of change and of the relationship of various factors—location, population size, specific culture, and exact composition of the decision-making group—to the kinds of change that have occurred.

From the early days of Euro-American contact and conquest, the peoples of the Pacific islands, particularly those in the area classified as Melanesia–New Guinea, have responded to the contact situation, which provided them with models for both material and nonmaterial culture, with a type of nativistic cult which is known in the Pacific area as the "cargo cult." [2]

The development of nativistic cults—or, as Anthony Wallace prefers to call them, revitalization movements[3]— is a recurrent feature of culture contact in societies whose members are in the throes of internal transition and in conflict about the acceptance or rejection of various parts of the diffusing culture. Typically, the nativistic cult provides a way in which the members of such a society can reconsolidate, at least temporarily, through the acceptance of a new all-embracing formula. The Ghost Dance of the American Indians is the classic North American example.[4] In the 1890s, with the breakdown of their own relatively recently established way of life (which itself depended on the horses, the guns, and the trade goods introduced by Europeans[5]), the Indians of the plains developed movements around a common core of beliefs: that the ancestors would return, that the supply of game would be replenished, that the white man would be driven away, and that the people would once more live in a state of goodness and plenty.

Nativistic cults vary in their dimensions from brief episodes in which a prophet or a new ritual activity temporarily seizes the imagination of a people[6] to situations in which an entire culture, under the direction of the cult ideology, is consciously remodeled along new lines.[7] As a response to change, they are not limited to contact between a primitive and a civilized people. They may, in fact, occur in any set of circumstances in which a group is faced with a major cultural breakdown and is under extreme pressure to copy foreign models or to invent new ones, as a result of which the group focuses its efforts on redefining the whole cultural situation, including man's relationship to the universe, to his fellow men, and to himself. Within this wider definition, the culture of Turkey after World War I,[8] the Soviet Union, modern Israel,[9] and contemporary mainland China[10] may each be classified as an all-embracing revitalization movement.

In the last forty years, the development of cults in response to culture contact has occurred with great frequency in the islands surrounding New Guinea as well as on the New Guinea mainland.[11] In fact, the cults which have developed have so many features in common that they may be considered a specific aspect of Euro-American contact with the natives of this area. The generic name, "cargo cult," derives from one of the central, recurrent beliefs—namely, a belief in the imminent arrival of cargo.

The essential features of a cargo cult manifestation are these: An innovator, inspired by a supernatural revelation, announces that in the near future an event will take place which will center on the arrival, by supernatural agency, of a cargo made up of a large assortment of objects emanating from the world of the European; at the same time, the invading whites will go away, or else they will be banished or reduced to the status of servants. The inauguration of the new order may be accompanied by some natural hazard —a flood or a period of darkness. To ensure that the new order will come about, those who will be its beneficiaries are urged to prepare themselves for the millennium by destroying their property, killing their domestic animals, eating up all their crops, building special houses, and so on. Acceptance of the prophecy usually is followed by a period of great excitement, often accompanied by convulsive seizures of a contagious nature. This is followed, in turn, by a period of increasingly unsatisfactory waiting for the miracle to take place and, eventually, by the dissolution of belief and expectation and by rejection of the prophet by his disappointed followers. At some point in the cycle countermeasures usually are taken by the responsible administrators for the colonial or the United Nations Trust government.

Cargo cults are endemic in the area. In terms of cultural macro-evolution, their general features may be explained in the light of the contrasts between the island cultures and the models of other cultures to which the islanders have been exposed, and the occurrence of cargo cults may be subsumed under a much more general process. At this level of discussion, there is no need to invoke the roles of specific individuals. The cult initiators can be examined under the general heading of "prophets," and they may be classified as to the appearance of various characteristics, such as mental instability, experience away from their own culture, and so on. And since cults are endemic, it may be maintained that cult outbreaks will occur each year in some part of the area with peak concentrations of occurrence which are explicable in relation to such an event as World War II and the consequent exposure of the native peoples to huge modern armies.[12] Quite possibly, we might be able to define the conditions under which the occurrence and various outcomes of these cults could be predicted with relatively high levels of probability, but in the areas predictively indicated by this level of analysis, there would be a spotty occurrence of actual outbreaks and outcomes. This spotty occurrence, which has been characteristic of cargo cult occurrences in an affected area, reflects the "cutoff" level of effective prediction at the level of macro-specification.

Cargo cult behavior has, in fact, become so well established in the area and covers such widely divergent constituent cultural units that it has now diffused as a model for cultural change among inland peoples of New Guinea who, up to now, have lacked the experience of direct contact with the overwhelmingly more complex culture of Europeans.[13] Recently, far up in the New Guinea Highlands, where people still cultivate their gardens with Neolithic tools, people have constructed "radio towers" for communication with the supernaturals who, in some magical way, will bring them greatly desired gifts.

It may be said, then, that cargo cults have become a potentiality of the entire area of New Guinea and the surrounding islands—a form of social behavior available to the individuals of many different local cultures in many different stages of Westernization.

Since World War II, however, there has developed in New Guinea another innovative form of social behavior, which may be called a "movement." Sometimes occurrences of this kind have been called "political movements" or even "forerunners of nationalism." [14] Characteristically, these movements include programs of directed change, modeled on Euro-American culture, that call for local autonomy, political identity, and the adoption of real (not merely symbolic) aspects of modern culture.[15] That is, people who are caught up in a cargo cult may set a table with a white tablecloth and a bouquet of flowers, and then, seating themselves around the table, they may stare studiously at a paper covered with print which, in fact, no one there can read. In contrast, people who have started a movement make definite plans for the incorporation of European features of housing, dress, and manners, and they make specific demands for schooling.

Colonial and Trust Territory administrations have reacted with concerted hostility to cargo cult manifestations; in official eyes they appear to be apocalyptic and unsatisfactory models of new behavior, which are doomed to collapse through internal failure and external power pressures. In contrast, the modernization movements express, often in most uncomfortable ways, the aspirations of New Guinea peoples toward a way of life which, in various and often conflicting forms, has been commended to them by administrators, missionaries, and the special advocates of new colonial policies among the external governing groups.

Sometimes cargo cults and movements have occurred in association; at other times they have occurred separately. But they do have several features in common.[16] For example, both are future-oriented. It is characteristic of these Oceanic nativistic cults that their adherents do not attempt to restore a lost past; instead, they seek immediate attainment of a more desirable future in which the relative positions of the native and the white man will be altered, but the local group will continue to enjoy all the benefits of contact. Similarly, the political movements are strictly oriented toward a future in which the participants and other members of their society will enjoy the benefits of a European style of life, and the condition of the natives— who now conceive of themselves as inferior only because they lack the material amenities of modern civilization— will be remedied.[17]

Leadership also is very important. But a movement, in contrast to a cult, makes very high demands on the qualities of intelligence and organizational talent in all those who undertake to program concrete change.

Whereas cargo cults had become endemic in the New Guinea area, political movements were epidemic in the immediate postwar atmosphere. Cargo cults depended on supernatural means of bringing about an immediate Utopia, and they thrived on dreams, visions, and suggestibility. In contrast, movements depended on politicoeconomic means of realization, and they thrived in the political atmosphere in which colonialism was being abandoned and technical assistance was becoming a moral imperative of the more highly developed countries as part of the newer effort to bring underdeveloped countries into the modern world.

In post-World War II New Guinea, the sociocultural conditions which were conducive to the occurrence and support of movements were well established in the ongoing political, social, and religious instrumentalities of the area, and a frame of reference within which modernizing change could be understood and supported existed in those agencies outside the area which were important to it—the United Nations Trusteeship Council, the Government of Australia, the Colonial Office of the United Kingdom, the South Pacific Commission, and so on. Consequently, it is possible to predict the continuing occurrence of native movements and, to some extent, the forms such movements are likely to take. It is possible also to outline what the consequences might be of such events as, for example, a change of party in political power in Australia, a shift to Communist hegemony in a nearby area, the relocation of a missile testing area by one of the Western powers, and so on.

In the New Guinea area, hundreds of small linguistic groups—hundreds of local cultures with no unifying forms of political organization beyond the loose alliances accompanying intermarriage and trade—were exposed to the same overall situation. However, although a knowledge of cults and movements, with their emerging institutional forms, has made possible certain generalized predictions, this knowledge does not make possible *specific* predictions of when or where or under what particular circumstances —in which small local culture—a cargo cult, a political movement, or some combination of the two will crop up;

and when such a manifestation does occur, it does not make possible specific predictions about its local course of development.

In the Admiralty Islands, where (in 1954) there were some 15,000 people speaking approximately 25 different languages, one of these cult–movement combinations did succeed beyond all possible expectation. This is the Paliau movement, which got under way in 1946, and, in time, unified the people of 32 different South Coast villages, including all nine villages of the Manus-speaking people. Earlier studies of the Manus people, carried out in 1928–29,[18] made it possible, in 1953–54, to trace the antecedents of the Paliau movement and the course of its successful development.[19] An analysis of this transformation[20] shows, essentially, the extreme complexity of the factors that made it possible for one extraordinarily gifted individual, Paliau, to realize the potentialities of his leadership within a group of dissimilarly gifted followers. (See Plate 8.)

The shift from a macro- to a micro-level of analysis, which is necessary for an appraisal of the Paliau movement, involves a dramatic change in focus. For now, instead of dealing with the Southwest Pacific and a time scale of several centuries, the center of attention is the small archipelago of the Admiralty Islands (usually called Manus) and, within the Admiralties, a cluster of villages along the South Coast and some tiny islands off the South Coast. As Australia represents a mainland to the island of New Guinea, and New Guinea a mainland to the islands of the Bismarck Archipelago, so the Great Admiralty—an island some 60 miles long—represents a mainland to the peoples living off the South Coast.

No complete census has been made of those involved in the Paliau movement, but the general relationships are known. Involved in the movement were the population of the island of Baluan (some 600 people), where Paliau himself was born, the whole population of the lagoon-dwelling, fishing Manus villages (some 1,500 to 1,800 people), about 2,000 recruits from the land-dwelling Usiai, and small splinter groups from among the land-dwellers on some of the other little islands. At its height the movement numbered only about 5,000 people. Paliau spoke Baluan (his mother tongue), Manus (the language of the largest group in the movement), and Neo-Melanesian (a lingua franca spoken all over the Territory of New Guinea). He knew no world language. The events relevant to my discussion occurred between 1946 and 1954, when Theodore Schwartz ended his study, but the movement continues to the present day.

Here in the Admiralties, instead of thinking about great men in relation to large entities—the inhabitants of the city–states of Greece or of nations like China or Japan or the British Empire—we have to reduce our scale to a handful of Neolithic men. In 1928, when the Manus were first studied and the present generation of adults were children, they lived in a geographical world which they conceived of as a giant saucer, with the waters of the sea sloping up and away on every side. Their conception of time was individual-centered. One counted backward from oneself to one's father's time, one's father's father's and his father's time, and forward to one's son's son's time. Life was unbounded in time or space. The passage of time was marked by the monthly appearance of fish over the reef. The people had no anchorage beyond their salt lagoons, and no history beyond the recital of the settlement of each of the eleven villages related to the parent village, Peri, where I worked in 1928.

The entry of this remote, savage, tiny group of people into the modern world was no less abrupt than the change of focus required of the Western reader who attempts to understand the striking and significant changes that occurred in their lives. Their new order began in 1946. Before this year no date was marked, but after 1946 faithful records were kept of month and day, and often hour of the day. Up to this time, this was a people who acknowledged only vague ties of common language and common custom within a language group and many individual ties that crossed language groups, all within the small world of the archipelago; but after 1946, they learned to place themselves in relation to the Trust Territory, with its capital at Port Moresby, to Canberra, and to the United Nations. The distance we have to go in imagination in order to treat such a tiny primitive group seriously is, in fact, a measure of how far they themselves had to come. At no other period in history would the contrasts have been so great, because only in this period has scientific progress been so greatly accelerated and only in this period have primitive, peripheral peoples been given physical and psychological access to a worldwide political system.

Immediately after the war, the South Coast villages in Manus presented a picture that was repeated hundreds of times in New Guinea villages elsewhere. Young men had been caught away from their own villages by the war that swept through the area, and their imaginations had been stimulated by the sights they had seen and by the way they were treated by both the Australian and the American armed forces—by outsiders who were burdened by no worry about how it would be possible to maintain a postwar labor system with a daily ration of one and a half pounds of rice, a weekly ration of a can of corned beef, and a monthly ration of one piece of cheap cotton cloth. The troops, relieved of any responsibility for the future, were free to treat the natives, who worked for them—

helped them, acted as guides, took them fishing, and carried the wounded on stretchers—as individual, competent human beings.

The tremendous paraphernalia of modern warfare provided a dramatic change in scale in the native picture of the white man's world, hitherto represented by the meager equipment permitted to a few isolated individuals living in the not too prosperous Trust Territory. Even the numbers of men were impressive, as few New Guinea natives had ever seen more than two hundred or so white men at a time, and during the war over a million men passed through Manus on their way to Eastern objectives. The whole wartime experience was enormously broadening and stimulating, shifting the scale of cargo cult possibilities from kerosene lamps to electronically controlled Naval searchlights, from pinnaces to cargo planes, from hand tools to bulldozers.

Behind the allied lines and behind the Japanese lines, the young men talked of the changes they would introduce when they reached home again: no more turning over their earnings to the old men for silly old-fashioned ceremonies; no more search for native valuables; no more backbreaking labor with poor tools. Instead they intended to live in a world in which natives could earn money to buy the goods they wanted, and, in turn, the goods would give them a better standard of living.

Meanwhile, in Canberra and Port Moresby, the immediate postwar climate of opinion was friendly to native development. The head tax had been abolished. Natives were to learn to be self-governing and able to administer local courts, villages were to be consolidated, public health services were to be modernized, and consumer cooperatives were to be set up. Native leadership was to be encouraged.[21] Schools were to be established, and experiments were to be conducted in creating new sources of income

—corporately owned larger boats to transport saleable products, sawmills and plywood factories, the planting of cacao and other tropical crops, and the establishment of new coconut plantations. A climate of opinion favorable to rapid change existed equally among the administrators at the top, who were sensitive to the postwar currents of world opinion, and among the enterprising younger people of New Guinea. The whole wartime experience kindled their imagination as it presented a kind of exposure of Neolithic populations to large-scale technological organization which was unprecedented in history.

In the Admiralties, the villages of the South Coast were subject to the same influences as those brought to bear in the other parts of the Territory, where later the Administration experimented with Councils and Cooperatives, local taxation for local purposes, new schools, and other new forms of organization. The young men returned to the South Coast—to the small islands, to the lagoon villages of the group that called themselves the Manus, and to the landbound villages of the Great Admiralty—eager for change of one kind or another. In many villages there were stirrings of attempted change. Each local leader had his own ideas about resisting the old ceremonial life, about rebuilding his village in modern style, about working for money. But the ideas for change were fragmented even from village to village, just as in the long Melanesian past each small group had specialized in a particular product or some special service. And the efforts of these local leaders were not strong enough to prevent the reinstatement of the old culture, modified, it is true, by fifteen years of mission work, by the abolition of warfare and the resort to violence in the settling of disputes, by some experience of British legal practices, and by the introduction of a limited amount of European goods—sail cloth to replace mat sails, cloth to replace bark cloth, iron for adzes, and metal for fishhooks. In each village, after the initial efforts of one young man or a group of young men had failed, there was every indication that the little societies would settle down to the expected compromise—a progressive attenuation of their old traditions and an exceedingly narrow relationship to the modern world. This relationship would be based on Territory-wide work-boy regulations and styles of behavior, on the slight contacts with a wider world provided by missionaries who were intent on preserving in the native peoples an innocence of the evils of modern life, and on traders who, rather than take the risk of bringing in new things that would lead to new wants, preferred to make huge profits from the sale of a few standard articles.

The whole archipelago is poor. It has few resources, and the land is poor, with only a limited amount suitable for plantations. The Admiralties had, in fact, been regarded as so backward that little modernization was planned for many years ahead. There was, of course, the possibility of a cargo cult, but among a people as isolated as the Manus, a cargo cult usually played itself out within a few months, and after a period of famine and disorder, the local society was much as it had been before. The most that could be expected in the way of change would be the introduction of more Australian currency in the bridal exchanges, some local ventures in starting retail stores (which would fail) or attempts (usually abortive) to obtain a boat or to buy a plantation.

Conditions like these were common throughout the Territory. Working in the tradition of entrepreneurial leadership so characteristic of this world of small political groups without hierarchies of authority, local leaders sprang up, persuaded a cluster of villages to move, attempted with government help to establish a viable economic base for change, ran into trouble with the local administration, and then finally settled down to maintain

their petty authority without any significant change of role
—or lost their power altogether.

For any analysis of what took place in the Admiralties,
it is important for comparative purposes to establish the
Territory-wide base line of the historical roles and expectations of the native peoples, as they reacted to the changes
brought by white men, and the policies that were being
developed at high administrative levels immediately after
the war. The extent of the contribution of the single group
and the single leader can then be judged within the macro-
specific context, without which no estimate of the contribution of the individual is relevant.

In the case of the Paliau movement, we can place the
contribution of a single individual within a cluster of local
leaders, within a known, particular cultural background,
at a period when change was radically favored by circumstance, and in this way we can bridge the gap between the
small-scale event and the possible larger consequences.

In the Admiralties, in 1946, events were proceeding as
in other isolated parts of the Pacific. When the men returned to the villages, they were a little older than was
usually the case; therefore, they were a little more eager to
pick up the threads of their traditional life—to get married
and to start involving themselves in the local trading and
exchange system. The village of Peri had been bombed by
American planes, and its inhabitants had temporarily scattered. Working as guides, they had helped the Americans
rout the Japanese out of the bush. Now, after the war, they
were busy rebuilding and repairing the village. New houses
were built in traditional style in the sea. The particular
local piece of progressivism in Peri was simply a demand
that work should be done for money and that the old dogs'-
teeth and shell currency should be abandoned. The leader
of the young men in this village effort was Banyalo, who
was one of the first natives to be trained to a minimal

knowledge of reading and writing and who had been a clerk in Rabaul for many years, but who was now retired for age. The young men held secret meetings. The old men, with heavy investments in a whole series of exchanges, rejected their idea. Peri, like all Manus villages, was Catholic, and the home of the resident mission priest was in this village. Following the tradition of relative noninterference in the local culture, which had developed as recommended mission practice in the first half of the century, the Mission married young couples decked out in native currency and almost completely restricted its teachings to religious subjects.

Lacking effective support in the village, Banyalo led a group of younger men off to work on a neighboring plantation owned by a trading company, and tried to persuade the planter's wife to set up a school. Under normal circumstances, these young men would rapidly have been drawn back into the engrossing financial transactions of their village life, daily fishing for the markets, large-scale fishing for big events, and the accumulation of native property through their participation in native events. They would have looked longingly at the European property they had acquired through the casual generosity of the Americans— folding chairs, one or two desks, enamel basins, sheets of plywood, pieces of corrugated iron, and large metal drums —and they would have realized that, once these things were broken or worn out, they would not be able to get any more.

Their imaginations had been fired by the Americans, whom they thought of as beautifully equipped technically, and they connected this high level of technology with a different kind of social organization. They contrasted their own endless quarreling over a single broken clay pot and the American willingness to spend any amount of money, time, and equipment to save the life of a single soldier.

They saw American Negro troops dressed, quartered, and paid as well as the white troops were, and they felt that the Americans had made the "men of Africa all right." They were caught up by the spectacle of so many people all alike, the great scale of the army barracks, the bulldozer constructions, and the great planes. They said shrewdly that the Americans cared less than they themselves did about material things because (as they told me eight years later) "you have so many more of them." They also had been caught up by the egalitarianism of the Americans, who treated them not as natives to be kept in their place, or as future plantation workers, or even as members of another race, but simply as amusing and competent companions. This gave the Manus the idea that in potential they were no different from the Europeans, in spite of the gap which, hitherto, had seemed fixed and unbridgeable.

All these perceptions were there, but there was no one to give them focus. Though each village produced at least one leader and one little, partial attempt to rebel against and negate tradition, the perception of their own potentialities and the little, abortive leadership attempts at change were not strong enough. It took a personality of a stature far above the best of these local leaders, a man with an imagination that transcended anything they had imagined, to transform these amorphous malcontents into a real political movement and to make something of the casual by-products of culture contact, which increasingly had left the peoples of the South Seas disinherited.

Such a man was Paliau. He was a native of the little island of Baluan, where some 600 people, who both fished and gardened, lived in close proximity to Mouk, one of the strongest of the Manus lagoon villages. In 1945 the people of Baluan received a letter from Paliau telling them to build a big meeting house. He was coming home and he had plans.

In Manus terms, the people of Baluan, living on their small fertile island, were a group of frivolous lightweights, unenterprising and unreliable. Paliau, however, claimed one Manus ancestor and, as a child, had spent much time among the Manus of Mouk. He had conceived a tremendous admiration for the Manus as a seafaring, enterprising people, but he pitied them because they had no land. From the time of his return with his program, which possessed an appeal far beyond anything the local Manus leaders had attempted, he tried to work with these local Manus leaders and so, from the start, his developing ideas absorbed their perceptions of the desirability and possibility of change and, particularly, their experience of the Americans.

Although his programmatic contribution was extraordinarily simple, it had the character of all great programs in providing a long time perspective and a larger context for the human beings to whom it was addressed. The central elements were three. First, it was his conviction that if the people of the Admiralties were to make progress and set up a modern society, they must eliminate the age-old distinctions between the lagoon dwellers (the Manus), the small-island people (the Matankor), and the inland gardeners (the Usiai) of the Great Admiralty. Miniature as this experiment in widening human sympathy was, it had an electrifying effect on a people bred to mutual contempt and antagonism between near-neighbors, who spoke different languages, fitted differently into the diversified ecological system, and had no political mechanisms to maintain any permanent political cohesion beyond the village but, instead, engaged in lethal, debilitating warfare. (A comparable lift is sometimes given when a new nationalism is forged on a racial basis.) It was Paliau's peculiar genius to make his talk of the "men of New Guinea" involve an immediate, practical breaking down of economic, residential, and social barriers among peoples already living close to one another.

His second programmatic point was that change could not be piecemeal. What was necessary was across-the-board change. Every item of the old culture would have to be overhauled and examined and, for the most part, rejected. Houses, clothing, manners, marriage forms, land use, trade, travel, funeral rites—everything would have to be changed, and every regression to an old form would have to be fought, since a lapse in one area would lead to regression in other areas.

As his third programmatic point he advocated long-time planning, systematic saving to accumulate capital funds, and a concerted hard-working effort directed toward a new way of life. This emphasis stood out in sharp contrast with the effortless immediacy of the cargo cult; it may, in fact, have helped to generate the cargo cult episode that followed on his first few months' unsuccessful recruitment and political agitation.

Out of the excitement generated by Paliau's plan—for which he gained very limited support—and out of the postwar ferment, a real cargo cult did develop on a South Coast island and spread rapidly from village to village. In each village people were seized with excitement, spoke in tongues, insisted on the destruction of the old, and awaited the promised arrival of the new—planes, ships, bulldozers. This upheaval, called the Noise, in which Paliau himself was barely involved, swept away much of his former opposition. Like people in a war-bombed country, who later found themselves better prepared for industrial innovation than their neighbors who had suffered less destruction, the people who had lived through the Noise, who had flung their possessions, old and new, into the sea, were ready to start again. With the exception of two individuals, every member of the lagoon-dwelling Manus people was now swept into the movement. In later months, smaller resonating cult outbreaks among the land people swept portions of their villages into the movement also.

Paliau himself believed that without the cult outbreak, with its excesses, excitement, destruction of property, and frustrated apocalyptic hopes, he might never have succeeded in establishing his movement. Additionally, the cult episode led to a break with the Mission. In this way the Mission, which would have been a strong ideological and intellectual center of opposition within the society, was transformed into an external enemy against which movement loyalties could be mobilized. The cargo cult also led to conflict with government, when the original prophet was murdered by his brothers after his promises had failed to materialize. This combination of Mission and local administrative hostility to the movement provided a whole set of external enemies, and their existence helped Paliau to define his movement as bounded: people either came inside or they remained outside.

Now, within the space of a few months, Paliau, amply seconded by a kind of cabinet drawn from the enterprising local leaders, began to transform the whole South Coast way of life. He invited the Manus people of Mouk to move ashore onto his ancestral lands on the island of Baluan. All the other Manus villages also moved ashore onto small islands or combined with the gardening Usiai who came down to the sea coast to join them.

A people who, under the old complex system of aid and ceremonial, had been able to build only two or three houses in a year, now built sixty houses in a little over two months. The new villages were designed to express the new concepts. Every house had the same dimensions and all had separate rooms for separate purposes. There was a central square in which meetings were to be held. Skeleton

versions of "docks," "customs," "hostels," "hospitals,"
"schools," and "banks" were set up. The old practices were
examined, and new rules were made about the amount of
expenditure that was appropriate for a wedding and a
funeral. Individual economic responsibility was introduced, together with community-wide use of unused lands
and community provision for widows and orphans and the
sick. A common treasury was established, and into this
went money made during the war, to be drawn upon for
the common good of the entire movement. As the break
with the Mission left the population without clergy, Paliau
took it upon himself to revise the Scriptures and to set up
standards of clerical behavior. By 1949, he had transformed
a Neolithic society into a very crude but systematic version
of a mid-twentieth century society.

It is now important to ask what manner of man was this
who could so transcend the achievements of leaders of
other societies of the same level, who could maintain and
continually reinforce a programmatic vision of social transformation, and who drew on every available resource—the
imagination of the Manus, the help provided by friendly
government officials, and on his own experience when,
under the "local leader" program, he was taken to Port
Moresby and was shown cooperative stores and well-baby
clinics. The complex vicissitudes of the Paliau movement,
which echoed up the corridors of history to the chancel-
leries of major countries, to the United Nations, and to the
Vatican, have been described in detail elsewhere. Here I
shall try to select those aspects of Paliau's history and performance that offer clues to the way in which this man,
with his unique capacities, met the hour of opportunity.

We know nothing of his childhood, except what he himself told us, and we have only meager records of his days
in the Territory police force. He was away at work in 1928
when I was first in Manus, and I met him for the first time

in 1953. Then both Theodore Schwartz and I spent many hours talking with him, and observing his relations with his lieutenants, with Europeans, and with the rank and file of his movement. Theodore Schwartz worked intensively on the movement, and collected a large number of accounts from other participants, compared penciled notebook records kept by men who had just learned to read and write, and tape-recorded Paliau's account of his life and his speeches to his followers. As he was an orphan, with no siblings alive, no comparison could be made with his immediate relatives.

This is how Paliau struck me in my first contact with him:[22]

I had first seen Paliau while attending a court case in Lorengau, where a man who had nearly killed Paliau with an axe was being tried. There I had been able to watch him from behind the barrier of my temporary identification with government, as the District Commissioner's lady and I chatted with the judge during the recess of the court. I had seen something of the way he was regarded on the government station as he stood, dressed very correctly in white ducks, with two or three other men, similarly dressed, at a distance from the court building.

During the court proceedings, when the judge instructed him to attend and listen to the evidence, I had watched Paliau stand, very still, and spiritually withdraw from the whole proceeding. His stocky frame was drawn in to the smallest possible compass, his face expressionless and nonparticipating. The trial of the man who had nearly killed him was conspicuously ignored, even while he stood and answered questions respectfully, coolly indicating it had, quite clearly, nothing to do with him. This behavior contrasted sharply with the picture which many of the officials involved still held of him. He was called, even in the notes made by officers on patrol, "The Emperor," whose attempted reign was illuminated with comparisons to Hitler and the Emperor of Japan. He was said to have maps of his proposed empire which would include not only the Admiralty Islands but New Ireland and New Britain as well! He was said to maintain a huge harem of women, to have his food served to him by a line of kneeling servitors—Japanese style—to have established a totalitarian régime which flouted every canon of free government and used such loathsome devices as drilling, bells, curfews, passes. He was said to have claimed to have been given a key to Heaven by God, with whom he was in personal communication, so that he could "drop in any time."

It seemed curious to watch this quiet man, that day in the court in Lorengau, dramatic only in his fixed intention to be non-dramatic, standing unostentatiously in the little local courtroom where the whole majesty and tradition of British law were concentrated —abstracted from the pageantry of the Old Bailey to come to life again in a little frame building on a South Sea island—and to know that he appeared to the Australians against the backdrop of their whole complexity of historical tradition, which carried the memories of long-dead kings and religious reformers, the lecheries of the Tudor Court, the combination of a revolt of the working man and non-conformity which was Wesleyanism in eighteenth-century England, the excesses of Hitler's totalitarian régime and of the partly modernized Japanese Empire. I wondered how Paliau saw himself, how much of this weight of history lay on his mind. One confusing little bit from a report I had read teased my mind. A government official who had had some dealings with Paliau had reported that the latter "asked me what he should do next." This little bit suggested some ground for the accusation that he was a man without a program, hungry for power. I had yet to learn that his peculiar genius consisted of drawing inspiration from every opportunity that came his way.

It took us a long time to understand the way in which he had to combine a sense of divine mission sufficient to focus the enthusiasm of the mystical fanatics in his following, an ability to make rational and effective plans that would keep the loyalty and admiration of responsible, intelligent lieutenants, and finally, an ability to work with government officials as someone anxious to learn all he could about their methods and goals. All three—the sense of mission of one who was fulfilling a divine plan, the sense of great intellectual competence in which he towered over his followers in statesmanship and planning, and a genuine puzzlement as to how his program was to be related to the wider world—all three of these threads in his complex personality were real and integrated. He, indeed, adeptly and responsibly, tried to be "all things to all men."

So Paliau stood in court and heard the man who had just failed to kill him given only nine months more in jail. Did he know, I wondered, that there were plenty of people who said the man ought to be executed for having *failed* to kill such a pestilential character, and that even those not so deeply involved would see the case as a kind of test between Paliau's assumed "power" and the constituted authorities, so that the lighter the sentence for the vaguely smiling psychotic assailant who stood in the dock and explained that he had not really meant to kill Paliau, only to hurt him badly—when he fell upon him unexpectedly and cut his chest open with an axe—the greater the victory for law and order.

Although Paliau's marriage (after a divorce) to the attempted murderer's wife had occurred much earlier, it made the attack into just the sort of mixture between the consequences of "imperial" debauchery and political subversion which served to confuse the whole issue of how the New Way was to be regarded. A light sentence was passed, the issue of the defendant's insanity taken into account in the only way open at present as an amelioration of the severity of the sentence, as there was in any case no place but the jail for the violent insane. And afterwards I was entertained with stories of what a theatrical act Paliau, carried into the station half-dead from a chest wound, had put on in the hospital. Meanwhile, Paliau never approached me, nor I him. He had been a boy when I went away, and a member of another tribe, inhabitants of an island on which I had had only a brief visit.

Then I returned to the South Coast and Paliau came to Bunai. After being prepared for the enormous importance of the occasion by private conferences with Samol, the "councillor" of Bunai, the Schwartzes first met Paliau accidentally, when he was wearing only a pair of shorts. He greeted them, they felt, with presence of mind, but some slight embarrassment. Theodore Schwartz asked him if he would make a tape recording, and this was agreed upon. That afternoon, the whole group, Paliau, Samol, and four of Paliau's Baluan associates—variously designated by European critics as his "court," his "lieutenants," and his "cabinet"—accompanied by Theodore Schwartz, appeared without warning in Peri, where they were greeted by our Peri high officials without fanfare, in a state of informal undress. Only old Pokanau, "the old lawyer man within the village," went and got dressed up and hastened to prepare some food.

Paliau and his group entered my house and accepted cigarettes, Paliau at ease, charming, completely master of the situation. It was not until a little later, as I watched him speak to other people or help me out of a canoe with just the very slightest extra flourish, that I realized what there was about him that had perhaps contributed more than any political aspect of his New Way to the title of "Emperor." For his manner was definitely "vice-regal," not "regal," merely vice-regal, but a native who can play a vice-regal role skilfully—with style, without any subservience, wearing his higher allegiance like an accolade—carries an air of aristocracy about him which is especially detestable to many Australians in the prevailing egalitarian climate. . . .

After the first interchange of amenities as we established the fact that we had never met and that Paliau had been away at work as a young boy when I had been on Baluan, on an impulse I went and got an article in which I had published a picture of a small naked Peri child, Ponkob, sitting on a chair trying to write with pencil and paper [see Plate 7]. "This is the picture," I told Paliau, "with which I have ended my talks about Manus. I showed it to Americans and said, 'The way the Manus meet the white man is to try to *do* what the white man *does*.'" His eyes lit up, and I saw for the first time the strength of the imagination which had conceived the possibility of skipping five thousand years of history. "You *knew!*" he exclaimed. "You knew, you understood

twenty-five years ago what we only knew much later."
I was to learn that he was especially caught by the
appearance of foreknowledge of any kind. The first
precursor of an idea carried a heavy weight of emotion for him, one which it would be easy for devoted
followers, imbued with partly understood Biblical
doctrine, to endow with even greater force of prophecy. There were many tales told of the way he had
foretold Japanese attacks in the early days of the
war.

The next day, when he made the tape recording
giving an account of his life, I was to see, as he concluded his speech, another facet of his particular kind
of genius, his ability to seize the materials offered
by a situation and use them: "We—my generation
—were born too late—what we want is to *make a
good chair for our children to sit down on,*" and the
photograph of small sturdy Ponkob, his toes tensed as
he imitated the writing of the white man, was trans-
muted into a symbolic statement. No wonder the
Manus, themselves possessed of a language shorn of
habits of spontaneous metaphor, had found Paliau's
oratory irresistible, when he spoke, to use the new
words which have been coined to describe such speech,
in "talk picture."

During the week that he stayed in Bunai, held fast
by an unfavorable wind which made the crossing to
Baluan impossible, among us, we saw several other
sides of his multi-faceted personality—the gracious
guest at a feast, the angry leader betrayed and humili-
ating his followers for putting on a dance in which
men still "dressed as women," wearing *laplaps* [loin
cloths] instead of trousers (for Paliau understood that
to wrest treatment as equals from trousered white
men, trousers worn properly would in the end be

essential), the "experienced" parliamentarian drilling the council members who were novices, the law-giver upbraiding a habitually adulterous woman who attempted to misrepresent her case. The ambiguity between what he demanded and that which his followers insisted on according him remained. Yet when he left I was surprised to see that, while small groups of people brought farewell presents as they did to any departing canoe in Peri, he left with little fanfare but with a gesture of grace and an intrinsic sense of himself as a person. Much of his charismatic power to lead was said to have dimmed by this time. James Landman described the tense excitement which used to grip the group when he spoke, standing high on a lighted stage. Now, sobered by the small, humdrum tasks of local administration, he less often reached such heights.

Paliau's earlier history has to be reconstructed from his own words. He was born about 1910; in his autobiographical statement, he said:[23] "When I was born to my mother and father, they were still 'backward.' They couldn't make known to me the time or the month that I was born in." He was orphaned when he was about seven years old, and he remembered his childhood as a lonely one. He "just drifted around," though two relatives, his mother's sister and Joseph Pati, a clan brother of his father, tried to take care of him:

> I was in the middle between the two. But I wasn't properly cared for. Why? My parents were dead. . . . But it was characteristic of me even as a child, I didn't stay put. . . .
>
> While I was still young my eyes saw clearly all the big feasts they used to make before . . . It is like this. If I am "rubbish" in having no dogs' teeth, no

food and no pigs, then I can't make this dance. This is the mark of men who have much wealth, who raise many pigs, and who make large gardens. All of us children were schooled in this custom. Some learned and some didn't. I didn't learn. Why? Because I knew it was no good . . .

When they made the feasts and when the feast was over a strong sickness used to break out in the village. When a feast was finished and the sickness occurred it used to kill 20 or 30 men. Later they used to say that ghosts kill us . . . if one man dies first, his ghost takes all of us. . . .

By the time I was a little older I found that all my age mates had died from this way of life. If an older man pulled them into it later they died from it . . . But I didn't believe this talk about the spirits of the dead. Why didn't I believe it? It was the way of children; they are ignorant. When I was a child my parents died. I never used to conform properly to any belief. Times when there was much sickness, the time of rain, darkness, thunder, and lightning, all the kin of my father and mother would be cross with me. . . . I wouldn't listen, I wouldn't stay put. If there was a big rain and they spoke to me, I would go out in the rain. Why? It is the way of children. They are ignorant. They can't be afraid. That's how it is, that when I was older I didn't believe in ghosts. I said this talk of ghosts is a lie.

Time passed, then I was more grown up. I think I was about 15 years old when they put me down for government tax. I wasn't finished with all of these ideas. What ideas? The idea that I wouldn't accept the talk of the big man who said there were ghosts in the village and my thoughts about all the big feasts . . . Now, at this time I didn't travel by canoe.

I didn't go to the big place [the Great Admiralty]; I just stayed with the men of the island. Just once, when I was younger, I heard the name Lorengau, and I thought it was one of the big places of the white men. Then once I was taken in a canoe. We went to Lorengau. When I arrived, I saw it was just another place like our own . . . As for Mouk, all the old men of before had said that I had an ancestor there. When I was still small my father used to take me to Mouk. It is the way of children. If their father goes they cry to go with him . . . And almost until I was 15 I just stayed in the village. Then I was marked to pay taxes to the government.

I heard this from the patrol officer who collected the tax. I stood up before his eyes and he said, "Next year you will pay tax, now you cannot." Then I thought, "I am not a fully grown man yet, and they have marked me to be taxed." Then I thought about finding money. I started working for a Chinese named Leyu. I worked for two years. I didn't have whiskers yet. I was a young boy, not a young man. This Chinese looked at me and said I wasn't capable of hard work, I was just capable of cooking. He said I was too small. He wanted to send me back, but I was persistent. Why? Because the patrol officer had said I was to be taxed. I wouldn't have any money . . . Soon Leyu dismissed me as his cook and sent me to Akan [a second Chinese]. I worked as cook for him for two years. During this time that I cooked for him I received two shillings a month, one length of cloth per month, and two sticks of tobacco, a little matches, and a little soap each week. When I finished, I was given £5 for these two years. When I finished my work I was angry, while I was at work also I was angry. My anger was for this reason, these two Chinese didn't pay well.

I was angry, but I didn't quarrel with them. I wasn't lazy about work. I just kept it to myself. When I had finished the two years I divided the £5. For £2.10 I bought myself some things in the store. The other £2.10 I brought to the village. I gave it to Joseph Pati and all the kin of my father and mother. When they saw that I had come back, and they came to see me, they all cried . . . When Joseph Pati saw all these people he opened my box that I had bought at the store. He took all the small things that I had brought along with this £2.10 and he divided it among all these relatives of my father and mother who had come.

What I have just told is the same for all the men of Manus. The first time that I went to work I saw that this was not right. Why did I see it wasn't right? I went to find money for the government tax, so that I wouldn't go to jail over it. I had also bought a few little things such as *laplap* [a length of cloth worn as clothing, like a wrap-around skirt from waist to knees, worn by both men and women] and some other things from the store also. Then Joseph Pati divided it up among all these people, and I am again rubbish. I no longer have anything. This sort of thing didn't just happen to me; it happened to all the men of Baluan and Manus together. Others who had gone among the white men previously had come and received the same treatment also. They couldn't hold on to a single thing. They all thought it was all right. But I understood now, and I thought it was wrong. It made nothing of me. Why was this? They all valued all this money from before that belonged to our ancestors—dogs' teeth and shell beads. They all valued all the ornaments of the past, the grass skirts and the leaves used for adornment. The women used leaves. The men pounded the bark of a tree and wore it. They all thought about all these things, then when they went to work for the white man and came back they threw away all their money on their kin. Now I was poor. Now what? I was angry in my mind, but I didn't express anger with my mouth. Soon the *kiap* [government officer] would come for money and I had none.

I thought again of going to ask this Chinese if I could work for him. I went with him again for another two years . . . When the two years were up I received again £5 . . . I sent the money to the village, but I didn't go. Another Chinese wanted me again. He was named Akim. He wanted me to go shoot pigeons for him with a shotgun. I cooked, too. I stayed with him for six months . . .

I went back to my village. My money was gone. They had already divided it up among all the brothers, sisters, and other relatives of my mother.

I had no money. Now I wanted to go to work as policeman. I joined for two years the first time. When I went away to the police I still did not have whiskers yet. I wasn't able to have the full outfit of a policeman. I just went with the *kiap*. After one year I was given the full equipment of a policeman. I worked in the bush [the interior, away from the European centers]. I worked at finding this *masta* that they had killed, Master Bom. He was looking for gold and was killed by the natives of the bush. We went to right this wrong. We caught the natives, many of whom went to jail. They were not jailed to be killed but to teach them the ways of the white man and of the coast. When they had learned we brought them back to tell those who were in the bush. The men of the interior had no knowledge of the coastal area. The white men called them the Kukakuka. When they saw us they wanted to kill us, too. I worked in this part of the interior in teaching them and pacifying them for two years. . . . I had finished two years now, and I returned to my village. While I worked as a policeman I was paid the same as when I had worked for the Chinese. When I was finished, I spent all this money on buying things. My box was full. I brought it all to Baluan. There was no difference. It was just the same. All the relatives came, and the old man Joseph opened my box and gave out everything. Joseph had taken the place of my dead father. All the Baluans are alike in this custom, should Joseph be different? He was the same as the rest. The Manus of the sea were the same. The Mouks, too, all the same. . . .

I stayed in the Admiralties for two years at this time. I just hung around. I went along with anyone who was going anywhere, just coming and going. If they made a big feast on Lou, I went along to observe. When they made a feast, I ate with them all. That in my mind I knew it all to be wrong, this I kept to myself . . .

I went to see every part of Manus. For what reason did I go around observing like this? I thought that this practice of letting everything of value be dispersed among everyone, does it exist only in Baluan or is it everywhere in the Admiralties? I didn't speak out about it, I just thought about it like this. This way of doing things cannot help us. The way of our distant ancestors is still with us. It was becoming clearer in my mind. The white man has long been in our midst. Always he puts us to some task. When the patrol officer comes among us and one man isn't clean, the officer will be angry. If the government sends word to clean the road, and if they do not clean it, they will go to jail. With houses, too, if they don't build their houses well, they can go to jail. If they don't have money for taxes they go to jail. If there is no *house kiap* [a rest house in the village for government officers on patrol] or no latrine, there will be jail. Many of us have been in jail. But they don't learn. They persist in all these ways of the past that I have already mentioned. I saw that everywhere in the Admiralties; it was the same as in Baluan.

When two years had passed I joined the police again for another two years. This time I went to Rabaul. As policeman I was sent out to work among the natives of the bush. Everything about the natives around Rabaul was not different in kind from the Admiralties. It was the same. All the specific customs were somewhat different, but as far as making big feasts and losing money as if it were something of no value, this was the same as in the Admiralties. When I went back to work as a policeman, I didn't do it for nothing. I did it from anger at the natives of the Admiralties. This was in my mind. When I left I thought that I would never go back to Baluan. I found that I didn't like the way of life of the Admiralties. I could never go back. But when I went to Rabaul it was the same as in the Admiralties. I left Rabaul and went to Salamoa. It was the same there. I went as policeman to Madang. I took in all the ways of the natives of Madang. It was just the same. I went to Finschaven and observed the customs of the natives there. It was again the same. Lae, also, and Kavieng were the same. Then I thought, our cultures are only of one kind. Now where does this leave me? Well, I just stayed at work as policeman. I stayed for 12 years altogether. If I saw a man

from Baluan I asked him, "The ways of the old men
of Baluan, do they still exist or are they finished?"
And he would say, "They still exist and what is wrong
with this? It is still our culture." . . . [After Paliau
had been away three years, he took leave to visit
Baluan again.] After three years I wasn't just vaca-
tioning. I came to look again at the Baluan culture
and I came to bring a little money.

While Paliau was in Baluan he established a loan fund,
which he left in the care of local government appointees,
to pay the taxes of men who might otherwise have to go
to jail. At first he used his own money, but later he persuaded others to contribute also. In his account of these
years, we see a prefiguration of his inclusive attitude toward neighboring peoples in the instructions he gave for
the use of this revolving loan fund: "Take care of all
men from Lou, Pwam, and Mouk."

At the beginning of the war in the Pacific, Paliau, with
several thousand natives from various islands, was caught
on the island of New Britain, back of the Japanese lines.
After hiding out in the bush for over a year, Paliau gave
himself up. Then, under Japanese direction, he helped to
organize the several thousand indentured laborers into
self-sufficient groups, supervising their planting of food.
This gave him further organizational experience.

When the end of the war came, there was a day of
reckoning for all natives who had worked in any way
with the Japanese. Since New Guinea was a Trust territory, no one could be accused of treason, but a conspicuous individual like Paliau could be tried as a war criminal.
Paliau maintained that the departing Australians had told
them that the Japanese would be the government and
must be obeyed. He was able to prevent his own conviction and that of other natives, but his days in the police

force were over. He even experienced considerable difficulty in returning to the Admiralties. Then, as he said in his narrative, "I began to wonder what I would do next." At this time he sent home the letter telling the people of Baluan to build a big meeting house, for he had a plan. Later he told of a dream he had had (before the war) about such a meeting house:[24]

> I dreamt of something that rose up almost to the sky. It was very long. There were two things that projected down from the top. They looked like megaphones that are used for shouting. They started at the top and came down. It [this building] was very red. It looked red at the top. It came down, down, down straight upon this piece of ground here near the store [in the center of Lipan Village]. When it came down and reached the ground it looked like a cloth surrounding us. It had taken the form of a building. We were inside and its door was shut. It was a house with a door. I wanted to open the door to go outside, but the door was stuck. I pushed the door three times, but it was as if a man, though it was no man, pushed back. That was all. I found an image here according to which I could make a house.

As the movement developed, absorbing and retaining some of the mystical elements of the cult, Paliau remained to many of his followers a mystical as well as a temporal leader. Myths grew up about him and about his miraculous power of prophecy—claims which he neither affirmed nor denied. A mythical genealogy was elaborated, giving him links with different parts of the Admiralties, and so the lines of inspiration and lineage blended.

In the early days of the movement he spoke tirelessly, for hours, drawing his audience in with the vividness and strength of his oratory. He was especially the master of a style of speech rich in parables, extended analogies, and metaphor, as can be seen in his own reconstruction of his speech about the new meeting house on his return to Baluan:[25]

> I pictured a house. I said this house is a good thing. As for the function of this house I said, "Look at the framework of this house, all these timbers are the bones of this house; they are like the bones of us human beings. This beam that rests at the top of the house is like our backbone. These, which form the sides, are like our ribs. The bones of the side are attached to the backbone. The floor inside the house is like the abdomen of men. The part of the house that has the front ladder is like the head of a man. There is a door in the other part that is like the anus of man. The windows of this house are like the ears and nose by which man gets his breath. The posts that support the house are like the legs and arms of men. Everything that is inside of the house is like all the organs and the heart of man. Why is it that everything in the house is just like everything in men? The part of the house that is like the anus of us men has another door that leads to the cook-house. The door near the house ladder is like the mouth of us men; as it leads back to the door of the cook-house, it is like the bowels of men. All the fastenings that bind the house together are like the muscles, ligaments, tendons, and blood vessels of our bodies. Everything for building a good house is needed also for making a good man. Who does this building? It is God Himself who builds man. He knows that you and I, who are men, cannot sleep unprotected on the ground or the sea; we must sleep in houses. His building is to build the souls of us men that

sleep within our bodies, which are their houses. If our bodies are broken, our souls have no houses and must go back to God, our Father. Why? The breath of the souls of men is the breath of His mouth. While our souls are inside our bodies, these are their houses. But where are our bodies to sleep? The house is like the 'skin' of the body. If our bodies had no house, we couldn't sleep. Would our bodies sleep under stones? No! Would they sleep on the water or on the ground? No! They must stay in houses, to protect them from the rain, to hide them from the sun. That is why we live in houses. When we talk, do we talk under a stone or do we sit down to talk on the water, or do we just sit on the ground? No, we must make a house in which men can talk.''

Paliau is, I believe, an example of the kind of man who can make a crucial difference in the course of cultural micro-evolution, and so, if the time is ripe, in the direction of cultural macro-evolution also. The speed of the cultural change which he was instrumental in bringing about in Manus provides the modern world with a unique example of the possibility of rapid transformation—and this at a period in history when the philosophy of planned change in developing countries is itself in a state of sensitive and responsive transition.

Born a hundred years earlier, Paliau would have had no such access to the variety of experience as work boy and police boy. He would not have taught himself to read and write, and he would not have been able to observe and weigh the claims of the different missionary groups. Certainly he would not have been provided with materials with which to think about the place of New Guinea in the wider world; in fact, there would have been no such wider world to relate to. He might have had the same high sensitivity to cultural contrast and to the possibility of culture change, for the whole of the Admiralties have a high degree of cultural awareness. The situations which led to his initial loneliness—his orphanhood and his repudiation of the feasting style of his people—might have led him to emigrate to a South Coast Manus village, where he might have become a local leader or where, just possibly, his immense superiority might have precipitated a crisis in which he would have perished without making any mark.

His tremendous intellectual superiority over all the men of the archipelago with whom it was possible to compare him was indubitable. It was this which gave him his sense of being always alone. With a mind comparable to that of Franklin Roosevelt, Paliau lived in a world which consisted of a handful of almost illiterate people. Yet, had he become widely literate and had access to one of the great traditions of the world, the wealth of organized thinking might have swamped his thinking and blunted his unique capacities. Paliau's insulation from any written tradition and from contact with those who lived within such a tradition (aside from his Chinese employers, a few police officials, a few officials in the administration, and a few missionaries) also gave him an extraordinary freshness.

The Schwartzes gave him a series of projective tests, and these he seriously and imaginatively bent to his own purposes:[26]

> Presented with a Rorschach (ink-blot test) card, he would use each card plausibly, competently, would relate it as a whole to an ethical theme, not concerning himself with the small details but assigning top and bottom, middle and sides to roles in the drama between good and evil. On the Thematic Apperception Test he also turned each incipient theme into an item in social reconstruction. On one card a group

of young native girls were represented standing outside a hut, while one stood at a distance. After identifying himself with the lonely one, he then went on to give a lecture on the education of women. He skilfully avoided personal content, and worked with the experimenter through the gross morphology of card structure. He worked two days on his Mosaic test, building a beautifully balanced statement of good and evil. In each case he performed in such a way that his percept, although part of his own system, could not be challenged by the structure of the card.

Born a hundred years later, Paliau might have found himself selected from the children of all the peoples of the world to be trained in a special school for the extraordinarily superior. In such a school, matching his wits and his abilities against those of others equally gifted, his contribution would certainly have been very different.

As it is, he is living at a moment in history when his peculiar gifts could enter into an interplay with history through his sense of being alone and his capacity for self-propulsion combined with a constructive use of anger. The repercussions of his life will be heard for decades to come, as the theory of cultural change evolves in a world in which the progress of any given people is the concern of all.

In 1954, my first estimate of Paliau's impact was as follows:[27]

We will need many more detailed studies before the role of a personality like Paliau's will become clear to us. To be as intrinsically superior to his fellows as Paliau was to every other one of his people lays a burden of loneliness on any man. It establishes a sense of precipice, of distance, which may lead to madness and despair, or to greatness. Paliau sees his own childhood in such terms, fatherless, remote, and as a boy too young for the police work for which he succeeded in volunteering, sitting by himself, wondering. All his imaginative enthusiasm was for the Manus, to whom he proudly traced one ancestral line, and he saw them as a great and terribly unfortunate people because they had no land.

For his own people of Baluan he had far less enthusiasm. These were his grasping relatives who stripped him of his earnings each time he returned from work. When he went away to work, the people of his village had not yet been fully Christianized, and Paliau, alone of all the people he led, had never been christened and had no Christian name. He had been trained in no mission school, and during his work-boy days his experience of missions had been mixed and unsystematic. He had learned to write from no teacher who carried the authority of an orderly education, a right to teach the mysteries of education. Instead, with help from his fellow police boys, he had taught himself to write and had developed not the characterless printing or script of an unsuccessful schoolboy which most Manus use but a distinctive script and a real signature. Even his most ambitious organization experience, providing for the homeless masses of native laborers left over in New Britain after the Japanese conquest of Rabaul, he saw as something which he had to work out himself.

PALIAU'S SIGNATURE

Perhaps most important of all, he had practically no contact with the Americans. The experience of the American way of life which had caught the imagination of the people whom he led was unreal to him. His vision of a world remade came from the same sources as the ideals which his countrymen sensed behind the imperfect actualities of American behaviour—human brotherhood, human consent to be governed, the dignity of each individual man, and the benefits of civilization, education, medicine, law. But his was a distillation from other sources, mediated by his long experience of working with Australians. So he brought his impassioned pleas for a New Way to a people whose imagination had been quickened by a different reality—the American occupation of Manus —in which he had no part.

Speaking in a language which was not his mother tongue, Manus rather than Baluan, he led a stranger people, whose spirit he admired extravagantly, whose landless fate he pitied far more than it deserved, whose vision of a world in which all children who were born lived, and no man's hand was turned against another, and no human being sacrificed for gain, he met with his vision of a unified people, whom he must lead toward a limited earthly paradise to be realistically attained only by hard work and controlled behavior.

The Paliau movement is named after its originator, and the contribution of this exemplar to the developing world must be so named. Yet it would be a mistake to describe the situation as if Paliau, who was crucial to the situation, had also created it in its entirety. The success of the movement was dependent on the organizational ability of men of Manus culture. It was they who became Paliau's lieutenants and, leading them, he drew on their cultural style and their stimulated imaginations. The width of his own imagination made him raise the level of change, so that where, before, each small village rose or fell—the course of attempted change in each one dependent on the talents of its best leader and those who were willing to follow him—Paliau could draw on the concerted talents of all these men. Among them there were those who had the ability to lead several villages, as Samol of Bundai led the villages near the coast of the Great Admiralty. There were those who could share his vision and also had the strength and the obstinacy to oppose Paliau—men like Lukas of Mouk. There were the young men who were not rebellious against the past, but who were emerging with opened eyes into the present and the future—men like Peranis Cholai of Peri.[28] In a different fashion, the course of the movement depended also on the particular bent of the various government officials who were charged with obstructing or guiding its leaders, particularly James Landman, who guided the movement through its early days after a government council had been granted. In still another fashion, the cargo cult, inaugurated by a prophet without other leadership characteristics, periodically revived by the mystical minded, and perpetuated by the stubborn, was an essential part.

It is not enough to delineate the period and the place. It is not enough to describe an endemic phenomenon like the cargo cult, or an epidemic phenomenon like the post-World War II political movements. The actual combination of particular individuals must also be invoked if the processes of cultural evolution are to be understood. We must add to Kroeber's statement[29] that "geniuses are the indicators of the realization of coherent pattern growths of culture value," the possibility (which Kroeber recognized) that "most of the potential geniuses born are never realized," and also, going beyond this, that they may *not* be born, that they may die before their time comes to act, and that they may be born in a context in which it is other *individuals* (rather than the right level of culture, or the right cultural climate) who are needed but are not present or able to act. The solitary genius may perhaps be a precursor, but in culture change the whole context is relevant to the initiation and outcome of a significant innovation.

PART III

10. The Conditions
of Conscious Participation
in the Evolutionary Process

INCREASINGLY in recent years thinkers concerned with contemporary problems have sought a place for man in the evolutionary process in which he is no longer the wholly unconscious or the half-conscious most recent development in a cosmic process but instead, having obtained some understanding of the nature of evolution, begins himself to direct its course.[1] Yet all too frequently discussion of the problem breaks down because of unexplored differences in the viewpoint of those who are temperamentally inclined to think in terms of controlling the processes of nature and of those who are temperamentally inclined to envisage a role for man which is dependent on cooperative understanding of some cosmic design. At one extreme are those who, arguing for control, foresee that as man gains greater knowledge of genetics it will be possible by gene manipulation to control the kinds of individuals who will be born, or that, with a greater knowledge of drugs, it will be possible to control population size, or, in more elaborate fantasies, that it will be possible by the propagation of test-tube tissue to order a dozen "Churchills" to fill the needs of a dozen political positions.[2] The other extreme is best represented by the prophets of apocalyptic cults and by those who, accepting man's limitations, see history as a set of recurrent cycles, each as futile as the last, or see man's role as that of a gambler, taking a desperate chance on a seat in Heaven, or see man as a static figure, elegantly and pessimistically living out his existence.

We may examine these two versions of man's future possibilities in terms of their contemporary reference. Until the time when biological research has advanced far enough so that control can be assumed over plants, animals, and men, there are very few steps that can be recommended. One of these would be to make the modifications in the educational system that are necessary to produce more scientists to work on the problem. Meanwhile, the daydream of biological control has the reverse effect of a kind of nightmare, an alarming depiction of a world to come in which practically no one now alive would wish to live. The daydreamers themselves do not speak of genetic control as something by which they too would be controlled; instead, they picture men and women like themselves, in some future age, manipulating the germ plasm of others in ways guaranteed to improve the caliber of mankind to a point where problem solving on a huge scale would be very easy to accomplish.[3]

The suggestion that we replace man's long, slow, fumbling attempts to control the environment and to develop styles of life wherein he becomes increasingly more human by automatic controls of various kinds—including not only those resulting from breeding or propagation but also those resulting from the application of somewhat crude and only partly known rules of behavior to a conditioning process—is an image that functions in the present as a deterrent to enthusiastic commitment to the future.[4] In addition, it is curiously out of step with the dominant feature of this age—that is, with the vast increase in man's freedom to travel, to know, to understand. The transmutation of this great increase in freedom, this enlargement of the stage upon which every individual acts, into a picture of a future of rigid and predetermined controls involves a regressive flight from freedom of the kind that Fromm diagnosed for Nazi Germans,[5] or a continuation of reliance on strong but hated authority of the kind that characterized Old Russia and is still dominant in the Soviet Union,[6] or a conceptualization of human beings as machines, and human life as a machine-like process, a temptation to which Americans are very vulnerable.

Viewed as a new kind of mechanized power, man's greater control over biological evolution invokes a future in which more and more poultry will live out their lives crowded on beds of wood shavings. It invokes a future in which human mating will become a centrally controlled mechanism—whether this takes the form of artificial insemination or selective birth control ensured by the use of drugs—for the production of the right kind of individual to develop and exercise more control. This mechanized image has great repellent power for most of the human race and has attraction only for those who, in such a situation, can comfortably see themselves in positions of power. Mechanization of this kind may be feasible. But viewed in the perspective of man's present situation, the image does not function to increase men's willingness to view their future state with enthusiasm and imagination or their readiness to undertake sacrifices for the future.

Perhaps not accidentally, those who are willing to hand over complete control of their destiny to some outside power emphasize divisiveness. Whether this abnegation of control is phrased in terms of predestination, or the attainment of Nirvana, or the dignified enactment of a role robbed even of tragedy by its meaningless culmination in a gratuitous act,[7] or the acquisition of the last few seats in Heaven reserved for Jehovah's Witnesses, an image of the future which is based on a conception of man's essen-

tial powerlessness has the effect of cutting off the individuals who pursue such a goal from all other men. The
Christian born to be saved though other men are damned,
the Existentialist turning the power of his imagination
inward to feed on his own pride and despair, the Burmese
Buddhist distributing alms for the sake of his own soul
or entering a monastery to break his ties with everyday
life—all roles of this kind are insufficiently inclusive. Acceptance of any of these positions tends to produce an
elite group, the members of which pursue their way in
disregard of the ways of lesser men as they seek a goal
which is defined by its accessibility only to the insightful
or the chosen.

The inference is clear. Neither from those who dream
of gaining power by genetic manipulation, by the manipulation of a behavioristic psychology, or by the use of a set
of precisely operating drugs, nor from those who, individually and without regard for their fellow men, seek
to ally themselves with or resign themselves to a power
they are helpless to alter do we obtain an image of the
future that is capable of inspiring the man of today to
become an active and responsible participant in the world
of tomorrow.

Yet at present an understanding of the evolutionary
process can lead us at least to recognize that, over and
over again, species have reached points of significant divergence—a possibility of evolution of too great specificity, for example, the outcome of which has determined
whether a species has survived or has disappeared leaving
open a zone into which species whose evolution has proceeded differently can expand. That these points of divergence have occurred in a context of mutation and cyto-
plasmic alternation and within the conditions set by the
environment, while man's choices may be made in conferences held in the Kremlins and Pentagons of rival

states, does not change the overall nature of the argument. Our knowledge of evolution suggests that any species may progressively become more, or less, able to survive.[8] And our knowledge of the process gives us an opportunity to exercise choice hitherto unknown on this planet, but it provides no guarantee that men will make the kinds of choices necessary for the survival of *Homo sapiens* and the intricately contrived cultures he has evolved as a result of his special methods of accumulating generational gains.

An examination of the history of past civilizations, the sure traces of many small and fragile human societies that have completely vanished, suggests that the "instinct of self-preservation," invoked so facilely by physical scientists in their moments of optimism,[9] has not yet been incorporated into human culture in any reliable way. That human societies rely on developing in crucial members a combination of self-oriented and other-oriented behaviors is fully documented, but up to the present the combination in each society has remained an unstable constellation, in which the cultural style has been inadequately directive of the diversity of individuals who have been called upon to discharge their culturally determined and evolutionarily significant roles as kings and chiefs, prime ministers, judges, prophets and preachers, artists, poets, philosophers and, in very recent days, scientists.

Stated simply and bluntly, there is no anthropological evidence of an adequately evolved and reliable *cultural* method of assuring the survival of a society or the survival of the human species. For the past, before we became involved in a worldwide network, the model must be the single society, and we can consider how single societies, through time, using their culturally developed mechanisms of political choice, have sometimes made choices that have assured the continuation of their culture or the physical survival of their constituent members. But as we approach the point at which, for the first time in human history, the social community and the membership of the species *Homo sapiens* are coterminous, the inadequacy of existing mechanisms for survival choice becomes glaringly apparent. This truth is brought home to us by any review of the slowly and painfully evolved political mechanisms—the structural inventions like tribal councils, chiefs, kings, oracles, generals, as well as royal commissions, international conventions, and attempts to create international organizations and bodies of international law—and of those cultural conventions of individual behavior that have invoked support of political institutions —protection of the women and children of the tribe, allegiance to a liege lord, patriotism, honor, and bravery as characteristic of certain classes in a society—or of the ideological identifications that require martyrdom, wisdom, peacemaking, and giving sanctuary as aspects of special roles or places. At certain times and in certain places, each of these has facilitated the survival of a given society in competition with or in cooperation with other societies. But none, so far, has proved to be continuingly reliable.

If we look at these social inventions in their ecological settings, we find that even remarkably stable protections, such as bulk of population or strategic position on an island or among mountains, have ceased to insure social continuity in the face of technological change. Having evolved the means of destroying all mankind and not having as yet evolved a mechanism through which a sufficient section of mankind can be saved to insure genetic and cultural continuity, mankind exists today in a state of great precariousness.

This statement is based only on our scientific evidence; it does not in any way involve metaphysical systems that transcend the scientific evidence. As such, it is a warning to those who wish to use *scientific* evidence in predicting the future and in expressing optimism about the future of the earth. A remark such as that made by I. Rabi, "I trust man's instinct of self-preservation," [10] would be appropriate if it were translated to mean, "I trust God's plan for man." But our scientific knowledge of the functioning of human societies produces no basis for a statement of this kind. From the collapse of the tiniest tribe on a South Sea island to the collapse of Nazi Germany when Hitler ordered the sewers of Berlin to be flooded, from the pact made by Montezuma and Cortez[11] to the Irish Free State choice of independence from the British Commonwealth, the history of human societies has demonstrated that the available social forms and human motivations have failed to insure the welfare or even the mere survival of a society.

Linking a metaphysic to our scientific knowledge makes it possible to portray all man's partial successes and partial failures as steps in a cultural evolution in which ultimate success is inevitable, and this viewpoint can be made compatible with all our knowledge of human evolution to date. The glaring failures of given societies to achieve survival can then be seen as steps on the road toward a human society to which each smaller society has made some evolutionary contribution; so regarded, failure is as much a contribution to the whole as is success. From this point of view the inadequately organized society, too small or too large and unwieldy, the hypertrophied institution that is no longer appropriate, the infant institution that is not yet sufficiently developed to be viable—all these go down, but the sweep of cultural evolution continues. Man's ability to comprehend his world and conceptualize his place in it grows ever greater, and when lethal competition between social groups has no further evolutionary value or involves too great a risk, the next step will occur. But for different groups the next step is very differently defined—in the belief, for example, that all men will finally hear the voice of one god; in the conviction that communism will triumph over all other forms of social organization or that worldwide adoption of contraception will solve the population problem; or in the hope that unilateral disarmament, as a kind of beneficent act of redemption, will insure the world against disaster. A construct may have the grandeur of Père Teilhard de Chardin's conception of a universe, at the Alpha point, aeons ago in the lithosphere, unfolding until the planet is clothed first in life and then in consciousness, which after millions of years of further evolution will finally fold in upon itself again at an Omega point of perfect finality.[12] But grand or trivial as these constructs may be in their conceptualization, they permit contemporary men to evade responsibility for cultural invention and to substitute trust or faith, blind loyalty or enlightened obedience, for an active search for solutions to our present dilemma.

When any one of these certainties, which are outside the realm of science and cannot be generated by science, is added to our knowledge of evolutionary history and our definition of man's situation, men are able to visualize a future in which neither man's power over man and over biological processes nor man's helplessness is overemphasized. Furthermore, the advocates of disarmament, or the Communists, or those who see the Christian as a participant in the great scientific adventure of exploring the universe[13] can build into their program the idea that those who believe must get to work on research and on actions of various kinds in order that the inevitable may be fulfilled more quickly. This possibility in itself gives these optimistic ideologies great compelling power over the human imagination. So any one of these inclusive doctrines of redemption may contribute to the survival of the species.

In contrast, the apocalyptic pessimism of the evangelical cult, the pessimistic philosophical nihilism of the sophisticated, and the cynical greed of the man in the street who has been left without any metaphysical guidance serve to enervate and paralyze men's will and imagination.

If the problem were simply one of commitment—a struggle between those who believe survival to be certain and those who believe it to be both unlikely and undesirable, so that the degree of commitment of the optimists would carry them on to the next cultural invention—we would at this moment have little cause for anxiety. Some group of human beings, highly motivated and sustained by faith in evolution, would continue to extend our knowledge of human behavior until they had built a safe social structure for all mankind. Then only those who smothered all curiosity and denied the importance of all scientific endeavor, or so perverted it that it became self-defeating and only destructive (the real danger of Nazism), would be dangerous to the future of mankind in those cases in which they combined hostility to knowledge with an ability to use the dangerous products of the science which they also decried. Even then we might reasonably hope that continuous and patient research, pursued under the favoring climate of some absolute faith, would provide the knowledge necessary to create those evolutionary structures essential to man's survival under contemporary conditions of global communication and accessibility to destructive weapons.

However, the absolute faiths that can generate the trust and the optimism necessary for the pursuit of suitable and essential research have one unfortunate characteristic; their inclusiveness of ideals is not combined with a reliable inclusiveness of social practice. Each lacks the necessary cultural forms that would make it possible for believers to put their vision into effect in such a way as to protect the whole of threatened mankind. Philosophers of a humanism based on science alone may preach responsible surrender, while a contest between world powers is being pursued with modern thermonuclear and biochemical weapons that endanger not only civilization but the entire species and possibly all life. But these advocates of surrender lack sufficient knowledge of human behavior to recognize the political hopelessness of their task without the large-scale conversions to their point of view that would be necessary for success.[14] Communism, too, has failed to develop techniques of internal and external persuasion adequate to implement its optimistic historical determinism. Consequently, Communists have relied on techniques of coercion, both of the citizenry of Communist states and of whole nations brought arbitrarily under Communist rule, which are themselves at least partly self-defeating. As the pacifist who seeks converts in new contexts and with a new rationale of the possibility of world destruction is ignored or turned upon by his society and is subjected to ridicule or even imprisonment, so also the Communist enthusiast has generated a type of coercion which is equally self-defeating when viewed from the standpoint of hopes of preventing a worldwide holocaust. And the Church, whose message of universal responsibility for the lives of men and the life of the world provided a metaphysical background for Teilhard de Chardin's magnificent incorporation of a cosmic view of evolution, forbade him to teach or to publish. Disobedience to his superiors would have meant the severance of his connection with the sources of his all-pervading trust, within which his researches could be made meaningful to all mankind. Ecclesiastical obedience robbed the Western world, at a crucial moment in history, of his evolutionary formulations.[15]

Meanwhile other groups, lacking the comprehensive philosophies within which our increasing knowledge of evolution and the evolutionary possibilities inherent in mankind could be developed, are unable to include the whole of mankind in their concerns and continue to be swayed by schismatic religious beliefs, narrow nationalisms, institutionalized chauvinism. Armed and assertive, they are fully able to launch, or at least to trigger, a catastrophic war.

We are therefore faced with a more urgent need so to involve ourselves consciously in evolution that we may be able to make the necessary inventions for the survival of mankind. In whatever field we would seek solutions initially, a first step is the straightforward admission that we do not have them. We do not know how to find the kinds of leaders we need; we do not know how to construct the kinds of social organization we need; we do not know how to persuade a large enough body of people to follow any course of action without simultaneously generating opposition to that very course of action. We do not know how to institutionalize a worldwide ideology so that the way in which it is structured does not defeat its stated goals. Most important, perhaps, we have not yet created, even on a pilot experimental basis, a type of social organization capable of finding, recruiting, educating, and providing for the innovative intelligence we need. Yet there is little doubt that among our living population as mankind is constituted—without resort to controlled eugenic manipulation—there is a sufficient number of highly gifted individuals who, given the proper cultural conditions in which to work, could go on to make the necessary innovations.

It is my conviction that although we have not begun to do so, we have enough knowledge to set about the task of creating the necessary conditions, and in the remaining chapters of this book I shall discuss some aspects of this problem. We do not have to wait until discoveries of drugs or possibilities of genic manipulation put greater power into the hands of men who lack an adequate social structure to limit and modulate that power. Nor do we have to risk the accumulation of apathy and the privatization of goals by which a democracy like ours is threatened when its citizens feel themselves powerless before forces over which they have no influence.

In an open society like ours, in which there are so many not bound by absolutes, men are sustained by their sense of the alternative paths that may be taken. Democracies of our type are characterized by this sense of choice that is wide and can be widened; related to this is a specifically American attitude toward having room to move around in. "Don't fence me in" is a meaningful colloquialism. For Americans, particularly those Americans for whom dependence on science has become an article of faith, the recognition that the emergency is real and desperate, that devices for dealing with it do not exist and must be developed, and that, in developing them, we can make no blueprint of what they must be, should provide the impetus for genuine commitment and optimism. If we can free ourselves from the obsolete hierarchical arrangements that have made the practitioners of one science feel superior to those in other sciences and can treat the knowledge we have with respect, we can start work. The act of making a start can, at least on the American scene, engender the kind of trust in the future which we must have in order to work for that future with conviction.

11. The Conditions of Scientific Participation

IN THIS DISCUSSION I have argued that the unit of cultural micro-evolution is a cluster of interacting individuals who within the special conditions provided by period and culture make choices which set a direction—a channel—in which events tend to flow until other points of divergence are reached. Further, I have considered the specific cultural conditions under which a given innovation is made possible, as well as the way in which period—the state of knowledge and the types of existing interaction among people—provides a context in which clusters of individuals act. For evolutionary activity, each of these conditions is essential. Cultural conditions and favorable period will not of themselves ensure that an outstanding man, the genius after whom a significant change is likely to be named, will actually make a contribution. Still less can they provide for the composition of the cluster of which he is a part.

The task of conscious participation, in which we put to use our existing knowledge of the nature of cultural evolution, necessarily includes an assay of each of these conditions and an estimate of the points at which intervention would be possible. Consequently we need accurate analyses of the particular cultural system in which we plan to work, analyses that focus on the particular cultural capacities for innovation and the particular cultural neutralities and actual blocks.

We may consider a few examples of this kind of analysis. It would be necessary to locate sources of conservatism in a society in order to know whether the locus of conservatism was in those groups in the population among whom there had been very little change for many generations or in new and mobile groups who had recently attained a desired status which, though they did not yet fully understand what it stood for, they were ready to defend violently. Also, it would be important to locate groups whose members displayed the kind of extreme resistance to change that characterizes people who have undergone some historical trauma that has segregated them from the main currents of cultural development through serfdom, slavery, peonage, caste-like peasantry, and so on. It would likewise be necessary to locate those groups in the society who were overwilling to change rapidly, careless of the responsibilities that change entails. One would also have to consider whether the potentialities of a given society were sufficiently pronounced and uniform so that it would be advisable to concentrate all the cultural potential on one type of innovation, political or artistic or technological, or on one stage of the innovative process, on first insights or approximations, or on development rather than initial invention. In studying a very large, complex society, such as the United States, the United Kingdom, the Soviet Union, India, or China, it would be necessary to consider whether concentration and specialization should be organized regionally or through some other type of subgroup and how a desirable evolutionary balance might best be obtained in a large overall cultural system in which a common language and a national culture facilitated communication among groups representing different versions of the culture, with different potentialities for innovation, development, skepticism, and hardheaded conservatism.

Up to the present, no one has fully worked out such

relationships within a specific national culture or between different national cultures.[1] As yet we are dependent on various special investigations such as studies of the industrialization of Japan;[2] the progress of the Soviet Union in implementing an earlier, highly developed abstract level of science;[3] the success of the United States in putting original inventions into large-scale production; the capabilities of the United Kingdom, France, and Italy in developing finished and intricate models on a small scale. In these partial investigations, attention has focused on technological innovation and occasionally on political innovation, but little attention has been given to other relevant aspects of the culture or to a successful innovation as a generator of further change of evolutionary significance.[4]

Traditionally, the assessment of period has been the particular concern and has fallen within the special competence of the historian.[5] The fact that elapsed time has been a necessary part of the methodology of history complicates the problem of assaying the period in which we are now living and the coming period in which all the peoples of the world will participate. Until World War II, it was possible for historians to treat period very partially. Even if it was known, for example, that there had been intellectual contacts between China and Europe at a certain time, it was possible to analyze a period of European history as if, in terms of period, the two areas were relatively independent of each other and, vice versa, to consider periods in Chinese history without direct reference to periods in European history.[6] Indeed, for some parts of the world, notably the American continents in pre-Columbian times and the islands of the South Pacific and aboriginal Australia before the voyages of the sixteenth and seventeenth centuries, considerations of worldwide periods were essentially irrelevant since, before Europeans came into these areas, the inhabitants did not participate in the determining historical events that shaped the fate of peoples in other parts of the world. Between the time in the history of mankind when overall conditions may have affected all the representatives of the early hominidae and the present, when the world has become one—physically, as fallout follows on nuclear explosions, and politically, insofar as every population on earth is vulnerable to the acts of other populations—historical periods were localized in their significance.[7]

Because we have treated historical period locally and partially, we do not as yet have a framework within which we can systematically characterize a decade of world history by means of exact indicators of a large number of states of parts of the total system. We do have a growing body of worldwide statistics which can encompass such things as climactic change, radiation effects, population change, nutritional status, agricultural potential in relation to existing technologies and systems of land tenure, and so on, but we do not have a framework within which each of these partial kinds of knowledge would fit. Furthermore, we have only very slightly developed a methodology for making retrospective experimental analyses in which only one element—a crop failure, the death of a key political figure, the passage of a new immigration law, or a delay in completing an innovation—is treated as a significant variable. Rigorously applied, with full use of existing long runs of accurate data on different variables, such retrospective analyses would begin to provide us with devices for setting the limits within which development can take place in the next decade and give us some measure of accurate projection.[8]

At present, our attempts to characterize a coming period have met with dramatic failure—for example, the prediction that the birthrate in the United States would fall [9] (which was based on naive extrapolations of a short-time trend), or the prediction that with a rising standard of living in regions of the world undergoing new development the birthrate would fall.[10] Even in situations calling for very short-time predictions there have been conspicuous failures, such as the failure of the opinion polls in 1948 to predict the election of President Truman[11] or, in the market research field, the failure to predict the popularity of a new style of automobile.[12] The skepticism and caution bred of these failures have hindered the search for new significant variables and for closely correlated patterns of events, such as are needed for the prediction of longer trends.

For example, the various uses of uranium now have worldwide political, biological, and medical significance. These could be examined for their predictive value as, over a long period, economists were once able to base predictions on the uses made of gold. In the case of gold, price was the principal indicator, but new discoveries of gold, the location of these discoveries in political units, the methods by which gold was processed, and the state of rival elements and types of currency also had to be considered for purposes of prediction.[13] In a parallel way, the locations of raw supplies of uranium, the kinds of decisions made about the production of nuclear weapons, the development of uses of atomic power for peacetime energy needs, the technology of specific uses of atomic power, the involvement of atomic power in space technology, the condition and availability of rival sources of power, the responsiveness of worldwide public opinion to radioactive risks and benefits, all would have to be taken into account in examining the usefulness of uranium as an indicator and in working out the particular combination of factors relevant to prediction.

Or we might find that biological indicators—for example, the location and proportion of those under age ten in

1963 who develop kwashiorkor[14] or other less extreme forms of protein malnutrition—might serve to project the quality and the geographical location of kinds of political initiative three decades into the future. To the extent that protein malnutrition in early childhood has irreversible effects, this is a future condition of the world population about which we can be informed today.

In a recent cross-cultural study, David McClelland [15] has attempted to correlate themes of achievement in elementary school textbooks with predictions of entrepreneurial talent and economic growth decades later, with which he has combined retrospective analyses to increase the predictive value of his hypotheses.

At present our ability to characterize the period in which we live and to prefigure a coming period is also dependent on the geographical segmentation of areas of large-scale integrated research. Gunnar Myrdal—outside of Sweden—worked on one set of problems in the United States, a second set for the Economic Commission for Europe (under the Economic and Social Council of the United Nations), and still another set in India. In Myrdal's case, these disparate researches have been united through the development of an encompassing theory.[16] But, more commonly, economists who are concerned, for example, with the consequences of automation in the United States are surprised by sudden political upheavals in Africa. Or the calculations of professional students of trade unionism in socialist countries are thrown off balance both by automation and by nationalist revolutions. Clearly, we have not yet developed a framework for looking at the entire world simultaneously or for developing solutions on a worldwide basis.

In order to identify choice points at which change is possible, it is not enough for us to develop methods of characterizing the period in which we are the living actors.

We need also to develop methods by which we can simultaneously cross-check intraperiod sequences that arise from unique and only relatively predictable events. For example, a catastrophe like an earthquake, which causes thousands of deaths and great destruction of property, not only affects the society in which it occurs but also, given a worldwide system of communication, raises the level of awareness (or, if many earthquakes occur in rapid succession, may blunt interest) in other parts of the world.[17] Such changes in social perception may have far-reaching political consequences in influencing measures of soil conservation, flood control, dam construction, and technical assistance, as well as potential shifts in political orientation in countries desiring economic aid, differential allotments of public funds for education, defense, underground nuclear testing, and public works, the location of capital cities of new countries, and so on. However, we can arrive at an accurate understanding of the complex process by which a single event of this kind alters the state of the whole system only if the immediate effects are studied soon after the event and the later effects are also followed up. Furthermore, we shall need to assess rates of response to events of different magnitudes as these responses vary from one country to another, closer to and farther away from the place where a particular event has taken place.

Once we have developed methods of period analysis, based on very careful experimental retrospective studies and cross-checking simultaneous studies that measure the repercussions of single events throughout the system, we shall be able to work out prefigurative indicators. These may or may not be single complexes, such as the uses of gold or uranium. Their purpose will be to indicate significant types of fluctuation in the whole system in which points of divergence may be developing.

It is my argument that the points of divergence, the

points of greatest freedom in the system, may precede the peaks of significant change which later are defined as the turning points in history. The significance of a peak of this kind (for example, Darwin's presentation of the theory of evolution) is not that it determines a course of development, of which it is more likely to be the culmination than the origin, but rather that it gives direction to the *next* step in an evolutionary sequence. One purpose for which we need to develop methods of doing retrospective experimental analysis is to make possible a re-examination of the familiar arguments about the anticipation of particular famous men. So one might by experimental reconstruction work out the course of development without, specifically, Darwin or Freud or Marx. Actually, of course, such situations have occurred historically, as in the case of Mendel, whose work was virtually unknown and its significance overlooked when it was published,[18] and in the case of Stolypin.[19] Purposive, conscious, and responsible intervention in cultural evolution must be carried out in terms of a worldwide system, with awareness that events in any one part of the system will have repercussions on other parts of the system. This means that the prefigurative indicators must have reference to the whole and must give us information both about those developments which are already past the point at which intervention can be successful and those points at which intervention is possible (Plates 12, 13).

As in modern society the sciences are taking over the ancient and respected role of the prophet, the vicissitudes of prophets in earlier ages become relevant. The prophet who led his people safely to the Promised Land; the prophet who, like Cassandra, could only discern a train of events long after the events were hopelessly in train, who could aggravate but not change the situation; the prophet who produced a self-fulfilling prophecy that became an active component of the system with which he was working—

all these are analogues of what the application of scientific research to prediction may produce. It is possible that by harnessing both description and prediction to a worldwide system, we may acquire some control over the competitive distortion that comes about when nations or industrial complexes are free to create their own "public" information.[20]

The state of a given culture, including the extent to which it is changing and is capable of change under new conditions, and the state of the world are both conditions in which cultural evolution takes place. An event that may become of evolutionary importance is not in and of itself something that can alter either the particular culture or the state of the world. However, if a particular event of potential evolutionary significance does set in motion a train of events, it will affect the later state of the culture and later periods in the world. It is more difficult for us to accept the culture, with its potentialities for certain types and rates of change, and the period, with its already inevitable contemporary characteristics, as *given*, than it is for us to deal with a desired change as if it had already occurred and at the same time to recognize that the small, potentially innovative detail is part both of a given culture and of the state of the world. We need a time–space model which makes simultaneous provision for various aspects of the future, including those aspects of the future which have already been determined by past events (for example, the upper limits of the world population between the ages of thirty and forty, twenty years from now), those aspects which allow for a limited number of alternatives (for example, the availability of different kinds of fuel), and those aspects which are completely unpredictable, at least in the present state of our knowledge (for example, the appearance of a new highly resistant virus, or an accidental major atomic explosion). And we need information about the ways in which the anticipation of future trains of events are, or may become, operative in the present.

Considerable work has been done on ways in which an individual's or a people's view of the past affects the present, but comparatively little work has been done on an individual's or a people's view of the future as a component in the present.[21] Yet any conscious attempt to bring about change becomes a component, however inconspicuous, of the present. Consequently, the likelihood that a next step in evolution will occur can be estimated not only from the state of the culture (particularly the accumulation of knowledge and skills and frames of reference) and the conditions of the period (particularly the conditions of interrupted or uninterrupted communication, peaceful cooperation or active conflict, and so on), but also from existing germinal conscious attempts at innovation.

The population "explosion" provides us with one example. Even though no precise attempt is made to determine trends, statistical extrapolations of the present world population demonstrate very clearly that the changing ratio between men and natural resources will bring about other changes of a magnitude which may be expected to have evolutionary significance. This would be so even though actual demographic conditions went completely unrecognized by anyone. However, the population explosion has been recognized in many parts of the world, and this recognition has had significant effects at many levels on the relations between nation-states, as a factor in the preservation of peace, in orienting our thinking about food production, on the structure of the family, on the acceleration of space exploration, whether this is conceived of as a remedy for overpopulation or as a means of rescuing man from the disasters that will accompany overpopulation, and, finally, on our estimates of mankind and our estimates of the value of other men, our own family line, our own stock, our own nationality, the relative value of those already born and those not yet born, the near and the distant future, freedom of choice or central control.[22]

The issue of what shall be done to meet the problem is one that looms large and will loom larger, and we can be saved from facing this issue neither by natural catastrophe nor by the possibility of a man-made catastrophe of nuclear or biochemical war in which mankind may be wiped out. We can see shaping up around the world some of the main lines of response, already hardening, in part, to inevitability. The choice point in the position on traditional methods of contraception taken by the Roman Catholic Church has been passed. The selection of the issue of contraception by non-Catholics as a weapon against Catholicism has had the predictable effect of hardening the stand of the Roman Catholic Church. So, too, there is an apparent hardening of the general lines of strategy that will be pursued by those countries in the Free World which have a high standard of living—encouragement of the use of contraception by *other* peoples in poor and underdeveloped countries within their sphere of influence while, at the same time, they pride themselves on their own large families. The Communist countries may be expected to pursue a strategy of controlling the birthrate in their own countries by arbitrary measures for and against abortion or contraception while, at the same time, they make light of arguments advanced by the Free World about the impossibility of indefinitely expanding food production.[23] These three positions have given rise to various countersuggestions; for example, a suggestion that if it were not for the opposition of the Roman Catholic Church, the practice of contraception would rapidly spread around the world, and a suggestion that the number of children born can be limited by state-controlled sterilization, compulsory or voluntary, or by the deferment of marriage, and so on.[24]

Quite clearly, the principal positions and the counter-suggestions are totally inadequate approaches to the over-all problem of population limitation. Roman Catholics recommend deferred marriage and increased abstinence, but they have no means of commending their recommendations outside their own communion. New nations boast of their growing populations and are affronted by suggestions that they, but not Europeans or North Americans, should practice population control. The Communists at one time promote and at another discourage population increase as an adjunct of their world policy.[25] As things now stand, even if there are great improvements in existing agricultural practices, in the allocation of land, and in the types of crop grown, there will inevitably be an increase in malnutrition and its accompaniments—disease, differential death rates, impairment of functioning, and enlightened bitterness.

Population growth will provide a condition for evolutionary change. But the direction of change and the greater or lesser likelihood of mankind's survival may be determined by purposive intervention.

Within the whole complex it is possible to locate certain areas of activity. There are, for example, those who are experimenting with oral contraceptives with reversible effects; those who are experimenting with techniques which produce irreversible—and also reversible—sterility; those who are concerned with devising methods of international cooperation which override national boundaries in such ways that differences in population between nation–states lose some of their significance; those who are experimenting with ideas for limited warfare with "clean" bombs and various methods of biochemical warfare which have a high potential for wiping out part or all of the world's population; those who are developing a space technology adequate for the establishment of space colonies so that, independent of events on earth, a portion of the human species can be preserved; those who are concerned with the simplification of the expensive, heavy, and bulky technology of the contemporary world in order to increase people's mobility and decrease their consumption of irretrievable resources and use of energy; those who are experimenting with new sources of food to short cut the present complicated food production cycle, eliminate expensive forms of transportation, and produce nutriments at enormously lowered cost and expenditure of natural resources. And, finally, there are those who are concerned with the overall ethical, philosophical, and religious implications of the choices that individuals must make in deciding whether or not to have children, whether to set a higher value on the welfare of their own unborn children than on the welfare of other children who are already born or, alternatively, to surrender—voluntarily or by coercion —some of their rights over their own individual reproductivity.

Interdisciplinary and worldwide exploration would greatly extend a list of this kind, and in extended form it could provide a basis for purposive innovation. Whether we then look at the population problem from the standpoint of the currents of world opinion that would be set in motion or from the standpoint of individual career choice, the relevance of what is done becomes salient. Individually, a biochemist may choose to work on the elaboration of biochemical warfare, the development of methods of oral contraception, or the production of new, less expensive, more compact foods, suitable for feeding enormous populations or for use in outer space. The sciences concerned with human behavior may direct their efforts toward the construction of new forms of international cooperation, such as world food banks, or they may undertake research on the consequences of the individual's reproductive status for his total health, or they may attempt to provide a scientific background for the kind of choice that must ultimately be made on the basis of a total world philosophy. Between precise knowledge of the possible consequences of a particular course of action for individual personality, on the one hand, and a world philosophy of human action, on the other, particular cultures, religious systems, and ideologies are the mediating variables of which account must be taken. Childlessness means one thing in a culture in which failure to reproduce means a loss of status in this world or the next. It means quite a different thing in a culture in which having children is regarded as a suitable reward for having worked to achieve a reasonable standard of living, and something different again in a culture in which a newly awakened sense of national identity requires each individual to make a personal contribution to his country's strength. It means still something else in a religion devoted to final annihilation of the personal self, and a different thing again in a religion in which individuality is a religious value and embodiment as a human being is a final actualization of a soul. And the fusing of children and cars and television sets in the secular rewards for economic conformity has still other consequences.

We already have the necessary methods for studying the overall problem at all these levels and for acquiring information on the individual psychological consequences of the kinds of choices that are made in different cultures and by those with different religious and ideological orientations. At every stage of any change in world orientation, the particular significance of change will be determined by the cultures and the religious and ideological groups which initiate, promote, and accept any particular type of solution. It would be possible for us to group areas of research so that they would have mutually reinforcing significance.

For example, research on new foods could be grouped with research on oral contraceptives; or research on space colonization with research on the new uses of nuclear energy; or research on the individual with research on group correlates of different patterns of reproductivity. This kind of categorization would enable us to arrive at a division of labor whereby problems could be assigned to those parts of the world in which the culture, the religion, and the political ideology would foster a particular kind of research. For example, research on new, inexpensive foods to replace our present highly expensive methods of producing animal protein would encounter continuous obstruction in the Americas and Europe, but it might well be heavily supported in a country like China. Similarly, research on methods of sterilization might receive its greatest cultural support in Japan, the country which for many centuries has articulately faced population problems. And passionate agnosticism might be a suitable background for research on oral contraception, and so on.

A strategic assay of the world situation, a definition of the state of the period, and a systematic analysis of the potential for evolutionary change, or obstruction of change, in each part of the world's population, in national cultures, local scientific traditions, different religious and political orientations—these are the first steps we can take in planning for immediate and responsible participation in cultural evolution.

12. Difficulties in
Creating Evolutionary Clusters

A RECOGNITION of the state of the world and the potentialities of different cultures in the world can be a first step in the process of conscious participation in evolutionary change. Were our situation less precarious, it might be wise to postpone further action until the necessary research organs were established for obtaining comparable, simultaneously collected data encompassing the whole, as data were made available by the organization of the International Geophysical Year. There are two arguments against delay. One objection is the failure of most social scientists even now to realize that in the single network in which the societies of the world are today involved simultaneity of research is necessary. The other objection is simply one of time. Even with adequate financing and urgent prosecution of plans, it would take several years to get research actually under way. Meanwhile we are living in a period of extraordinary danger, as we are faced with the possibility that our whole species will be eliminated from the evolutionary scene.

One necessary condition of successfully continuing our existence is the creation of an atmosphere of hope that the huge problems now confronting us can, in fact, be solved —and can be solved in time. There are, indeed, systems of faith and hope in different parts of the world. But the way in which each system is organized in absolute opposition to each other system not only reduces the effectiveness of each one but also, in some cases, adds to the danger, as all-or-none dichotomies are presented to the peoples of the world so that, apparently, the only choice is between "atheistic Communism and Christianity" or between "Communism and Imperialistic Capitalism," and so on. During the 1930s, just such a forced alignment to Left or Right—which distorted or left without clear definition the hopes and fears of many of the peoples of the world—provided the ideological dynamism through which we were eventually plunged into World War II. We need, now, a view of the future that neither minimizes the immediate peril nor generates despair. For only a view of the future which permits each segment of the world's people to believe that mankind has the intellectual resources to make a forward step in cultural evolution will engender the spiritual commitment without which we cannot hope to make the earth safe for the cultural inventions the human species has already made.

I have discussed how evolutionary change proceeds through the actions of clusters of individuals, the members of a small primitive village or the cabinet of a great nation. Each such cluster is characterized by a discernible relationship to a particular cultural potential and period and by a peculiar combination of abilities. The most distinctive characteristic of an evolutionary cluster is the presence in it of at least one irreplaceable individual, someone with such special gifts of imagination and thought that without him the cluster would assume an entirely different character. An individual of this kind we are likely to classify as a genius, that is, someone whose exceedingly rare combination of gifts appears to be a genetic and experiential accident but who makes a contribution to evolution not by biological propagation but by the special new turn he is able to give to the course of cultural evolution.

The effectiveness of a genius appears to be highly dependent not only on the state of the culture and the period in which such an individual is born but also on the exact position in the social structure which he occupies and the exact composition of the cooperative face-to-face group within which he acts. This last condition is the one most consistently overlooked. In focusing our attention on a central figure like Christ or St. Paul, we miss the significance of the Twelve Apostles. So, also, in recent history, we tend to overlook the early Bolshevik leaders or the group that surrounded Hitler. Or we emphasize one of the Founding Fathers of the United States at the expense of the others.[1] Or, in other situations, we emphasize those who have broken away from a group, especially during its formative stages, at the expense of those who remained to make up a continuing cluster. The effect of this neglect of the importance of clustering is that social scientists no less than the naive public persist in searching for "leaders," and a great deal of research effort goes into the attempt to define the characteristics of individual college students or young businessmen or young politicians that enter into "leadership."[2] Yet these searches have been singularly arid and sterile. A country that is "looking for leadership" is immediately recognizable as a country in a parlous state. Although lengthy discussions about different kinds of leadership in different situations serve, indirectly, to explain why science has not solved the problem of identifying leaders, they serve no further constructive purpose.

Instead, we can take the position that the unit of cultural evolution is neither the single gifted individual nor the society as a whole but *the small group of interacting individuals* who, together with the most gifted among them, can take the next step; then we can set about the task of creating the conditions in which the appropriately gifted can actually make a contribution. That is, rather than isolating potential "leaders," we can purposefully produce the conditions we find in history, in which clusters are formed of a small number of extraordinary and ordinary men, so related to their period and to one another that they can consciously set about solving the problems they propose for themselves.

The initial procedure is, of course, familiar to everyone who has worked in the natural sciences in the last two decades. There is, for example, the organizational technique which the British, in World War II, called "operational research," [3] in which scientists of proved intellectual capacities were formed into groups and set to solving new problems, often well outside their fields of specialization. In the United States the Manhattan Project was an enterprise of the same kind,[4] in which first-rate scientists were brought together to produce as a group something which no one of them, within a limited time, could have produced alone. One of the motivations for forming a team of this kind has been the "freshness of approach" of a well-trained scientist working on a new problem; another has been the "cross-fertilization" that takes place when several disciplines work together on a task. It is doubtful whether either of these is essential; certainly the underlying problems can be dealt with in other ways. Lacking an individual with the specific scientific training to tackle a new task, one can make a virtue of preliminary ignorance and use the freshness incidental to learning about the particular problem as an asset in group research. And where the relevant disciplines have been so fragmented by the archaic academic organizations of science that it is impossible to get essential information without drawing on specialists in several fields, the difficulty can be turned into an advantage insofar as well-presented, new material from unfamiliar fields is regarded as a stimulant. However, neither original ignorance of the matters in hand nor specialization that has resulted in ignorance of essential work in other fields is a necessary condition for team work.

Here I should like to point out a characteristic of the sciences that deal with man's social behavior which is a great handicap in the human scientist's effort to capture the attention of the scientific and the responsible lay world. Inventions in the field of human behavior must draw directly and fully on existing forms of human behavior. Communication must initially be couched in a natural language. Research and development must in large part conform to existing types of social action. These things are, of course, equally true of the natural sciences, for the rituals of communication in scientific publications, scientific meetings, and academic departments are deeply traditional in character. But the results of activities in laboratories or projects in the natural sciences are ultimately expressed in formulas about the nonhuman world or about human beings phrased in the terms of genetics or organ systems, and so on. After the results are so formulated, whatever experience has been gained about the way in which trained and specially gifted individuals work together then sinks in a limbo of ideas about "common sense" or rules for running a laboratory. All that remains available to the organizers of such projects is a large set of premises which are unsystematic, unexamined, and capable of influencing behavior only at an inexplicit and traditional level.[5]

But when human behavior itself is the subject of scientific investigation, something very different occurs. The behavioral scientist not only is a part of what he studies and must attempt to regularize, he is also conscious of his part.[6] His recommendations must be accepted and put into practice by other human beings who are already involved in some way in the very activities he has been investigating, whether they are making judgments about other persons, recruiting a suitable staff, bringing up children to use their minds, or resolving failures to function adequately in work or in personal relationships. Every problem for which the human scientist is asked to find a solution is already being solved *after a fashion* in the society in which he himself has a functioning place. People do judge each other's potentialities; staff are found and employed; groups with a job to do somehow get on with one another; children are taught something in schools; individuals with heavy loads of anxiety and distorted views of the world continue to hold jobs, destroy the work of other men, and try to maintain personal relationships.

Therefore, when the human sciences come on the scene, they enter a functioning system which its members must defend in proportion to the precariousness with which it is working. Just as the farmer will prefer a low-yield crop which is relatively certain to produce a harvest to a new crop which, although highly recommended, is uncertain, so human beings are likely to cling to modes of behavior which have been found to work at least part of the time. The hazards of change are so great that men are likely to approach a new idea much as they approach magic, either by rejecting the new idea altogether as too dangerous or by regarding it as a panacea whose effectiveness is determined by absolute, blind faith.

The natural scientist can retire with his formulas and laboratory instruments and experiment until he has perfected some process; the human scientist cannot do this. The subject matter of his research can be no other than his fellow human beings in all their particularity and intransigency. In order to carry with him those who must someday make use of his discoveries, he must carry them with him all the time, creating in the midst of the very situation which he hopes his research will alter the conditions necessary for using his discoveries once they are made. His public, among whom are included natural scientists, humanists, statesmen, politicians, and all sorts of men of affairs, make certain demands upon him, demands that reflect the peculiarly human fear that change will invade and destroy traditional forms of behavior. Two kinds of reception are given the human scientist's discoveries. On the one hand, a discovery is denigrated by the assertion that it is "common sense put into jargon"; on the other hand, some small part of a developing insight—some temporary "instrument" like a questionnaire or a test or some special improvement in group procedure—is reified into a kind of magical solution. That these bits and pieces of the human science repertoire are, in fact, treated as magic is obscured by the particular form of magic, by the fact that acceptance invokes our contemporary belief in the omnipotence of science. But the public, including many other social scientists who seize upon this ragtag and bobtail of instruments and methods, have too little understanding of science to respond with discrimination. They take "science" on faith and apply the adjective "scientific" uncritically and without relation to the issues involved. So a ritualistic picture of science is built up as quantitative, necessarily involving "experiments," objective, "necessarily excluding most parts of the personality of the investigator," absolutely certain in its predictions, and so on. This is a conventional view of science that is uncritically shared by most scientists.

In this unfavorable climate of opinion, the new kind of insight which the application of scientific method, as opposed to scientific ritual, can produce is regularly abused, obscured, or vulgarized. Three instances must suffice here. In the 1930s, in the course of an investigation of the effect of different kinds of lighting on the work output of manual workers at the Hawthorne Works, a Western Electric

Company plant in Chicago,[7] the researchers stumbled onto an unexpected circumstance, namely, that there was an improvement in work output among the girls—whether changes for the better or the worse were made in their work environment—all of whom were personally interviewed. From this observation of the effect of interviewing, there developed a special style of interviewing which was a complicated and highly developed social technique, as complex as Roberts Rules of Order or psychiatric interviewing. In this technique, the interviewee was selected by the interviewer; the employee was interviewed on the job, on company time, and was permitted to talk himself out through many hours; the interviewer was continuingly present in the group; absolute rules of privileged communication protected the worker, but the interviewer had the duty of making recommendations, in general, to management if the interviews revealed the need for some alteration in plant procedure which might practically be carried out; and, finally, the interviewer did not have any specific theoretical psychological frame of reference. The Hawthorne Experiment, as the report on these procedures came to be known, demonstrated that with this type of interviewing a good proportion of the workers worked out solutions to the various problems that bothered them. Yet the technique did not survive.

Instead, the method was applied in various diluted and unorganized forms, and traces of the Hawthorne Experiment are found today embedded in theories of nondirective interviewing, in the special type of interviewing used by Eliot Chapple in the Interaction Chronograph study,[8] and in various interviewing procedures which do not include the series of interrelated controls that were used by Roethlisberger and his associates in the original study. There was no social mechanism by which those who made the original discoveries could insist on the fact that there is a systematic relationship among the various elements in their procedure, that only when all the elements are present does the procedure have the special therapeutic and morale effects that had been found, and that if the technique is to be used effectively, it must be used as a whole.

Psychoanalysis in many ways presents a systematic contrast to the Western Electric–Hawthorne Experiment type of interviewing. The patient must seek out the analyst; the patient must pay for every minute of the analysis; the patient's time is rigorously limited to a "fifty-minute hour"; the analyst must have an exhaustive theoretical and experiential grasp of the processes with which he is dealing; and the analyst is neither required nor expected to take any action in the real world that might alter conditions having an impact on the patient's life.

In contrast to the Hawthorne Experiment, the methods of Freudian analysis have been preserved and transmitted in an apprenticeship situation, but expensively, by the establishment of a cult atmosphere and with a very low level of communication between the psychoanalytic theoretician and the rest of the human sciences.[9]

Another illustration is the fate of the word "feedback" in that part of social psychology which owes its original inspiration to Kurt Lewin and which is popularly known as Group Dynamics. In 1946, a Macy Foundation interdisciplinary conference was organized to use the model provided by "feedback systems," honorifically referred to in earlier conferences as "teleological mechanisms," and later as "cybernetics," [10] with the expectation that this model would provide a group of sciences with useful mathematical tools and, simultaneously, would serve as a form of cross-disciplinary communication. Out of the deliberations of this group came a whole series of fruitful developments of a very high order. Kurt Lewin (who died in 1947) took away from the first meeting the term "feedback." He suggested ways in which group processes, which he and his students were studying in a highly disciplined, rigorous way, could be improved by a "feedback process," as when, for example, a group was periodically given a report on the success or failure of its particular operations. In this very special form, feedback became part of the jargon of Group Dynamics, which has also assumed many of the characteristics of a cult in the efforts made to conserve some of the rigor of procedure with which Kurt Lewin and the experimentalist, Alex Bavelas,[11] had attempted to imbue it. In this case, far from serving as a catalyzing, high-level theoretical tool, the term feedback has become a jargon-catchall for any kind of report back to government, management, the subjects of an experiment, subjects during an experiment, and so on. Stripped of its intellectual potential, the term knocks about the corridors of Unesco and for the most part those who use it have no idea that this bit of enjoined, Group Dynamic-recommended behavior is in any way related to the forbidding cross-disciplinary integration known as cybernetics.

These are almost uniformly discouraging findings. The survival of a carefully developed, new form of applied human science, based on rigorous and lengthy observations, seems at present to depend on the establishment of a cult;[12] alternatively one must resign oneself to the fragmentation of the form into catchwords, part procedures, and blindly applied recipes. The present Glueck test for juvenile delinquency[13] and the indiscriminate use of such methods as the Rorschach, the lie detector, and sodium amytal are all examples of this kind of fragmentation. One is led to ask whether social invention at this level is possible, whether there is any hope that the social scientist, in the kind of society which initially welcomes and then distorts his researches, will be able to meet the demands that are made on him.

We are lacking any evidence that controlled social invention fares better in the Communist world, where the problems of power are felt more acutely by the authorities, and discoveries that are effective in altering the course of human history have to be severely scrutinized in terms of party policies. Isolated techniques of "brain washing," which are not the products of science but are the historical outcome of police methods in special Russian[14] and Chinese[15] contexts, can be identified, labeled, and propagated within the political system, but examination of their use does not justify the belief that they are the outcome of scientific research. The belief that they are, is based in part on the paranoia that is fed by the contemplation of unlimited power and in part on attempts made by American and Canadian human scientists to explore, scientifically, some of the consequences of pushing isolation techniques to the extreme.[16]

In the last forty years we have seen an enormous increase in the indiscriminate use of a great variety of methods of influencing human behavior. Where there is enough power, as in the Communist countries, or enough money, as in parts of the Western world, behavior can be influenced. Subjected in sufficient measure either to the threat of torture or its actuality or to continuous, unrelenting pressure, men retract their dearest beliefs and even embrace the beliefs of their enemies. Under sufficient, continuous pressure from their associates, the converts to a new religion or a new political ideology can keep themselves and each other on their toes, alert, guilty, or exalted. Bombarded day and night by billboard pictures, by the persuasive techniques of radio and television advertisements, the public learns the name of one brand rather than another and at the same time absorbs the message behind the message—that doctors are authorities, that advertisements and many other messages as well are to be treated with casual cynicism. Because the various techniques of mass and individual terror and persuasion have been developed in an era in which the capacity to threaten and blazon abroad has come into the hands of those who have large political or economic power, the techniques themselves have been confused with the technologies that serve them, and a kind of pseudo-scientific aura glows around them. Techniques of torture and confession that were well known at the time of the Spanish Inquisition are attributed to the researches of Pavlov,[17] and the successes of modern advertising are attributed to the findings of Freud.[18] On the whole, these are empty claims. Although tremendous advances in the human sciences have been made in the last hundred years, almost no advance has been made in their use, especially in ways of creating reliable new forms in which cultural evolution can be directed to desired goals.

Do we then face a dilemma somewhat like the one faced by those who wish to increase communication among men by inventing new and simpler languages? It is not difficult to invent special languages—languages that consist of partly specialized vocabularies or a whole logic or a system of mathematics—for the use of specialized groups; nor is it difficult to learn them. But the invention of a language that will include not only the highly specialized aspect of a formal discipline but also the whole personality of any human being has so far proved to be an intractable problem. The redundancy contributed by the speech of the stupid, the groping, the inarticulate, the wise, and the poetical, which makes a natural language a suitable vehicle for whole communication, is as intrinsic to a natural language as is the rigor, the narrow definition, and the absence of redundancy to mathematical and chemical formulas.[19] We can isolate, if we wish, one aspect of human behavior in the laboratory. We can seat ten engineering students around a specially built table and experiment with forms of intercommunication and their efficiency.[20]

Or we can invent "instruments," that is, controlled situations in which individuals are asked to react, and can draw inferences from the behavior under study. We can even measure the correspondence between the behavior style of an individual and the behavior style demanded by some position in a social structure for which the individual is being selected.[21] But we have no methods of assuring the kind of management structure that would make efficient use of the results of such testing, even in a small, highly controlled setting. In the same way, although we could specify fairly rigorously measurable characteristics that should exclude a man from consideration for public office, we have at present no way of using such criteria.

But considering this disappointing welter of experiences with projective tests, small group research, personality profiles, interview schedules, matching-choice techniques, subliminal advertising, and hypnotic techniques, and the hopes and fears that have gone into their invention, their use and misuse, it is possible to make a few clear statements. It is not now possible to simulate real situations in all their natural redundancy, with all the irrational and unacknowledged and unidentified elements present. If we want to know what Polish soldiers will do in a real situation, no amount of analyzing Polish culture and character and resynthesizing the analytical elements back into "the Polish soldier" will serve as well as the presence of an actual group of Polish soldiers.[22] If we want to turn into food an unappetizing brown paste, made according to nutritionally sound practices out of some high protein source, the simplest way of doing it is not by means of a complicated analysis of the food practices of various peoples, but by giving batches of the brown stuff to cooks of the appropriate nationality and letting them cook it.[23] Stated very simply, because of the intractability and complexity of most elements in the social processes of a real society, the more we can rely on already existing socially established behaviors in carrying out the experiments necessary for a new scientific insight, the better are our chances of success.

Consequently, each set of discoveries about human behavior must be regarded as an unstable and potentially explosive aggregate, destined for unsystematic and uncontrollable diffusion throughout a society or, today, the world. We may carry on basic scientific research into the nature of the patient–physician relationship,[24] the importance of the structure of a communications network,[25] the existence of invariant elements of style in an individual's interaction with others,[26] the effects of various types of error-free learning,[27] the regularities in the behavior of individuals reared in one culture,[28] the reliability of certain kinds of sampling of large populations,[29] but the more intensive our efforts to adapt the findings of such basic research to actual procedures suitable for real life situations, the greater the difficulty becomes. The transference situation, as a single aspect of an ambulatory patient's whole life, or the recommended diet in which every gram of protein is significant, or the small intimate conference in which everyone must observe certain rules for interlocking behavior[30]—each proves to have a precision requirement that leads to an attempt to form a group consisting of those who "understand" how to use the discovery. Faced with the danger that the original complex set of discoveries will be fragmented and misused or will be used in some harmful way, the little group of cultural innovators form a cult and, turning inward, relate more and more to each other and less and less to outsiders. As they depend on jargon and often on unexpressed and inexplicit assumptions, apprenticeship learning becomes more necessary. Each article of faith and each procedure, originally dictated by genuine scientific discovery, now, by virtue of this continual elaboration in a closed and unrealistic system, becomes less assimilable when it is diffused as a single item.

Vivid examples of the evils of this kind of diffusion can be found in the way certain items of psychoanalytically derived practice spread through American society in the 1920s. Freud's finding that childhood is a period of intense emotional response and that childhood responses are patterned and given form by the behavior of parental figures is a profoundly important one. But, half-understood, the translation of this finding into a recommendation that the whole family go self-consciously nude, or that the child be encouraged to eat dirt, or that all sensed impulses should be carried out at once, was a travesty on the actual discovery; more than this, the loosely floating ideas were dangerous and destructive.

Similarly, when a new course in mathematics or literature or biology, based on painstaking research and closely articulated so that one part is dependent on another,[31] is torn apart and the little pieces are injected into a more traditional course, this, too, may do harm rather than good. Even though pupils who are taught by the new methods may have made outstandingly superior records, other pupils, taught by an irresponsible mixture of old and new methods, may do less well than those who are traditionally trained. Conceived of as a whole, an inclusive new system of learning, progressive education disintegrated in practice into a loose assemblage of bits— seats that could be moved around, field trips, chumminess with a teacher, having fun in school (which is a very different thing from the conception of joy in self-directed learning). Diffused as bits and pieces, these ideas led to the destruction of the old system without the possibility of creating a new one, and in the 1950s each bit in turn became a target for attack and a ground for returning to an outmoded system.[32]

So far, no matter how soundly grounded in scientific research these socially relevant insights have been, no matter how great the need has been to incorporate them into ongoing human behavior, not one has survived except where some small interacting group of fully indoctrinated individuals has been formed into a miniature society with a localized "center." This is, in effect, the moral of a book like *Walden Two*.[33] Each new insight is so dependent on each other one in the creation of the whole that only in a closed institution—whether this is a school, a prison, a hospital, a ship, or an autonomous self-sufficient colony—can the desired new state of affairs be carried out.

For anyone who believes it is possible to apply our knowledge of how cultural evolution has occurred to the preservation of mankind and the facilitation of human well-being, the problem becomes one of establishing this possibility so that it can be effectively used by contemporary society, can stay alive, and can resist distortion. Each new idea is immediately transformed into the ethical problem of the form in which it should be communicated so that its effects will be least harmful and most useful.[34]

If evolutionary advances do in truth occur in face-to-face groups, in which the imagination of the most inordinately gifted is implemented by special kinds of interaction with others—those able to understand, criticize, resist, acquiesce, and execute the development of the idea or program or plan—then, obviously, a series of steps can be taken to create the conditions in which such groups can form.

Furthermore, if we are agreed that our contemporary

period and culture are favorable to great forward steps in social invention, as well as subject to great danger, and if we are agreed that the need is urgent, then any steps that can be taken to foster social inventions should be taken—and quickly.

It has often been informally proposed that we should have a series of Manhattan Projects in the social sciences, in each of which first-class minds, hopefully including one or two of genius caliber, will be gathered together to work on special tasks: how to end war, maintain peace, eradicate mental illness, keep the population of the world to a manageable size, and so on. If the unit of cultural evolution is a group of the kind that has been described, surely out of our thousands of highly talented and highly trained men and women we can construct clusters of individuals who, by working together on important problems, will come up with some inventions for solving the problems of peace. If such Manhattan Projects for Peace could not gain government support, surely foundation support could be found for these groups in which we could mobilize what we know and combine it with our best desires for mankind.

Unfortunately, the construction of a socially viable procedure, a procedure that will have an effect on world peace, is extraordinarily unlike the construction of an atom bomb. The Manhattan Project operated in secrecy; those who commissioned the group were those who would use the product if the group succeeded in its task; and the ultimate product was a piece of hardware.

None of these conditions would obtain in groups charged with the development of a next step in social organization. Secrecy in carrying out the tasks would have the effect of psychological warfare. The groups that backed the effort would not be the groups that would have to carry out the recommended solution. The more complexly interrelated the parts of the solutions that were developed, the less chance the solutions would have of surviving any kind of diffusion.

Yet it is essential that man's conscious participation in cultural evolution should begin not only under the impetus of the idea itself, as Julian Huxley has suggested,[35] but also in the form of social inventions suitable for stabilizing a highly vulnerable, worldwide intercommunicating system. Clearly, the simple creation of artificial clusters of gifted, highly trained, and experienced individuals, in an attempt to simulate the conditions under which evolution has occurred in the past, will not suffice. Since it will not, are there other steps?

13. An Evolutionary Focus for Thinking

IF A FIRST STEP in activating evolutionary thought is the creation of living intellectual networks which will be conducive to the formation of evolutionary clusters, then one may consider whether the kinds of problems around which such networks would be organized would not also, indirectly, assure the formation of clusters for their solution. At the present time in the Middle East, for example, archaeologists who are working on the past and technicians who are attempting to solve contemporary problems are likely to have relatively little contact with one another. The findings of archaeologists, derived from industriously sorted potsherds and beads and laboriously excavated ruins, are more likely to be communicated to other archaeologists working on comparable problems in other parts of the world than to technicians who are attempting to make the desert bloom again and are not immediately concerned with questions of time depth. Instead of emphasizing this kind of lateral, intragroup communication, it would be possible to combine the several kinds of investigation that are being pursued concurrently in order to facilitate the solution of problems with which the different disciplines are concerned. By considering together the problems resulting from the drenching and souring of the small oases of arable land in Saudi Arabia, the lessons to be learned from man-created deserts, the best methods of measuring the age of water found in aquifers, and the most economical methods of distilling salt water to produce fresh water, a greater impetus would be given each investigator to use the technical resources of the others and to contribute his own skills to the combined results.[1]

But there may be even more explicit ways in which the focus of intellectual activity may be related to evolution. In order to consider what these may be, one apposite question would be the following: *Do we have at present any means, means that involve no new complex inventions, for diffusing and so safeguarding the evolutionary gains mankind has already made?*

Ever since the nineteenth-century prophets of doom began to envisage types of warfare that could wipe out civilization, there has been a burgeoning of the "sealed casket" fantasy of protecting the most precious and crucial products of civilization. The fantasy has taken a variety of forms, the simplest of which is the deposition, deep underground, of complete records of our most complex achievements so they can be replicated by other men in some postdisaster period. In another form, it has involved the careful selection of a small group of living men who carry the crucial knowledge of civilization in their own heads; packed off, complete with model instruments, logarithmic tables, blueprints, Shakespeare, and the Bible, this group would have the responsibility of preserving the laboriously built and possibly unique construct we call civilization, which for thousands of years has enabled successive generations to begin where their predecessors left off. Given the conditions of modern warfare, the fear that "civilization" might be wiped out has been transformed into a fear that all men on the planet might be wiped out; correspondingly, the sealed casket fantasy has been transformed into a fantasy involving the launching of space colonies. So defined, the image of the space colony as an instrument of wider exploration is lost, and an acceptance

of the need for a constricted, man-made world to preserve "all that is left" involves an acceptance of catastrophe
which breeds its own antidotes of apathy and indifference.
In this context, then, we may expect that the establishment of space colonies adequate to preserve the traditions
of human civilization will proceed only very slowly.

For the present, however, there appears to be a greater
risk that all civilization will be destroyed than that all
mankind will be destroyed. Placing their faith in man's
marvelously intricate brain, biologists are cheered by the
probability that even after a catastrophic war, representatives of *Homo sapiens* would survive in very remote
parts of the earth, far from major explosions or centers of
diffusion of biochemical warfare, on islands, in inaccessible
jungles, in deep, secluded valleys.[2] And there, in some
fashion, civilization would begin again. Many anthropologists are less sanguine, for in their work among primitive
peoples they have seen how men with brains fully as good
as our best have been hopelessly limited by the level of
their culture and the lack of any of the conditions through
which change can be brought about.

The basic human repertoire—language, the family,
simple tools, art, some cosmological system, methods of
subsistence and cultural transmission, rudimentary forms
of group organization—this would endure. No matter
which group of existing representatives of *Homo sapiens*
survived, these basic inventions would endure because,
in some form, all of them are common to all mankind
today. But as yet we have no grounds for believing that
any small human society would *necessarily* take the steps
that would in time lead on to what we call civilization.
Given a combination of conditions such as the improved
use of land, ideas about the division of labor, and a population that is both fairly dense and fairly diversified, so
that diversification of response is assured, it is easy to

demonstrate that certain trends are already set which quite probably would culminate in a more or less viable form of civilization with some kind of script for record keeping, political devices suitable for the organization of large units, complex forms of economic exchange, and the possibilities of an improved technology.

But the conditions that can lead to such increases in the density of population may be absent. Even where they are present—as in the highlands of New Guinea, where much larger, intercommunicating groups could survive on the available land and with the existing technology—the political institutions necessary for the effective integration of larger groups may be absent.[3] So, too, specialization in one aspect of a culture may affect development in other aspects. The aboriginal inhabitants of Australia and Tasmania gradually multiplied and occupied more of the continent, but their preoccupation with incest taboos and with the biological differences between the sexes and between the old and the young led to a kind of circular elaboration of ideas in which they became trapped.[4] Similarly, the Eskimo, for all their recurrently demonstrated ability to recognize the complex, made very selective use of European technology to elaborate their basic culture rather than making use of the new possibilities to take evolutionary steps.[5] In West Africa,[6] complex political structures were built up without the use of writing (even though, through trade relations, the idea of script for record-keeping was available), with consequent limitations on further development. In North Africa[7] and in Melanesia,[8] the hypertrophy of trade relations was a condition that was unfavorable to political integration.

When we look at the whole range of human cultures and follow out the types of multilinear evolution that have been traced by Steward, Sahlins, and Service[9] in their analyses, the evolutionary potentialities of human culture seem very high indeed. So, also, when we follow out the cultural development that has occurred in some one part of the world over a relatively long period of time, as Karl Wittfogel has done in his studies of "hydraulic" cultures,[10] the rather monotonous potentiality for civilizations to develop in one direction is striking. But if we begin at an earlier stage and follow out the steps from food gathering to horticulture and from horticulture to the domestication of animals, these steps seem far less determined and much more precarious. The lower in the scale of cultural evolution we go—and this means reliance on the more widespread aspects of early culture—the greater is the possibility that a culture will be caught in a blind alley, as when a people become preoccupied by obsessive ritual, or find a stop-gap solution to the food problem, or build in a politically limiting institution like headhunting.

Keeping these things in mind, the task of preserving mankind's evolutionary gains in the face of possible catastrophe depends on our ability to answer two basic questions: First, how can we preserve large enough groups of human beings to be certain that our biological heritage will be protected? How large a group this would have to be is a problem that must be solved by geneticists and demographers. And second, how can we preserve our existing cultural gains, the product of thousands of years of human inventiveness and creativity, so that, in any catastrophe which was not complete, the surviving members of the human species would *not* have to begin all over again?

For it must be recognized that a surviving group could not, in fact, "begin all over again" in the same way. The earth on which they would have to build a new technology has been almost stripped of many of its more readily utilizable resources, and the minds of men would be shadowed by the memory of almost total disaster. This might in time be muted to the dimensions of the Biblical account of the Flood—but with a difference. For, in the recent past, a greater knowledge of the natural world permitted men to free their imagination from the implications of a literal "flood," but in the future, greater knowledge would eventually force upon men some recognition of a man-made catastrophe.

Clearly, we cannot leave to chance the possibility that mankind would once more travel the long road to civilization; nor need we do so. But when we consider the question of how we can assure that as long as there are living groups of human beings on earth they will be the heritors of a viable civilization, we can see that the answer does not lie in the endless elaboration of peaks of scientific endeavor alone. Rather, it lies in the invention of devices for the most rapid and thorough dissemination of the basic inventions of civilization on which the survivors of a world disaster would be able to build anew. To accomplish this will be a scientific task of no mean dimensions, but it is one to which effort and funds and government support can be directed without rousing the deep opposition that makes it so difficult to bring about intentional, scientifically based social change in a modern society.

Such a task would have a twofold purpose. There is first the necessity of ensuring that all the peoples of the world are equipped to carry on cultural evolution—that no disaster shall be so great as to destroy mankind's ability to create viable cultures through which cultural evolution will be furthered. And second, there is the necessity of ensuring that all the peoples of the world are equipped to participate in the further development of the civilization we cherish. In both its purposes, this task is inevitably directed toward the same populations—those peoples who, because they live farthest from modern industrial centers, participate least in twentieth-century culture and who, by the same token, would be most likely to survive an almost worldwide nuclear holocaust. In addition, because they are farther removed from the lines of intellectual development that have finally merged in the formation of the modern world, they are also our best possible sources of new variations.

At present, however, these peoples living on the fringes of civilization—on islands, high in mountain ranges, on deserts, and in jungles—are poor and doubtful custodians of any future we would care to hope for. Their present chances of participation in and contribution to ongoing civilization are also very poor. Many of them live in groups so small that there is slight real hope of finding a genius among them. Yet if highly trained and gifted members of higher civilizations could be persuaded to work on the problem, the contributions which a small band could not otherwise make might nevertheless be channeled into our knowledge of man's diverse possibilities.

The most immediate task would be to work out a set of preconditions for the highest development of civilization, based on our knowledge of both the ancient and the modern world. This then could be systematically diffused to the alert and eager primitive and peasant populations of the world, recognizing that the steps by which men acquire knowledge now need not be those about which we know historically, as in the past men laboriously invented the ideas of script, number, the arch and the wheel, the lever and the loom. (The Manus, because of such apparently unrelated behavior as the parental insistence that a child take full moral responsibility for his physical acts, had no difficulty in accepting, understanding, and using machines.[11]) However fructifying pictographs and magical symbols may once have been, these would not

need to be diffused so that nonliterate peoples might experiment with them; rather, we would diffuse the idea
of what writing is and how records are kept. Nor would
a people linger at a "manuscript stage" of writing books;
knowledge of how books are produced would be more
important. The idea of the wheel, so basic and yet missing
from the New World and many remote areas, could be
diffused through toys and small tools in which the wheel
principle was so explicit that it could not be lost.[12]
Ideas of number and measurement could be cast in forms
that could be readily disseminated, that would be likely
to survive under primitive conditions, and that would be
capable of generating anew the great systems we now have
at our command.

Such an effort can be phrased, as Evelyn Hutchinson
has suggested to me,[13] as lowering the entropy of the whole
system in the interests of survival; but it need not be
regarded merely as a precautionary measure. The problem
of analyzing the essential forms of our present civilization is one that would necessarily involve our most highly
trained minds, and the task of adapting these essential
forms to the capacities of the most primitive, isolated, and
traumatized peoples would in itself provide a center of
evolutionary endeavor in our own society. The task would
have to be carried out by clusters of men and women with
fertile and imaginative minds, different kinds of compe-
tency and experience, drawn from the humanities as well
as from the physical, biological, and social sciences, working in cooperative situations, including field stations in
various parts of the world.

The problems that must be solved are fundamentally
technical, and therefore they are amenable to solution.
One such problem might be concerned with music. If one
wished to preserve and diffuse, in some embryo form, the
great musical styles of the past and present, what in the

way of musical knowledge would have to be diffused, and in what instruments would that knowledge have to be embodied for worldwide diffusion and ultimate survival? (One possible answer is suggested by the work in glotto-chronology[14] and the research now being done by Alan Lomax:[15] the most conservative musical form is the lullaby that is sung generation after generation.) Or, to take another basic problem, what ideas would one have to introduce about nutrition, and in what forms, in order to lay the groundwork for eventual questioning and testing of a traditional diet? Or, what are essential ways of looking at the universe—fixed directions, a calendar geared to celestial bodies, the idea of space–time? How could the rudiments of hierarchical forms of social organization, necessary for all large undertakings, be condensed so as to be available to all peoples? In this case, the answer may in part be contained in something as simple as a graduated adjectival form, including a superlative.

Discussion of such an enterprise serves several useful purposes. First, the problem of how we are to assure the continuity of civilization is one to which we must give serious attention. Second, we need to bring the contributions of all peoples into the world stream of civilization. And third, it is vitally necessary for us to find the means of creating the evolutionary clusters for which problems like these provide a focus. Let me, for a moment, analyze what a project of this kind would entail.

To strip down a whole complex—geometry, or nutrition, or mechanics, or representative government, or the metric system, or currency and banking, or Pavlovian learning theory, or metric poetry, or genetics, or photography—to a condensed precursor or prefigurative form would require not only the play of highly imaginative minds from many fields but also, necessarily, cooperation with other highly imaginative minds. Furthermore, elucidation of a problem of this kind would be sufficiently difficult and unusual that it would not be enough for a participant to be a practicing poet or a trained psychologist. It would be necessary to acquire concrete material on actual learning experiences and attempts to teach certain kinds of things to the uneducated, the poorly educated, and the preliterate. So, also, it would be necessary to analyze the ways in which ideas are dependably embodied in different aspects of living—house forms or tools, seating plans or ways of treating the dead—in many parts of the world. Those who were working conjointly on such a problem would have to see and hear, touch and taste, walk among and upon the same things, so they would be sensitized, systematically, to one another's responses. By facilitating communication at every level, from the most abstract to the most concrete and multidimensional, the thinking of such a group would take on some of the mastery that is now found in a single mind with the added gain of diversity and the advantage of rapid, structured criticism and elaboration of each idea.

The task set would involve the deep commitment of those highly endowed individuals who value the miracle of man's progress on earth, a miracle that enlists our deepening wonder the more we know of the infinitely large and the infinitely small. As our increasing knowledge makes it possible for us to set side by side galaxies and genes (as Beadle did in his presidential address to the American Association for the Advancement of Science[16]), the place of man in such a system is neither reduced nor demeaned, as some men have felt who have kept their eyes trained on the telescope or the microscope but have failed to look at man himself; rather, it becomes steadily more awe-inspiring. The evolution of a creature who is finally able to comprehend the system out of which he has emerged to consciousness (whether

we see consciousness as finally folding back on itself in
an Omega state or as enduring the extreme tension of facing unimaginable vistas) is miraculous if it is unique—
but perhaps more miraculous if it is not unique. The
preservation of this miracle can be as demanding of our
commitment as is, among various peoples of the world,
the imperative to preserve wife and child, fellow tribes-
man and territory, nation–state, or wider-spread religion.
The very sentences we learned in school provide us with
a phrase for the expansion of our commitment: that human civilization and the human species "shall not perish
from the earth."

14. Ongoing Social Forms

WHAT OTHER CONSIDERATIONS are important in looking at the role of the human sciences in cultural evolution? I have discussed some of the attempts made in the last hundred years to develop viable forms of application of research on human behavior to the welfare of human beings and the improvement of society. Where the research has been conducted in isolation from other disciplines and from the ongoing human scene in which it can be applied, it has tended to be too self-contained, and the possible applications—expressed in rules of human behavior rather than through artifacts—have been too intricate to be preserved intact. The invention, however sound, has proved to be incapable of diffusion except by cult formation, which has limited usefulness as a method, or by fragmentation. If neither cult formation nor initial intricacy and ultimate fragmentation can provide us with the necessary means, are there other contemporary cultural practices that are better suited to the purpose?

Let me reiterate that the simplest method of ensuring acceptance of a change is to embody it (at least in part) in some ongoing social form. The hazards are, of course, great.[1] The cooks who are given a new synthetic or dehydrated food may invent new and palatable dishes that fit into the accepted style of a people's food habits; but in doing so they may ignore an instruction that was designed to ensure the use of boiled water or long enough cooking to destroy harmful bacteria. The nursery attendants who are carrying out a plan to give babies greater freedom of movement, as part of a Soviet government campaign against swaddling, may nevertheless cut holes in the middle of the nursery tables and seat the babies in them.[2] Ongoing social forms have their own inherent intractabilities.

The experience of the last twenty-five years has taught us the futility of launching a new cultural invention without forethought as to the hazards it will encounter. An attempt of this kind is likely to be as ineffective as would be the launching of a small boat laden with synthetic food, oarless and rudderless, in rough waters off a rocky coast. The boat itself would be battered to pieces, its broken planks would float ashore as driftwood, and the freight would be eaten by various unspecifiable fish. Every new, purely social invention needs developmental care, whether the invention is a set of originally good ideas for improving communication with a large audience,[3] a method of training apprentices through socially replicating situations,[4] or a way of reactivating the pleasant and once articulate memories of a disjointed group of immigrants.[5] This is true even in those cases in which the invention finds expression not in a set of rules but in some object which seems to be more foolproof.

When the loudspeaker for platform use was invented, a new and terrible advantage was given to the speaker, the more frightening because it could be used not only in churches, where religious sanctions had raised the authority as well as the pulpit platform of the preacher far above the layman's power to answer him, but also in meetings, where hitherto the man on the floor not only could but did reply to the man on the podium. With the invention of the floor microphone, some measure of freedom was restored to those in the audience, but experience has shown that while the floor microphone increases the possibility of discussion it does not of itself ensure freedom of reply from the floor. It is still necessary to supervise the placement of the microphone where it can be used, to make certain that the members of the audience know how to signal their desire to speak, and to provide opportunities for them to get to the microphone—or to get the microphone to them—when they wish to speak.

The one-way vision screen used in nursery schools, psychological testing rooms, and mental hospitals for teaching parents, students, and medical residents can be an effective instrument for protecting the integrity of the experience that is under observation or, on the contrary, it can be a means of aggravating the anxiety of those who are observed and of hardening the insensitivity of the observers.[6] If the individual under observation is told in an uncomplicated way that there are people behind the screen, he will ignore the screen and their presence behind it most of the time, and the screen will fulfill its purpose.[7] But the mere existence of the screen does not determine its use. It can give extra protection to a small frightened child, who need not be brought before strange adults in a crowded staff meeting room. Or it can be an extra violation of human dignity, when an applicant for a professional position is brought into a rigged waiting room and is put under unacknowledged observation.

Even when a new invention in material form has been designed with certain expected human behavior in mind, such as a new kind of outpatient clinic into which the architect has built a desired type of patient–nurse–doctor relationship, it has been found necessary for the planning unit to retain supervisory rights until the new form has been incorporated in the way intended into the habits of the professional group, who can then embody it and transmit the relevant behavior to others.[8]

So while the embodiment of a new cultural invention

in a specific object—a floor microphone, a one-way vision screen, a special form of recovery room, a teaching machine, a panel-shaped table, a system of simultaneous interpretation, a two-way closed television circuit, a projector with capsule loading so that a teacher can use film easily, a plastic feeding bottle that permits a child to move about as it drinks—provides for new possibilities, only responsible and cherishing vigilance can prevent the patterns of behavior which the new invention was designed to alter from being reinstated because they are supported by so many other aspects of the behavior of the users. This objection is, of course, the case for a complete transformation from an old to a new pattern. But transformation is feasible only under the special conditions of a change of level in a society, a move from country to city, a total change of occupation, and so on.[9] Our more common model of change must be the introduction of new methods of teaching and learning and intercommunicating, healing and helping, predicting and preventing, into ongoing systems.

In making a cultural innovation, then, the first question one must ask is whether there is an existing form that can be used with some slight modification or whether some radical new invention must be made. This is itself an ordinary form of mildly innovative behavior. When the nation faces an emergency, those who are preparing to take action look over the available repertoire of special emergency committees, commissions, congresses, local branches, and so on. Experiments of various sorts are made, and then either the effort dies or someone hits on a workable formula capable of enlisting sufficient backing in the national community, such as the vast, interlocking complex of commissions, and so on, concerned with getting food to Europe during and after World War I, held together largely by the efforts and experience of Herbert

Hoover,[10] or the Committee to Defend America by Aiding the Allies, in World War II.[11] These are natural-history examples of our task, as we attempt to find ways of facilitating creative evolutionary change without inventing formulas that are so intricate that they must be protected by cult rules to prevent their rapid fragmentation.[12]

Returning to the search for existing forms in which the cultivation of evolutionary clusters can be pursued, there is, in addition to the Manhattan Project and its many offspring, a large number of activities that can provide gifted individuals of different kinds with an optimum climate for the development of their special talent or genius. There are, for example, a great many interdisciplinary projects, developed within the grant-giving limitations and interests of special agencies, which permit or require cooperation among members of an institution who formerly did not interact with one another. For a project of this kind, it is usually necessary to import some scientific personnel from elsewhere—a psychologist or a sociologist who is selected because he is available at the salary offered and by training should be the kind of person who will contribute to the enterprise. But the general aridity of this project approach, with its initial emphasis on possible sources of funds to have a project *with* and research that ignores most of the characteristics of the people who work together, has been amply documented.[13] A group aggregated to carry out research because a grant-giving agency has a program,[14] some individual scientist is ambitious, and other scientists, needed technically, are hired primarily for their formal training, only by accident ever becomes a locus of creative activity. The mushrooming of research projects around the world, following the American grant-giving pattern, undoubtedly has had the effect of providing additional training for many individuals, but as a design for productive group activity the interdisciplinary research project seems to lack the potential necessary for participation in the evolutionary process.

Another possibility is the institute to which individuals of some distinction are invited, which provides them with opportunities to work on projects in which they are interested in association with others like themselves. In a setting of this kind, the crucial element seems to be freedom, or its lack. If the underlying intention of the institute's program is to bring together certain *disciplines,* rather than to nurture the talents of particular *individuals,* the process seems to lead to failure—to the building of more useless fences than those it was hoped such a program might break down. The Yale University Institute of Human Relations is a case in point.[15]

Another possibility is the residential setting in which gifted people are brought together without commitment to produce anything specific. Individually or in groups, persons of demonstrated high research ability are asked to come and live for a given period of time on a university campus or, as in the most notable experiment of the kind, at a special center like the Center for Advanced Study in the Behavioral Sciences.[16] At the outset a plan of this kind may have an aura of spontaneity. The individual who is invited to come is asked when he would like to come, with whom he would like to work. Seniors may select young people with whom they would like to work, and juniors also may select seniors with whom they would like to engage in long, fruitful conversations. But over time the plan tends to become more formal. The choice of one individual by another becomes suspect; it is merely a way of getting one's own work done. Applicants are selected not for the originality of their thought but on the basis of their current status. Such an institution, organized in a burst of spontaneous enthusiasm as a place where hungry minds really will be fed on the heavenly manna of good conversation, is likely in time to settle down in more formal and conventional patterns.

Still another arrangement for bringing together good minds is the interdisciplinary seminar. One example of this is the set of interlocking University Seminars, originated by Frank Tannenbaum at Columbia University, some of which have been in continuous existence since 1945.[17] In running seminars of this kind, individual members of a university faculty, faculty members from other nearby institutions, and other suitable individuals, brought together by invitation, form a group who meet regularly, sometimes for many years, sometimes working on a special problem, sometimes merely exchanging ideas evoked by a single presentation. Such seminars are a new invention for shaking up the members of a large university faculty. They give an opportunity for people to meet who otherwise might not come to know each other, and sometimes students are permitted to participate. Most important, perhaps, the University Seminars provide a physical setting in time and place where people can be sure of coming together.

A variant of this invention, before these valuable sequences of meetings were arbitrarily discontinued, was the conference series organized under the sponsorship of the Josiah Macy, Jr. Foundation. Each one was a convocation of fertile minds, interested in a subject from many angles, who met once a year, two or three days at a time, over a five-year period to discuss many facets of a many-faceted problem. The focus could be a very general one, for example, Problems of Consciousness.[18] For a conference of this kind it was not necessary to take the precautions that are mandatory when one is inviting an individual to become a resident in an institution or when one is inviting a colleague from another department to join a group. Participants in the conferences were asked to drop their jargon and to avoid the use of special technical languages that had gone beyond jargon—to translate what they had to say into English. The style of discourse, in which interruption was almost mandatory, encouraged flights of imagination, small precise insights, and the formation of permanent friendships between people, widely separated in space, whose characters were complementary to each other. Those who became adept in the conference technique were likely to be invited to become part of some other conference. Special guests moved freely in—and out if the setting was uncongenial. The conferences took place in pleasant quarters. No one was paid anything beyond his expenses, but everyone assumed the onerous and time-consuming obligation to edit his own contribution and send it back for publication. This meant that there was a geometrical relationship between the amount an individual contributed to a conference and the amount of work he had to do afterward. The morose and uncommunicative, who, while they sat through a conference, took but did not give, were sent a great green transcript, obstreperously demanding and too large for any file, which required very little work of them. Those who intervened frequently had the additional task, later, of fitting the stenotypists' version of what they had half-said —when context, expressive hands, and free-floating images provided meaning—into some sensible form that would not distort the equally-to-be-edited next remark. The published transactions of the Macy conferences provide one of the closest approximations of an account of creative intellectual conversation that, with all our paraphernalia of tape recording and stenotyping, we have yet been able to produce.

A formula distilled from these experiences would come to something like this: A conference would provide a guaranteed opportunity to meet some vividly first-class people in a noncompetitive and intense atmosphere. The conversation would come to an end and would be resumed. There would be freedom to talk and freedom to listen, and the web of meaning would be woven as we talked, making a new pattern before our eyes. No one would be paid, and there would be no permanent commitment. Those who could not continue would be free to drop out, without guilt. The more one gave, the more would be asked of one. A larger number of experienced people would develop the ability to talk with other scientists in a given style, and as the formidable barriers in the styles of discourse of different European countries and different disciplines dropped away, individuals would develop a capacity for finely modulated communication in which their minds really worked together. The very temporary nature of these contacts—three days, with the interchange ending almost in the middle of a sentence—was essential to the pattern.[19]

Out of this fluid meeting, talking, and parting—now under the formal heading of Cybernetics and now under the formal heading of Problems of Consciousness, sometimes in the setting of a Macy conference and sometimes at a conference that is similar in style but takes place in a different setting[20]—one can sometimes see emerging something that is more than an idea in one man's mind (though the margins of the scratch pads may turn into so many frames for new insights) and more than the sudden recognition by two minds that their style of thinking is parallel or complementary. In a group of four or five it is sometimes possible to see, as it is happening, the formation of a new and potentially stable cluster of individuals— individuals who now can speak together with tremendous speed, for whom sentences no longer need to be finished, whose conversation gives shape to ideas that do not grow separately in each single mind but, instead, grow simultaneously in every mind and in the conversation going on among the speakers.

For such an emergent cluster no precise formula can be written. The only possible formulation is a delimitation of the conditions within which clusters of this kind can come into being. The existence of these conditions, or the hope that they may exist, is the reason why high civilization flourishes in cities, however far the latter-day beneficiaries of civilization may flee into the suburbs at night. In a city, especially a city in which there is provision for many kinds of people to meet in clubs and cafés, in theaters or at the opera, the gifted are drawn together by no master plan, but they move toward one another as inevitably as moths toward light.

The cry of loneliness that goes up from human scientists almost everywhere in the Free World is not the cry of starving men but of men with an insatiable taste for the kind of contact they have experienced at conferences, on expert committees, in study groups, in consultant groups, or on the boards of scientific societies. All of these settings—if the people who take part in them are good enough—provide occasions for meeting with others whose work is developing, whose ideas are germinating and growing, not yet clipped and shaped by the hard lattices of customary styles of publication. Unfinished work, work not yet begun, the first glimmer of a new hypothesis, the picture for which only a sketch has been made, the poem that is a tantalizing image, an opening rhythm in the poet's mind, the unexpected side result of an experiment no one as yet understands—it is all this which creates a nexus of thought and imagination. It is here that new ideas are somehow born, like culture itself, not by direct physical transmission but by a process of diffusion and original invention from the contributions gifted minds can make only when the setting is right.

15. Possible Forms of Centers with an Evolutionary Potential

IF WE ARE indeed to participate in evolution not merely by creating new technology, new medical techniques, new kinds of foods, and new forms of communication, but more specifically by participating in the very process of culture creation, what hope does our accumulated experience of the last thirty years give us?

I have shown how important scientific insights, too fully elaborated, have to be wrapped in cult precautions if they are not to fragment destructively as they become part of the climate of opinion, now so volatile in response to the mass media. I have also considered the conscious creations of certain innovative groups which have been charged with finding solutions to the problems facing the world, and I have reviewed some of the difficulties faced by such groups as they must, in most instances, report to a part of the world which did not help establish them and is not equipped to use their findings. Established by those with power, groups of this kind become absorbed in the power struggle. Established by those without power, their battle to gain acceptance turns into another attempt to propagate a cult or else results in the dispersion of still more free-floating fragments. This in turn increases the confusion and the likelihood that a puzzled public will turn in self-defense to a know-nothing philosophy.

Analysis of the past suggests that the combination of an atmosphere of freedom and choice and a setting in which spontaneous and wholly voluntary commitments can be made provides the conditions within which intellectual friendships and clusters form from which we may expect ideas of evolutionary significance to emerge. At present, however, there is a paradoxical relationship between the freedom of choice of ideas, the type of contribution, the length and fullness of one's participation, and the intellectual excitement that can be generated. A group of individuals may work very well together, but if they are then confined within the walls of an institution in which administrative lines harden or if they are organized to carry out a project from which scientifically respectable rather than world-shaking results are expected, the outcome of their efforts will not be the same.

I find myself returning to the model of the city or the great university in a city and to the model of the meeting place to which certain people go often enough so they may hope to meet one another but not so often that the element of surprise and excitement is lacking.[1] In the modern American setting, seminars and small shared projects (provided these do not become a new set of confining walls within which development is subordinated to the timely completion of the project) replace the cafés and coffee houses that we have never been able to reproduce. The single university, by itself, does not seem to provide the necessary kind of nearness *and* distance *and* choice. It may be too small; then the same people meet too often, aimlessly or routinely. It may be too large; then, thinking they can always meet tomorrow, people never meet today, or else at every meeting there are too many people. In a university, also, the isolated musician or artist who is expected to give sustenance to his more academic colleagues is himself cut off from long, free communication with other musicians and painters.

A cluster of institutions like the Menninger Foundation

and its associates in Topeka, Kansas, comes closer to the kind of setting in which new ideas come easily.[2] Here, in a city which is also the state capital, are two large private clinics, one for adults and one for children, to which come the privileged and the rich. Here also are a great veterans' hospital, a state hospital, a state treatment center for children, an industrial school for boys, and a rehabilitation center for the blind. There is a small university interested in the arts, a large air base with its complement of professional people, and a community theater. There are teachers, lawyers, and other professional men and women, and the institutions necessary to keep such a complex group going. The city is large enough so that it is not a mere appendage of the institutions in and around it, and it is small enough so that people meet frequently in different combinations.

The cluster of institutions is directed toward definite purposes—care, therapy, education—and it has a central focus of work within a growing body of theory and practice so closely joined that it is almost impossible to distinguish them. It is open to the outside world. Each July a class of residents, who have taken their training all over the city, leave for other parts of the United States and other regions of the world, South America, the Near East, and the Far East, and a new class enters. Senior people move from one institution to another, or leave after many years. New senior people come, often from Europe. Dotted over the campus of the several institutions are small rooms where coffee is served at more or less fixed hours, and here, with the breath-taking speed that is so characteristic of American life, plans are hatched, ideas are briefly challenged, a reference to some remote work is given and received. "I didn't quite understand what you meant the other day; can you give me a reference?" Later there arrives a large envelope on both sides of which are imprinted little boxes saying *To* and *From,* already half filled with names, so that one has a sense of being part of a network of communication; inside is a book or a paper, a written reference, a paragraph on the idea, the first draft of a paper, or a note to ask someone else who will know more.

Sometimes, of course, the project style seizes on some part of this network. It may happen then that those who are committed neither to the development of theory nor to therapy but to work on some grant may find themselves temporarily imprisoned by its artificial limits, and so walled off from their fellows. But this is rare. The urgency of the tasks—caring for the very ill and training young men and women who have already given many years to preparation for their work—and the excitement that comes from continual interaction of theory with practice keep a high flame burning, a higher flame than can be produced simply by the resources of a city in which the same number of institutions (or many more) exist without a real pattern of interrelationships.[3]

Every day, in Topeka, bulletins appear in each of the large institutions, in which, in addition to the announcements of strictly intramural affairs, there are announcements of what is going on elsewhere, in other parts of the city or the state, the nation or the world. Announcements are made of meetings that draw together the members of one profession for an intensive discussion or of staff meetings that bring together members of many disciplines; other announcements herald the arrival of out-of-town visitors, who usually come both to teach and to learn; still others mention those who have gone away to attend conferences elsewhere, and those who are consulting, traveling in India or Israel, talking with state and national agencies, examining some rare clinical case, or giving a paper to a small group in some tiny college. In the central auditorium there is an intercommunication system so that the staffs of remote state hospitals may listen in and participate by asking questions during the question period after a lecture. Extensions of this system also make it possible for those in other institutions to take an hour to listen to a lecture without using up a valuable hour driving to the auditorium.

Those who easily see how a change of pattern on the wings of drosophila[4] represents the process of evolution and who greet a change in the pigmentation of a moth in industrial England as a marvel of adaptation[5] nevertheless find it hard to see the small, potentially decisive changes in our accustomed institutions which contain the ingredients of retrogression or advancement. The overt evidence often is no easier to see than the darkened moth against the smoke-darkened tree trunk, and the innovation may be an alteration in the patterning of many small familiar bits, each a part of the known scene. Taken piece by piece, there is not one startling or revolutionary feature about the Menninger School of Psychiatry. It is the unique combination that matters.

In other cities, residents work in associated institutions, seminars are held, reading groups are organized, research goes on, patients are admitted and treated, certain of the staff and the residents are "in analysis," analysts meet at late parties, visitors are invited to come to lecture and to learn. Where such a structure is presided over by an imaginative focusing figure and the group is small enough, a close coherent body of people is formed, rather like an extended family—an extended family with many purposes and an immense diversity of resources. Where the structure is good, it is an extended family that has the potential for growth of a single family. The young are well nourished and are sent forth. The life of the elders is renewed because there are new young. Such an institution is the

the University of Cincinnati Department of Psychiatry.[6] Where in a *zadruga* of the Balkans it was the annual clearing of the land and the care of the crops and the cattle that kept the group focused,[7] here it is the education of the young and the care of the patients that does so. Institutions like these, feeding on their own diversified resources, have this potential of growth.

The Merrill–Palmer Institute in Detroit, another unique institution, housed in a cluster of old buildings, provides us with a related model.[8] The overarching purpose of the school, the training of undergraduate and foreign students in child development and home economics, has brought into being a set of activities designed both to train and to provide research materials that are reabsorbed into the program, enriching the understanding of teachers and students. Among these activities are a well-baby clinic which provides a focal point for studies of growth, a nursery school which has been deeply influential in the development of nursery school practice in the United States, a nutrition clinic, after-school groups, and a camp in which the further development of the nursery-school children can be followed out, and a marriage-counseling service to which former nursery-school children, now grown up and the parents of a new generation, can come for advice. Here, as in Topeka and in Cincinnati, provision is made for small conferences, for visitors from abroad. Here also research is carried out, partly as an ongoing process and partly piecemeal, with the sometimes stultifying support of special grants. The first nursery-school children now belong to the grandparental generation, and the school, now seventy-five years old, has played an important intellectual role in Detroit, as one program after another has been inaugurated within its walls. Its only limitation is that it is somewhat too small and too concentrated in its program. The personality of the director is crucial, and the individual members of the staff must form a very tightly interlocking group. Even though the man who is currently studying growth can make little of the viewpoint of the current psychologist, he must nevertheless sit and discuss his project with him. Moreover, the general atmosphere of human responsibility generated by a program centered around the care of young children and young students casts a protective mantle over any intellectual deficiencies of the staff. Occasionally there are not enough senior students, genuine graduate students with minds capable of challenging a staff many of whom grow somnolent with the years, nor is there in general enough active, diversified participation with other institutions in Detroit. But from Merrill–Palmer have come many innovations in the practices affecting the teaching and care of young children, in the introduction of these new child-care practices into new countries. Innovations in practice, however, have not been equally matched by research contributions, mainly because the professional staff is too small.

Descriptions of experiments like these can be multiplied, but not manyfold. Yet the experience we have gained from them should make it possible for us to design settings for new evolutionary clusters. Though it would be an interesting experiment to build at least one institutional cluster from the ground up, it is not necessary to create entirely new institutions. Any city having a number of institutions devoted to higher education, medicine, and the arts would be suitable as a setting in which a group of institutions, isolated from each other, each too small, too compartmentalized, too partial to be effective as a single unit, could be transformed into a living network of change.[9] With one proviso—it cannot be a city that is basically dependent on these institutions for vitality or its very existence; it must be a city that has a life of its own, diversified, complex, changing.

The overall plan must involve several diversified institutions. Among them there must be some in which change of membership is inevitable—because there are graduate students and fellows, shifting residencies, short-term undertakings, and so on. The intellectual life of the community must be free in the sense that each member of it earns his daily bread by teaching, therapy, technical work in long-term research that is part of the ongoing purpose of an institution, by writing novels or producing plays, by editing or illustrating new work. The membership will then have many bases and will be bound to the vicissitudes of many different institutions, so that the whole will have a flexibility that will protect it against a single disaster, and the enterprise will be proof against the efforts of any one individual to wreck it—a precaution we are just beginning to recognize as a desperate necessity.

A connective living network must of course have some central purpose, some reason why students are exchanged, lectures are given cooperatively, intercommunication systems are put into operation, some reason why it is important for people on the different campuses and institutional grounds to know who is in town, for what purpose, and what is happening here and there. Experience suggests that a network of this kind is kept alive by having human beings with recurrent needs at its center—infants, school children, patients, graduate students, senior technical people from other countries who must learn a great deal in a limited time. It is also possible for people from many institutions to focus their work on the problems of a small growing community, on urban rehabilitation, or on the internal difficulties of old and new industries, but programs of this kind are less manageable. At most, urban renewal occurs once in a generation, and once the task has been accomplished the small clusters of interested, innovative people must go farther afield and are likely to be dispersed. Should technical assistance to underdeveloped countries become a focus of attention, field stations abroad would have to be built into the program.

Those who have been paying attention to the development of new programs may object to the idea of considering such plans as innovations because of the many activities now underway. Cornell University has had field stations in Thailand and an experimental hacienda in Peru[10] and organizes field trips to the Indians of the Southwest for students of technical change. Each of the departments of psychiatry of the five medical schools in Philadelphia shares in the research and the teaching going on at the Eastern Pennsylvania Psychiatric Institute. Active cooperation has created links between Clark University, the Worcester State Hospital, and the Worcester Foundation for Experimental Biology. Precisely because programs such as these do already exist, comparatively small alterations in organizational styles might make a very great difference. For without a central focus, all cooperation tends to break down under the pressures of institutional pulling and hauling and the struggle for power, prestige, funds, and simple convenience.

Whatever the program may be, whatever its institutional form may be, whether it is the program of the interdisciplinary University Seminars at Columbia University, the Menninger School of Psychiatry, or the joint investment of departments of psychiatry in the Eastern Pennsylvania Psychiatric Institute, or the long series of Macy conferences, or the Merrill–Palmer program of studies of infancy, the network can survive only if there is some active, zestful, and vested interest in its continuation and growth. This means that there must be one person or one group of persons (usually it is one individual who has the decisive combination of zest and creative imagination) completely committed to the existence of the network. Where the network is devoted to sufficiently diverse and growing purposes, the enthusiastic network designer may quite safely possess a large number of empire-building drives without the usual disadvantages of such drives. For the very nature of the total structure will make it impossible for the most inveterate empire-builder to strengthen one institution without strengthening the others.[11] The need for a design for such interdependent institutions is urgent.

The network must have living creatures continually within its shared interest—birds, deer, children, patients, foreign technicians. In addition, it must have a shared production interest with the highest intellectual content, but a production interest that is always associated with the lives of men and the life of the society so that the connection between theory and practice, which is absolutely essential in the life sciences, will remain intact. If the contribution to evolution is to be an immediate one, the focusing interest must be relevant to one of the central concerns on which our immediate future survival rests—methods of international cooperation, rapid cultural change, mental health, education for the new era, population control, food and nutrition, space, planetary peace.

The structure must allow also for the individual who wants to work almost entirely alone but who requires good resources. Furthermore, the shared interest must be wide enough to encompass a great many smaller, more limited research interests, to make room for every discipline in the sciences, the humanities, and the arts. For example, in a program in which the focusing interest was population control, one part of the work would be carried on in the laboratory by physiologists and biochemists, but an integral part of the work would also consist of discussions with theologians about the ethical issues, with psychiatrists about the difficulties encountered in sterilized subjects and in repetitive unmarried mothers, with historians and economists and sociologists about the social consequences of population growth and decline, with anthropologists about contrasting cultural solutions, with artists and poets whose responses to the prospects opening out could be important in a newly developing climate of opinion. In each program, in every network, specific provision must be made for the inclusion of the sciences, the humanities, and the arts if we are to bring to an end the sterile isolation and mutual suspicion in which the three groups now live and obstruct each other.[12]

Representation of these many aspects of cultural life must be accomplished on the basis of individual interest and involvement. The person, not the discipline, must be central. Too often planners say, "We must have a theologian" or a "biochemist." But the individual who is selected because of his disciplinary classification without regard to who and what he is, as himself, is demeaned thereby and may well limit his participation in a group to a destructive defense of his own narrow training and bias. In a large community where there are many theologians and many biochemists, some will spontaneously become interested and ask to come into the program; others will have worked closely with someone who is already interested. This would mean that a thinking and working group would seldom be stuck with anyone who was there for any reason other than genuine interest and commitment. In a group of this kind only the necessary organizers and dispatchers would be paid; everyone else would draw his basic livelihood from something else. So the method of recruitment must be either self-selection or person-to-person selection, as friend or colleague talks with enthusiasm about the focal interest that is being pursued and rouses a corresponding enthusiasm and potentiality for commitment in his listener.

Even this cannot protect the thinking cluster from the man who is stupid, difficult, obsessed, or boring. But it is my assumption that a genuine evolutionary group must very early come to terms with representatives of exactly these intellectual possibilities. The exasperating inability of a stupid man with a good education in one discipline to understand anything new is a living example of one of the barriers to the acceptance of a new idea. The individual who cannot speak well or understand any one of the languages of international communication or who lacks basic education is encountered at almost every level of international meeting today. The touchy newcomer, who feels discriminated against because of race, religion, or sex, has just the prickly, oversensitive surface which, a little later, may prevent some important idea from ever being put into practice. The zealot and the fanatic need somehow to be represented—hopefully in small doses. It is difficult to make a case for the inclusion of the boring; yet perhaps the one imperfection that is most likely to keep men of genius from making their full contribution to cultural evolution is a contemptuous impatience toward their fellow men.[13] And a bore is simply a person to whom one can find no tolerable level of response.

Certain of the organizational requirements of such a network can also be indicated. The network must, for example, be localized in space. There must be some place where meetings can be held, messages left, materials stored, services arranged for.[14] This need not be a center that is devoted only to the activities of a network, as in the case of the New York Academy of Sciences.[15] It may, instead, be one of the cooperating institutions. Both methods pose problems; each may lead to rivalry and accusations of imperialism. If the network is to have a center devoted wholly to its wide and multiple purposes, precautions should probably be taken to prevent it from taking on other functions, such as becoming a secondary graduate school or a project-administrating agency.

Yet ideally it should have better organizational facilities than has any one of the cooperating institutions from which individual members are drawn. For here, in the network, people will work freely, for pure intellectual delight or out of commitment to the needs of mankind, and give their time and energy and often also their money to make such a network possible. In return they should be able to work in the best possible conditions. All the complex and wonderful new inventions for projection, duplication, simultaneous translation, and intercommunication should be available to them. Or if working conditions must be Spartan, everyone should be permitted to share in the acceptance of the Spartan fare, as a poor thing but their own, something with which they themselves are willing to make do. The pleasures of one of the beautiful new conference centers or the rigors of an overheated basement can underwrite high-level, voluntary, free intellectual life. It is the sloppy, ineffective middle position that is intolerable. The conference room that is not cleaned in the morning, in which the smoke of last night lingers over the table, the dreary meal in a dreary restaurant that precedes so many scientific meetings, the bad coffee or lukewarm cocoa that a meager and grudging budget provides, the equipment that is inadequate, that breaks down and is neither repaired nor replaced—these are the things that dampen not only the spirit but the imagination also.

Great intellectual advances have been mapped out in cafés, in coffee houses, at high tables, in laboratories threatened by bombardment or starvation. It is these small extra increments of challenge or delight that make the difference between stagnation and swiftly blossoming thought. Intellectual advances have always taken place in settings that had an intrinsic style, that reinforced or provided contrast to the other dreams that were being elaborated at high tables, behind prison walls, in hidden cellars.

16. Invoking the Future

THE HISTORY OF SCIENCE as well as the history of religion is filled with accounts of the way the future lays a life-giving or a deadening hand on the present. The images of what life may be like for our children and our children's children provide the impetus to work for, to hasten or to fend off, the future that is prophesied. Originally so fragile that words alone or mathematical symbols alone can invoke them, the images are entrusted first to the mathematicians and poets and painters, then to the engineers. Grown a little more tangible, they are finally ready for the mock-up of an enclosed city on the moon. From the laboratories of the world come rumors that life can be made new, as conceivably once, incredibly long ago, it came into being. The distance to the stars has changed in the few short years since Ruth Benedict wrote:[1]

> The star that loosed this arrow down the dark
> Is centuries-long extinguished, and its ray
> Clean as a pinpoint, perfect to the mark,
> Shivers not yet to void. Bodies decay,
> Life being put asunder, and sweet sound
> No longer holds the air where streams are bound,
>
> Only this gleam is fathered of the dead,
> A goblin birth, having no source in heaven
> Nor in men's eyes, a disinherited
> And phantom thing, that soon shall scatter even

Its slight and tapered essence, and the dark
Close down at length over its gutted spark.

Preposterous years, held taut in nothingness
To carry so a futile beam to earth,
Though night be nothing profited, no less
Outstare our trivial doubting. Death and birth
Are whimsies of the wind; nothing avails;
Yet till its term is spent, no star beam fails.

Time is now measured in generations, and men dream of new journeys, infinite extensions of the pilgrimages to Mecca on which men died and children were born, for on these journeys none of those who set out together will be alive at the end, but only their descendants, who will themselves have no living memory of the earth that was left behind. Like those who are born blind and have to learn from those with sight, mediated and interpreted by those who late in life are blinded, what color is and what men mean by a sunset, a rainbow, or the velvet night, so the imagined children born in space will have to combine lessons learned from film and tape with memories carried in their parents' voices, voices which are themselves only echoes of voices heard in childhood.

Thinking wonderingly how strange this would be not only changes our sense of time, as light years are converted into the span of human life, but also throws new light on the road we ourselves have traveled, and, without the facsimile of photography and magnetic tape, the life our ancestors lived is also an echo of echoes, given form and substance because our feet stand, or so we think, on the same road, or because a scrap of wall, a worn coin, the faint outline of a house site testifies they were once here.

The twin fears in man, which in some unfortunates become so obsessive that their lives are twisted and distorted in response to them—the fear of being closed in and the fear of open spaces—meet in the contemplation of outer space, where the future colony is pictured both as totally enclosed and as floating in nothingness. Those whose sense of themselves is dependent on the natural world look with even deeper affection at the robin and the squirrel on the lawn as they realize what life would be like in a space colony which had to synthesize its own food and in which no animal life except human life could be supported—not a worm, not a toad, not a bumblebee to mediate between men and algae. So, in the present, although there are as yet no space ships and no space colonies, the imagination of the denizens of the mid-twentieth century already differs from that of their fathers.

An old Plains Indian spoke of taking peyote and watching the colored images on the feather fan that formed a screen before his eyes. Then he spoke of his children, who would be able to read and write and who would not need peyote to realize their visions.[2]

We are indeed a generation who have come unprepared into a world we never made nor ever dreamed of "to pay the debt we never promised."[3] But we do not need to rely only on images of the future, however skillfully conjured up with words and numbers, paint and wire. There is another way for us to draw life from the future through an intensive preoccupation with the growing thought of young children, the denizens of the twenty-first century.

Evolutionary content which can quicken the process of evolutionary thought is to be found in the exploration of children's minds, minds already attuned to a world about which we have learned with wonder and alarm after we have become old enough to know how strange it is. But our children are habitués of a world in which possible total catastrophe, the peregrinations of satellites, the simultaneous presence of father-by-the-fireside and father-on-the-television-screen are commonplace. They have grown up in an age in which the death of a child comes about almost always by accident rather than through illness, and they see natural death further away and violent death closer to than their parents do. Casually twisting the dial of the television set or the transistor radio, images and messages from all over the world, the preserved or recreated voices of the past, and the imagined voices of the future come to them simultaneously. The other side of the world is where father was yesterday or will be tomorrow, only one sleep away from here where he is leisurely planting a rose bush. The point of the story of the wicked stepmother who sent the little stepdaughter out to find strawberries buried under the snow is lost for them, forever, for strawberries ripen somewhere all the year round, and the back of the north wind and the other side of the moon are places they can think of reaching without magic.

Like all other explorations that can contribute most safely to evolutionary advance, such explorations should not be pursued starkly nor with the simple end in view of somehow burning children's unlived days to provide a fire by which to see our own dreams more vividly.[4] Rather, the intensive study of how children's minds develop, combined with the lively delight of teaching them in new and suitable ways, should itself provide a medium in which evolutionary imagination can flourish. The young physicist, who now talks only with other young physicists and never with a postman or a poet, would find, if he were enlisted in the task of teaching pre-physics to all children, those who will someday make good physicists, those who will be poets, and those whose greatest ambition is perhaps to be postmen. He would be forced to keep his own rare and special language closer to the natural languages of men.[5] The walls that now separate him from his fellows, even most educated men, would crumble first in his own mind, as he faced the fact that if he could not answer the questions of a bright four-year-old, he had not really discovered what he was talking about. Straining to meet a growing mind that has been born into a world already transformed, while one is also providing it with new and better ways of thinking, begets a new kind of creativity in those who teach. When this will be combined with research of a delicacy of which we have as yet only a few visible hints, then the whole evolutionary process will become available to us.[6]

The lines of exploration have been laid down, the specification of individuality in each mother–child couple, the variation in the sensory modalities with which each child is met and itself meets the world, the tremendous consequences for later life as one stage or phase, rather than another, is emphasized by the culture, the complications of learning that space–time makes all events irreversible or that all events are reversible. Psychoanalysis has mapped the ways in which impulses, once phylogenetically appropriate to a very different kind of hominid, must be integrated in each member of *Homo sapiens,* now equipped with a long learning period, a delayed puberty, and the huge accumulation of knowledge that his brain and length of learning make possible.[7] The new science of ethology provides clues to some of the instinctive variations that may be necessary conditions for profound individual differences.[8] Margaret Lowenfeld, through the transformation device provided by a "world" built with sand and water and miniatures of "everything" in the world, has invented a way for the child's early thought, so different from the sequentially coded thought of the secondary process, to be expressed.[9] The work of Edith Cobb suggests that human beings need to perceive and recreate internally and expressively what they perceive of the universe in which they are growing—that they have in fact a "cosmic sense." [10] But all this is still in its infancy.

Meanwhile we are faced with new demands. How early can we discern and describe the special gifts and capabilities of a child? What is the relationship between the acceptance of an abstraction in a child's first words and its later ability to learn abstractions? How will a muting or, alternatively, an intensification of sensory contact, in the child's best or its least sensitive mode, affect its power to learn— perhaps turning into a hyperactive little monster of destructiveness a child who otherwise might have built better than anything we know.

Today our approaches to children are fragmented and partial. Those who care for well children know little of children who are sick. The deep knowledge that comes from the intensive attempt to cure is separated from the knowledge of those whose main task is to teach. Those who teach the blind child or the brain-injured child are separated from those who teach the "superior" child. The kind of cross-penetration of knowledge that comes when felicity and calamity are placed side by side hardly ever occurs. Those who teach the children of impoverished homes have no experience of what an intellectually lively home can contribute to learning, and the two extremes of culturally determined precocity and retardation are never put on a single scale.

Here especially there is urgent need for the creation of living networks, connecting institutions of many sorts, all of them involving children. Such a network will make it possible for many thinkers to share the experience of the same child, watching through a one-way vision screen, studying one film over and over in entranced contemplation of a world that, like art, represents a transformation of experience, listening to a tape of a child's voice until the pattern—there in sound, in inflection, in cadence, in words—comes clear, watching a skilled teacher instructing the same child whom one has watched at play.

These are the sources on which we can draw to increase our participation in evolution, even as we are creating new forms of education which will produce those better fitted than we to meet the complexities of the future. If we can create living networks of the diversely gifted and the diversely trained whose concern it is to safeguard our present heritage and to learn from and teach those who will be the carriers of this heritage, we shall automatically focus our inventiveness on the very center of the evolutionary process.

Looking back and visualizing the whole slow accumulation of inventions that have made us human beings and, finally, civilized human beings, we find, salient among them, man's developing ability to include in the conception of his own group ever more people living at a greater distance: his clan, his tribe, his nation, his religion, his part of the world. Step by step the intricate inventions have been made by which men have moved from the invocation of undemonstrable common descent, by which one's brothers could be numbered in the hundreds or even thousands, to allegiance to one liege lord or king, together with thousands or millions of others, to the gathering together of the children of one God, whereby the lines dividing one kingdom from another could be crossed, to nationhood, in which those who once formed separate units or who came from different lands could be joined together by the hundred million, to a world ideology which can encompass nation–states, different races, and different religions in one allegiance for which men are still perilously asked to die. Each step has meant greater potentialities and greater danger. Each time we have increased the number of those whom we would protect, whose death at our own hands we would call murder, we have increased the number of those who could become, in a body and overnight, without further identification, our mortal enemies whom it would be virtue to destroy.

Finally, with the invention of modern weapons, we have reached the end of the road that can be traversed in the simple dichotomy of "ours," whom we protect, and "they," the enemy, against whom we protect our own. Abruptly we are brought face to face with the stark reality that we cannot protect our own children unless we protect their children also, not before a declaration of war or after a peace treaty as in the past, but while the enmity exists, so that the war will never be declared. So the individual member of each nation, each group of nations pledged to some position in the world which is denied or threatened by some other nation or group of nations, becomes his enemy's keeper, as well as his brother's, his neighbor's, his fellow national's, and his fellow believer's, with whom he shares a common ideology. This is something no men on earth have as yet learned how to be. And when we have learned, a new grade of evolution will be reached. For the relations between such peoples, who are of necessity the keepers of each other's children, no words that now exist will be wholly appropriate.

In the past, men gathered together out of choice to meet the challenge of danger that came from other men. Now, for the first time, each side is equally dangerous to all. Each nation with the power to precipitate total warfare must become, of necessity, as it seeks to protect its own, the protectors of those against whom its fatal armaments are arrayed. We have come full circle. Our human situation no longer permits us to make armed dichotomies between those who are good and those who are evil, those who are right and those who are wrong. The first blow dealt to the enemy's children will sign the death warrant of our own. The processes of evolution have kept us one species, and now the technical advances of cultural evolution, having power to destroy us, have made it necessary for us, at last, to make the invention that will protect every member of the human species with the sanctions that once stretched no farther than a stone could be thrown. Having come so far, can we make the next invention in time?

Illustrations

Plate 1. Wabe holding a *balugasi'*—a symbolic request for a feast from his sister's son. Arapesh, Alitoa Village, 1932.

Plate 2. A symbolic statement that a man forbids his wife to feed any more pigs, made of a bark pig trough, taro, and assorted spearheads and arrows. Arapesh, Alitoa Village, 1932.

Plate 3. Stylized drawings of animals and human beings by a Mountain Arapesh boy, 1932.

Plate 4. Nonseaworthy model of a European ship made by Beach Arapesh children, 1932.

Plate 5. Drawing of a European ship by a Manus boy, 1928.

Plate 6. Manus boy sailing
accurate models of
European ships, 1928.

Plate 7. Manus child, 1928. Statement of Manus relationship to European models.

Plate 8. Paliau of Manus, 1954.

Plate 9. Change within one generation, Manus, 1953.

Plate 10. Pokanau and his son, Manus, 1928.

Plate 11. Pokanau in 1953.

Plate 12. Stolypin, 1911.

Plate 13. Lenin on the schoolroom wall, USSR, 1963.

Plate 14. A three-second episode from a work sheet in *A Natural History of an Interview,* by Norman A. McQuown and others. Kinesic recording by Ray L. Birdwhistell; linguistic recording by Norman A. McQuown. In this scene (frames 792–864) the mother (D), with the child (B) seated before her, addresses the interviewer (G). As D speaks, B plays with a toy gun and lets it fall to the floor.

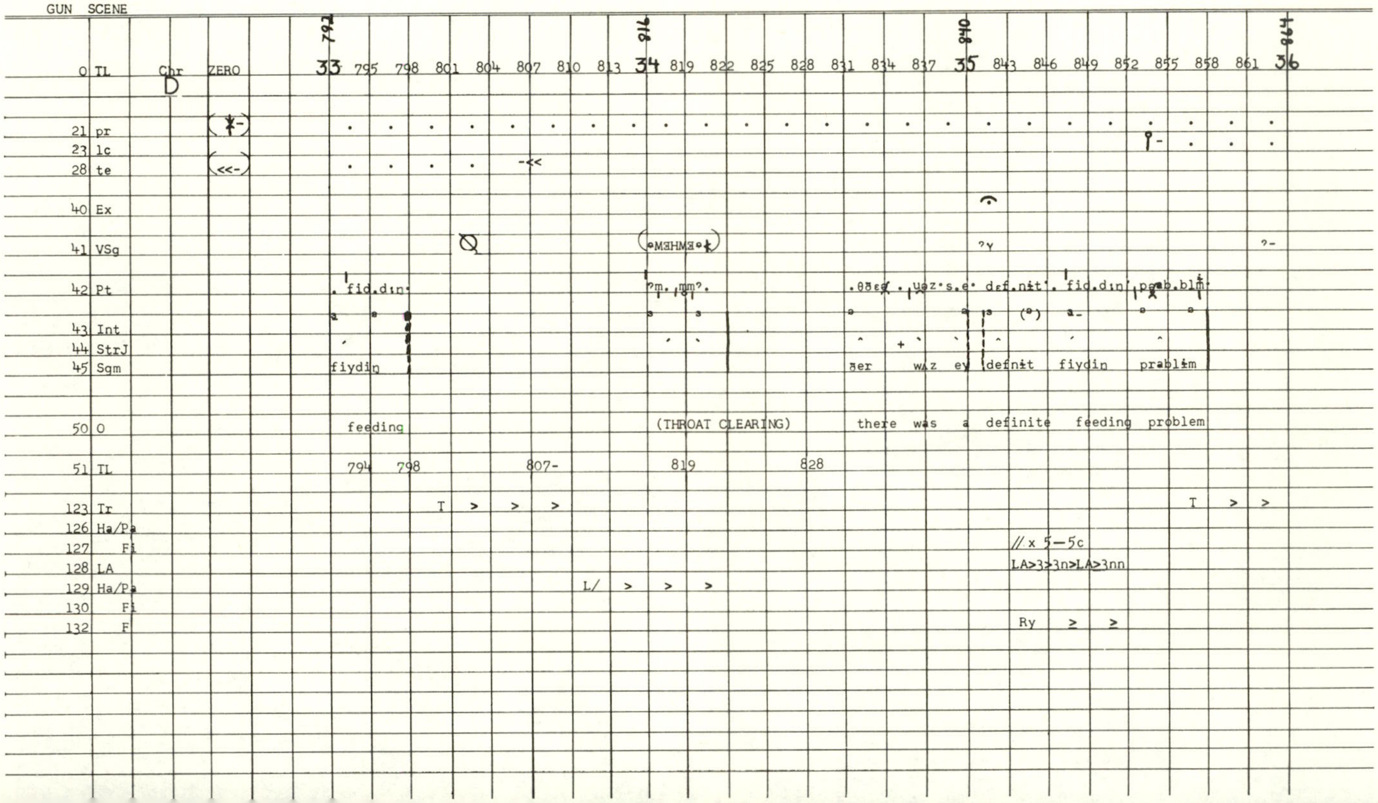

138 VA
139 BA
140 CCh   (internalizing)
141 Com

51 IL   (L/12) cig
129 Ha/Pa

138 VA
139 BA
140 CCh
141 Com

51 IL   Hv2
113 He

116 E   O Ov > > >

126 Ha/Pa
127 Fi
129 Ha/Pa
130 Fi

138 VA
139 BA
140 CCh
141 Com

(E-)
(↘)

(internalizing)

(kinesic shift)

adpersonalizing

editorial >

(eye rub)

(rolls cigarette)

(smokes)

*Gregory continues to roll cigarette
to make different lip contrl to 921.

R/1c4c >
gun

OO
gun

L/11
cig

L/12*
cig

794 798 800

798 800

828 830

821

828 830

856

856

Z00
gun**

(blink)

** Gun falls to floor.

Plate 15. Child watching artist at work, Bali, 1937.

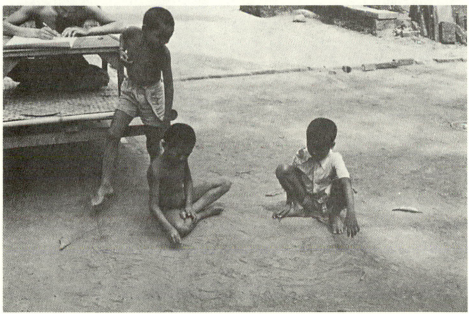

Plate 16a, b. Children drawing on the ground as artist works, Bali, 1937.

Plate 17a, b. Mario teaching, Bali, 1936.

Plate 18. Mario teaching a visiting dancer from Malabar, Bali, 1937.

Plate 19. The visiting Malabar dancer teaching Mario, Bali, 1937.

Plate 20. Mario dancing in Bali, 1937.

Plate 21. Mario's troupe in New York City, 1957.

APPENDICES

Appendix A

Micro- and Macro-Cultural Models
for Cultural Evolution[1]

THEODORE SCHWARTZ
AND MARGARET MEAD, 1961

WE WERE ASKED to discuss non-evolutionary typology. Considering the non-evolutionary, however, we decided that a typology of whole cultures is either evolutionary or trivial. What might constitute a non-evolutionary classification? It is possible to make classifications of cultures that would not have been considered evolutionary as long as evolution was taken as limited to unilinear or multilinear sequences of progressive stages. Very recently the concept of evolution has become more inclusive, to the extent that most of the interests of cultural anthropologists are embraced by this concept. Biological evolutionists such as Huxley[2] and Simpson[3] have long conceived of evolution as encompassing not only general progress and multilinear regularities of sequence but also the divergence of species and other taxa that do not lead to higher grades and that do not parallel the course of other lineages.

In anthropology, it is only recently that those concerned

with historical or diffusionist studies, with acculturation, with typologies, for example, of kinship systems, languages, social character or cultural goals, could recognize fully the relevance of their studies to evolution. Those more explicitly evolutionists had considered these studies as historical, non-evolutionary, even anti-evolutionary. Sahlins and Service in their recent book, *Evolution and Culture,* remove one of the bases of the old polemic by the inclusion of such lines of study as I have mentioned.[4]

The distinction Sahlins makes between specific and general evolution corresponds to Huxley's divergence and advance, and to Simpson's expansion and progress. These are seen as two aspects of a unitary process, sometimes more sharply differentiated as two directions or even two kinds of evolution.

Specific evolution, according to Sahlins and Service, treats of populations diversifying through adaptive modification—actual, historical lineages of new forms differentiate from old forms, advancing in the relative sense of specialization toward a particular environment. General evolution deals with classes of representative forms arranged in levels according to the criterion of thermodynamic advance with a series of related structural criteria. It is said that specific and general evolution involve two different taxonomies—the former, phylogenetic, the latter, non-phylogenetic and discontinuous.[5] This basic formulation and its derivative laws leave many issues. We could contend that general evolution should be taken as a special case of specific evolution, but the important point for this paper is that this inclusive view of evolution should lead us toward completion of a unified theory of cultural evolution. Evolution, more inclusively conceived, has become more or less identical with general determinism in which even historical determinants are conceded their role, that is, the effect of specificities of time, place, and personnel in the interstructuring of events. The evolution-transforming effect of convergent diffusion is emphasized and even stability and continuity become problems of evolutionary dynamics.

Completion of a general theory of cultural evolution requires both micro- and macro-evolutionary amplification. General macro-evolutionary laws must be specified for the phases of evolution to which they apply. Phase changes, that is, changes in the process of change, have often been noted in evolution, most often in the alteration of process and mechanisms occurring with the transition between biological and cultural evolution.

In biological evolution there have been other alterations of evolutionary process. Major adaptive radiation of phyla was followed by a relaying of forms of lower taxonomic order.[6] The production of new inter-group variation diminished, while behavioral variability developed as the adaptive specialization of one phylogenetically continuous line from which man and culture emerge.

Similarly, in cultural evolution, one great adaptive radiation with migration of human groups throughout the world still at relative primitive stages of cultural development, produced the great areal cultures and their internal differentiation. Increasingly larger systems of transactional groups are formed, within some of which the lead of progressive evolution of culture is relayed, culminating in a single historical evolution of a national industrial multistate complex. Convergence through cultural transmission is greatly accelerated making the non-literate, non-industrial cultures pre-literate and pre-industrial. Movement toward communicational integration of a world culture, a single transactional unit of further cultural evolution, indicates a new phase of literally unilinear evolution dependent upon internal variation rather than on variation among partially isolate cultures as in earlier phases.

It is such intra-systemic properties, processes and mechanisms that lack explicit elaboration in micro-evolutionary theory. The discovery of the coding, storing, and transmission mechanisms, the genotype–phenotype relationship and the genetic structure of Mendelian population,[7] has provided biological evolution with its firm micro-evolutionary foundation. Anthropological experience with cultural data on particular cultures, culture change and the personality–culture relationship, has not yet been reflected in a conceptual model of culture adequate for micro-evolutionary theory. This model should include the internal variation and distributive structure of a culture.

Culture is usually conceived in terms of that which the members of a society have in common; personality, in terms of that which is unique to the individual. Much of culture is not common to all members of a society and much of the content of the individual personality is not unique to the individual. The familiar concept of culture that is based on the criterion of commonality of content leads the anthropologist to homogenize the cultures that he studies and to ignore or exclude much that is not different in kind or significance from that which he does study except that its distribution among the members of a society is heterogeneous. Our concept of culture must take into account the distribution of the contents of a culture among the members of a society or sub-societal group.

Each individual derives implicit cognitive–affective–evaluative constructs from his participation in the events that make up his life history. We call the individual's total set of implicit constructs an "idioverse." [8] The idioverse is roughly analogous to the total genotype of the individual in genetics, but it is not derived from this analogy which is not highly productive. The individual's experiential idioverse is affected by his "bio-idioverse" (his genotype–phenotype make-up) to the extent that this modulates his experience. The idioverse does not involve a reduction of culture to individual psychology. In the on-going experience of the individual these idioversal constructs are constantly undergoing formation, replication, and transformation as they are activated in communication and enter into the structuring of events.

The concept of culture based on the "idioverse" starts from the assumption of heterogeneity rather than of commonality and offers a more complex model for the structure of commonality to be found within the heterogeneity of culture. Any subset of idioverses (of any size, from pairs to societies, to multi-societal complexes) has an intersect which contains the constructs common to all the idioverses of the subset. What any group has in common makes up their intersect. The great number of different intersects to be found among the idioverses of the individuals of a society may be ordered into levels of commonality. A culture contains a highly complex structure of commonality and *not* a unitary body of common content. This structure of commonality formed by all idioversal intersects exists within a culture and is not itself to be defined as the culture. A culture is defined as a "multiverse" which is a set of idioverses and not just the intersects among these idioverses. It includes not only what these individuals have in common but also what any subset of them have in common. A multiverse includes also that which lies outside of any intersect—those idioversal constructs which may have some unique component, but which potentially may enter into communication and into the determination of events. The constructs comprising the idioverses of each member of the personnel-set of an event are all available for the structuring of that event regardless of whether or not these constructs are held in common by the members of the personnel-set.

The volume of a given intersect depends upon the criteria we adopt for "commonality." Some of the important criteria will be: formal identity or partial identity of constructs, complementarity of constructs (as in constructs having reference to related behaviors, at least one of which implies the others), and co-affect, which means, briefly, similarity of associated affect, value, or behavior-determining valences.

Cutting across the idioversal structure of a culture are interrelated systems of constructs which comprise supra-individual institutional patterns. While such patterns are our usual subject matter little is known of the distributive structure of such institutions because we tend to make the leap too quickly from field or survey data to the higher order patterns. A more systematic building-up of these patterns upon their distributive loci in no way limits our arrival at patterns of higher order. It calls only for a successive mapping of higher levels against a micro-cultural base. Rather than not seeing culture for its variance, we include the variance in culture as an important basis of micro-evolutionary process. We may exemplify some of the more familiar multiversal levels with such terms as: status cultures, family cultures, local culture variants, areal cultures, phase, period, or generation cultures, civilizations. Any idioverse or multiverse presents with others a surface of contact differentially permeable to communication. The communicational boundaries, isolate mechanisms and transactional linkages should be studied.

After this exercise of imagining culture in idioversal–multiversal form let us imagine the form of a total macro-evolutionary typology of cultures and of the property space in which they evolve. Cultures may be classified according to a great number of attributes. Take each of these as a variable or dimension of a multidimensional property space. Some of our dimensions will be sets of categories, classes, or types. If there is more than one proposed set of types, assign a dimension for each. Some of our dimensions will be continuous quantitative variables such as amount of energy in use. We add time and location to the already enormous dimensionality of this space. Each culture (each idioverse and all multiverses of any order) has a set of co-ordinates unique in its totality but part of an overlapping structure of commonality as previously defined. The space itself is not the same for all of the units mapped on it—in two ways. First, subsocietal units cannot be mapped against societal variables, and second, the dimensionality of the space increases in the course of evolution (a growth which could be measured in logons—units of structural information[9]), but as any one culture in progress amplifies the space, the added dimensionality exists potentially for all others. Our space is structured. Variables are grouped into areas by similarity of reference. More importantly, their determinate interrelatedness can be indicated by the angle between them using a system of polar coordinates so that the higher the correlation in the distribution of cultures among the set of variables, the smaller the angle they form in the space.[10] The interrelatedness is indicated in another way. As a culture moves from one position to another on any variable, its path of movement describes a vector running along that variable then branching out to intersect other variables with some lag until it has described a chain of causal accommodation through part of the space.[11] There is a variable density in the distribution of cultures and of causal vectors—areas of high density as well as empty spaces. In evolution cultures move through this space with different rates of change on the various dimensions. Continuity and change involve transformation of the culture's coordinate position. On a micro-evolutionary scale the component idioverses may respond differentially describing a more complex trajectory for the culture. The evolutionary advancement of a culture at any point in its historically continuous transformation depends upon its position on some few selected dimensions which are themselves part of the space, such as energy utilization.

In the course of evolution the property space itself changes. We may speak of a phase change where the pattern of evolution itself changes—when, for example, in the variable density distribution of cultural transformations in the macro-evolutionary space, there is a general shift from divergent to convergent paths with a downward general radiation of causal vectors from higher to lower cultures with sharply altered chains of accommodation and lag (inverse lag, as Service puts it[12]) within cultures.

The property space as we have constructed it so far does not yield a typology, but it does represent the universe of possible typologies and their substructions[13] within which the transformation trajectories of cultures in evolution are distributed and upon which our typological operations are performed.

Huxley and others have pointed out that cultural evolution will be increasingly transformed by the conscious, purposive intervention of man in the direction of his own course of development. Our field study of rapid culture change in Manus impressed us with the importance of the consciously held, self-reflexive culture constructs of the Manus.[14] Brought into intensive contact with the increasingly integrated world culture, the Manus moved actively toward inclusion, projecting ahead of them a transformal construct of their desired goal–culture and making a vehicular culture of their immediate cultural state, to carry them through change toward a goal which they will discover, is also moving. This is a general trend in cultural evolution. Anthropology responds to the rapid evolution of its object of study. It becomes impossible to restudy, with current means and concepts, the classical primitive culture, relatively intact, relatively homogeneous and self-contained, to which so much of our thinking remains attached. Our ethnographies become a paleontological record. With decrease of inter-cultural variation we may have to look to internal micro-cultural variation within world culture for our sources of cultural richness, complexity, and further evolutionary progress—to discover and fulfill human potentialities and values in the continuing evolutionary thrust provided by science.

Appendix B [a]

Seven Pacific Cultures

IN THE FOLLOWING NOTES I have attempted to provide some brief orientation for the reader on the seven Pacific cultures on which I have done field work: where the various peoples are, when and under what circumstances my own work was done, and what sort of knowledge exists about them in published sources. Where published materials are extensive, only selected sources will be cited.

Each culture presented different problems. In Samoa I worked alone; there had been much work done before, and more has been done since. There were a dictionary and a grammar, and English could be used to learn the language. In Manus, in 1928, we had to analyze the language, using pidgin English as the interpreting language, and this was also true of Arapesh, Mundugumor, and Tchambuli, and of Gregory Bateson's original work in Iatmul, which I was able to use as a background. Balinese has been extensively analyzed, but with the help of an English-speaking linguistic assistant we found it more satisfactory to make a new analysis along the lines used with a totally unknown language. In all cases the language was learned, a base was established in a native village, and one village was intensively followed and studied. A gen-

[a] Abridged and adapted from *Male and Female* (New York, Morrow, 1949), Appendix 1, with additional references. All seven cultures listed here are discussed in *Male and Female*.

eral discussion of the Sepik Aitape district in which Arapesh, Mundugumor, Tchambuli, and Iatmul are located will be found on pp. 153–66 of "The Mountain Arapesh, I. An Importing Culture" (see below, Section 3).

Detailed discussions of field methods may be found in appendices and introductions to my various publications. The most important methodological sources follow.

Selected Sources

Mead, Margaret, *Coming of Age in Samoa,* New York, Morrow, 1928; reprinted 1949, Mentor MP418, New York, New American Library, Appendix 2, pp. 152–55.

————, *Growing Up in New Guinea,* New York, Morrow, 1930; reprinted 1953, Mentor MD255, New York, New American Library, Appendix 1, pp. 165–72.

————, "Living with the Natives of Melanesia," *Natural History, 31*:1 (1931), 62–74.

————, "More Comprehensive Field Methods," *American Anthropologist, 35*:1 (1933), 1–15.

————, "Native Languages as Field-Work Tools," *American Anthropologist, 41*:2 (1939), 189–205.

————, "Researches in Bali 1936–1939, I. On the Concept of Plot in Culture, II. Methods of Research in Bali and New Guinea," *Transactions of The New York Academy of Sciences,* Ser. II, 2:1 (1939), 24–31.

————, "The Mountain Arapesh, II. Supernaturalism," *Anthropological Papers of The American Museum of Natural History, 37,* Pt. 3, New York, 1940, 325–38.

————, "Anthropological Data on the Problem of Instinct," *Psychosomatic Medicine, 4*:4 (1942), 396–97.

————, "The Mountain Arapesh, V. The Record of Unabelin with Rorschach Analyses," *Anthropological Papers of The American Museum of Natural History, 41,* Pt. 3, New York, 1949, 293–302.

————, "Research on Primitive Children," in *Manual of Child Psychology,* ed. Leonard Carmichael, 2d ed., New York, John Wiley, 1954, pp. 735–80.

1. Samoa

My material on Samoa was gathered during a nine-month field trip in 1925–26 as a Fellow in the Biological Sciences of the National Research Council, on a research project designated as the study of the adolescent girl.

The Samoan Islands, with a population in 1926 of 40,229, are peopled by a Polynesian group, a people with light brown skin and wavy black hair who speak a Polynesian language. The islands were Christianized in the first half of the nineteenth century and were administratively divided between a League of Nations Mandate under New Zealand called Western Samoa, which comprised the islands of Upolu and Savaii, and American Samoa, which was governed by the United States Navy.

All my detailed work was done in the remote islands of the Manua group, principally in the village of Taū on the island of Taū.

Selected Sources

Cook, P. H., "The Application of the Rorschach Test to a Samoan Group," *Rorschach Research Exchange, 6:2* (1942), 51–60.

Copp, John, and Faafouina I. Pula, *Samoan Dance of Life,* Boston, Beacon, 1950.

Durand, J. D., *The Population of Western Samoa,* Reports on the Population of Trust Territories, STSOA/Series A/no. 1, Lake Success, N.Y., United Nations Department of Social Affairs, Population Division, 1948.

Ember, Melvin, "The Nonunilinear Descent Groups of Samoa," *American Anthropologist, 61:4* (1959), 573–77.

Fraser, John, "On Some Folk-songs and Myths from Samoa" (by T. Powell and G. Pratt, with introduction and notes by John Fraser), *Journal and Proceedings of the Royal Society of New South Wales, 24,* Art. 12 (1890), 195–217.

———, "Some Folk-songs and Myths from Samoa," trans. G.

Pratt, with introduction and notes by John Fraser, *Journal and Proceedings of the Royal Society of New South Wales,* *25,* Art. 6, 10, 11, 18 (1891), 70–86, 96–146, 241–86; *26,* Art. 12 (1892), 264–301.

———, "Some Folk-songs and Myths from Samoa," *Journal of the Polynesian Society,* 5:19 (1896), 171–83; 6:21–23 (1897), 19–33, 67–76, 107–22; 7:25 (1898), 15–29.

Gray, J. A. C., *Amerika Samoa: A History of American Samoa and Its United States Naval Administration,* Annapolis, Md., United States Naval Institute, 1960.

Hiroa, Te Rangi (Peter H. Buck), "Samoan Material Culture," *Bernice P. Bishop Museum Bulletin, 75,* Honolulu, 1930, 1–724.

Holmes, Lowell D., *Ta'u: Stability and Change in a Samoan Village,* Reprint of the Polynesian Society, 7, Wellington, N.Z., Polynesian Society, 1958.

Keesing, Felix M. *Modern Samoa: Its Government and Changing Life,* Stanford, Stanford University Press, 1934.

———, and Marie M. Keesing, *Elite Communication in Samoa,* Stanford, Stanford University Press, 1956.

Krämer, Augustin, *Die Samoa-Inseln,* 2 vols., Stuttgart, Naegele, 1902.

Mead, Margaret, *Coming of Age in Samoa,* New York, Morrow, 1928; reprinted 1949, Mentor MP418, New York, New American Library.

———, "A Lapse of Animism among a Primitive People," *Psyche, 9*:1 (1928), 72–77.

———, "The Role of the Individual in Samoan Culture," *Journal of the Royal Anthropological Institute, 58* (1928), 481–95.

———, "Samoan Children at Work and Play," *Natural History, 28*:6 (1928), 26–36.

———, "Americanization in Samoa," *American Mercury 16*:63 (1929), 264–70.

———, "Social Organization of Manua," *Bernice P. Bishop Museum Bulletin, 76,* Honolulu, 1930, 1–218.

———, "Two South Sea Educational Experiments and Their

American Implications," in "Eighteenth Annual School-men's Week Proceedings, March 18–21, 1931," *University of Pennsylvania School of Education Bulletin, 31*:36 (1931), 493–97.

——, "The Samoans," in *Cooperation and Competition among Primitive Peoples,* ed. Margaret Mead, New York, McGraw-Hill, 1937; rev. ed. 1961, BP123, Boston, Beacon, pp. 282–312.

——, "Cultural Contexts of Puberty and Adolescence," *Bulletin of the Philadelphia Association for Psychoanalysis, 9*:3 (1959), 59–79.

——, "Weaver of the Border," in *In the Company of Man,* ed. Joseph B. Casagrande, New York, Harper, 1960, pp. 175–210.

O le tusa paia, o le Feagaiga Tuai, ma le Feagaiga Fou lea na Faasamoaina, trans. from the original languages, with marginal references, London, British and Foreign Bible Society, 1862; rev. ed., 1887.

Pratt, George, *Grammar and Dictionary of the Samoan Language,* 4th ed., Malua, Samoa, London Missionary Society, 1911.

Rowe, Newton A., *Samoa under the Sailing Gods,* New York, Putnam, 1930.

Steubel, Oskar, "Samoanische Texte," *Veröffentlichungen aus dem Königlichen Museum für Völkerkunde, 4*:2–4 (1895), 55–241.

Stevenson, R. L., *Vailima Letters,* Chicago, Stone and Kimball, 1895.

——, *In the South Seas,* New York, Scribner, 1911.

Su'apa'ia, Kipeni, *Samoa: The Polynesian Paradise,* New York, Exposition Press, 1962.

Sullivan, Louis R., "A Contribution to Samoan Somatology," *Memoirs of the Bernice P. Bishop Museum, 8*:2, Honolulu, 1921, 81–98.

——, "Marquesan Somatology, with Comparative Notes on Samoa and Tonga," *Memoirs of the Bernice P. Bishop Museum, 9*:2, Honolulu, 1923, 141–249.

2. The Manus of the Admiralty Islands

A. FIRST EXPEDITION, 1928–29

In 1928, when we made our first study, the Manus people were a group of about 2,000 living in eleven autonomous villages along the south coast of the Great Admiralty, the central island of the Admiralty Archipelago, an island group located between 1°50′ and 3°10′ S. and between 146° and 148° E.

The people are light brown in color, tall and well built, with the frizzy hair of the Melanesian, and speak a Melanesian language. In 1928 their villages were built in lagoons adjacent to their fishing grounds and, with the exception of the village of Mbuke, which made pottery, and a few sago grounds won in war from the land people of the Great Admiralty, they depended on fishing and trading for their entire livelihood. Wood for house building, bast for fishing lines, and utensils and tools were all traded from the other peoples of the Admiralties, the transportation of trade articles in Manus deep-seagoing canoes being an important item in what they had to offer other peoples. In spite of their peripheral position, with no land except small built-up platforms and occasional precipitous little islands, the Manus were a dominant, wealthy people, preferring trade to war, but competent warriors when they did engage in war.

The Admiralties came under European control as part of German colonization, and passed to an Australian Mandate after World War I. In 1928 the Manus had not yet been missionized. Many Manus had, however, served in the native constabulary, even in German times, and most adolescent boys who had not yet been away to work spoke pidgin English.

Field work was conducted by Dr. Reo F. Fortune and myself during a six-month period in 1928–29, when I held a Fellowship from the Social Science Research Council. This was my first culture in which pidgin English had to be used as the intermediate language, so that pidgin had to be learned from a Manus-speaking schoolboy with an understanding, although hardly any speaking knowledge, of English at the same time we were working on the Manus language.

Selected Sources

Bühler, A., "Versuch einer Bevölkerungs– und Kulturanalyse auf den Admiralitätsinseln," *Zeitschrift für Ethnologie, 67* (1935), 1–32.

Fortune, Reo F., "Manus Religion," *Oceania, 2*:1 (1931), 74–108.

———, "A Note on Some Forms of Kinship Structure," *Oceania, 4*:1 (1933), 1–9.

———, *Manus Religion,* Philadelphia, American Philosophical Society, 1935.

Mead, Margaret, *Growing Up in New Guinea,* New York, Morrow, 1930; reprinted 1953, Mentor MD255, New York, New American Library.

———, "Melanesian Middlemen," *Natural History, 30*:2 (1930), 115–30.

———, "Water Babies of the South Seas," *Parents' Magazine, 5*:9 (1930), 20–21, 61.

———, "Living with the Natives of Melanesia," *Natural History, 31*:1 (1931), 62–74.

———, "Savage Masters of the Sea," *Safety Education, 10*:9, Sec. 1 (1931), 228–30.

———, "Two South Sea Educational Experiments and Their American Implications," in "Eighteenth Annual Schoolmen's Week Proceedings, March 18–21, 1931," *University of Pennsylvania School of Education Bulletin, 31*:36 (1931), 493–97.

———, "An Investigation of the Thought of Primitive Children, with Special Reference to Animism," *Journal of the Royal Anthropological Institute, 62* (1932), 173–90.

———, "Kinship in the Admiralty Islands," *Anthropological Papers of The American Museum of Natural History, 34,* Pt. 2, New York, 1934, 183–358.

———, "The Manus of the Admiralty Islands," in *Cooperation and Competition among Primitive Peoples,* ed. Margaret

Mead, New York, McGraw-Hill, 1937; rev. ed. 1961, BP123, Boston, Beacon, pp. 210–39.

Meier, Joseph P., "Mythen und Sagen der Admiralitätsinsulaner," *Anthropos, 2* (1907), 646–67, 933–41; *3* (1908), 193–206, 251–71; *4* (1909), 354–74.

Nevermann, Hans, *Admiralitäts-Inseln,* III: *Ergebnisse der Südsee-Expedition 1908–1910,* ed. G. Thilenius, Hamburg, Friederichsen, 1934; see also for extensive bibliography.

Parkinson, Richard, *Dreissig Jahre in der Südsee,* Stuttgart, Strecker and Schroeder, 1907.

Spitz, R. A., "Frühkindliches Erleben und Erwachsenenkultur bei den Primitiven, Bemerkungen zu Margaret Mead 'Growing Up in New Guinea,'" *Imago, 21* (1935), 367–87.

B. SECOND MANUS EXPEDITION, 1953–54

In 1953 I made a second expedition to the Admiralties, accompanied by two graduate students, Theodore Schwartz and Lenora Shargo Schwartz (now Lenora Foerstal). The Admiralty Island Expedition of The American Museum of Natural History, 1953–54, was made possible by a grant from the Rockefeller Foundation, with supplementary grants from the Frederick G. Voss Anthropological and Archeological Fund of the Museum. I spent six months in the field, and my collaborators fourteen months.

In the twenty-five year interval between the first and the second study, the Manus had been converted to Roman Catholicism and had received a minimum of schooling. During World War II they had experienced the departure of the Australians, occupation by the Japanese, the eviction of the Japanese, occupation by Allied forces (Americans with Australian civil government attachés) and, finally, the return to the Admiralties of the Australian Administration, now part of the Trust Territory of Papua and New Guinea. In the years after the war the Manus people had, on their own initiative, carried through a social revolution which was triggered by one of the recurrent Oceanic cargo cults. Led by Paliau, an extremely unusual man from the small island of Baluan, the people moved ashore, revised their traditional culture, and set up a

simplified version of Western culture as they had experienced
it. In 1953 it was possible for me to restudy the village of Peri
and to see the actual transformation which had taken place
within and among individuals whom I had known as children
twenty-five years earlier.

In this new study it was possible to use complicated instruments of research and recording—tape recorders, moving picture film, a massive collection of still photographs, projective
tests, and somatotyping—not yet in existence or not adapted
to field research in 1928, and a conceptual framework that had
developed in the human sciences in the intervening years.

Selected Sources

Bogen, Emil, "The Admiralty Islands and the Admiralty
Islanders: Incidental Observations at a Southwest Pacific
Naval Base, 1944–1945," n.d. (manuscript).

Lowenfeld, Margaret, *The Lowenfeld Mosaic Test,* London,
Newman Neame, 1954.

Mead, Margaret, "Manus Revisited," *Annual Report and Proceedings, Papua Scientific Society,* Port Moresby, 1953, pp.
15–18.

————, "Cultural Discontinuities and Personality Transformation," *Journal of Social Issues, Suppl.* Ser., no. 8 (1954),
3–16.

————, "Manus Restudied: An Interim Report," *Transactions
of The New York Academy of Sciences,* Ser. II, *16*:8 (1954),
426–32.

————, "Twenty-fifth Reunion at Manus," *Natural History,*
63:2 (1954), 66–68.

————, "Energy Changes under Conditions of Culture
Change," *Sociometry and the Science of Man, 18*:4 (1955),
201–11.

————, "Applied Anthropology, 1955," in *Some Uses of Anthropology: Theoretical and Applied,* Joseph B. Casagrande
and Thomas Gladwin, eds., Washington, Anthropological
Society of Washington, 1956, pp. 94–108.

————, *New Lives for Old: Cultural Transformation—Manus,*

1928–1953, New York, Morrow, 1956; reprinted 1961, Mentor MT324, New York, New American Library.

———, "Cultural Determinants of Behavior," in *Behavior and Evolution*, Anne Roe and George G. Simpson, eds., New Haven, Yale University Press, 1958, pp. 480–503.

———, "Cultural Factors in Community–Education Programs," in *Community Education*, ed. Nelson B. Henry, Chicago, University of Chicago Press, 1959, pp. 66–96.

———, "Cultural Determinants of Sexual Behavior," in *Sex and Internal Secretions*, 3d ed., ed. William C. Young, Baltimore, Williams and Wilkins, 1961, pp. 1433–79.

———, and Theodore Schwartz, "Political Structures of the Admiralty Islands," 1955 (manuscript).

———, and Theodore Schwartz, "The Cult as a Condensed Social Process," in *Group Processes*, Transactions of the Fifth Conference 1958, ed. Bertram Schaffner, New York, Josiah Macy, Jr. Foundation, 1960, pp. 85–187.

———, J. M. Tanner, Theodore Schwartz, and Barbara H. Heath, "The Physique of the Inhabitants of Manus (New Guinea) Village, Assessed by Anthropometry and Somatotypes," n.d. (manuscript).

Schwartz, Lenora Shargo (Lenora Foerstal), "Cultural Influence in Perception," unpublished Master's Essay, Stella Elkins Tylor School of Fine Arts of Temple University, 1959.

Schwartz, Theodore, "The Paliau Movement in the Admiralty Islands, 1946–1954," *Anthropological Papers of The American Museum of Natural History*, *49*, Pt. 2, New York, 1962, 207–422.

———, "Systems of Areal Integration: Some Considerations Based on the Admiralty Islands of Northern Melanesia," *Anthropological Forum*, 1:1 (1963), 56–97.

———, and Margaret Mead, "Micro- and Macro-cultural Models for Cultural Evolution," *Anthropological Linguistics*, *3*:1 (1961), 1–7; see also Appendix A, this volume.

Smythe, William, "The Languages of the Admiralty Islands," n.d. (manuscript).

C. THIRD MANUS EXPEDITION, 1963–

A third Admiralty Island expedition is now projected, beginning in the summer of 1963, under a grant from the National Institutes of Health. On this expedition a field station will be maintained by Theodore Schwartz, my collaborator in 1953–54, and Lola Romanucci Schwartz; and I shall join the expedition periodically for joint work. In this restudy after ten years, it is proposed to place the language and culture of the Manus within the larger framework of the areal culture, whose languages and cultural variations are the focus of this research.

3. The Arapesh

The Arapesh are a Papuan-speaking people, brown skinned and fuzzy haired, who occupy a wedge-shaped piece of territory on the northwest coast of New Guinea, reaching from the Pacific Coast over the triple range of the Prince Alexander Mountains, down into the plains that form the watershed of the Sepik River. The borders of the territory are indeterminate, the people have no name for the whole group, and the word "Arapesh" was coined by the anthropologist from the native word for human beings. They live in three different environments: on the beach, where they garden, fish, and trade with the adjacent islands; in the mountains, where they eke out a very precarious livelihood with hunting, gardening, and sago-working; and on the plains, where they are in active contact with headhunting peoples and have large yam gardens. Their number has been very loosely estimated at about 8,000. As part of the old Mandated Territory of New Guinea, recruiting began in this area after World War I, and in 1931 all adolescent boys expected to go away to work.

The Mountain Arapesh were studied intensively by Dr. Reo F. Fortune and myself during seven months in 1931; this research, as well as field work among the Mundugumor, the Tchambuli, and the Iatmul was supported by grants from the Frederick G. Voss Anthropological and Archeological Fund of The American Museum of Natural History. Dr. Fortune made a return visit to the Arapesh in 1936.

Sources

Fortune, Reo F., "Arapesh Warfare," *American Anthropologist, 41*:1 (1939), 22–41.

———, *Arapesh*, Publications of the American Ethnological Society, 19, New York, Augustin, 1942 (texts and grammar).

———, "Arapesh Maternity," *Nature, 152*:3849 (1943), 164.

———, "The Rules of Relationship Behaviour in One Variety of Primitive Warfare," *Man, 47*:115 (1947), 108–10.

Mead, Margaret, "The Marsalai Cult among the Arapesh, with Special Reference to the Rainbow Serpent Beliefs of the Australian Aboriginals," *Oceania, 4*:1 (1933), 37–53.

———, "Where Magic Rules and Men Are Gods," *The New York Times Magazine,* June 25, 1933, 8–9, 18.

———, "How the Papuan Plans His Dinner," *Natural History, 34*:4 (1934), 377–88.

———, "Tamberans and Tumbuans in New Guinea," *Natural History, 34*:3 (1934), 234–46.

———, "Where Sorcerers Call the Tune," *Asia, 34*:4 (1934), 232–35.

———, "The Mountain-Dwelling Arapesh," in *Sex and Temperament in Three Primitive Societies,* New York, Morrow, 1935; reprinted 1950, Mentor MP370, New York, New American Library, pp. 15–118.

———, "The Arapesh of New Guinea," in *Cooperation and Competition among Primitive Peoples,* ed. Margaret Mead, New York, McGraw-Hill, 1937; rev. ed. 1961, BP123, Boston, Beacon, pp. 20–50.

———, "The Mountain Arapesh, I. An Importing Culture," *Anthropological Papers of The American Museum of Natural History, 36,* Pt. 3, 1938, New York, 139–349; "The Mountain Arapesh, II. Supernaturalism," same series, *37,* Pt. 3, 1940, 317–451; "The Mountain Arapesh, III. Socio-Economic Life, and IV. Diary of Events in Alitoa," same series, *40,* Pt. 3, 1947, 163–419; "The Mountain Arapesh, V. The Record of Unabelin with Rorschach Analyses," same series, *41,* Pt. 3, 1949, 285–340.

———, "Cultural Determinants of Sexual Behavior," in *Sex*

and Internal Secretions, 3d ed., ed. William C. Young, Baltimore, Williams and Wilkins, 1961, pp. 1433–79.

———, "The Bark Paintings of the Mountain Arapesh of New Guinea," in *Technique and Personality in Primitive Art,* Museum of Primitive Art Lecture Series, 3, New York, Museum of Primitive Art, 1963, pp. 7–43.

4. THE MUNDUGUMOR

The Mundugumor people of New Guinea, some thousand in number, speak a Papuan language that bears some marks of being simplified by having been a trade language. They live in two hamlet clusters, four on one side and two on the other of the swiftly flowing Yuat River, which joins the south bank of the Sepik River at Yuarimo in the Sepik District of the old Mandated Territory.

Dr. Fortune and I worked among the Mundugumor for three and a half months in the autumn of 1932. In the division of labor in the field, I worked principally on child behavior and material culture. At this time, although not missionized and only so recently brought under government control that children of ten and eleven had been cannibals, they presented the picture of a broken culture. Ceremonies were infrequent; many men were away at work; only a few of the first group of recruits to go away had come home. The Mundugumor were missionized at some time between 1933 and 1938, when I had an opportunity to see again my principal informant, Omblean of Kenakatem, the village in which we had made our headquarters.

The published studies on the Mundugumor, in addition to *Male and Female,* are:

Mead, Margaret, "Tamberans and Tumbuans in New Guinea," *Natural History, 34:*3 (1934), 234–46.

———, "The River-Dwelling Mundugumor," in *Sex and Temperament in Three Primitive Societies,* New York, Morrow, 1935; reprinted 1950, Mentor MP370, New York, New American Library, pp. 119–63.

———, "The Mountain Arapesh, I. An Importing Culture,"

Anthropological Papers of The American Museum of Natural History, 36, Pt. 3, New York, 1938, 139–349.

5. THE IATMUL

The Iatmul people of the Middle Sepik represent one of the most noteworthy cultures of New Guinea. Their villages occupy country on both banks of the Sepik River from about 150 to about 250 miles from the mouth of the river. They speak a complex Papuan language which also has a simplified form used as a trade jargon by neighboring tribes. Their magnificent villages, with great pile dwellings and impressive men's houses, were under water part of each year. The separate villages were loosely interrelated by a complicated cosmological and totemic system of names and by theories of origin that traced one village back to another. But there was no central political organization, and even in the villages, the largest of which had 500 people, an uneasy form of order was maintained only by pitting subgroups against each other. Although some villages traded with bush people, in markets and for special commodities like pots, stone axes, and ocher, the Iatmul were on the whole self-sufficient, practicing a rich range of crafts and arts—basketry, carving, bark painting, modeling on skulls, etc.

Our intensive knowledge of the culture is based on four field trips by Gregory Bateson: a short expedition up the river for collecting and reconnaissance in 1929; work in the village of Mindimbit, 1930; work in Kankanamun and Palimbei in 1932–33; and an eight-month stay in 1938 in Tambunum on which I accompanied him, studied the children, and cooperated in collecting photographic records to provide comparative materials for Bali. All the specific materials on children come from this Tanbunum field trip and are related to the differentiation of Tambunum culture from the up-river Iatmul culture on which *Naven* is based.

Sources

Bateson, Gregory, "Social Structure of the Iatmul People of the Sepik," *Oceania,* 2:3–4 (1932), 245–91, 401–53.

———, "Music in New Guinea," *The Eagle* (St. John's College, Cambridge), *48*:214 (1934) 158–70.

———, "Culture Contact and Schismogenesis," *Man, 35*:199 (1935), 178–83.

———, *Naven*, Cambridge, Cambridge University Press, 1936; 2d ed. 1958, Stanford, Stanford University Press.

Mead, Margaret, "Public Opinion Mechanisms among Primitive Peoples," *Public Opinion Quarterly, 1*:3 (1937), 5–16.

———, "Character Formation in Two South Sea Societies," in *Transactions of the American Neurological Association, Sixty-Sixth Annual Meeting . . . 1940*, Richmond, Va., William Byrd Press [1940], pp. 99–103.

———, "Conflict of Cultures in America," in *Proceedings of the 54th Annual Convention of the Middle States Association of Colleges and Secondary Schools . . . 1940*, Philadelphia, Middle States Association of Colleges and Secondary Schools, 1940, pp. 30–44.

———, "Administrative Contributions to Democratic Character Formation at the Adolescent Level," *Journal of the National Association of Deans of Women, 4*:2 (1941), 51–57.

———, "The Family in the Future," in *Beyond Victory,* ed. Ruth Nanda Anshen, New York, Harcourt Brace, 1943, pp. 66–87.

———, "Age Patterning in Personality Development," *American Journal of Orthopsychiatry, 17*:2 (1947), 231–40.

6. THE TCHAMBULI

The Tchambuli people of New Guinea are a small tribe—only 500 in all—who live on the edge of the Tchambuli lake, under the Tchambuli mountain. Two waterways connect the lake with the Sepik River about 180 miles from its mouth. They speak a difficult Papuan language which is not understood by the people around them, whose languages they have to learn.

At the time Dr. Fortune and I studied them, in 1933, they had been under control by the government of the Mandated Territory of New Guinea some seven or eight years, and just previously they had fled their ancestral territory, in fear of the warlike Iatmuls, and gone in three separate groups to live with bush people. Now, under the Pax Britannica and with iron tools, they were involved in a cultural renaissance, building a series of elaborately decorated men's houses along the shore, and great family dwelling houses inland. They had a few gardens, but depended mainly on fishing and on trading for other food in periodic markets. The planned division of labor in field work was the same as in Mundugumor.

Except for the discussion in *Male and Female,* the only published study is:

Mead, Margaret, "The Lake-Dwelling Tchambuli," in *Sex and Temperament in Three Primitive Societies,* New York, Morrow, 1935; reprinted 1950, Mentor MP370, New York, New American Library, pp. 164–89.

7. BALI

A. FIRST EXPEDITION, 1936–38, 1939

The people of Bali contrast strongly with all the others discussed here. They are not a primitive people, but Indonesians speaking a Malay language who for many hundreds of years have been exposed to the high cultures of Southeast Asia and China. Almost a million people on their tiny island—only 2,905 square miles in size—east of Java, they have lived in a society that in many ways resembled the Middle Ages in Europe, or did so until Netherlands rule was instituted at the beginning of this century. The country was divided into small kingdoms, in which rulers of Kesatria caste presided loosely over a Brahman priesthood; they exacted mild tribute from a prevailing casteless peasant population who lived in villages, each of which had a perfectly organized self-sufficient social structure that regulated land tenure, irrigation, and all types of social organization except those few which reigning princes had arrogated to themselves. Hinduism had penetrated the religious structure deeply, but there were also many traces of old Buddhism. Caste, believed to have been brought in from Java when the Hindu Javanese fled the spreading power of Islam, sat rather lightly in Bali, where it was possible for high-caste men to marry low-caste women and yet bequeath some caste to their children.

In spite of the conspicuous differences between prince and peasant, between Brahman priest and local village temple officiant, between the crude Mountain craftsman and the Plains artisan, in its ceremonial and its symbolism, a great part of Balinese life was available to every Balinese. So although we find extreme and detailed differences between one part of Bali and another, or between the formal behavior of different castes, or between different priestly sects, the character structure seems to be extremely homogeneous, with little difference between the villages whose inhabitants never go into trance and those where almost everyone goes into trance.

The first Balinese expedition was conducted from 1936 to 1938 and, after a nine-month break for work among the Iatmul of New Guinea, during a return visit in 1939. The expedition was financed by the Frederick G. Voss Anthropological and Archeological Fund of The American Museum of Natural History and by grants from the Social Science Research Council and the Committee for Research in Dementia Praecox supported by the Thirty-Third Degree Scottish Rite, Northern Masonic Jurisdiction.

Study of such a complex society is of necessity a very different task from the recording, at most by two people, of the culture of some small, just discovered and already disappearing primitive culture. In the years in which Gregory Bateson and I worked in Bali, based in the mountain village of Bajoeng Gede, we were heavily indebted to Jane Belo, Colin McPhee, and Katherine Mershon, and to the insights of the artist, the late Walter Spies.

In Bali we developed our modern intensive method of using still photography (28,000 stills) and moving picture records and the method of working with a variety of cross-cutting samples of the culture: one community study, one study of each of the two highest castes in a given setting, a longitudinal study of a set of children, studies of ceremonials in different parts of the island, and samples of drama, carving, painting, and so on. With these new methods—developed in part with the hope of bringing a multidisciplinary team to Bali for further research—we moved from the kind of record which could be worked up by the field worker on a ratio of two years of desk work to one year in the field to a record, based on the rapid accumulation of materials, which made possible a ratio of some twenty years of analysis to one year in the field.

B. SECOND BALINESE EXPEDITION, 1957–58

In 1957, accompanied by Ken Heyman whose primary field of interest is photography, I made a brief reconnaissance visit to Bali, under a grant from the National Institutes of Health. During the twenty years since 1937 the Balinese had experienced Japanese occupation, in World War II, the war of liberation against the Netherlands, and the changes brought about by the formation of the Republic of Indonesia. It was possible to visit the villages in which I had worked in the 1930s; there we filmed and photographed the children, now grown up, with their children, and the artists, now twenty years older, and made a preliminary assay of the changes that had occurred among a peasant people who were coming to have a sense of participation in the modern world.

This restudy has provided a valuable contrast to the restudy of the much simpler culture of the Admiralty Islands, and the groundwork has been done for a projected long-term study within another five to ten years.

Selected Sources

There is a great literature on Bali, both technical and popular. Netherlands scholars have studied the law, and have constructed archaeological sequences from detailed studies of archaeological remains. I shall cite here only references to my own and Gregory Bateson's work, such work of our collaborators as we ourselves drew on, and subsequent work that has drawn on our work.

Abel, Theodora M., "Free Designs of Limited Scope as a Personality Index," *Character and Personality*, 7:1 (1938), 50–62.

Bateson, Gregory, "An Old Temple and a New Myth," *Djawa*, *17*:5–6 (1937), 1–17.

————, "The Frustration–Aggression Hypothesis," *Psychological Review*, *48*:4 (1941), 350–55.

————, "Bali: The Human Problem of Reoccupation," New York, Museum of Modern Art, 1942 (mimeographed).

————, "Bali: The Value System of a Steady State," in *Social Structure: Essays Presented to A. R. Radcliffe-Brown,* ed. Meyer Fortes, Oxford, Clarendon Press, 1949, pp. 35–53.

————, and Margaret Mead, *Balinese Character,* Special Publications of The New York Academy of Sciences, 2, 1942; reissued 1962.

Belo, Jane, "The Balinese Temper," *Character and Personality*, *4*:2 (1935), 120–46.

————, "A Study of Customs Pertaining to Twins in Bali," *Tidschrift voor Ind. Taal-, Land-, en Volkenkunde,* 75:4 (1935), 483–549.

————, "A Study of a Balinese Family," *American Anthropologist, 38*:1 (1936), 12–31.

————, "Balinese Children's Drawings," *Djawa, 17*:5–6 (1937), 1–13; reprinted 1955 in *Childhood in Contemporary Cultures,* Margaret Mead and Martha Wolfenstein, eds., Chicago: University of Chicago Press, pp. 52–69.

————, *Bali: Rangda and Barong,* American Ethnological Society Monographs, 16, New York, Augustin, 1949.

————, *Bali: Temple Festival,* American Ethnological Society Monographs, 22, New York, Augustin, 1953.

————, *Trance in Bali,* New York, Columbia University Press, 1960.

————, "Balinese Paintings," n.d. (manuscript).

Franken, H. J., and others, *Bali: Studies in Life, Thought and Ritual,* Selected Studies on Indonesia by Dutch Scholars, 5, The Hague, Van Hoeve, 1960.

Geertz, Clifford, "Form and Variation in Balinese Village Structure," *American Anthropologist, 61*:6 (1959), 991–1012.

Geertz, Hildred, "The Vocabulary of Emotion: A Study of

Javanese Socialization Processes," *Psychiatry,* 22:2 (1959), 225–37.

Holt, Claire, "Les Danses de Bali," *Archives Internationales de la danse,* Pt. 1 (April 15, 1935), 51–53; Pt. 2 (July 15, 1935), 84–86.

———, "Théatre et danses aux Indes néerlandaises," in *Catalogue et Commentaires, 13,* Exposition des Archives internationales de la danse, Paris, Masson, 1939, p. 86.

———, "Analytical Catalogue of Collection of Balinese Carvings," New York, The American Museum of Natural History, n.d. (manuscript).

McPhee, Colin, "The 'Absolute' Music of Bali," *Modern Music, 12*:4 (1935), 163–69.

———, "The Balinese *wajan koelit* and Its Music," *Djawa, 16* (1936), 1–50.

———, "'*Angkloeng* Music in Bali," *Djawa, 17* (1937), 322–66.

———, "Children and Music in Bali," *Djawa, 18*:6 (1938), 1–15; reprinted 1955, in *Childhood in Contemporary Cultures,* Margaret Mead and Martha Wolfenstein, eds., Chicago, University of Chicago Press, pp. 70–94.

———, "Figuration in Balinese Music," *Peabody Bulletin,* Ser. 36, no. 2 (1940), 23–26.

———, *A House in Bali,* New York, Day, 1946.

———, *A Club of Small Men,* New York, Day, 1947.

———, "Dance in Bali," *Dance Index,* 7:7–8 (1948), 156–207.

———, "Five-Tone Gamelan Music of Bali," *Musical Quarterly, 35*:2 (1949), 250–81.

———, *Music in Bali,* New Haven, Yale University Press, 1964.

Mead, Margaret, "Public Opinion Mechanisms among Primitive Peoples," *Public Opinion Quarterly,* 1:3 (1937), 5–16.

———, "Researches in Bali, 1936–1939, I. On the Concept of Plot in Culture, II. Methods of Research in Bali and New Guinea," *Transactions of The New York Academy of Sciences,* Ser. II, 2:1 (1939), 24–31.

———, "The Strolling Players in the Mountains of Bali," *Natural History, 43*:1 (1939), 17–26, 64.

———, "The Arts in Bali," *Yale Review, 30*:2 (1940), 335–47.

———, "Character Formation in Two South Sea Societies," in

Transactions of the American Neurological Association, Sixty-Sixth Annual Meeting . . . 1940, Richmond, Va., William Byrd Press [1940], pp. 99–103.

———, "Conflict of Cultures in America," in *Proceedings of the 54th Annual Convention of the Middle States Association of Colleges and Secondary Schools . . . 1940,* Philadelphia, Middle States Association of Colleges and Secondary Schools, 1940, pp. 30–44.

———, "Social Change and Cultural Surrogates," *Journal of Educational Sociology, 14*:2 (1940), 92–109.

———, "Administrative Contributions to Democratic Character Formation at the Adolescent Level," *Journal of the National Association of Deans of Women, 4*:2 (1941), 51–57.

———, "Community Drama, Bali and America," *American Scholar, 11*:1 (1941–42), 79–88.

———, "Educative Effects of Social Environment as Disclosed by Studies of Primitive Societies," in *Environment and Education,* Human Development Series, I, Supplementary Educational Monographs, 54, Chicago, University of Chicago Press, 1942, pp. 48–61.

———, "The Family in the Future," in *Beyond Victory,* ed. Ruth Nanda Anshen, New York, Harcourt Brace, 1943, pp. 66–87.

———, "Age Patterning in Personality Development," *American Journal of Orthopsychiatry, 17*:2 (1947), 231–40.

———, "Children and Ritual in Bali," in *Childhood in Contemporary Cultures,* Margaret Mead and Martha Wolfenstein, eds., Chicago, University of Chicago Press, 1955, pp. 40–51.

———, "Bali in the Market Place of the World," *Proceedings of the American Academy of Arts and Letters and the National Institute of Arts and Letters,* Ser. II, no. 9 (1959), 286–93.

———, "Cultural Determinants of Sexual Behavior," in *Sex and Internal Secretions,* 3d ed., ed. William C. Young, Baltimore, Williams and Wilkins, 1961, pp. 1433–97.

———, and Frances C. Macgregor, *Growth and Culture,* New York, Putnam, 1951.

Zoete, Beryl de, and Walter Spies, *Dance and Drama in Bali,* New York, Harper, 1939.

Films

Bateson, Gregory, and Margaret Mead, *A Balinese Family,* Character Formation in Different Culture Series, New York University Film Library, 16 mm., 17 min., sound, 1952.
———, *Childhood Rivalry in Bali and New Guinea,* ibid., 16 mm., 20 min., sound, 1952.
———, *Karba's First Years,* ibid., 16 mm., 20 min., sound, 1952.
———, *Trance and Dance in Bali,* ibid., 16 mm., 20 min., sound, 1952.

Appendix C

Bibliographical Considerations

THOSE OF US who work on the growing edge of knowledge and rely heavily on interdisciplinary conferences as a form of orientation are faced with a peculiar problem of documentation. I have estimated that it now takes some 30 hours to document an article that can be written in two hours, because so many of my own reference points are to oral accounts of research whose published versions may not appear for several years. The problem is, moreover, inextricably bound up with the question to which this book is addressed, that is, the way in which communication, at many levels of codification and expressed through different sensory modalities, can facilitate the process of cultural evolution.[1]

This book is not a compendious review of the literature, nor is it an attempt to present a separate and idiosyncratic theory designed to replace all other theories. I have written in the light of theoretical work by psychologists, anthropologists, and ethologists, and I have attempted not to make any statement that might be called into question by *work* in other fields. Theoretical pronouncements which do not flow specifically from actual work but are by-products of a theoretical position —such as Hebb's attacks on psychoanalysis[2] or Steward's statement that culture influences personality but personality does not influence culture[3]—I propose to deal with only if they have in some way illuminated the questions I am asking. Nor do I propose to become entangled in the discussions of those coteries of self-reference—for example, Bidney, Hallowell, Kluckhohn, Kroeber, and Spiro—in which a small group of human scientists, writing primarily for one another, cite a minimum of evidence but present a maximum of contradictory arguments *ad argumentum,* as in Spiro's "Culture and Personality, the Natural History of a False Dichotomy." [4] I realize that there are groups of human scientists who recognize only this form of discussion, and it may well have a function in sharpening the attention of the student who hopes to make a contribution out of ratiocination and erudition rather than basic field research. Franz Boas used to warn us that it was a mistake to publish a new theoretical statement in a monograph, where no one would ever recognize it for what it was. I think he was right to the extent that most of one's colleagues do not recognize an unlabeled theory. But I do believe that in the long run theoretical work that flows directly from research has a different kind of usefulness from theoretical work that is essentially a secondary elaboration of other scientists' primary research.

At the same time, just as no good anthropologist will undertake a detailed exploration of one aspect of a culture without having a working knowledge of the whole culture, its history, its place in an area, and so on—as far as these things are known—I believe it is unjustified to undertake a discussion of part of a field unless one has a working knowledge of the whole. However, if I were to describe fire-walking in Fiji, for example, I would not feel that I would have to include in that particular discussion accounts of Melanesian or Polynesian cultures or discussions of fire-walking and related behavior in other parts of the world.

At times the kind of inclusiveness used by an anthropologist in focusing on a single institution is not completely understood in other disciplines. It seems useful, therefore, to provide a single illustration here, taking fire-walking in Fiji as a subject, to indicate what it would be necessary to take into account:[a]

> In considering the institution of fire-walking in Fiji, it would be necessary to place Fiji as an archipelago of some 200 to 250 islands (the total count varying by the size of the atoll that is given the status of an island), with a total land area of some 7,083 square miles; the archipelago in turn would be placed in the Pacific, where the extent and number of other archipelagos are known. The physical type of the Fijians, their height range and skin color and the astonishing frizziness of their hair would be placed within our existing knowledge of all the races of mankind, particularly the physical types found in Polynesia and Melanesia, as the Fijian Islands lie on the boundary between these two culture areas.
>
> The physical features of the islands, which vary from mountainous islands of volcanic origin to small coral atolls, would be specified. This would be done within the context of what is known about the relations between life on volcanic islands and life on hurricane-swept atolls, with the implications for nutrition, types of agriculture and fishing, and the availability of natural resources and opportunities for trade and exchange, and also the consequences of these for different choices in types of social organization.[b] These physical features would also be viewed in relation to the evidence provided by blood-group studies, theories of Pacific migration, specific local disease conditions, etc.
>
> The languages spoken in Fiji would be designated as belonging to the Malayo–Polynesian family, with spe-

[a] The reference on Fijian fire-walking will be cited at the foot of the page on which they occur; publications cited only in connection with fire-walking will not appear in the consolidated list of references.

[b] Douglas L. Oliver, *The Pacific Islands*, Cambridge, Harvard University Press, 1952; Marshall D. Sahlins, *Social Stratification in Polynesia*, Publications of the American Ethnological Society, Seattle, University of Washington Press, 1958.

cific relationships to Polynesian and Micronesian languages.[c]

The extent of our historical knowledge would be stated, including the date of discovery by European mariners and the type of contact that immediately followed on discovery, when Polynesian Tongans, armed with recently acquired firearms, extended their earlier attempts at hegemony over the population, and also the consequences of this admixture of populations and cultural traits.[d]

It would be necessary to take into account the specific type of social organization. The institutions of sacred chieftainship, of sister's son's rights, and of ceremonial, economic, and political relations between cross-cousins would be placed both in the wider context of this part of Oceania[e] and in the context of similar institutions in the world.[f]

So each statement would contain, explicitly or by implication, a sense of the whole—an indication of the place of these islands, this climate, these people, and their institutions within the context of the known and recorded aspects of human life in the known world.

Then, turning to a discussion of a particular institu-

[c] Arthur Capell and R. H. Lester, "Local Divisions and Movements in Fiji," *Oceania, 11*:4 (1941), 313–41, and *12*:1 (1941), 21–48; also George W. Grace, "The Position of the Polynesian Languages within the Austronesian (Malayo–Polynesian Language Family)," *Bernice P. Bishop Museum Special Publication, 46*, Honolulu, 1959.

[d] Buell Quain, *Fijian Village*, Chicago, University of Chicago Press, 1948; see especially Ruth Benedict's introduction, pp. xi–xvii. See also Laura Thompson, *Fijian Frontier*, Studies of the Pacific, 4, New York, American Council, Institute of Pacific Relations, 1940.

[e] Margaret Mead, "Social Organization of Manua," *Bernice P. Bishop Museum Bulletin, 76*, Honolulu, 1930, 1–218 (especially for further bibliography); also Mead, "Kinship in the Admiralty Islands," *Anthropological Papers of The American Museum of Natural History, 34*, Pt. 2, New York, 1934, 183–358.

[f] A. M. Hocart, *Kingship*, London, Oxford University Press, 1927; Robert H. Lowie, *Primitive Society*, New York, Liveright, 1920; George P. Murdock, *Social Structure*, New York, Macmillan, 1949.

tion, i.e. Fijian fire-walking, it would be necessary to place this custom itself in a complex context. It would be presented as a custom which has also been reported for Bulgaria, Spain, Trinidad, Mauritius, Japan, India, Straits Settlements, Bali, Tahiti, etc.,[g] and as a custom which has two characteristic forms—the specific practice of walking on hot stones (the form taken by Fijian and Tahitian fire-walking) and walking on hot coals. Further, it would be necessary to take into account its relationship to ordeals by fire[h] and to the use of fire as an earnest of some specified connection with the supernatural (as in Balinese trance dancing, when the little *sangiang* dancers trip across hot coals or remain impassive when hot coals fall onto their skin[i]).

And, finally, the Fijian institution itself would be described.[j] A full discussion would include an attempt to

[g] F. Arthur Jackson, "Fire-Walking in Fiji, Japan, India, and Mauritius," *Journal of the Polynesian Society, 8*:3:31 (1899), 188–96; see also Wilmon Menard, "Fire-Walkers of the South Seas," *Travel, 62*:2 (1933), 18–23.

[h] James G. Frazer, *The Golden Bough*, 3d ed., Part VII: *Balder the Beautiful*, 2, London, Macmillan, 1914, pp. 1–15.

[i] Jane Belo, *Trance in Bali*, New York, Columbia University Press, 1960.

[j] W. L. Allardyce, "The Fijians and Their Fire-Walking," *Proceedings of the Royal Colonial Institute, 35* (1904), 71–77; Charles R. Darling, "Fire-walking," *Nature 136*:3439 (1935), 521; J. W. Davidson, "The Legend of the Vilavilairevo (Fire-Walking) of the Island of Bengga, Fiji," *Journal of the Polynesian Society, 29*:2:114 (1920), 91–94; "Demonstration of Fire-walking," *Nature, 136*:3438 (1935), 468; "Fire-Walking: Scientific Tests," *Nature, 129*:3520 (1937), 660; Robert Fulton, "An Account of the Fiji Fire-Walking Ceremony or Vilavilairevo with a Probable Explanation of the Mystery," *Transactions and Proceedings of the New Zealand Institute 1902, 35* (1903), 187–201; A. M. Hocart, Correspondence, "Fire-Walking," *Man, 37*:150 (1937), 118–19; T. M. Hocken, "An Account of the Fiji Fire Ceremony," *Transactions and Proceedings of the New Zealand Institute, 31* (1899), 667–72; Albert G. Ingalls, "Fire-Walking," *Scientific American, 160*:3 (1939), 135–38; F. Arthur Jackson, "A Fijian Legend of the Origin of the 'Vilavilairevo' or 'Fire Ceremony,'" *Journal of the Polynesian Society, 3*:1 (1894), 72–75; Andrew Lang, Correspondence, "The Fijian Fire-Walk," *Folk-Lore, 14*:1 (1903), 87–88; J. W. Lindt, "The Fire Ordeal at Beqa, Fiji Islands," *Transactions of the Royal Geographical Society of Australasia (Victoria Branch), 11* (1894), 45–58; Harry Price, Correspond-

measure the "genuineness" of the fire-walkers' immunity from burning. In conclusion, there would be the possibility that a full understanding of this particular institution on a remote Pacific island archipelago might contribute to our knowledge of man's psychological capacities.

Just as in an analysis of *fire-walking in Fiji*, I do not feel it necessary or desirable to include the full background (as outlined above) in my discussion, I do not feel called upon to write long discussions of the work on evolution, ethology, cultural anthropology, Oceanic ethnology, linguistics, the psychology of learning, artistic style, and so on, on which I have drawn, in order to place my own observations in context. In the complexities of the present world, any student who attempts to place a discussion in a wide context has to depend on some organized procedure to which aspects of the wider literature in a field are immediately relevant.

In this volume I have followed a few rather simple procedures in my references. First, I have not used a secondary source where a primary source is available on a point (i.e. I have preferred Sigmund Freud to Otto Fenichel,[5] Charles Darwin to Loren Eiseley,[6] Jean Piaget to David Rapaport,[7] Gregory Bateson to Gardner Murphy,[8] Konrad Lorenz to John P. Scott.[9] Second, I have relied very heavily on those members of other disciplines with whom I have had an opportunity for protracted face-to-face exchange, either separately or in the many interdisciplinary conferences in which it has been my good fortune to participate. The small intimate multi-

---

ence, "Fire-Walking," *Nature, 139*:3526 (1937), 928–29; James Purves-Stewart and David Waterston, "Observations on Fijian Fire-Walking," *British Medical Journal,* 2:3912 (1935), 1267–69; Thomas S. Reed, "The Maoris and Their Land," *Proceedings of the Royal Geographical Society of Australasia (South Australian Branch) 1907–08, 10* (1909), 48–66 (especially 65–66); Kingsley Roth, "The Fire-Walk in Fiji," *Man, 33*:49 (1933), 44–49; also Roth, "Oceania: A Note on the Fijian 'Fire-Walking' Ceremony from an Ethnological Standpoint," *Man, 36*:235 (1936), 172–73; Colin Simpson, "The Fire-Walkers of Fiji," in *Islands of Men,* Sydney, Angus and Robertson, 1956, pp. 213–48.

disciplinary conference has become one of the major communication devices of the twentieth century.[10] In conferences like the ones conducted for many years by the Josiah Macy, Jr. Foundation,[11] clarification can be obtained immediately, and multisensory modalities are available for those who are accustomed to drawing on living sources rather than on coded sources. So I refer more often to the proceedings of those conferences of which I was a member—to those conferences where, in fact, I listened and looked—than to others of equal importance. For example, I refer to the proceedings of the cybernetics conferences,[12] but I would not be likely to refer to the Hixon Symposium[13] unless one of my living sources referred to the Hixon Symposium as a better source of something mentioned only cursorily at a conference I did attend.

But primarily I depend on my own field work, for here I know the full extent of the materials and do not have to waste paper lamenting the omissions of colleagues who are interested in other problems. Seven primary Pacific field trips, one American Indian field trip, and two further restudies of Pacific Island cultures have provided me with sufficient variety to illuminate those matters which I feel competent to discuss.[14]

An Arapesh example of the handling of noun classes might not be as fully rewarding as an example taken from a Bantu language—if I had the same range of information about learning among the Bantu. But for my purposes I consider the Arapesh example a better one. If I were writing an even-handed textbook and knew neither Arapesh nor Bantu at first hand, I might choose quite differently. But I believe it is worth while to work from living models[15] whenever it is possible to do so.

Notes

NOTES TO PREFACE

1. Thomas Henry Huxley and Julian S. Huxley, *Touchstone for Ethics,* 1947.

2. Charles Darwin, *The Origin of Species,* reprint of the first edition, 1951.

3. C. H. Waddington and others, *Science and Ethics,* 1942.

4. Gregory Bateson, *Naven,* 1936.

5. G. K. Noble and H. T. Bradley, "The Mating Behavior of Lizards: Its Bearing on the Theory of Sexual Selection," *Annals of The New York Academy of Sciences,* 1933.

6. C. R. Carpenter, "A Field Study of the Behavior and Social Relations of the Howling Monkeys (*Alouatta palliata*), *Comparative Psychology Monographs,* 1934.

7. J. M. Tanner and Bärbel Inhelder, eds., *Discussions on Child Development,* 4 vols., 1957–60.

8. Bertram Schaffner, ed., *Group Processes,* 5 vols., 1955–60.

9. Margaret Mead, *Male and Female,* 1949.

10. Margaret Mead, "Cultural Determinants of Sexual Behavior," in *Sex and Internal Secretions,* 1961.

11. Anne Roe and George G. Simpson, eds., *Behavior and Evolution,* 1958.

12. Margaret Mead, ed., *Cooperation and Competition among Primitive Peoples,* 1937.

13. Bateson, *Naven.*

14. Report of the Committee on Food Habits, "Manual for the Study of Food Habits," *National Research Council Bulletin,* 1945.

15. Margaret Mead, "Cultural Determinants of Behavior," in *Behavior and Evolution,* 1958.

16. Margaret Mead, *Coming of Age in Samoa,* 1928.

17. Margaret Mead, *An Anthropologist at Work: Writings of Ruth Benedict,* 1959.

18. Margaret Mead, "Apprenticeship under Boas," in *The Anthropology of Franz Boas,* 1959.

19. See, for example, Michael Banton, ed., *Darwinism and the Study of Society,* 1961; S. A. Barnett, ed., *A Century of Darwin,* 1958; Marston Bates and Philip S. Humphrey, eds., *Darwin Reader,* 1956; Frederick C. Bawden and others, eds., *Symposium on Evolution,* 1959; "Centennial, April 1959," *Proceedings of the American Philosophical Society,* 1959; "Darwin–Wallace Centenary," *Journal of the Linnean Society of London, Zoology,* 1958; Loren Eiseley, *Darwin's Century,* 1958; John C. Greene, *The Death of Adam,* 1959; Betty J. Meggers, ed., *Evolution and Anthropology,* 1959; Russell L. Mixter, ed., *Evolution and Christian Thought Today,* 1959;

"The Origin of Species—A Centennial Symposium," *Australian Journal of Science,* 1959; Sol Tax, ed., *Evolution after Darwin,* 3 vols., 1960.

20. Marshall D. Sahlins and Elman R. Service, eds., *Evolution and Culture,* 1960.

21. Theodosius Dobzhansky, "Eugenics in New Guinea," *Science,* 1960; D. Carleton Gajdusek, "Kuru: An Appraisal of Five Years of Investigation," *Eugenics Quarterly,* 1962, and bibliography in this article.

22. Hudson Hoagland and Ralph W. Burhoe, issue eds., "Evolution and Man's Progress," *Daedalus,* 1961.

23. C. H. Waddington, *The Ethical Animal,* 1961.

24. Hoagland and Burhue, issue eds., "Evolution and Man's Progress."

25. Peter H. Knapp, ed., *Expression of the Emotions in Man,* 1963.

26. L. S. B. Leakey and Clark Howell, "The Discovery by L. S. B. Leakey of *Zinjanthropus boisei,*" *Current Anthropology,* 1960.

27. Loren Eiseley, *The Immense Journey,* 1957, pp. 127–41.

28. G. E. Hutchinson, personal communication; see also, Margaret Mead, "Cultural Determinants of Sexual Behavior," 1961.

29. Charles Darwin, *Expression of the Emotions in Man and Animals,* 1955.

30. Theodore Schwartz and Margaret Mead, "Micro- and Macro-cultural Models for Cultural Evolution," *Anthropological Linguistics,* 1961; see also Appendix A, this volume.

31. Sigmund Freud, *Totem and Taboo,* 1918.

32. Margaret Mead, *"Totem and Taboo* Reconsidered with Respect," *Bulletin of the Menninger Clinic,* 1963.

33. Margaret Mead, "The Menninger Foundation: A Center of Innovation," *Menninger Quarterly,* 1961.

34. Harold A. Abramson, ed., *Problems of Consciousness,* 5 vols., 1951–55; Heinz von Foerster, ed., *Cybernetics,* 5 vols., 1950–56; Bertram Schaffner, ed., *Group Processes,* 5 vols., 1955–60.

35. Anne Burgess and R. F. A. Dean, eds., *Malnutrition and Food Habits,* 1962; Mary Capes, ed., *Communication or Conflict: Conferences: Their Nature, Dynamics and Planning,* 1960; *Mental Health in International Perspective,* 1961; Kenneth Soddy, ed., *Mental Health and Infant Development,* 2 vols., 1955.

36. Tanner and Inhelder, eds., *Discussions on Child Development.*

37. Evelyn S. Stewart, "The Merrill–Palmer Institute: Deep Probe in the Science of Living," *Michigan Yearbook 1961.*

38. L. K. Frank and others, "Teleological Mechanisms," *Annals of The New York Academy of Sciences,* 1948; Margaret Mead and others, "Man in Space," *Annals of The New York Academy of Sciences,* 1958; "The New York Academy of Sciences Its History and Activities," in *Science Center New York,* n.d.

39. American Association for the Advancement of Science, *Directory of Officers and Activities for 1962,* pp. 62–125.

40. *Bulletin of the University of Cincinnati Graduate Training Program in Psychiatry 1961.*

41. Frank Tannenbaum, "University Seminars: Anniversary Report," *Graduate Faculties Newsletter Columbia University,* 1960.

42. Margaret Mead, "The Comparative Study of Culture and the Purposive Cultivation of Democratic Values," in *Science, Philosophy and Religion, Second Symposium,* 1942; Mead, "The Comparative Study of Cultures and the Purposive Cultivation of Democratic Values, 1941–1949," in *Perspectives on a Troubled Decade: Science, Philosophy and Religion, 1939–1949, Tenth Symposium,* 1950.

NOTES TO INTRODUCTION

1. Gregory Bateson and Margaret Mead, *Balinese Character,* 1942.

2. Margaret Mead and Frances C. Macgregor, *Growth and Culture,* 1951.

3. Efforts to resolve the problem of the extent to which culture change can be attributed to identified individuals have been an integral part of the long process by which, during the present century, anthropologists have attempted to free modern thought of the idea of a series of inevitable stages of cultural evolution and to present evidence countering the claim that there is any form of permanent association between any race and any culture or any level of cultural development, or between any codified product of culture (e.g. language) and the rest of culture, or between such a codified product and the race of those who are its carriers (i.e. the speakers of a language).

The resolution of this problem has also been part of the struggle to document the hypothesis of the psychic unity of mankind and to demonstrate the existence of essentially rational processes of thought among the culturally simplest and most primitive groups of mankind. Thinking about these different aspects of human capacities and of culture merged in the tendency to treat expressions of originality—genius and its products—as the by-products of time and space, the culture of a period and the organization of a society acting upon and through a reliably recurrent and often unused supply of superior individuals.

Boas, writing in *The Mind of Primitive Man* (first published in 1911, but summarizing two decades of thinking), pointed out that "originality is a trait which is by no means lacking in the life of primitive people" (p. 112), but also that "the mind of even the greatest genius is influenced by the current thought of his time" (p. 113). He concluded that "our brief consideration of some of the mental activities of man in civilized and primitive society has led us to the conclusion that these functions of the human mind are common to the whole of humanity," but he also commented prudently, "I do not believe that we are able at the present time to form a just valuation of the hereditary mental powers of the different races" (p. 122).

Contemporaries of Boas were working on related aspects of the problem, and younger anthropologists continued to struggle with the various issues that had been defined. Edwin R. A. Seligman published *The Economic Interpretation of History* in 1902, and some time later William Ogburn became interested in the question of the inevitability of invention (William F. Ogburn and Dorothy Thomas, "Are Inventions Inevitable," *Political Science Quarterly*, 1922). In *Culture and Ethnology* (1917), Robert Lowie, having argued that "psychology, racial difference, geographical environment, have all proved inadequate for the interpretation of cultural phenomena," concluded that "the inference is obvious. Culture is a thing *sui generis*" (p. 66). Later, in discussing "knowledge and science" in *An Introduction to Cultural Anthropology* (1934), Lowie emphasized "cooperation" in pointing out that "a science depends not only on other sciences and on skilled mechanics but on the whole organization of society" (p. 338), and he sheered even farther away from the idea of individual contribution in his final statement that "science, like all of culture, is not the work of one or two favored nations or races but of humanity as a whole" (p. 341), a conclusion which emphasized instead the cumulative nature of knowledge. Still later, in the expanded version of this book (revised edition, 1940), Lowie dealt with the problem of "race and variability" and with the specific question of "those distinctive features that so sharply set off industrial civilization from its predecessors and contemporaries" (p. 533) by recognizing, on the one hand, the importance of "individual variability" and, on the other, the pre-eminence of the cultural context, as suitable or unsuitable to a particular kind of innovation at a particular time and place. In the same period, beginning in the 1920s, A. L. Kroeber worked on the voluminous materials that led to the publication of *Configurations of Culture Growth* (1944), a study in which he made a deliberate effort to "disregard personalities except as inevitable mechanisms or sources of cultural expression" (p. 10). In his conclusions (p. 839), he stated:

> It is the clustering of recognized genius in time and space and common speech which is the basis of the value–growth appraisals which have been outlined in this book.
>
> This implies a definition of genius supplementary to the customary or popular one that a genius is an individual who is eminently superior in his mental endowment. A social definition of genius may also be offered. Geniuses are the indicators of the realization of coherent pattern growths of culture value.
>
> A corollary is that most of the potential geniuses born are never realized, so far as history or human values are concerned.

Inquiries like these, in seeking to emphasize the equal dignity of men of all races and all levels of culture, denigrated the importance of great men, as individuals. Boas' interest in family lines and in the merging of ancestry in small inbred communities (*The Mind of Primitive Man*, see especially revised edition, 1938, pp. 52–73) and even his discussion of the fact that individuals inherit their specific traits from their particular ancestors, not from a population (anticipating in this present-day discussions of small breeding groups within large populations), had little effect on contemporary attitudes. The prevailing assumption, implicit in the work of the period, was that any discussion of identified individuals (who would inevitably come from one ethnic group rather than another) as significant for culture change would in some way contradict the basic hypothesis of the psychic unity of mankind.

The rejection of the doctrine of the superiority of any group of identified persons can also be seen in the way in which Kroeber, in contrast to Herbert Spencer, came to use the term "superorganic." In discussing the concept of the superorganic, David Bidney (*Theoretical Anthropology*, 1953, pp. 34–39) points out that as the term was used by Spencer to apply to the "processes and products" of group interaction, it could be used to describe social process among "bees and wasps, bird communities, and gregarious animals" as well as men (p. 34). But in Kroeber's use of the term, the stream of culture is divorced from its carriers, as when, in "The Superorganic" (*American Anthropologist*, 1917, p. 186), he stated:

> All civilization in a sense exists only in the mind. Gunpowder, textile arts, machinery, laws, telephones are not themselves transmitted from man to man or from generation to generation, at least not permanently. It is the perception, the knowledge and understanding of them, their ideas in the Platonic sense, that are passed along.

The attempt to distinguish between culture and its carriers at all stages of evolution has led to the positions on cultural evolution taken by anthropologists like Leslie White and Julian Steward. At another level the partially resolved controversies are reflected in distinctions currently made between a sociological approach (in which the units are individuals, groups, or formal relationships) and a cultural approach (which is conceived of as independent of identified individuals or an identified social group). Discussing the intellectual background of "The Superorganic" in *The Nature of Culture* (1952), Kroeber commented that "what was hanging over the study of culture, as I sense it now, was [not the dominance of the biological explanation, but] rather a diffused public opinion, a body of unaware assumptions, that left precarious the autonomous recognition of society, and still more that of culture" (p. 22). In actual field work the study of culture and the study of social structure are inextricably combined. But the failure, on the part of the cultural anthropologist, to distinguish between "culture" and "a culture," and, on the part of the social anthropologist, between formal social relationships and a living group of individuals, continues to cloud the issue, and so leaves unclear the theoretical evaluation of the actual contributions of identified individuals.

Another by-product is related to the fact that the struggle to demonstrate the psychic unity of mankind was conducted in a period of renascent racism and eugenic uproar (see, for example, Madison Grant's *The Passing of the Great Race,* 1918), which increased in the 1920s until it reached a climax in the period of racial myths and genocide, 1934–45 (for writing on this period, see Ruth Benedict's *Race: Science and Politics,* 1959), and which continues in the 1960s in the rejoined battle, along new as well as old lines, to establish racial superiority. This is the contemporary tendency to identify any discussion of individual attributes that can be ascribed to heredity, rather than to culture, as ipso facto destructive of the new ideals which are today grounded in (not producers of) our growing scientific knowledge of man as one species. So charges of incipient racism are one form taken by opposition to any discussion of the significance of somatotype, or to explorations of the precursors of *Homo sapiens* which hypothesize that man may be a polytypic species, or to suggestions of the kind made by Hermann Muller ("Should We Weaken or Strengthen Our Genetic Heritage," *Daedalus,* 1961) that when *artificial* breeding is undertaken, as in artificial insemination, eugenic choices should be made.

It is instructive to see how a scientific struggle to deal with the new evidence based on field work among living primitive peoples, which *preceded* our knowledge that all living peoples are members of a single species, led to the development of an ethical ideal which is congruent with the aspirations voiced in the United States in reaction to the eighteenth century European claims to superiority over any and all denizens of the American continent. Thus Jefferson, in his *Notes on the State of Virginia* (as quoted in *The Golden Age of American Anthropology,* Margaret Mead and Ruth Bunzel, eds., 1960, pp. 75-81), quotes Buffon's opinion that in North America all nature, including man, is inferior to Europe (p. 75):

> "Although the savage of the new world is about the same height as man in our world, this does not suffice for him to constitute an exception to the general fact that all living nature has become smaller on that continent . . ."

Jefferson then undertook to refute this theory (pp. 79-80):

> Before we condemn the Indians of this continent as wanting genius, we must consider that letters have not yet been introduced among them. Were we to compare them in their present state with the Europeans North of the Alps, when the Roman arms and arts first crossed these mountains, the comparison would be unequal, because, at that time, those parts of Europe were swarming with numbers; because numbers produce emulation, and multiply the chances of

improvement, and one improvement begets another. Yet I may safely ask, How many good poets, how many able mathematicians, how many great inventors in arts or sciences, had Europe North of the Alps then produced? And it was sixteen centuries after this before a Newton could be formed. I do not mean to deny, that there are varieties in the race of man, distinguished by their powers both of body and mind. I believe there are, as I see to be the case in the races of other animals. . . .

So far the Count de Buffon has carried this new theory of the tendency of nature to belittle her productions on this side of the Atlantic. Its application to the race of whites, transplanted from Europe, remained for the Abbé Raynal. "One must be astonished (he says) that America has not yet produced one good poet, one able mathematician, one man of genius in a single art or a single science."

In refutation of this criticism, after comparing America's small population and short time span with the large populations and long historical time span of France and Britain, Jefferson concluded his strictures (p. 81):

The present war having so long cut off all communication with Great-Britain, we are not able to make a fair estimate of the state of science in that country. The spirit in which she wages war is the only sample before our eyes, and that does not seem the legitimate offspring either of science or of civilization. The sun of her glory is fast descending to the horizon. Her philosophy has crossed the Channel, her freedom the Atlantic, and herself seems passing to that awful dissolution, whose issue is not given human foresight to scan.

Thus these older struggles, both scientific and passionately ideological, recur to complicate our ability to use new formulations demanded by new scientific findings.

4. See Appendix B, Second Manus Expedition, 1953–54, for a list of published materials.

NOTES TO CHAPTER 1

1. Margaret Mead, "Closing the Gap between the Scientists and the Others," *Daedalus*, 1959.

2. Robert H. Lowie, *History of Ethnological Theory*, 1937.

3. H. G. Wells, *Jean and Peter: The Story of an Education*, 1935, pp. 59–101.

4. Madison Grant, *The Passing of the Great Race*, 1918.

5. Frederick Engels, *The Origin of the Family*, 1902.

6. See Edward Westermarck, *The History of Human Marriage*, 1921. The appositeness of such theorizing to human demands for importance is equally well attested to by Harlow Shapley's glee whenever the need for the intervention of God is moved one step farther away in the chain

of possible creation. In a discussion of man's several adjustments of his relationship to the physical universe ("Man's Fourth Adjustment," *American Scholar,* 1956), he stated that today "the many researches of the past few years in the field of macromolecules have made it unnecessary any longer to postulate miracles and the supernatural for the origin of life" (p. 457). This sense of protest is also reflected in the sermon of a Protestant minister (Rector of St. David's Church, Topeka, Kansas, Spring 1959), who had fully accepted the idea of evolution and a universe of great time depth but who, after describing the countless ages before man emerged from the sea, went on to say: "And all this was part of God's plan for us today, right here in Kansas. All this occurred so that we, here today, celebrating our hundredth anniversary, might be part of God's church."

7. William Alfred Hinds' *American Communities* (1961), first published in 1878 and based on visits to several still surviving utopian communities, is valuable for the picture it gives of the different national as well as ideological origins of these nineteenth-century attempts to create the perfect society in the New World.

8. Lewis H. Morgan, *Ancient Society,* 1877; see also Bernard J. Stern, *Lewis Henry Morgan: Social Evolutionist,* 1931.

9. Walter Goldschmidt, ed., *The Anthropology of Franz Boas,* 1959; Margaret Mead and Ruth Bunzel, eds., *The Golden Age of American Anthropology,* 1960.

10. A. L. Kroeber, *Configurations of Culture Growth,* 1944; also Kroeber, *A Roster of Civilizations and Culture,* 1962.

11. Margaret Mead, unpublished lecture notes, Spring 1923.

12. Boas' viewpoint is exemplified in *Primitive Art,* 1927. In the opening paragraph of the Preface, he wrote:

> The treatment given to the subject is based on two principles that, I believe, should guide all investigations into the manifestations of life among primitive peoples: the one the fundamental sameness of mental processes in all races and in all cultural forms of the present day; the other, the consideration of every cultural phenomenon as the result of historical happenings.

In opposing the thesis "of a single unilateral development of cultural traits the world over," he took the position (p. 5) that: "critical study of recent years has definitely disproved the existence of far reaching homologies which would permit us to arrange all the manifold cultural lines in an ascending scale." At the same time, in discussing the specific historical problem of the development of art styles, he pointed out (p. 7):

> There are very few parts of the world in which we can trace, by archaeological or comparative geographical study, the growth of art styles. Prehistoric archaeology in Europe, Asia, and America shows, however, that, as general cultural traits are in a constant state of flux,

so also do art styles change and the breaks in the artistic life of the people are often surprisingly sudden. It remains to be seen whether it is possible to derive generally valid laws that control the growth of specific art styles.

13. A. C. Haddon, *Evolution in Art,* 1895.

14. Franz Boas, "Decorative Designs of Alaskan Needle-Cases: A Study in the History of Conventional Designs, Based on Materials in the U.S. National Museum," *Proceedings of the U.S. National Museum,* 1908.

15. Robert H. Lowie, "Reminiscences of Anthropological Currents in America Half a Century Ago," *American Anthropologist,* 1956.

16. A notable victim of this prejudice was William Christie MacLeod. His preoccupation with the problem of possible Asiatic origins of American Indian cultures (see, for example, "Certain Mortuary Aspects of Northwest Coast Culture," *American Anthropologist,* 1925; "On the Southeast Asiatic Origins of American Culture," *American Anthropologist,* 1929, in which MacLeod discussed Dixon's *The Building of Culture;* "The Nature, Origin, and Linkages of the Rite of Hookswinging: With Special Reference to North America," *Anthropos,* 1934; and, above all, *The American Indian Frontier,* 1928) made him thoroughly unpopular. At one period he was given inappropriate refuge in the Wharton School of Business Administration through my father's interest in his work; but today his work is virtually unknown.

17. Elsie Clews Parsons, "Nativity Myth at Laguna and Zuni," *Journal of American Folk-Lore,* 1918; Parsons, "Pueblo-Indian Folk-Tales, Probably of Spanish Provenience," *Journal of American Folk-Lore,* 1918; Parsons, "Spanish Elements in the Kachina Cult of the Pueblos," *Proceedings of the Twenty-third International Congress of Americanists,* 1930.

18. Melville J. Herskovits, *The Myth of the Negro Past,* 1941 (see also bibliography).

19. Boas, *Primitive Art.*

20. Edwin R. A. Seligman, *The Economic Interpretation of History,* 1902.

21. This is a perception that pervades discussions of Marxist and Leninist strategy without specific identification. At the present time see, for example, the ongoing discussions between the Soviet Union and mainland China.

22. For a discussion by White of the development of his position on evolution and for references to his principal articles on the subject (beginning with "Energy and Evolution in Culture," *American Anthropologist,* 1943), see Leslie A. White, *The Evolution of Culture,* 1959, p. ix.

23. William F. Ogburn, *Social Change,* 1922.

24. Sigmund Freud, *Civilization and Its Discontents,* 1930; also Karl Menninger, *Love against Hate,* 1942.

25. Lawrence K. Frank, "Cultural Coercion and Individual Distortion," *Psychiatry,* 1939; Martha Wolfenstein, "Fun Morality: An Analysis of Re-

cent American Child-Training Literature," in *Childhood in Contemporary Cultures,* 1955; also, John Dewey, *The School and Society,* 1900.

26. James Harvey Robinson, *The Mind in the Making,* 1921.

27. George Dorsey, *Why We Behave like Human Beings,* 1926.

28. See Introduction, Footnote 3.

29. B. F. Skinner, *Walden Two,* 1948; Skinner, *Science and Human Behavior,* 1953; Skinner, "The Science of Learning and the Art of Teaching," in *Programmed Learning: Theory and Research,* 1962.

30. Eliot D. Chapple, "Personality Differences as Described by Invariant Properties of Individuals in Interaction," *Proceedings of The National Academy of Sciences,* 1940.

31. W. Grey Walter, *The Living Brain,* 1953.

32. Konrad Z. Lorenz, "The Comparative Method in Studying Innate Behaviour Patterns," in *Physiological Mechanisms in Animal Behavior,* 1950.

33. N. Tinbergen, *The Study of Instinct,* 1951.

34. D. S. Lehrman, "A Critique of Konrad Lorenz's Theory of Instinctive Behavior," *Quarterly Review of Biology,* 1953.

35. See, for example, in *An Appraisal of Anthropology Today,* Sol Tax and others, eds., 1953, the discussion (especially the comments, p. 165) of J. M. Tanner's paper, "Growth and Constitution," in *Anthropology Today,* ed. A. L. Kroeber, 1953.

36. An amusing sidelight on the way in which a package of ideas tends to diffuse can be seen in the stand taken by W. Grey Walter on the subject of historical matriarchy in the face of contemporary anthropological opinion that there is no factual basis for such a stage (Tanner and Bärbel Inhelder, eds., *Discussions on Child Development,* 1958, p. 24). This may be regarded as a component in a package which is diffused and over-determined, in that Walter's identification with Pavlov carries with it Marxist elements that are irrelevant anthropological accretions.

37. Howard Scott, *Technocracy: Science versus Chaos,* 1933.

38. But an invention made in a society with one type of social organization may have profound effects on another society which borrows the invention; see Lynn White, Jr., "Tibet, India, and Malaya as Sources of Western Medieval Technology," *American Historical Review,* 1960.

39. Leslie A. White, *The Evolution of Culture.*

40. V. Gordon Childe, *Man Makes Himself,* 1936.

41. John Dollard and others, *Frustration and Aggression,* 1939.

42. In the 1930s a new concept of democracy was emerging in the United States. Under the pressure of widespread poverty and an extreme lack of funds, new means had to be found to implement the growing determination to better social conditions. Private voluntary institutions such as the American Red Cross and the Julius Rosenwald Fund, government agencies such as the United States Office of Education, and the various bureaus of the Department of Agriculture all began to emphasize the value of local effort. The initiative of the small group, often carefully stimulated from

the outside, was seen as the means of providing the necessary impetus to action. During World War II these attempts to stimulate community action were extended to new fields—nutrition, youth work, the care of service men's wives, etc.—and community planning became more widespread and better organized. See, for example, Muriel W. Brown, *With Focus on Family Living,* 1953; Edwin R. Embree and Julia Waxman, *Investment in People: The Story of the Julius Rosenwald Fund,* 1949; Jean Ogden and Jess Ogden, *Small Communities in Action,* 1947; Walter Pettit, *Case Studies in Community Organization,* 1928 (an account of how the Red Cross got a program going in a rural community); and *The Schools and Community Organization,* 1944.

43. For Germany see, for example, Gregory Bateson, "Cultural and Thematic Analysis of Fictional Films," *Transactions of The New York Academy of Sciences,* 1943; Bateson, "An Analysis of the Nazi Film *Hitlerjunge Quex,*" 1945; "Germany after the War: Round Table—1945," *American Journal of Orthopsychiatry,* 1945; and Talcott Parsons, "The Problem of Controlled Institutional Change," *Psychiatry,* 1945; and for Japan, George C. Allen, *A Short Economic History of Modern Japan, 1867–1937,* 1962; Ruth Benedict, *The Chrysanthemum and the Sword,* 1946; Douglas G. Haring, ed., *Japan's Prospect,* 1946; and J. Stoetzel, *Jeunesse sans chrysanthème ni sabre,* 1954; also unpublished work by Ruth Benedict, Gregory Bateson, Clyde Kluckhohn, and Arnold Meadow.

44. See, for example, Ruth Benedict, "A Note on Chinese Culture and Personality," 1943; Benedict, "Rumanian Culture and Behavior," 1946; Benedict, *Thai Culture and Behavior,* an unpublished War Time Study Dated September 1943, 1952; Erik H. Erikson, "Hitler's Imagery and German Youth," *Psychiatry,* 1942; Geoffrey Gorer, "Themes in Japanese Culture," *Transactions of The New York Academy of Sciences,* 1943; and Gorer, "Burmese Personality," 1943.

45. For discussions of method, selections from research carried out, and bibliographies through 1954, see Margaret Mead, "The Study of National Character," in *The Policy Sciences,* 1951; Mead, "National Character," in *Anthropology Today,* 1953; Mead and Rhoda Metraux, eds., *The Study of Culture at a Distance,* 1953; and Mead and Martha Wolfenstein, eds., *Childhood in Contemporary Cultures,* 1955. On Russia see, for example, Mead, *Soviet Attitudes toward Authority,* 1951; Geoffrey Gorer and John Rickman, *The People of Great Russia,* 1950; and on China, Ruth Bunzel, "Explorations in Chinese Culture," 1950.

46. Julian H. Steward, "The Economic and Social Basis of Primitive Tribes," in *Essays in Anthropology Presented to A. L. Kroeber,* 1936; Steward, ed., *Handbook of South American Indians,* 1946–59.

47. Julian H. Steward and others, *The People of Puerto Rico,* 1956, p. 14.

48. Margaret Mead, ed., *Cultural Patterns and Technical Change,* 1953; also Edward H. Spicer, ed., *Human Problems in Technological Change,* 1952.

49. Conrad M. Arensberg, "Report on a Developing Community, Poston, Arizona," *Applied Anthropology,* 1942.

50. Bateson, "An Analysis of the Nazi Film *Hitlerjunge Quex.*"

51. Ray L. Birdwhistell, "Family Structure and Social Mobility," *Transactions of The New York Academy of Sciences,* 1958.

52. Eliot D. Chapple, "Personality Differences as Described by Invariant Properties of Individuals in Interaction"; Chapple, "The Interaction Chronograph: Its Evaluation and Present Applications," *Personnel,* 1949; Chapple and Conrad M. Arensberg, "Measuring Human Relations: An Introduction to the Study of the Interaction of Individuals," *Genetic Psychology Monographs,* 1940.

53. Morton H. Fried, *Fabric of Chinese Society,* 1953.

54. Geoffrey Gorer, *The American People,* 1948; Gorer and Rickman, *The People of Great Russia.*

55. Felix M. Keesing and Marie M. Keesing, *Elite Communities in Samoa,* 1956.

56. Margaret Mead, "Professional Problems of Education in Dependent Countries," *Journal of Negro Education,* 1946.

57. Steward and others, *The People of Puerto Rico.*

58. Charles Wagley, *Amazon Town,* 1953.

59. International Preparatory Commission, *Mental Health and World Citizenship,* 1948.

60. Gregory Bateson, "The Pattern of an Armaments Race, I. An Anthropological Approach, II. An Analysis of Nationalism," *Bulletin of the Atomic Scientists,* 1946; Margaret Mead, "The Ethics of Insight-giving," in *Male and Female,* 1949; Lewis F. Richardson, *Arms and Insecurity,* 1960; also Richardson, *Statistics of Deadly Quarrels,* 1960.

61. These observations are based on my own unpublished interviews made within the first week after Hiroshima and on audience responses to discussions of atomic energy in lectures given in the period between Hiroshima and the publication of Hersey's book, *Hiroshima,* 1946.

62. Although American perceptions began to alter at the time Hersey's book was published in 1946, the popular view that atomic bombing resulted in a "quick death" was still very widely held around the world for some time—for example, in France, in 1947 (unpublished interviews, Paris, Summer 1947).

63. In fact, however, concern for the effects of radiation, including physiological effects and chromosomal alteration, far antedates the present crisis. In April 1928, a program of investigation was presented to the Division of Biology and Agriculture, National Research Council, and a committee, known as the Committee on Radiation, was formed. The early interest of industry in the research was made evident by the support given colloquia, and that of social scientists and educators by the fact that a major publication, *Biological Effects of Radiation,* edited by B. M. Duggar (1936), was financially supported by the General Education Board, the Rockefeller Foundation, and the Commonwealth Fund (Duggar, pp. v-vi).

64. *The Biological Effects of Radiation,* 1956, p. 18.

65. See Fyodor Dostoyevsky, *The Brothers Karamazov,* 1950, a conversation (p. 291) in which Ivan poses the question:

> Tell me yourself, I challenge you—answer. Imagine that you are creating a fabric of human destiny with the object of making men happy in the end, giving them peace and rest at last, but it was essential and inevitable to torture to death only one tiny creature—that baby beating its breast with its fist, for instance—and to found that edifice on its unavenged tears, would you consent to be the architect on those conditions? Tell me, and tell the truth.

On this point, see also C. H. Waddington, "The Biological Effects of Bomb Tests," *New Statesmen and Nation,* 1957.

66. William L. Laurence, "You May Live Forever," *Look,* 1953.

67. See, for example, P. B. Medawar, *The Future of Man,* 1960; also Hermann J. Muller, "The Guidance of Human Evolution," in *Evolution after Darwin, 2,* 1960; and Muller, "Should We Weaken or Strengthen Our Genetic Heritage," in "Evolution and Man's Progress," *Daedalus,* 1961.

68. Charles G. Darwin, "Address: The Physical Universe," in *Man's Contracting World in an Expanding Universe,* 1960.

69. Interest in the distant past is diffuse rather than concentrated, and is reflected in the popularization of subject matter (e.g. early man, or the early civilizations of the Middle East, for example) and books (especially in the new paperback editions) which, only a few years earlier, were of interest mainly to specialists.

70. See, for example, Rachel Carson, *The Sea around Us,* 1950.

71. Personal communication, based on reports by teachers working with students in junior high schools in New York City in 1957–58 and 1958–59.

72. Arnold J. Toynbee, *The Study of History,* 2 vols., 1947, 1957.

73. This stands out clearly in the work of serious writers of science fiction, some of whom are themselves scientists; see, for example, Isaac Asimov, *The Naked Sun,* 1958; Arthur C. Clarke, *Childhood's End,* 1953; Fred Hoyle, *The Black Cloud,* 1959; Chad Oliver, *Shadows in the Sun,* 1954; Vercors, *You Shall Know Them,* 1953; W. Grey Walter, *The Curve of the Snowflake,* 1956; John Wyndham, *The Midwich Cuckoos,* 1957.

74. Shapley, "Man's Fourth Adjustment."

75. George W. Beadle, "Uniqueness of Man," *Science,* 1957.

76. See Introduction, Footnote 3. Lytton Strachey, in England, and Emil Ludwig, in Germany, exemplified this viewpoint in their biographies, however much they differed in their style and choice of subject.

77. William F. Ogburn and Dorothy Thomas, "Are Inventions Inevitable," *Political Science Quarterly,* 1922.

78. Theodore Abel, "The Element of Decision in the Pattern of War," *American Sociological Review,* 1941.

79. Harold A. Abramson, ed., *Problems of Consciousness,* 1955, p. 159.

80. Gardner Murphy, *Human Potentialities,* 1958.

81. Edith Cobb, "The Ecology of Imagination in Childhood," *Daedalus,* 1959.

82. Richard M. Brickner, "Telencephalization of Survival Characteristics," in *The Frontal Lobes,* 1948.

83. Brickner, "Telencephalization of Survival Characteristics," pp. 660–63.

84. R. H. Codrington, *The Melanesians,* 1891; Robert R. Marett, *The Threshold of Religion,* 1929.

85. Reo F. Fortune, *Manus Religion,* 1935.

86. "The personalized sword is invariably one of the possessions of a hero . . . Magic swords are talismans; they protect against injury and always kill or wound an opponent. They may render the owner invisible; they grow or shrink at need; they give the magic power to travel great distances. The magic sword brings up the wind (Chinese), speaks (Celtic), emits fire (Chinese) . . . [and] it becomes discolored or runs with blood when unfaithfulness or death occurs" ("Swords," *Funk and Wagnalls Standard Dictionary of Folklore, Mythology and Legend,* ed. Maria Leach, 1950).

87. Norbert Wiener, *The Human Use of Human Beings,* 1950; also, Wiener, "Some Moral and Technical Consequences of Automation," *Science,* 1960; and A. L. Samuel, "Some Moral and Technical Consequences of Automation—A Refutation," *Science,* 1960.

88. In a personal communication, John M. Stroud wrote:

> It is possible to approach the problem of life by *defining* life rather than by asking the traditional question, "What is life?" Any question implies an infinite answer and though one learns a great deal by asking questions and it is vastly profitable to do so, "answers" are not acquired in this fashion. . . . The definition of Life that I use is: *Life is that domain of space–time to which the notion of negative entropy or information demonstrably applies.*
>
> Our present knowledge of this domain presents it as a single, multiply-interconnected domain, a four-dimensional "fishnet" rather severely rent.
>
> If we divide the mechanisms of control and communication involved into two classes—"genetic mechanisms" and "extragenetic mechanisms"—the domain defined by genetic mechanisms alone is identical with the domain of the Darwinian hypothesis. The domain of geneless artifacts is that of cultural organizations of men and machines and other genetically structured but partially extragenetically controlled organisms.
>
> Such a definition, however, does not define living "things" as we typically envision them—"material" objects like bodies, in an older world view; "physical" objects whose dimensions are those of mass, length, time, inductivity, etc., in a more recent view—but as systems

of informed and controlled action, which are "dimensionless" in a classical physics or "spiritual" in a still older world view.

Illustratively, in this view neither the bodies of men nor the bodies of machines are a part of life—they are the implements or instruments of life. Only the *actions* could be part of life, and those actions which are demonstrably controlled, informed actions are, in this definition, part of life, and it is a matter of only secondary concern which of the two broad classes of instruments is involved in the execution of the action.

89. Marjorie H. Nicolson, *Science and Imagination*, 1956, especially Chapters 1 and 6; for references to earlier discussions, see pp. v–vii.

90. Marjorie H. Nicolson, *Voyages to the Moon*, 1960; it is an interesting comment on the ebb and flow of interest in ideas that few current readers of science fiction have any knowledge of this extremely popular genre at any period before 1900.

91. For nontechnical review of many of these methods, see R. N. C. Bowen, *The Exploration of Time*, 1958; for a more specialized description of methods, see M. J. Aitken, *Physics and Archaeology*, 1961. See also Willard F. Libby, *Radiocarbon Dating*, 1955.

92. John Bradford, *Ancient Landscapes: Studies in Field Archaeology*, 1957.

93. C. H. Waddington, *The Strategy of the Genes*, 1957.

94. Konrad Z. Lorenz, "The Role of Aggression in Group Formation," in *Group Processes*, 1959.

95. See, for example, W. H. Thorpe's discussion of the chaffinch, *Learning and Instinct in Animals*, 1963, pp. 420–26; see also his references to other studies, pp. 418–20.

96. Theodosius Dobzhansky and Joseph B. Birdsell, "On Methods of Evolutionary Biology and Anthropology," *American Scientist*, 1957.

97. White, *The Evolution of Culture*.

98. Gregory Bateson, "The Science of Decency," *Philosophy of Science*, 1943.

NOTES TO CHAPTER 2

1. Julian S. Huxley, "Evolution, Cultural and Biological," in *Current Anthropology*, 1956, p. 3.

2. Huxley, "Evolution, Cultural and Biological," pp. 10–11. This statement in full reads:

I must first justify the view that what evolves in the psycho-social phase is not the genetic nature of man, or individuals, or society, or minds-in-society, but a new supra-organismic entity, demanding an appellation of its own. *Culture* is the appellation by which anthropologists denote this central subject of their science.

Culture, if I understand it aright, is a shared or shareable body of material, mental and social constructions ("artifacts, mentifacts, and socifacts") created by human individuals living in a society, but with characteristics not simply explicable or directly deducible from a knowledge of the general psychological or physiological properties of human individuals, any more than the characteristics of life are simply explicable or directly deducible from a knowledge of the general chemical and physical properties of inorganic matter, or those of mind from a knowledge of the properties of neurons. Culture has a material basis, in the shape of resources of food, raw materials, and energy; but though the quantity and quality of material resources available will influence or condition the character and development of a culture, they do not determine it in detail, so that differences between cultures are no more explicable or deducible from a knowledge of their material basis than from that of their psychological basis in the minds of individuals.

3. Huxley, "Evolution, Cultural and Biological," pp. 11–12.

4. Earnest A. Hooton, *Up from the Ape,* 1947.

5. See Introduction, Footnote 3.

6. Zellig S. Harris, *Methods in Structural Linguistics,* 1951; Margaret Mead, "Review of *Methods in Structural Linguistics,* by Zellig S. Harris," *International Journal of American Linguistics,* 1952.

7. Ernst Haeckel, *The Evolution of Man,* 1910.

8. W. N. Kellogg and L. A. Kellogg, *The Ape and the Child,* 1933.

9. Cathy Hayes, *The Ape in Our House,* 1951.

10. Arthur Koestler, *Reflections on Hanging,* 1957.

11. Margaret Mead, "Brushes of Comets' Hair," *Menninger Quarterly,* 1962.

12. The French writer, Vercors, raised this question directly in his science fiction fantasy, *You Shall Know Them,* 1953.

13. Lawrence K. Frank, *Society as the Patient,* 1948.

14. The interplay of man's recognition of himself as a separate kind of creature with his sense of a shared creatureliness with all living things is complex and revealing. For example, in societies in which there is strong caste feeling—where, by cultural definition, members of some groups are regarded as in some way not belonging to the same species as one's own group and attempts are made to create various kinds of breeding barriers—this may find expression in violent preferences in food. Thus, in the Southeastern United States, white cornmeal is for human consumption but yellow cornmeal is fit only for animals. In Europe there are equally violent repudiations of various foods which appear to grow out of the dichotomization of human beings, highly differentiated by class, and animals. Thus, in Poland, potato parings are specifically food for *pigs.* (See Margaret Mead, *Male and Female,* 1949, pp. 183–85.)

An even more striking example of this interplay is the treatment, in

India, of wandering autistic children, who are culturally described as children who have actually been stolen and reared by wolves. Extensive investigation finally has produced a fairly definitive account of what, in fact, happens. Infants who are carelessly exposed in the fields are destroyed by wild animals. Autistic children either wander away from home or are abandoned. When such a child is found, the myth of a nearby wolf is invoked and the child can be re-accepted into the society by which it had been neglected or abandoned, under the pretext that its disabilities have been brought about by wolf-rearing. (See William Fielding Ogburn, "The Wolf Boy of Agra," *American Journal of Sociology,* 1959.)

15. See, for example, Weston LaBarre, *The Human Animal,* 1954.

16. I owe this recognition to discussions with G. E. Hutchinson.

17. Bertram Schaffner, ed., *Group Processes,* 1955–60; see especially Konrad Z. Lorenz, "Morphology and Behavior Patterns in Closely Allied Species," in *Group Processes,* 1955; also Lorenz, "The Role of Aggression in Group Formation," in *Group Processes,* 1959.

18. Huxley, "Evolution, Cultural and Biological," p. 23.

19. Ibid., Footnote 9.

20. Julian H. Steward, *Theory of Culture Change,* 1955.

21. Marshall D. Sahlins and Elman R. Service, eds., *Evolution and Culture,* 1960.

22. A. L. Kroeber, *The Nature of Culture,* 1952.

23. Thus, Huxley ("Evolution, Cultural and Biological," p. 18) states that "the biologist is driven to view culture historically, as cultural evolution, and to see cultural evolution as a part, albeit a special part, with its own peculiar methods and results, of the evolutionary process as a whole"; but he also concludes (p. 22) that, in man, "the capacity for the cumulative transmission of experience marked a critical point in the evolutionary process—the passage from a biological to a cultural mode of evolution."

24. Steward, *Theory of Culture Change.*

25. Frederick Lehman, "Some Anthropological Parameters of Civilization: The Ecology and Evolution of India's High Culture," 1959.

26. George P. Murdock, *Social Structure,* 1949; also Thurlow R. Wilson, "Randomness of the Distribution of Social Organization Forms: A Note on Murdock's *Social Structure,"* *American Anthropologist,* 1952.

27. See, for example, Felix M. Keesing, *Culture Change,* 1953; Margaret Mead, ed., *Cultural Patterns and Technical Change,* 1953.

28. Ruth Benedict, "Psychological Types in the Cultures of the Southwest," *Proceedings of the Twenty-third International Congress of Americanists,* 1930.

29. Margaret Mead, "Personality, the Cultural Approach to," In *Encyclopedia of Psychology,* 1946.

30. Steward, *Theory of Culture Change.*

NOTES TO CHAPTER 3

1. Students of our own society, who have found some of the conceptions of cultural anthropology more useful than others, sometimes speak about the "culture" of a hospital, or the "culture" of the armed forces, or the "culture" of the lower class in a given region of the country. This usage, in which the focus is upon one specially identified group or institution within a larger whole, blurs the distinction between culture, defined as a system of behavior transmissible from one generation to another, in which the biological completeness of the social group (including both sexes and at least three generations bound by ties of consanguinity and affinity) is an intrinsic part of the system, and other forms of learned social behavior. While social groups within a society can simulate this process of cultural transmission through methods of absorbing immigrants, adopting war captives, or formalizing novitiates or initiations, it appears to me useful to maintain the distinction between the part and the whole. That is, in setting off the behavior of a subgroup, it is better to speak not of subcultures but of subgroups within a society with different *versions* of the same culture.

2. See, for example, Sidney Morgenbesser, "Role and Status of Anthropological Theories," *Science*, 1958, and the discussion of this paper by Gregory Bateson, Paul Bohannan, David E. Hansen, and Sidney Morgenbesser in "Letters: Anthropological Theories," *Science*, 1959.

3. Julian S. Huxley, "Evolution, Cultural and Biological," in *Current Anthropology*, 1956, p. 9; see also, David Bidney, *Theoretical Anthropology*, 1953, p. 33.

4. John Buettner-Janusch, "Boas and Mason: Particularism versus Generalization," *American Anthropologist*, 1957. As background for this discussion, see Verne F. Ray's "Review of *Franz Boas: The Science of Man in the Making*, by Melville L. Herskovits," *American Anthropologist*, 1955, the comments on this review by A. L. Kroeber ("The Place of Boas in Anthropology") and Robert H. Lowie ("Boas Once More"), Ray's "Rejoinder," and Murray Wax' "The Limitations of Boas' Anthropology," all appearing in the *American Anthropologist*, 1956.

5. Franz Boas, "The Central Eskimo," 1888, and Boas, "The Eskimo of Baffin Land and Hudson Bay," 1901; A. P. Elkin, *The Australian Aborigines*, 1954; A. R. Radcliffe-Brown, *The Andaman Islanders*, 1922; and on the Bushman, Elizabeth M. Thomas, *The Harmless People*, 1959.

6. A. R. Brown (see Radcliffe-Brown), "Three Tribes of Western Australia," *Journal of the Royal Anthropological Institute*, 1913, p. 148.

7. David Rapaport, "Technological Growth and the Psychology of Man," 1947.

8. John E. Frisch, "Research on Primate Behavior in Japan," *American Anthropologist*, 1959; Kinji Imanishi, "Social Organization of Subhuman Primates in Their Natural Habitat," *Current Anthropology*, 1960;

Junichiro Itani, "On the Acquisition and Propagation of a New Food Habit in the Natural Group of the Japanese Monkey at Takasaki-Yama," *Primates*, 1958; Paul E. Simonds, "The Japan Monkey Center," *Current Anthropology*, 1962.

9. Here I am concerned merely with different levels of transmission skill, and with the probability that early man took as models for his cultural inventions various kinds of species-characteristic behavior of other organic creatures.

10. Franz Boas, *Anthropology and Modern Life*, 1928, p. 66.

11. Boas, in his discussion, was dealing with the problem of open and closed societies and hostility toward the stranger; it is now known that other, related types of learning behavior occur in the wild among cognates.

12. For a summary discussion of experimental work on chaffinches by Thorpe and others, see W. H. Thorpe, *Learning and Instinct in Animals*, 1963, pp. 400–01, 419–27.

13. C. P. Richter, "The Self-selection of Diets," in *Essays in Honor of Herbert M. Evans*, 1943.

14. John C. Lilly, *Man and Dolphin*, 1961; also Winthrop N. Kellogg, *Porpoises and Sonar*, 1961.

15. William L. Thomas, Jr., and others, eds., *Man's Role in Changing the Face of the Earth*, 1956.

16. Gertrude Hendrix, "Learning by Discovery," *Mathematics Teacher*, 1961.

17. See Ruth Benedict's notes on Boas' "Methods" lectures, in Margaret Mead, "Apprenticeship under Boas," in *The Anthropology of Franz Boas*, 1959, p. 38.

18. Ray L. Birdwhistell, "Contribution of Linguistic–Kinesic Studies to the Understanding of Schizophrenia," in *Schizophrenia: An Integrated Approach*, 1959; also Birdwhistell, "An Approach to Communication," *Family Process*, 1962.

19. Margaret Mead, "Research on Primitive Children," in *Manual of Child Psychology*, 1954.

20. G. B. Grinnell, *The Cheyenne Indians, 1*, 1923, 110–16.

21. Margaret Mead, "Our Educational Emphases in Primitive Perspective," *American Journal of Sociology*, 1943.

22. In *Man and Culture* (1923), Clark Wissler defined a culture trait as follows (p. 50):

> The field-worker in anthropology begins his study of tribal culture by concentrating upon one or two points. Thus, he may set out to see how fire is kindled, observing that it is made by boring one stick into another, but that these simple looking implements are fashioned according to a specific pattern and that the procedure is likewise fixed as in any handicraft. Yet, it is not enough to say that fire is kindled

by wood friction; the individuality of the implements and the accompanying procedures must be recorded and representative objects collected. Thus, the fire-making implement, accompanied by photographs and field notes, becomes the objective record of a unit of observation. Such is, for practical purposes at least, a unit of the tribal culture and is spoken of as a *trait*. This term is also applied to mannerisms and to concepts of whatever kind. Thus the custom of a man marrying his wife's sisters may be observed, and, if so, is set down as a trait of the tribal culture. It follows then that a tribal culture is characterized by the enumeration of its observable traits and that the culture of one tribe is distinguished from that of another by differences in these traits.

Discussing the "meaning of culture," Wissler gave the following illustration (p. 2):

> We say that the Eskimo has a culture of his own because, from almost whatever angle we view his daily activities, we see new and surprising practices not to be found among other groups of people. Thus, he lives in a snow house, uses a peculiar boat called a *kayak*, rides upon sleds drawn by dogs, heats his houses with seal oil lamps, wears fur clothing of peculiar styles, etc., etc. Likewise, his methods of greeting strangers, his ideas of hospitality, beliefs concerning the heavenly bodies, ethical ideals, standards of beauty, methods of checking crime, training the young, etc., are peculiarly different from those found among other peoples. In view of all this, we say that there is an Eskimo culture.

Wissler's is a summary statement, but the *style* of enumeration (enlarged and much amplified because traits and clusters of traits are described) is characteristic of the work of some ethnographers. In compilations (for example, the enormous *Handbook of South American Indians,* ed. Julian H. Steward, 1946–59), which draw on the most various sources, trait-list descriptions of cultures are almost unavoidable as a principal basis of comparison of a very large number of cultures.

23. Uriel Weinreich, *Languages in Contact,* 1953.
24. Reo F. Fortune, *Sorcerers of Dobu,* 1932, pp. 106–07.
25. Geoffrey Gorer, *Himalayan Village,* 1938.
26. Allan R. Holmberg, "Nomads of the Long Bow," 1951.
27. "Urbanization and Standard Language," *Anthropological Linguistics,* 1959.
28. Margaret Mead, "The Mountain Arapesh, I. An Importing Culture," 1938.

NOTES TO CHAPTER 4

1. Gregory Bateson, "Social Planning and the Concept of Deutero Learning," in *Science, Philosophy and Religion*, 1942; John Dollard and N. E. Miller, *Personality and Psychotherapy*, 1950; E. R. Hilgard, *Theories of Learning*, 1956.

2. Konrad Z. Lorenz, "Comparative Behaviorology," in *Discussions on Child Development*, 1956.

3. G. Tarde, *The Laws of Imitation*, 1903.

4. John P. Scott, *Animal Behavior*, 1958.

5. Peter H. Klopfer, "An Experiment on Empathic Learning in Ducks," *American Naturalist*, 1957.

6. Margaret Mead, *Growing Up in New Guinea*, 1930.

7. Margaret Mead, *New Lives for Old*, 1956.

8. Lenora S. Schwartz, "Cultural Influence on Perception," 1959.

9. Mead, *New Lives for Old*, see Plate 7, Figure 3, "Ponkob playing at being a European, 1929."

10. Margaret Mead, *Male and Female*, 1949.

11. G. H. Seward, "Studies in the Reproductive Activities of the Guinea Pig, II. The Role of Hunger in Filial Behavior," *Journal of Comparative Psychology*, 1940.

12. Margaret Mead, *Moeurs et sexualité en Océanie* [1963], see "Danse phallique a l'occasion d'une grande distribution (Iles de l'Amirauté)," opp. p. 79.

13. Ibid., see "Garçonnet des Iles de l'Amirauté (Manus) se livrant a une danse phallique," opp. p. 231.

14. Twenty-five years later, in 1953, only the dart-throwing game, with a piece of palm trunk as the target, was left; now women as well as men and children played the game.

15. Peter Freuchen, *Eskimo*, 1931, pp. 8–9, 11.

16. Ruth Landes, *The Ojibwa Woman*, 1938, p. 109.

17. In Freuchen's account (*Eskimo*, p. 11), the woman who has built an emergency snow house includes both these ideas in her explanation to her husband: " 'Just an attempt of a simple woman to put some blocks together,' Iva replied. 'Do you think, Mala, that women can't build houses at all?' "

18. G. Morris Carstairs' discussion, in *The Twice-Born* (1957), of the perceptions of one caste by another is the fullest account we have of the mechanisms by which individuals orient themselves in terms of possible and impossible goals; see, for example, his description (pp. 100–02) of the occasional complete withdrawal of a man from all caste and family responsibilities, culminating in a "burial."

19. G. B. Grinnell, *The Cheyenne Indians*, *1*, 1923, 110–16.

20. For a summary history, see Robert H. Lowie, *Indians of the Plains*,

1954; see also, for example, John C. Ewers, "The Horse in Blackfoot Indian Culture," 1955; Oscar Lewis, *The Effects of White Contact upon Blackfoot Culture,* 1942; Bernard Mishkin, *Rank and Warfare among the Plains Indians,* 1940; Frank Secoy, *Changing Military Patterns on the Great Plains,* 1953.

21. Dudley Kidd, *Savage Childhood: A Study of Kafir Children,* 1906.

22. Mead, *Male and Female.*

23. Mead, *Growing Up in New Guinea.*

24. Mead, *New Lives for Old,* 1956 ed., p. 116.

25. Franz Boas, "The Central Eskimo," 1888.

26. It has been reported by Asen Balikci (personal communication), in discussing Eskimo children who had been brought down into Canadian hospitals, that children under six years of age learned the new language and the culture, as experienced in the hospital, with ease, but that older children had a kind of fixed quality which seemed to prevent them from learning it—as if they were Eskimo adults in miniature, only waiting to grow up.

27. Colin McPhee, "Children and Music in Bali," *Djawa,* 1938; Margaret Mead, "Children and Ritual in Bali," in *Childhood in Contemporary Cultures,* 1955.

28. Margaret Mead, *Coming of Age in Samoa,* 1928.

29. Margaret Mead, *The School in American Culture,* 1951.

30. These are cultural complexities within which the possible variations in biological maturation, as pointed out by G. Evelyn Hutchinson ("A Speculative Consideration of Certain Possible Forms of Sexual Selection in Man," *American Naturalist,* 1959), may be given further expression; see also A. Comfort, "Sexual Selection in Man—A Comment," *American Naturalist,* 1959; Gregory Bateson, "The Biosocial Integration of Behavior in the Schizophrenic Family," in *Exploring the Base for Family Therapy,* 1961.

31. Michael Balint, *Thrills and Regression,* 1959.

32. Ruth Fink, "The Changing Status and Cultural Identity of Western Australian Aborigines," 1960.

33. Margaret Mead, *The Changing Culture of an Indian Tribe,* 1932.

34. Obviously, the recognition of such differences may be phrased in a great variety of ways: They do not do something that we do; they do something that we no longer do; we do something that they do not do yet; and so on. Here I am concerned not with an exploration of the variations in this negative model setting by different peoples, ethnic groups, castes, or classes but with a learning type.

35. Margaret Mead, "The Mountain Arapesh, I. An Importing Culture," 1938.

36. Gregory Bateson, *Naven,* 1936, pp. 229–31.

37. Theodore Schwartz and Margaret Mead, "Micro- and Macro-cultural Models for Cultural Evolution," *Anthropological Linguistics,* 1961; see also Appendix A, this volume.

38. Margaret Mead, "The Mountain Arapesh, II. Supernaturalism," 1940.

39. Geoffrey Gorer suggested that I should have included here forbidden ways of learning as well as forbidden models. An exploratory discussion of ways of learning that are disallowed would have included the taboo on learning by smell. In our culture children are taught very early not to smell objects as a way of identifying their owners. The taboo on the identification of objects by taste is only less stringent. Also important—and much more complex—is the taboo on arriving at a conclusion intuitively, without being able to specify the intermediate steps. In our culture this behavior is treated with great severity by teachers and colleagues; the more successful the act, the more severe the disapproval. In other areas of learning, rote memory or the substitution of rational categories for memory may be either approved or disapproved. The prohibition of any type of exploratory behavior in early childhood, including prohibition of the use of the left hand, may have paralyzing effects in some area of learning. It would be most useful to have a systematic cross-cultural survey of children's exploratory attempts to learn through the use of particular senses and in particular modes.

NOTES TO CHAPTER 5

1. Personal communication, Homer Barnett. As an example of the quick-wittedness of the Angmagsaliks (Eskimos of East Greenland), Captain Holm, the first European to make contact with this people, in 1884, commented:

> They knew well how to use the things . . . which were washed up by the sea. I may mention . . . that they used the bolt-sockets on a large brass mounting which was fixed to a boat which had been found crushed in the ice the year before, as ferules to keep the iron heads of bird darts in place. They thoroughly understood how to use and economize iron. Small fragments that could not be used for knife-blades were riveted to other bits of iron for the purpose of being furnished with a handle. [G. Holm, "Ethnological Sketch of the Angmagsalik Eskimo," in *The Ammassalik Eskimo,* ed. William Thalbitzer, 1914, pp. 112–13.]

2. Discussing the detailed knowledge which the Angmagsaliks had of their region and their geographical sense, Holm remarked that "they are able to point out exactly the good things which specially belong to each separate place; thus in one place there are many narwhals, in another many bears, harbour seals, gulls or even sea-weed" ("Ethnological Sketch," pp. 108–09). See also Franz Boas, "The Central Eskimo," 1888; Edmund Carpenter, "Eskimo Space Concepts," *Explorations,* 1955; Peter Freuchen and Finn Salomonsen, *The Arctic Year,* 1958.

3. Personal communication, Ray L. Birdwhistell.

4. F. Frazer Darling, *A Herd of Red Deer*, 1937; see also William R. Thompson, "Social Behavior," in *Behavior and Evolution*, 1958, p. 303.

5. Or, alternatively, we can adapt modern techniques—for example, air photography—to remap a "lost" landscape or recover a "lost" town; see John Bradford, *Ancient Landscapes*, 1957, which deals with the techniques of air archaeology.

6. This example was supplied by Col. Raymond Sleeper.

7. Col. Sleeper gave the following illustrative explanation:

> If you are traveling at Mach 5, you are traveling at one half the speed of sound in the medium (air). Your speed at Mach .5 is relative to the speed of sound, which is a function of the ambient temperature at that time and place. To calculate the actual distance traveled in the specified time, one must either know the ground speed from radio, radar, or visual references (either to the surface of the earth or to celestial bodies) or ground speed calculated from indicated air speed (Mach .5), temperature, pressure (altitude), and wind direction and velocity. The sound barrier is not a distance. It is a popular and romantic name for the unique aerodynamic phenomena that occur at the time when an accelerating or decelerating aerospace vehicle's speed is equal to the speed of sound in the environment (air).

8. In *Ancient Voyagers in the Pacific*, 1956, Andrew Sharp writes (p. 159) about the limitations even of precise knowledge: "The Caroline and Marshall Islanders had built up a precise knowledge of the currents, landmarks, meteorology and star courses on every journey to every island within their contact areas, and handed on the knowledge to younger pilots . . . [But] the knowledge had to be sustained by continued voyaging and instruction."

9. This information was given me by specialists on the subject during an official visit to the United Kingdom in 1943.

10. Jules H. Masserman, "Anxiety and the Art of Healing," in *Current Psychiatric Therapies*, 1961, p. 221.

11. Moyra Williams, *Horse Psychology*, 1956.

12. G. E. Hutchinson, "The Importance of Ornithology," in *The Itinerant Ivory Tower*, 1953. Discussing the satin bowerbird, studied by A. J. Marshall, Hutchinson writes (p. 61): "When the young are fledged, they are brought by the female to the bower, and for a week or two the family engages in communal display activities."

13. Joel C. Welty, *The Life of Birds*, 1963, pp. 269–81; Henry S. Williams, "Nest Building—New Style," *Natural History*, 1934.

14. W. H. Thorpe, *Learning and Instinct in Animals*, 1963, pp. 348–50.

15. Bruno Bettelheim, "Feral Children and Autistic Children," *American Journal of Sociology*, 1959; Bettelheim, "Rejoinder" [to Margaret Mead], *American Journal of Sociology*, 1959; Arnold Gesell, *Wolf Child and Human Child*, 1941; David C. Mandelbaum, "Wolf-Child Histories

from India," *Journal of Social Psychology,* 1943; Margaret Mead, "Feral Children and Autistic Children," *American Journal of Sociology,* 1959; William Fielding Ogburn, "The Wolf Boy of Agra," *American Journal of Sociology,* 1959; J. A. L. Singh and R. M. Zinng, *Wolf Children and Feral Man,* 1942.

16. John Kieran, *A Natural History of New York City,* 1959, p. 346.

17. James Fisher and R. A. Hinde, "The Opening of Milk Bottles by Birds," *British Birds,* 1949; Hinde and Fisher, "Further Observations on the Opening of Milk Bottles by Birds," *British Birds,* 1951.

18. Helen Blauvelt, "Dynamics of the Mother–Newborn Relationship in Goats," *Group Processes,* 1955; Blauvelt, "Neonate–Mother Relationship in Goat and Man," *Group Processes,* 1956.

19. Lauretta Bender and J. Allison Montague, "Psychotherapy through Art in a Negro Child," *College Art Journal,* 1947.

20. William J. L. Sladen, "Social Structure among Penguins," in *Group Processes,* 1956.

21. Margaret Altmann, "The Role of Juvenile Elk and Moose in the Social Dynamics of Their Species," *Zoologica,* 1960.

22. Lawrence K. Frank, unpublished series of lectures given at Mills College, 1949.

23. Margaret Mead, *Male and Female,* 1949.

24. Personal communication, Konrad Z. Lorenz.

25. J. M. Tanner and Bärbel Inhelder, eds., *Discussions on Child Development,* 1958, p. 85.

26. Margaret Mead, "Woman: Position in Society: Primitive," in *Encyclopedia of the Social Sciences,* 1935.

27. Te Rangi Hiroa (Peter H. Buck), "Samoan Material Culture," 1930; E. S. C. Handy and W. C. Handy, "Samoan House Building, Cooking and Tatooing," 1924; Margaret Mead, "Social Organization of Manua," 1930.

28. Gene Weltfish, *The Origin of Art,* 1953.

29. Franz Boas, *Primitive Art,* 1927.

30. Charles P. Mountford, personal communication.

31. Personal research in Australia, in 1951, among the participants in the experiment.

32. Carrolup Settlement Western Australia, "Aboriginal Children's Art," *Times Education Supplement,* 1950.

33. J. H. Hooykaas–Van Leeuwen Boomkamp, *Ritual Purification of a Balinese Temple,* 1960.

34. Jane Belo, "Balinese Paintings," n.d.

35. Augustus Hamilton, *The Art Workmanship of the Maori Race in New Zealand,* 1896.

36. Camilla H. Wedgwood, "Notes on the Marshall Islands," *Oceania,* 1942.

37. C. A. S. Williams, *Outlines of Chinese Symbolism and Art Motives,* 1941.

NOTES TO CHAPTER 6

1. Herbert M. McLuhan, *The Gutenberg Galaxy*, 1962; Margaret Mead, "Vicissitudes of the Study of the Total Communication Process," in *Approaches to Semiotics*, 1964.

2. Reo F. Fortune, *Arapesh*, 1932; Margaret Mead, "The Mountain-Dwelling Arapesh," in *Sex and Temperament in Three Primitive Societies*, 1935 (1950, pp. 15–118).

3. Arapesh is characterized by the familiar Oceanic type of linked instability of *r* and *l*, *k* and glottal stop.

4. Margaret Mead, *Coming of Age in Samoa*, 1928 (1949, p. 151); Mead, "Social Organization of Manua," 1930, pp. 4–5.

5. Margaret Mead, *Growing Up in New Guinea*, 1930.

6. Where words have traditionally supplied this type of ambiguous reference within which different individual experience supplied the detail, television, as a medium, does exactly the opposite. The attempt to replicate an event in the auditory–visual mode means that the viewer is not invited to add anything to what he experiences as he lives through the simulated event at the rate at which it would have occurred in actuality. Even the coding that is used in a museum miniature diorama, in which the number of leaves on a tree must be introduced disproportionately to the scale of reduction of the tree itself, stimulates some sense of distance, some effort of the imagination. Thus there is every danger that too much dependence on the new medium may reduce the type of stimulation and evocation which through the centuries have been provided by spoken and, even more, by written words. See Mead, "Vicissitudes of the Study of the Total Communication Process."

7. Robert Louis Stevenson, "Travel," in *A Child's Garden of Verses*, 1948.

8. See Margaret Mead, *Moeurs et sexualité en Océanie*, 1963, photograph opp. p. 78.

9. Margaret Mead, "The Mountain Arapesh, II. Supernaturalism," 1940, p. 425. In this account I have indicated by quotation marks the words that can be translated into Neo-Melanesian and thence into English (e.g. palm, coconut, wallaby, etc.), and I have left in Arapesh the words for which the Arapesh knew no Neo-Melanesian equivalents and of which I did not know the botanical or zoological names. Unfortunately, our Arapesh herbarium was damaged in transit; otherwise it would have been possible to shortcut this description by going directly from the Arapesh to the botanical names, eliminating Neo-Melanesian and English words.

10. For a description of Arapesh *tanggets,* see Margaret Mead, "The Mountain Arapesh, I. An Importing Culture," 1938, pp. 193–95, and Figure 9.

11. Mead, "The Mountain Arapesh, II. Supernaturalism," see "The girl who had no vagina" (pp. 375–76) and "The cassowary wife" (p. 398).

12. Ibid., p. 398.

13. Margaret Mead, "The Mountain Arapesh, V. The Record of Uni-belin with Rorschach Analyses," 1949.

14. Gregory Bateson, "Social Planning and the Concept of Deutero Learning," in *Science, Philosophy, and Religion*, 1942.

15. Rhoda Metraux, "Parents and Children," and "A Portrait of the Family in German Juvenile Fiction," in *Childhood in Contemporary Cultures*, 1955.

16. Helen Blauvelt, "Dynamics of the Mother–Newborn Relationship in Goats," in *Group Processes*, 1955; Blauvelt, "Neonate–Mother Relationship in Goat and Man," in *Group Processes*, 1956.

17. Gregory Bateson and Margaret Mead, *Balinese Character*, 1942.

18. See, for example, the two films produced by Gregory Bateson and Margaret Mead, *Karba's First Years*, 1952, and *Childhood Rivalry in Bali and New Guinea*, 1952.

19. *Karba's First Years; Childhood Rivalry in Bali and New Guinea.*

20. This description is based on my field work in Samoa in 1928–29. However, when Gloria Cooper went to Samoa in the fall of 1960, I asked her to investigate further the genesis of Samoan touchiness about etiquette, for which I felt I did not have an adequate explanation. Miss Cooper (personal communication) considers that this touchiness arises from the contrasting responses in formal and informal situations—being placated in a formal context and unmercifully cuffed in an informal one. As a result, any infringement of formality comes to be regarded as intolerable.

21. Colin McPhee, *A House in Bali*, 1946.

22. Reo F. Fortune, *Omaha Secret Societies*, 1932.

23. This peculiarity of Omaha folklore, as recorded by J. O. Dorsey ("Omaha Sociology," 1884) and by Alice C. Fletcher and Francis La Flesche ("The Omaha Tribe," 1911), led Ruth Benedict to suggest to Reo Fortune that he work on the Omaha in the summer of 1930. Fortune brought to this field work his experience of secrecy among the Dobuans (*Sorcerers of Dobu*, 1932); starting with a premise derived from work carried out far from the American scene, he solved the problem.

24. Ruth Benedict, "The Vision in Plains Culture," *American Anthropologist*, 1922; see also Paul Radin, "The Winnebago Tribe," 1923. Among the Winnebago, adults both urged young people to fast and instructed them carefully in what to expect; when they returned from a fast which ended in a vision experience, the adults helped to interpret the vision —and sometimes to reject an unsuitable vision (see especially the accounts of fasts, pp. 291–310).

25. C. H. Waddington, "Evolutionary Systems—Animal and Human," *Nature*, 1959; also Waddington, "The Human Evolutionary System," in *Darwinism and the Study of Society*, 1961.

26. Unpublished study made by Leo Haimson and Francis Rawdon

Smith in the late 1940s, for Columbia University Research in Contemporary Cultures.

27. For estimates of the population of the Territory of Papua and New Guinea, in 1957–58, see Brian Essai, *Papua and New Guinea*, 1961, Table 1, p. 240; for Netherlands New Guinea, in 1957, where the estimated population was 700,000, see *Worldmark Encyclopedia of the Nations*, 1960, pp. 700–01. The linguistic picture is a continually changing one, as new surveys are made or, sometimes, as the same analyst shifts the basis of his analysis (see S. A. Wurm, "The Changing Linguistic Picture of New Guinea," *Oceania*, 1960; also S. A. Wurm and D. C. Laycock, "The Question of Language and Dialect in New Guinea," *Oceania*, 1961). The linguistic map of New Guinea languages prepared by the Department of Education (Port Moresby) in 1955 (quoted by Wurm, "The Changing Linguistic Picture," p. 124) lists 501 languages known to exist at that time.

28. Bateson, "Social Planning and the Concept of Deutero Learning."

29. Mead, "Social Organization of Manua."

30. Ruth Benedict, *Zuni Mythology*, 1935.

31. Unpublished field work on Manus, 1953.

32. "Learning to Dance in Bali"; this film is in preparation.

33. See Margaret Mead, "Anthropology and the Camera," in *The Encyclopedia of Photography*, 1963.

NOTES TO CHAPTER 7

1. V. Gordon Childe, *Man Makes Himself*, 1936.

2. Leslie A. White, *The Evolution of Culture*, 1959.

3. Julian H. Steward, *Theory of Culture Change*, 1955.

4. Marshall D. Sahlins and Elman R. Service, eds., *Evolution and Culture*, 1960.

5. Frederick Lehman, "Some Anthropological Parameters of Civilization: The Ecology and Evolution of India's High Culture," 1960.

6. Karl A. Wittfogel, *Oriental Despotism*, 1957.

7. Charles E. Gray, "An Analysis of Graeco–Roman Development: The Epicyclical Evolution of Graeco–Roman Civilization," *American Anthropologist*, 1958; A. L. Kroeber, *Configurations of Culture Growth*, 1944; Kroeber, "Gray's Epicyclical Evolution," *American Anthropologist*, 1958; Kroeber, *A Roster of Civilizations and Culture*, 1962; Anthony Leeds and Robert Harrison, "Values and State of Knowledge in the Determination of Cultural Cycles—A Test of the Kroeber–Gray Hypothesis," 1960.

8. Lawrence K. Frank, *Society as the Patient*, 1948.

9. Oswald Spengler, *The Decline of the West*, 1932.

10. Ruth Benedict, "Psychological Types in the Cultures of the Southwest," in *Proceedings of the Twenty-third International Congress of Americanists*, 1930; Benedict, *Patterns of Culture*, 1934.

11. Kenneth E. Boulding, "Where Are We Going if Anywhere? A Look at Past-Civilization," *Human Organization*, 1962.

12. Frank Tannenbaum, "Men and His Institutions," in *Miscelania de estudios dedicados a Fernando Ortiz, por sus discipulos, colegos y amigos,* 1955–57.

13. Norman Cousins, *Modern Man Is Obsolete,* 1945.

14. Thomas Henry Huxley and Julian S. Huxley, *Touchstone for Ethics,* 1947; Julian S. Huxley, "Evolution, Cultural and Biological," in *Current Anthropology,* 1956. This position has been characteristic of Huxley's writing in the last fifteen years; see also "The Humanist Frame," in *The Humanist Frame,* 1962.

15. Winthrop N. Kellogg, *Porpoises and Sonar,* 1961; John C. Lilly, *Man and Dolphin,* 1961.

16. Jurgen Ruesch and Gregory Bateson, *Communication,* 1951.

17. Gordon H. Willey, "The Early Great Styles and the Rise of Pre-Columbian Civilizations," *American Anthropologist,* 1962; see also bibliography of this article.

18. The present world situation of Australia is a case in point. In the 1930s, Australia's dependence on sheep as a principal element in overseas trade, combined with the paucity of many natural resources necessary for twentieth century industrialization, made the prosperity of the Australian economy somewhat precarious. Added to this, the "white Australia" policy seemed to ensure for a long time to come Australia's relative isolation and relatively low ability to contribute cultural innovations.

But after 1935 the situation changed as the result of a whole series of events, in none of which Australian society was initially actively implicated. Among the relevant events were the rise of Hitler and the temporary successes of the Fascist states; the great number of European refugees who, both before and after World War II, were willing to emigrate from Europe; the new place of Australia in the defensive military strategy of the Western powers; the new political climate in which giving help to underdeveloped countries became an accepted style of behavior for technologically advanced countries; and, finally, the development of nuclear power. The possible evolutionary significance of Australian culture has been radically altered by this extra-Australian complex of events. The older fear that the country might be overrun by non-European immigrants was complemented by the new availability of European immigrants, many of them with professional skills. At the same time the change in military and diplomatic strategies involved Australia in unexpected relationships with her Asian neighbors. The discovery of large deposits of uranium-bearing ores provided a new power source.

Today, Australia has the combined advantages of educated and ambitious emigrants from many European countries, a new emphasis on scientific work which has come about because of the military situation and the availability of uranium, and a wholly unexpected openness to non-Europeans, following on the admission of large numbers of Asian students and the organization of technological aid operations under the Colombo plan. All this has changed the level of cultural interaction with the rest of the world, and now Australia's particular cultural gift for technical simplification, which once represented a kind of latter-day primitiveness begotten of the peculiarities of the settlement pattern in Australia's exacting physical conditions, may be a potential contribution to space technology.

19. White, *The Evolution of Culture.*

20. Steward, *Theory of Culture Change.*

21. Lawrence K. Frank, unpublished lectures on organized complexity.

22. Harrison Brown, *The Challenge of Man's Future,* 1954; Fairfield Osborn, *The Limits of the Earth,* 1953; Paul B. Sears, "The Processes of Environmental Change by Man," in *Man's Role in Changing the Face of the Earth,* 1956 (see also for bibliography).

23. Henry B. Collins, "The Origin and Antiquity of the Eskimo," *Smithsonian Institution Annual Report for 1950,* 1951; Collins, "Archeological Work in Arctic Canada," *Smithsonian Institution Annual Report for 1956,* 1957.

24. Robert C. Suggs, "The Archaeology of Nuku Hiva, Marquesas Islands, French Polynesia," 1959; Suggs, *The Island Civilizations of Polynesia,* 1960.

25. Allan R. Holmberg, "Nomads of the Long Bow," 1951.

26. L. S. B. Leakey, "Recent Discoveries at Olduvai Gorge, Tanganyika," *Nature,* 1958; Leakey, "Exploring 1,750,000 Years into Man's Past," *National Geographic,* 1961; Leakey and F. Clark Howell, "The Discovery by L. S. B. Leakey of *Zinjanthropus boisei,*" *Current Anthropology,* 1960.

27. For a recent discussion of some of the as yet unresolved problems, see F. Clark Howell, "European and Northwest African Middle Pleistocene Hominids," *Current Anthropology,* 1960; L. S. B. Leakey, "The Origin of the Genus *Homo,*" in *Evolution after Darwin,* 2, 1960; also Frank B. Livingstone, George Cowgill, and F. Clark Howell, "More on Middle Pleistocene Hominids," *Current Anthropology,* 1961.

28. Sigmund Freud, *Totem and Taboo,* 1918.

29. C. H. Waddington, *The Strategy of the Genes,* 1957; Waddington, "The Human Animal," in *The Humanist Frame,* 1961.

30. Huxley, "Evolution, Cultural and Biological."

31. Theodosius Dobzhansky and Joseph B. Birdsell, "On Methods of Evolutionary Biology and Anthropology," *American Scientist,* 1957.

32. We can reconstruct such a state of precarious relationship to the environment from the recorded experiences of Australian aborigines. In reply to my inquiry about this situation in Australia, Ronald and Catherine Berndt wrote (personal communication, February 1961):

> Over much of Aboriginal Australia the range of choice (as to what should be transmitted) was a narrow one. . . . Especially in the "desert," this was in fact the only way in which their survival could

be assured, as far as was humanly possible. They couldn't *neglect* to pass on all available information, whether or not it seemed immediately relevant to the local situation. Just as sacred knowledge was passed on gradually from the old through the not-so-old to the younger people, so in regard to ordinary everyday living the stress has been on this kind of continuity in handing on knowledge. . . .

Information about "abnormal" conditions is (or was) transmitted along with the general body of knowledge relating to "normal" conditions. Younger people are (or were) taught about "possibilities"—as a second or even third line of defense on which to fall back. E.g. adolescents living in or on the fringe of the "desert" can name foods which, although edible, are not "good"; they *can* be eaten, but one would not do so unless this were really necessary. And they have a fair idea of the places in which water is most likely, or least likely, to be found at certain seasons or in certain circumstances (e.g. after heavy rain, or after light rain, or when no rain has fallen for a certain time); how to gauge *where* rain is falling (direction, distance, places probably involved); and where and how to draw on such additional sources as frogs (which bury themselves underground, between rains), or the trunks or roots of various trees. . . .

To illustrate not only the variety but also the painstaking use of every possible natural resource. Some seeds are so tiny that a single seed is barely visible should it fall to the ground. The return, in terms of quantity, often seems out of all proportion to the time and energy spent in getting and preparing such foods. Even a termite mound (or "ant heap") is eaten without distaste, and so are the very small flies that are found in certain kinds of native fruit. There are several varieties of wild tobacco. . . . People like to chew them in dry stretches as a substitute for water—but one variety, which *can* be chewed, is used only as a last resort since it induces vomiting. There are other foods which make people giddy or lightheaded if eaten in any quantity, or cause them to urinate too frequently.

Today it is possible to document the kinds of break in continuity that are brought about through European contact. Other circumstances might have brought about similar breaks in the past, about which we have no records. So, the Berndts wrote:

When the Daly River rose during the wet season of 1945–6 and inundated most of the surrounding country, there was a great deal of talk about whether dry patches could be trusted to remain so. Although the Daly was expected to flood every couple of years, the levels varied; and the question asked was, "What parts remain dry even in the *biggest* floods?" The few local people who were old enough to have expert knowledge on this suggested several doubtful possibilities, but only one certainty; this last was completely untouched by the flood, which lasted almost a fortnight, and was at no time in any danger of being submerged.

33. Norman B. Tindale, "First Australian," *Pacific Discovery,* 1956; Tindale, "Culture Succession in South Eastern Australia from Late Pleistocene to the Present," *Records of the South Australian Museum,* 1957; for a summary discussion, see Grahame Clark, *World Prehistory,* 1962, pp. 240–47.

34. Collins, "The Origin and Antiquity of the Eskimo"; Collins, "Archeological Work in the Arctic"; also Collins, "Radiocarbon Dating in the Arctic," *American Antiquity,* 1953.

35. Bertram Schaffner, ed., *Group Processes,* 1955. In the published version of this conference, Lorenz himself does not use the phrase, but this and related images provide a recurrent theme throughout (e.g. comments by Lehrman, p. 114; Lorenz, p. 143; Schneirla, p. 191; Erikson, p. 213).

36. L. L. Whyte, "Developmental Selection in Mutation," *Science,* 1960.

37. Mavis Gunther, "Instinct and the Nursing Couple," *Lancet,* 1955.

38. In the Marquesas Linton and Kardiner postulated that a conspicuous difference in sex ratios was significant in determining the rather unusual form of polyandry, with its accompanying maternal neglect, and have suggested that this may have been a contributing factor in the Marquesan Islands population decline (see Abram Kardiner, *The Individual and His Society,* 1939, especially pp. 137–96 and 197–250). However, more recent field work (Robert C. Suggs, "Sexual Customs of the Marquesas," n.d.), combined with a recheck of earlier censuses suggests that the unbalanced sex ratio reported by Linton may have been a temporary phenomenon (see George H. L. F. Pitt-Rivers, *The Clash of Culture and the Contact of Races,* 1927).

39. Joseph W. Eaton and Albert J. Mayer, *Man's Capacity to Reproduce,* 1954; also Joseph W. Eaton and Robert J. Weil, *Culture and Mental Disorders: A Comparative Study of the Hutterites and Other Populations,* 1955.

40. Rhoda Metraux, "Effects of Cultural Anticipation and Attitudes toward Aging," in *The Neurologic and Psychiatric Aspects of the Disorders of Aging,* 1956.

41. Although it is unlikely, it is theoretically possible for a migrating group, the progenitors of a large population, to be selected on some basis that would establish a permanent difference in strength or weakness between the descendants of the migrants and those who remained behind. (See, for example, the slight evidence of specialization in the descendants of one of the *Bounty* mutineers, discussed by H. L. Shapiro in *The Heritage of the Bounty,* 1962.)

In fact, however, a situation of this kind is much too complex to make a full analysis of such possibilities feasible at the present time. For example, even though it were argued that the ancestors of the present

American Negro population had been subject to negative selection (as they included those whom fellow tribesmen were willing to sell into foreign slavery and those who were less skillful in evading capture), it would still be necessary to take into account the selective pressure of the slave ships and early plantation conditions, which would have screened out the weak as well as many of the able. To this would have to be added the unusual positive screening of those who had been sold for political reasons in Africa (as Melville J. Herskovits postulated for Haiti, in *Life in a Haitian Valley*, 1937, pp. 52–53; see also, his discussion in *The Myth of the Negro Past*, 1941, passim, for the United States), and in the New World the positive screening of the intelligent and the attractive as house servants, with resulting opportunities for protective miscegenation. In these circumstances it would seem that the positive selective factors would compensate for and possibly overbalance the negative ones.

Among French Canadians there was a steady selective process going on as those children who found most favor in the eyes of their landowning parents received a superior education or inherited the land, while those who found less favor tended to migrate away from the home community, often to the United States (see Horace Miner, *St. Denis: A French–Canadian Parish*, 1939). During World War II, marked differences in political attitudes were found between French Canadians and Franco-Americans, which might be attributed to the conservatism of those who had conformed most acceptably to their parents' desires and the less conforming attitudes of those who had been thrust out into the world (based on unpublished data from public opinion polls, during World War II). It is, however, exceedingly doubtful whether parental choices of this kind are based on any recognizable heritable qualities.

42. Edmund W. Sinnott, L. C. Dunn, and Theodosius Dobzhansky, *Principles of Genetics*, 1950, see Figure 73, Pedigree of hemophilia in the descendants of Queen Victoria of England.

43. Steward, *Theory of Culture Change*.

44. C. H. Waddington, *The Ethical Animal*, 1961.

45. Leslie White, in "The Concept of Culture," *American Anthropologist*, 1959, has proposed the term *symbolate* for "the class of things and events consisting of or dependent upon symboling" (p. 230); these when "considered in terms of their relationship to human organisms, i.e., in a somatic context . . . may properly be called *human behavior,* and the science *psychology*" and when "considered and interpreted in an extra-somatic context, i.e., in terms of their relationships to one another rather than to human organisms, we may call them *culture,* and the science *culturology*" (p. 231). Although I recognize the relevance of Professor White's argument about the need for a term like *symbolate,* I do not accept his statement that "cultural processes can be explained without taking human organisms into account" (p. 241); I would prefer to phrase this as "without taking *particular* human organisms into account." Profes-

sor White uses the illustration of mummification. To solve all the problems with which he is concerned, it is necessary to recognize that the process of mummification is not extrasomatic, in the sense that it is not related to human beings. Mummification is completely postulated on human organisms with defined properties which distinguish them, for example, from gorillas or bowerbirds and on the handling of dead human organisms in a particular way. Mummification is extrasomatic only in the sense that the *particular* properties of *particular* human organisms need not be specified because they are, as White points out, irrrelevant at this level of analysis.

46. For a discussion of the problems of language in various cultures, see "Urbanization and Standard Language: A Symposium Presented at the 1958 Meetings of the American Anthropological Association," *Anthropological Linguistics*, 1959.

47. In reply to my inquiry as to contemporary attitudes toward Gaelic Irish, the Rev. E. F. O'Doherty wrote, in part, as follows (personal communication, April 1963):

> Briefly, what has happened here is that the symbolic meaning of a "maternal language" has been forgotten by the many, though it was in a sense this very symbol which brought the nation together for the final push towards independence in the first quarter of the century. Now, by contrast, it has become in a sense a symbol of a minority, who refuse to come to terms with the twentieth century. . . . The actual number of people who speak Irish as a "mother tongue" has . . . fallen from perhaps half-a-million at the turn of the century to an estimated 10 or 11 thousand a few years ago. I think it could be shown that as long as learning the language was a voluntary effort on the part of the citizens, it acquired a symbolic meaning for them; it meant freedom, independence, their own way of life, overthrow of tyranny, etc. It actually symbolized the struggle for freedom. As soon as freedom was achieved however, the language was imposed on all citizens by an overzealous government. No choice was left to the parents or the children or the teachers. It became a necessary qualification for public office, etc. It thus came to symbolize tyranny rather than freedom, and "compulsion" was heard on all sides.

48. The small scale of events in primitive societies makes it possible to pursue an investigation of this kind in greater detail. Today the parts of New Guinea and the surrounding islands, which were once included in the territory known as the Bismarck Archipelago, Kaiser Wilhelmsland, and the German Solomon Islands, are a Trust Territory under the United Nations. In this Trust Territory formal government communiqués must be in English, and it is mandatory to teach English in schools. At a cultural macro-evolutionary level it would be possible to say that the trend

toward the use of English—not only in the islands administered by English-speaking nations but also in such adjacent territories as the former Netherlands New Guinea—is an inevitable part of local evolution in the Pacific. But if we examine the course of events in greater detail, we find a number of points of divergence.[a]

Before World War I, Australia had taken over the administration of the area known as Papua, or British New Guinea. In this area one native language, Motuan, was defined as an easy one for speakers of English to learn, and planters and missionaries who made their headquarters at Port Moresby learned to use it. The Papuan native peoples, who spoke many diverse local languages, also learned to handle Motuan as a lingua franca. But Motuan, a capriciously chosen local language, once spoken only by a very small tribe and a very small group of people, had no future as a language through which the native peoples of Papua could either enter a wider world or function efficiently as clerks, policemen, and so on, in the local system. A strong complementary movement for the teaching of English developed, and in this movement the position of one figure, Sir Hubert Murray, who was the first Australian Lieutenant-Governor (and who remained in control for thirty-seven years) was decisive. Under the pressure of the missions and the government and lacking a useful lingua franca, a few Papuans—but only a few—learned English.

Meanwhile, in the islands under German control, the German colonizers found in existence a pidgin which laborers had brought back from Queensland, where a pidgin used by the English colonizers and the Australian aborigines was already quite well developed. The idea of a pidgin had been adapted by the natives of German New Guinea to their own prevailing grammatical structure (that of the Melanesian languages) but with a prevailing English vocabulary. The Germans found it more convenient to treat this New Guinea pidgin as a foreign language, and to adapt and systematize it, than to teach the New Guinea natives German. Consequently, during World War I, when the Australian Expeditionary Force took over the German colonies, they found a going pidgin which Europeans and natives could easily learn.

New Guinea pidgin is easy to learn because it is uninflected (as are many Malayo–Polynesian languages) and because the development of a small number of available and expected circumlocutions makes unnecessary the mastery of a large vocabulary. For example, it is not necessary for two pidgin speakers to know the names of more than a very small number of objects. A conversation (the spelling of which has been anglicized for intelligibility) will go along like this:

[a] This discussion is based on my own field work. In regard to pidgin English see also Gregory Bateson, "Pidgin English and Cross-cultural Communication," *Transactions of The New York Academy of Sciences*, 1944; Robert A. Hall, *Hands Off Pidgin English*, 1955; Hall, "Colonial Policy and Neo-Melanesian," *Anthropological Linguistics*, 1959; and Margaret Mead, "Talk-Boy," *Asia*, 1931.

First speaker: Where stop tuptup?

Second speaker: Tuptup, he all the same what name?

First speaker: Tuptup? Oh, em he something belong fas(ten) em mouth belong bottle.

Second speaker: Oh! Now you look-out em tuptup?

First speaker: Yes, me like find em tuptup.

Second speaker: Tuptup belong what name bottle?

First speaker: Tuptup belong this fellow bottle all the time me savee capsize em whisky along em.

During the period between World War I and World War II, New Guinea pidgin became the lingua franca of the Mandated area, and whereas the Germans had regarded it as a New Guinea language, English speakers, using the English-derived vocabulary, moved it steadily toward a language which some linguists, taking their clues from the vocabulary rather than from the structure, would now classify as a branch of Indo–European.

But during this period there were still conflicts over education in the Mandated Territory. The League of Nations demanded that schools be set up, and halfhearted attempts were made to teach English to a few boys, but such efforts were defeated by the ready availability of a good substitute. Protestant missionaries who had entered the Territory had no idea how small and localized the language groups were, and they had laboriously translated the Bible into languages spoken by a few thousand, sometimes only a few hundred people. These local languages were then taught to new converts, a course which had the effect of triply depriving a newly converted tribe, since the new religion was not mediated in their mother tongue and not in a world language and not in a language which was becoming area-wide. In contrast, the Roman Catholic missions adopted pidgin for the catechism and the liturgy and for educational purposes.

Both these tendencies—quite "predictable" in terms of the historical separatism of the Protestants and the historical universalism of the Roman Catholic Church—were accentuated by the circumstance that the missions were German in their composition while the government was now adminis-tered by English speakers. A shift from pidgin to English would have involved more effort. However, it might have been accomplished if, at this point, a crucial member of the New Guinea administration had been strongly influenced by the Papuan colonial tradition or else had recognized that it would be possible to curb the power of the German missions by insisting on their using English. Instead, the most dynamic member of the administration was Sir Beaumont Phillips, who came to the Territory not from Papua but from the British Solomons where, under the influence of work boys' experience and propinquity to the German Solomons, a local version of pidgin had developed. Moreover, in the Mandated Territory, the traditions of Papua were invoked negatively rather than positively. In Papua the natives had to learn English (which of course they did not do) but they were not allowed to drive motor cars; in the Mandated Territory, they spoke pidgin and drove motor cars, and everybody was better off. Papua was run for the Papuans (pronounced Papúans when the natives were meant, and Pápuans when Europeans were meant). New Guinea was run for progress; that is, large extraterritorial enterprises were given more favor. Here again Sir Hubert Murray was involved in the development of these polarized attitudes. In the Mandated Territory the German missions were permitted to fill their ranks with German-speaking brothers and sisters who were nationals of other countries. As a result, in World War II, the Australian administration was faced with the existence of a network of enemy sympathizers, a situation which cost the lives of many Australian Coastwatchers.

Meanwhile, in the Netherlands East Indies, of which the third part of New Guinea (Netherlands New Guinea) was a neglected and unimportant part, another set of historically particular events was taking place. Before World War II the Netherlands paid little attention to Dutch New Guinea (as the Australians called it) or West Irian (as the Indonesians now call it). The lingua franca was Pasar Malay, a somewhat pidgin-like Malay which was used from Singapore throughout the Netherlands territories. At this period there was little contact across the borders between the two Australian parts of New Guinea, on the one hand, and Netherlands New Guinea, on the other. In acculturation—linguistically and in other respects —the natives of Netherlands New Guinea were oriented toward the East.

After World War II the efforts of a few enlightened Netherlanders turned to transforming the Dutch East Indies into part of the Netherlands Commonwealth, but they failed; with even a little more leadership they might have succeeded. At the settlement table the question of Netherlands New Guinea was laid aside as a bargaining point for later disposition; but with the hardening of relationships between the Netherlands and the new state of Indonesia, the New Guinea territory became a bone of contention. In the meantime, members of the old Dutch East Indies civil service were transferred to Netherlands New Guinea, as were many Eurasian former citizens of the Dutch East Indies who had elected to remain Netherlands citizens and for whom there was no place in the Netherlands. The new civil service began to use British models of colonization and to substitute English for Malay as the contact language.

This again was culturally predictable. The Dutch are members of a small maritime nation who have specialized in learning the languages of the larger powers. They have had long experience of the practicality of requiring language training, and they took this experience and expectation with them to the East Indies where, in the schools, after reading and writing were taught in the vernacular (Malay with a Western script was taught in the Middle School), Dutch, English, French, and German were taught in the higher schools. Furthermore, Malay was not the local, scriptless language of a small tribe (as Motuan was in Papua), but a language spoken by millions of people stretching from the mainland into the Pacific, with an impressive history and an ancient literature. So the peoples of the East Indies, when they became an independent state, treated Malay as a "real" language, and today there are over 90 million speakers of Bahasa Indonesian (which is a combination of the spoken Pasar Malay popularized by the Dutch as a lingua franca and the high literary and historical Malay). For the Malay-speaking people of Indonesia, Bahasa Indonesian is a standard language in the same sense that standard English or standard French is, replacing in written and spoken form the less mutually intelligible dialects.

The Netherlands, then deeply concerned to hold on to Netherlands New Guinea, adopted the English language and English methods of administration so that, in the world view, Netherlands New Guinea was part of New Guinea rather than part of "racially alien" Indonesia. Indonesian claims to the New Guinea territory could then be described as "brown imperialism"—a phrase to which Americans, on the one hand, and the Eastern and former colonial blocs, on the other, responded with emotion.

Meanwhile, the Mandated Territory of New Guinea, which during World War II had fallen to the Japanese and later had been recaptured by the combined Australian and American Expeditionary Forces, was transformed into a Trust Territory under the United Nations, but still with an Australian administration. This meant that such matters as education came up for review by members of the Trusteeship Commission of the United Nations. What, for example, was to be the language of education? The problem involves the future of almost a million and a half natives of the Trust Territory (almost two million, if Papua is included, as it is administratively), who speak over 500 mutually unintelligible local languages,[b] but who from year to year are becoming more proficient in speaking and writing pidgin, using highly variable but perfectly adequate local phonetic versions of the English alphabet. Anyone with experience in the Territory, when the question arose, knew that natives could learn to speak pidgin in a few weeks, and that children and adults could learn to read and write rapidly. Furthermore, pidgin provided a bridge to English; after writing was established, the common vocabulary made it quite easy to make the move.

But a whole set of pressures existed against the formalization of pidgin, each of which can be described in broad terms. There was the pressure for the use of English which came from Papua, strengthened when the administrative link to the Territory came into effect in 1949. There was the pressure for the use of English (or at least basic English) from the young "American" missionaries, both Protestant and Roman Catholic, who were engaged in intra-Mission battles with the old "German" missionaries. There was the historically determined sensibility of the Australians who, like Americans and Canadians, speak an English that diverges from the

[b] See Footnote 27, Chapter 6.

standard English of England. And, finally, there were the visitation committees from the United Nations, among whose members were non-
Europeans and others who were anticolonial in their viewpoint and sensitized to any kind of pidgin as a "slave language." All these pressures could
have been resisted by one strategically placed individual with a different
set of convictions—but they were not. The upshot is that the peoples of
New Guinea have been denied the kind of linguistic unification that
would have welded them into one people (as in the Dutch East Indies
the use of Malay was one of the preconditions for the establishment of
Indonesia).

It may, of course, be argued that the Australians wish to prevent any
idea of "nationalism" from spreading among the fragmented peoples of
New Guinea. But whatever the Australian viewpoint may have been, even
in the recent past, events involving West Irian (Netherlands New Guinea)
are hurrying the Australians toward some kind of token unity and autonomy in the Trust Territory, where the real language of communication
among the peoples is not even officially recognized by the Administration.
The proposal of the Netherlands government that Netherlands New
Guinea should also become a Trust Territory, had it been carried out,
would immediately have put the Australians, with their much more accul-
turated peoples, into an invidious position if their territories were not
also hurrying toward some form of self-government.

That there was still another thread in this complicated skein became
apparent during the discussions between the Indonesians and the Dutch,
which centered on the incorporation of West Irian as part of Indonesia.
These protracted and difficult negotiations—as also the expulsion of the
Dutch from Indonesia in late 1957 and the ill-fated Sumatran rebellion—
did great damage to a young state struggling to establish order. Throughout these events, the United States' views about the comparative legitimacy
of Dutch and Indonesian claims to the disputed territory were of crucial
importance in an overall national strategy in which the struggle with
Communism for Southeast Asia was the central theme. But the small
decisions in the Cold War have to be fought out with the specialists in
the appropriate agencies, and the judgments of foreign-service officials,
intelligence personnel, and the specialists of the various "desks" are taken
into account. The Dutch presented their view that the peoples of New
Guinea are of a different "race" from Indonesians, and that it would be
a perpetuation of "imperialism" to turn them over to Indonesia. The
Indonesians repeatedly stated their view that West Irian is part of Indonesia. Meanwhile, for higher-level policy, the crucial question was: How
far was it wise to back up the Sukarno government?

A different viewpoint might have been arrived at had one strategically
placed person argued the case in terms intelligible to Americans—namely
that Indonesian nationhood rests on the inclusion in Indonesia of all the
peoples of all the islands, who, for three hundred or more years, have

shared a Dutch contact culture. If one part is legitimately broken off, any other part—Bali or Sumatra—may equally well break away. Traditionally, at the signing of the American Declaration of Independence, Benjamin Franklin said: "We must all hang together, or assuredly we shall all hang separately." Had an appeal been made to Americans in terms of this essential, traditionally based and well-understood sense of solidarity, the Indonesian viewpoint would have been clarified and the United States might well have developed a different policy toward Indonesia in 1958. In this case, the negotiations might have ended in an acceptance of Indonesian claims, not in an appeasing gesture—as they did. This latter phrasing has now opened the way to new and dangerous territorial disputes in this part of the Pacific, and it poses new problems for the Australian administration of Papua and New Guinea.

Retracing our steps, we can see a number of real points of decision, that is, points at which the decisions made by two or three people could have changed the course of an actual historical sequence: the choice of Motuan and of English as the languages spoken in Papua; the choice by the Germans of a systematized pidgin English, instead of German, in old German New Guinea; the acceptance and continued government use of pidgin by the Australian administration in the Mandated Territory after World War I; the insistence by United Nations commissions on the abolition of pidgin after World War II; the final failure of the Dutch effort to retain Netherlands New Guinea after 1962; and the subsequent pressures for self-government in New Guinea among peoples whose languages of cross-cultural communication (Pasar Malay in West Irian, and pidgin in the Trust Territory) are not legitimate avenues of communication. In the mid-1950s, linguists and anthropologists made belated efforts to rename New Guinea pidgin "Neo-Melanesian" (as Pasar Malay was also renamed) to give it higher status as a language. But their efforts were made too late to influence crucial decisions.

The outcome of the larger sequence of events in Southeast Asia is not now predictable. But in twenty-five years, if it is necessary to take into account a New Guinea whose peoples speak to one another in one language but who receive communications from their government in another language (which they do not have the means of learning or of being taught), it will be easy enough to argue the inevitability of the sequence and the particular outcome. However, attention to the details of this event sequence will reveal that there were many points along the way at which the decisions of single individuals were crucially important, many points at which the pressures of differently informed and differently oriented individuals in key positions might have changed history.

49. "Measures and Weights," *Encylopaedia Britannica, 15,* 1956.

50. Charles Davies, *The Metric System,* 1871.

51. Ibid., pp. 60–62, 64.

52. Meanwhile the debate continues as, with the growth of industrializa-

tion, the cost of conversion mounts, and the difficulties of maintaining multiple system of measurement also mount. In a recent interview (William F. Freeman, "Decimal Inch Urged as Basic Measure," *The New York Times,* June 9, 1963), the director of research for a manufacturer of industrial fasteners pointed out that

> in the making of a simple bolt . . . special tools and gauging are needed for production of each variation of diameter, thread series and length [and he further commented] "probably the worst handicap is the reduced size of production lots incurred by splitting production between products made to the two systems. . . . It is unavoidable if we manufacture an appreciable number of our parts to the metric system. We can successfully absorb a few as 'specials.' The breakdown would come when the 'special' became commonplace."

But the continuing lack of rationality in this old debate appears when it is suggested that, since the cost of conversion to the metric system is prohibitive, Americans should instead adopt as a new system a decimal inch, pound, gallon, etc., which would still

> "leave the linear inch untouched. . . . Thus, the world would have two systems, metric and inch, the United States inch economy would not be weakened and the inch system ultimately could displace the metric system in the world economic competition."

NOTES TO CHAPTER 8

1. For a more technical discussion of this problem, see Theodore Schwartz and Margaret Mead, "Micro- and Macro-cultural Models for Cultural Evolution," *Anthropological Linguistics,* 1961; see also Appendix A.

2. Margaret Mead, "The Swaddling Hypothesis: Its Reception," *American Anthropologist,* 1954.

3. Solon T. Kimball, "Communication Modalities as a Function of Social Relationships," *Transactions of The New York Academy of Sciences,* 1963.

4. Margaret Mead, "Energy Changes under Conditions of Culture Change," *Sociometry and the Science of Man,* 1955.

5. Franz Boas, *Kwakiutl Tales,* 1910; also Boas, *Bella Bella Texts,* 1928; for a student of Boas, see Ruth Benedict, *Tales of the Cochiti Indians,* 1931.

6. Margaret Mead, *Coming of Age in Samoa,* Appendix 2, "Methodology of This Study" (Mentor Book MP418, 1949, pp. 152–55). This method was reidentified by Conrad M. Arensberg in "Behavior and Organization: Industrial Studies," in *Social Psychology at the Crossroads,* 1951.

7. William F. Ogburn and Dorothy Thomas, "Are Inventions Inevitable," *Political Science Quarterly,* 1922; see also Tertius Chandler, "Dupli-

cate Inventions?" *American Anthropologist,* 1960; and A. L. Kroeber, "Comment," *American Anthropologist,* 1960.

8. See Introduction, Footnote 3.

9. John Hersey, *The Child Buyer,* 1960.

10. Hermann J. Muller, "The Guidance of Human Evolution," in *Evolution after Darwin,* 2, 1960; also Muller, "Should We Weaken or Strengthen Our Genetic Heritage," *Daedalus,* 1961.

11. Leslie A. White, "The Concept of Culture," *American Anthropologist,* 1959.

12. Gunnar Myrdal, *Beyond the Welfare State,* 1960.

13. Margaret Mead, *New Lives for Old,* 1956; Theodore Schwartz, "The Paliau Movement in the Admiralty Islands, 1946–1954," 1962.

14. Karl Geiringer, *The Bach Family,* 1954.

15. Loren C. Eiseley, *Darwin's Century,* 1958.

16. Geiringer, *The Bach Family,* p. 197.

17. Ibid., p. 481.

18. Evaluation by Erasmus Barlow (personal communication), a great-grandson of Charles Darwin; see also Barlow, "The Dangers of Health," *The Listener,* 1956.

19. Peter Freuchen, *Eskimo,* 1931.

20. Elmer V. McCollum, "Stanley Rossiter Benedict 1884–1936," *National Academy of Sciences Biographical Memoirs,* 1952; see also C. P. Snow, *Science and Government,* 1962.

21. Nathan Leites and Elsa Bernaut, *Ritual of Liquidation,* 1954.

22. Bertram D. Wolfe, *Three Who Made a Revolution,* 1948.

23. Based on an unpublished analysis of a mountain-climbing team, made by Richard Emerson, University of Cincinnati.

24. L. C. Jouanneau, ed., *Discussions du Code civil dans le conseil d'État,* 1805–08; J. G. Locre, ed., *Procès-verbaux du conseil d'État, contenant la discussion du project de Code civil,* 1803–04.

25. Leslie R. Groves, *Now It Can Be Told: The Story of the Manhattan Project,* 1962.

26. Margaret Mead, "Patterns of Worldwide Cultural Change in the 1960's," in *Science, Technology and Development,* 7 [1963].

NOTES TO CHAPTER 9

1. Douglas L. Oliver, *The Pacific Islands,* 1952.

2. Peter Worsley, *The Trumpet Shall Sound,* 1958.

3. Anthony F. C. Wallace, "Revitalization Movements," *American Anthropologist,* 1956.

4. James Mooney, "The Ghost-Dance Religion and the Sioux Outbreak of 1890," *Bureau of American Ethnology, Fourteenth Annual Report, 1892–1893,* 1896.

5. See, for example, John C. Ewers, "The Horse in Blackfoot Indian Culture," *Bureau of American Ethnology Bulletin,* 1955; Oscar Lewis, *The*

Effects of White Contact upon Blackfoot Culture, 1942; Bernard Mishkin, *Rank and Warfare among the Plains Indians,* 1940; Frank Secoy, *Changing Military Patterns on the Great Plains,* 1953.

6. F. E. Williams, *Orokaiva Magic,* 1928.

7. Anthony F. C. Wallace, "Handsome Lake and the Great Revival in the West," *American Quarterly,* 1952.

8. Robert F. Spencer, "Culture Process and Intellectual Current: Durkheim and Ataturk," *American Anthropologist,* 1958.

9. Melford E. Spiro, *Kibbutz: Venture into Utopia,* 1956; also Spiro, *Children of the Kibbutz,* 1958.

10. However, cult movements linked with political movements are not new in China; see, for example, Li Chien-nung, *The Political History of China, 1840–1928,* 1956, pp. 54–55, for a description of Hung Hsiu-ch'uan and the background of the Taiping Rebellion.

11. E. W. P. Chinnery and A. C. Haddon, "Five New Religious Cults in British New Guinea," *Hibbert Journal,* 1917; P. Lawrence, "Cargo Cults and Religious Beliefs among the Garia," *International Archives of Anthropology,* 1954; Lawrence, "The Madang District Cargo Cult," *South Pacific,* 1955; Margaret Mead, "The Mountain Arapesh, V. The Record of Unabelin with Rorschach Analyses," *Anthropological Papers of the American Museum of Natural History,* 1949; also Mead, "Weaver of the Border," in *In the Company of Man,* 1960; F. E. Williams, "The Vailala Madness and the Destruction of Native Ceremonies in the Gulf," *Papuan Anthropology Report,* 1923; and Williams, "The Vailala Madness in Retrospect," in *Essays Presented to C. G. Seligman,* 1934.

12. Worsley, *The Trumpet Shall Sound;* Margaret Mead, "The Group as the Unit of Social Evolution," *Man,* 1958.

13. R. M. Berndt, "A Cargo Movement in the East Central Highlands of New Guinea," *Oceania,* 1952–53; R. M. Berndt, "Reaction to Contact in the Eastern Highlands of New Guinea," *Oceania,* 1954.

14. Jean Guiart, "Forerunners of Melanesian Nationalism," *Oceania,* 1951; Guiart, "John Frum Movement in Tanna," *Oceania,* 1952; Guiart, "The Co-operative Called 'The Malekula Native Company,' a Borderline Type of Cargo Cult," *South Pacific,* 1952.

15. Ian H. Hogbin, *Transformation Scene,* 1951; Hogbin, *Social Change,* 1958.

16. Theodore Schwartz, "The Paliau Movement in the Admiralty Islands, 1946–1954," *Anthropological Papers of the American Museum of Natural History,* 1962.

17. Sometimes, however, it is almost impossible to distinguish whether the element under discussion (e.g. marching in formation, or mustering a whole village into a line—both familiar practices of Administration patrol officers and plantation managers) is a bit of ritual, part of the behavior ushering in the utopian state, or is perhaps a sober but ill-advised attempt to imitate *all* the features of a Western way of life, as the natives have perceived it.

18. See Appendix B, pp. 342–43, for published work by Reo Fortune and by Margaret Mead on the 1928–29 expedition to Manus.

19. See Appendix B, pp. 344–45, for published work by Margaret Mead and by Theodore Schwartz on the 1953–54 expedition to Manus.

20. Schwartz, "The Paliau Movement."

21. Robert F. Maher, *New Men of Papua,* 1961.

22. Margaret Mead, *New Lives for Old,* 1956, pp. 190–91, 196–201.

23. The passages quoted here are considerably condensed (by omission) from the narrative by Paliau, "a close translation of a dictated autobiographical sketch," originally tape recorded by Theodore Schwartz, who commented ("The Paliau Movement," footnote, p. 239), "This account is remarkable in that it is an almost unbroken narrative by Paliau. I made no suggestions about the content, but simply stressed that I wanted a detailed story of his life on which he could spend as much or as little time as he wished." In these passages (pp. 239–42) I have translated a few terms from Neo-Melanesian.

24. Schwartz, "The Paliau Movement," p. 251.

25. Ibid., p. 251.

26. Mead, *New Lives for Old,* p. 200.

27. Ibid., pp. 209–11.

28. For detailed descriptions of these personalities, see Mead, *New Lives for Old,* and Schwartz, "The Paliau Movement."

29. A. L. Kroeber, *Configurations of Culture Growth,* 1944, p. 839. See also, Introduction, Footnote 3, for my discussion of this point.

NOTES TO CHAPTER 10

1. Julian S. Huxley, "The Humanist Frame," in *The Humanist Frame,* 1962.

2. William L. Laurence, "You May Live Forever," *Look,* 1953.

3. Hudson Hoagland and Ralph W. Burhoe, issue eds., "Evolution and Man's Progress," *Daedalus,* 1961; Sol Tax, ed., *Evolution after Darwin,* 1960.

4. Aldous Huxley, *Brave New World* and *Brave New World Revisited,* 1960.

5. Erich Fromm, *Escape from Freedom,* 1941.

6. Margaret Mead, *Soviet Attitudes toward Authority,* 1951.

7. Albert Camus, *The Stranger,* 1946; Nathan Leites, "Trends in Affectlessness," *American Imago,* 1947.

8. George G. Simpson, *The Major Features of Evolution,* 1953, pp. 206–12.

9. See "Symposium: The Physical Universe" (in which I. I. Rabi was a participant), in *Man's Contracting World in an Expanding Universe,* 1960.

10. Ibid.

11. Jan Ehrenwald, "The Return of Quetzalcoatl and Doctrinal Compliance: A Case Study of Cortes and Montezuma," *American Journal of Psychotherapy,* 1960.

12. Pierre Teilhard de Chardin, *The Phenomenon of Man,* 1959; Teilhard, *The Divine Milieu,* 1960.

13. John Hillaby, "Astronauts Get Blessing of Pope," *The New York Times,* 1956.

14. Bertrand Russell, *Has Man a Future?* 1962.

15. Julian S. Huxley, "Introduction," in *The Phenomenon of Man,* by Pierre Teilhard de Chardin, 1959.

NOTES TO CHAPTER 11

1. International discussions of the problems of technological change and industrialization in the newly emerging countries—especially recent discussions that incorporate the considerable experience of the postwar years (e.g. on a large scale, the United Nations Conference on the Application of Science and Technology for the Benefit of the Less Developed Areas, held in Geneva, February 1963; or, on a small scale, the conference held at the Center for the Study of Democratic Institutions, Santa Barbara, California, March 1962 [Carl F. Stover, ed., "The *Encyclopaedia Britannica* Conference on the Technological Order," *Technology and Culture,* 1962]) —are perhaps the best indicators we have of the lack of detailed, systematic, contextual analyses of this kind. It appears that the very necessity of drawing on existing experience, in the industrialized nations, is forcing us for the first time to come to grips with problems of fundamental cultural differences in the organization of technology.

2. See George C. Allen, *A Short Economic History of Japan, 1871–1937,* 1962; also, Allen, *Japan's Economic Recovery,* 1958, and Jerome B. Cohen, *Japan's Postwar Economy,* 1958.

3. See Eric Ashby, *Scientist in Russia,* 1947; also Ruth C. Christman, ed., *Soviet Science,* 1952; recent summary discussions tend to be specialized within particular fields; see, for example, Raymond S. Sleeper, "The Technological Conflict," *Air University Quarterly Review,* 1962–63.

4. In particular we are lacking studies that take key individuals into account; one example of a recent study of this kind, on a small scale, is Wilton S. Dillon's "Giving, Receiving and Repaying," 1962, which draws on the Marshall Plan experience of a French industrialist.

5. R. G. Collingwood, *The Idea of History,* 1946; also A. L. Kroeber, "History and Evolution," in *The Nature of Culture,* 1952.

6. See, for example, Joseph Needham, *Science and Civilization in China,* 2, 1956, for a discussion of periods of greater and lesser openness to contact with peoples and ideas outside China.

7. Lynn White's *Medieval Technology and Social Change,* 1962, is a particularly good example of the importance of combining research on artifacts and research on documents. But the training of the two sets of scholars who normally deal with these two types of source materials— historians, on the one hand, and archaeologists, ethnologists, and folklorists, on the other—has in general been such as to impede our knowledge of the way that Europe, Africa, and Asia have been interrelated throughout

the periods for which there have been written records. And even within a more restricted area, such as western Europe, specialization—as between, for example, the art historian and the historian working primarily with written and verbal records—has a very limiting effect; in contrast, the historian who can handle a wider range of source materials thereby is capable of both greater penetration and greater clarity. So, Phillipe Ariès' *Centuries of Childhood*, 1962, with its combined use of sources, illuminates the changing self-image in France and elsewhere in Western Europe.

8. Norbert Wiener, *Cybernetics*, 1948; also Wiener, *The Human Use of Human Beings*, 1950.

9. Frank Lorimer and Frederick Osborn, *Dynamics of Population*, 1934; W. S. Thompson and P. K. Whelpton, *Population Trends in the United States*, 1933.

10. The reasons given, however, might vary extremely. Compare (in the 1920s), Raymond Pearl, *The Biology of Population Growth*, 1925, and Charles E. Pell, *The Law of Births and Deaths*, 1921; see also Charles G. Darwin, "Address: The Physical Universe," in *Man's Contracting World in an Expanding Universe*, 1960.

11. Morris L. Ernst and David Loth, *The People Know Best*, 1949, pp. 136–40; also Frederick Mosteller and others, *The Pre-election Polls of 1948*, 1949.

12. John N. Brooks, *The Fate of Edsel and Other Business Adventures*, 1963.

13. Edward S. Meade, *Story of Gold*, 1908; John Maynard Keynes, *Treatise on Money*, 1930.

14. J. F. Brock and M. Autret, *Kwashiorkor in Africa*, 1952; Anne Burgess and R. F. A. Dean, eds., *Malnutrition and Food Habits*, 1962; B. D. Jelliffe, "Culture, Social Change and Infant Feeding: Current Trends in Tropical Regions," *American Journal of Clinical Nutrition*, 1962 (see also for further references).

15. David C. McClelland, *The Achieving Society*, 1961; and McClelland, "Business Drive and National Achievement," *Harvard Business Review*, 1962.

16. Gunnar Myrdal, *The American Dilemma*, 1944; Myrdal, *The International Economy: Problems and Prospects*, 1956; Myrdal, *Rich Lands and Poor*, 1957; Myrdal, *Beyond the Welfare State*, 1960.

17. See, for example, Martha Wolfenstein, *Disaster*, 1957; also G. W. Baker and D. W. Chapman, eds., *Man and Society in Disaster*, 1962.

18. Thus, in the case of William Bateson, the incorporation of the re-discovered work of Mendel into his own work—at a time when he was just approaching the same discoveries in the orderly pursuit of his own scientific interests—resulted in a kind of overemphasis, overpartisanship, and overacceptance of Mendel's work; the effect on his work might have been quite different if the discoveries had grown out of his own work or, on the contrary, if he could have built his thinking on the experimental

work already done by Mendel. See Beatrice Bateson, *William Bateson, F. R. S., Naturalist,* 1928.

19. For a recent discussion of Stolypin, see Edmond Taylor, *The Fall of the Dynasties,* 1963, pp. 161–62, 172–73, 188, and 406 (sources used in Chapter 9).

20. For an outstanding example see George Creel, *Rebel at Large,* 1947; also James R. Mock and Cedric Larson, *Words That Won the War,* 1939, especially Chapter 2, on Creel. As one response to "image making," see Daniel J. Boorstin, *The Image or What Happened to the American Dream,* 1962.

21. Rhoda Metraux, "Immigrants and Natives in the Space Age," unpublished paper presented at the annual meeting of the American Orthopsychiatric Association, 1963.

22. Harrison Brown, James Bonner, and John Weir, *The Next Hundred Years,* 1957.

23. Harrison Brown and E. K. Federov, "Too Many People in the World?" *Saturday Review,* 1962; for a summary of recent shifts and changes in Chinese policy, see Robert Trumbull, "Peking Opens a New Drive to Limit Population," *The New York Times,* June 16, 1963.

24. Clyde V. Kiser, ed., *Research in Family Planning,* 1962.

25. As, for example, in the interventions by the Soviet Union at the United Nations Conference on the Application of Science and Technology for the Benefit of the Less Developed Areas, held in Geneva, February 1963; for China, see Trumbull, "Peking Opens a New Drive to Limit Population."

NOTES TO CHAPTER 12

1. Esmond Wright, "Making History," *The Listener,* 1962.

2. See, for example, David C. McClelland, *The Achieving Society,* 1961 (see also for further references).

3. Norman Z. Alcock, *The Bridge of Reason,* 1961; C. P. Snow, *Science and Government,* 1962.

4. Leslie R. Groves, *Now It Can Be Told,* 1962.

5. We have as yet exceedingly few studies which make a real attempt at analysis; see, for example, Anne Roe, "The Psychology of the Scientist: A Definite Personality Pattern, Encompassing a Wide Range of Traits, Characterizes the Creative Scientist," *Science,* 1961.

6. Peter H. Knapp, ed., *Expression of the Emotions in Man,* 1963; see especially Ray L. Birdwhistell, "The Kinesic Level in the Investigation of the Emotions"; Felix Deutsch, "Sample: An Experiment with Associative Anamnesis"; and Margaret Mead, "Some General Considerations."

7. F. J. Roethlisberger and W. J. Dickson, *Management and the Worker,* 1939; T. N. Whitehead, *The Industrial Worker,* 1938; see also Henry A. Landsberger, *Hawthorne Revisited,* 1958.

8. Eliot D. Chapple, "Personality Differences as Described by Invariant

Properties of Individuals in Interaction," *Proceedings of The National Academy of Sciences,* 1940; Chapple, "The Interaction Chronograph: Its Evaluation and Present Applications," *Personnel,* 1949; Chapple and C. M. Arensberg, "Measuring Human Relations: An Introduction to the Study of the Interaction of Individuals," 1940; Joseph D. Matarazzo, George Saslow, and Ruth G. Matarazzo, "The Interaction Chronograph as an Instrument for Objective Measurement of Interaction Patterns during Interviews," *Journal of Psychology,* 1956; also Saslow and Joseph D. Matarazzo, "A Technique for Studying Changes in Interview Behavior," in *Research in Psychotherapy,* 1959.

9. Margaret Mead, *"Totem and Taboo:* Reconsidered with Respect," *Bulletin of the Menninger Clinic,* 1963.

10. L. K. Frank and others, "Teleological Mechanisms," *Annals of The New York Academy of Sciences,* 1948; Heinz von Foerster, ed., *Cybernetics,* 1950–56.

11. Alex Bavelas, "Communication Patterns in Task-Oriented Groups," in *The Policy Sciences,* 1951.

12. Under the heading of cult formation I would include those disciplines that deal with phenomena with which other disciplines also deal, but which have barricaded themselves in a walled system of jargon intelligible only to members of a given discipline.

13. Sheldon Glueck and Eleanor Glueck, *Family Environment and Delinquency,* 1962.

14. Nathan Leites and Elsa Bernaut, *Ritual of Liquidation,* 1954.

15. Robert J. Lifton, "Chinese Communist Thought Reform," in *Group Processes,* 1957; Lifton, *Thought Reform and the Psychology of Totalism,* 1961.

16. For an example of this kind of distortion see William Sargent, *The Battle for the Mind,* 1957.

17. Ibid.

18. Ernest Dichter, *The Strategy of Desire,* 1960.

19. Bertram Schaffner, ed., *Group Processes, 1,* 1955, see especially pp. 236–41.

20. Alex Bavelas, "Group Size, Interaction, and Structural Environment," in *Group Processes, 4,* 1959.

21. Eliot D. Chapple and Leonard R. Sayles, *The Measure of Management,* 1961.

22. Since this chapter was first written, one further step has been taken in the discussion of the relationship between simulated and natural situations. The group who prepared the report, "Science and Human Survival," *Science,* 1961, were well aware of the advantages of the natural history approach, when time and circumstances permit, but we also recognized that there are situations, such as nuclear warfare, in which no one could risk a real-life experiment, so that—whatever the defects of the method—simulation must be used in research. Consequently, the social

sciences which have based their work on real situations must provide materials which the experimentalists who use a natural science model must be prepared to use.

23. Experiments of this kind were conducted under the auspices of the Committee on Food Habits, National Research Council, during World War II; see Report of the Committee on Food Habits, "Manual for the Study of Food Habits," 1945.

24. For various approaches to the problem see, for example, Gartley E. Jaco, ed., *Patients, Physicians and Illness,* 1958; see also William Caudill, *The Psychiatric Hospital as a Small Society,* 1958.

25. Bavelas, "Group Size, Interaction, and Structural Environment."

26. Chapple, "Personality Differences as Described by Invariant Properties of Individuals in Interaction."

27. B. F. Skinner, *Science and Human Behavior,* 1953; Skinner, "The Science of Learning and the Art of Teaching," in *Programmed Learning,* 1962.

28. Margaret Mead, "National Character," in *Anthropology Today,* 1953.

29. See, for example, Philip M. Hauser, *Population Perspectives,* 1960; also Philip M. Hauser and Otis D. Duncan, eds., *The Study of Population,* 1959.

30. Mary Capes, ed., *Communication or Conflict: Conferences: Their Nature, Dynamics and Planning,* 1960.

31. Gertrude Hendrix, "Learning by Discovery," *Mathematics Teacher,* 1961.

32. Criticism of almost all aspects of formal education has burgeoned in recent years, and criticism of the critics has only added to the confusion; as an example of various points of view about the teaching of the teachers, see Report of the Second Bowling Green Conference, *The Education of Teachers: New Perspectives,* 1958.

33. B. F. Skinner, *Walden Two,* 1948.

34. Margaret Mead, "The Ethics of Insight Giving," in *Male and Female,* 1949, pp. 431–50; also Mead, "The Implications of Insight—II," in *Childhood in Contemporary Cultures,* 1955.

35. Julian S. Huxley, "The Humanist Frame," in *The Humanist Frame,* 1962.

NOTES TO CHAPTER 13

1. Margaret Mead, "Patterns of Worldwide Cultural Change in the 1960's," in *Science, Technology, and Development,* 7 [1963].

2. I have noticed that the cursory reader is decreasingly able to deal with "as-if" phenomena. I wish to emphasize, therefore, that I am not making a statement that the only survivors of a nuclear holocaust would be primitive, preliterate peoples. Obviously there are other possibilities, including such highly specialized portions of high civilizations as miners

and merchant marine personnel. Nor am I making a statement about probabilities in the event of a nuclear catastrophe. Rather, I am using the figure of a certain kind of nuclear holocaust to highlight specific current problems—the problems that the custodians of the peak developments of modern civilization must face in diffusing that civilization to the entire population of this planet. Isolated, preliterate peoples provide the most clear-cut case and, as an anthropologist, I am most competent to discuss this aspect of the larger problem of diffusion. The question of how the rudiments of our high civilizations are to be diffused to the peasant and proletarian members of civilized societies is, of course, of great practical importance, but it does not provide so clear a model situation.

3. Kenneth E. Reed, "Leadership and Consensus in a New Guinea Society," *American Anthropologist*, 1959.

4. Géza Róheim, *The Riddle of the Sphinx*, 1934.

5. Homer Barnett, personal communication.

6. T. Edward Bowdich, *Mission from Cape Coast Castle to Ashantee*, 1819; E. W. Bovill, *The Golden Trade of the Moors*, 1958.

7. Francisco Benet, "Explosive Markets: The Berber Highlands," in *Trade and Market in the Early Empires*, 1957.

8. Margaret Mead, "The Mountain Arapesh, I. An Importing Culture," 1938.

9. Julian H. Steward, *Theory of Culture Change*, 1955; Marshall D. Sahlins and Elman R. Service, eds., *Evolution and Culture*, 1960.

10. Karl A. Wittfogel, *Oriental Despotism*, 1957.

11. Margaret Mead, *Growing Up in New Guinea*, 1930.

12. A. L. Kroeber, "Stimulus Diffusion," in *The Nature of Culture*, 1952.

13. Personal communication, G. Evelyn Hutchinson.

14. Robert B. Lees, "The Basis of Glottochronology," *Language*, 1953; Morris Swadesh, "Lexicostatistic Dating of Prehistoric Ethnic Contacts," *Proceedings American Philosophical Society*, 1952; Swadesh, "Towards Greater Accuracy in Lexicostatistic Dating," *International Journal of American Linguistics*, 1955; see also, D. H. Hymes, "Lexicostatistics So Far," *Current Anthropology*, 1960; Knut Bergsland and Hans Vogt, "On the Validity of Glottochronology," *Current Anthropology*, 1962; and "More on Lexicostatistics," *Current Anthropology*, 1962.

15. Alan Lomax, "Folk Song Style," *American Anthropologist*, 1959; Lomax, "Song Structure and Social Structure," *Ethnology*, 1962.

16. George W. Beadle, "Uniqueness of Man," *Science*, 1957.

NOTES TO CHAPTER 14

1. Margaret Mead, ed., *Cultural Patterns and Technical Change*, 1953, section on "Nutrition."

2. Margaret Mead, "What Makes the Soviet Character?" *Natural History*, 1951.

3. For example, the loudspeaker, the floor microphone for audience use, panels, buzz sessions, etc.

4. Ronald Lippitt, "The Psychodrama in Leadership Training," *Sociometry*, 1943; Alvin F. Zander and Ronald Lippitt, "Reality Practice as Educational Method," *Sociometry*, 1944; U.S. Office of Strategic Services Assessment Staff, *The Assessment of Men*, 1950.

5. Rachel DuBois, *Get Together Americans*, 1943.

6. Henry A. Murray and others, *Explorations in Personality*, 1938.

7. As used in diagnostic work with children at the Menninger Foundation.

8. *Nuffield House, Musgrave Park Hospital, Belfast*, 1962.

9. Margaret Mead, "Cultural Factors in Community-Education Programs," in *Community Education*, 1959.

10. Frank M. Surface and Raymond L. Bland, *American Food in the World War and Reconstruction Period*, 1931.

11. William Allen White, *Objectives of the Committee to Defend America by Aiding the Allies*, 1940. This and other pamphlets provide background on the Committee, but there is no good account of the Committee's organization, etc.

12. It should be noted that Communist party organization consists of a set of specific social inventions, based not on scientific analysis but on the purposeful application of a consistent ideology in a particular society; this can be very widely diffused as long as the cult rules, including the rules of initiation and excommunication, are observed. The institutionalization of ideas in other contexts—as in the great religious orders of the Roman Catholic Church or the kibbutzim of Israel—have met the same conditions, i.e. rigid requirements for admission and provision for the exclusion of the heretic, the backslider, and the dissenter. On only a slightly milder scale, these methods are also used by the social sciences, where the departmental Ph.D., in the United States, serves the purpose of exacting recruitment to a discipline. In contrast, the lives of individual men who have attempted to break away from institutionalized ideas and their institutionalized settings provide us with insight into the difficulties of breaking away from one setting and creating a new one. See, for example, Erik H. Erikson, *Young Man Luther*, 1958; also Erikson, "The First Psychoanalyst," *Yale Review*, 1956.

13. Margaret Mead, "Recommendations for the Organization of Group Research," in *The Study of Culture at a Distance*, Margaret Mead and Rhoda Metraux, eds., 1953.

14. Margaret B. Luszki, *Interdisciplinary Team Research Methods and Problems*, 1958.

15. James R. Angell, "The Yale Institute of Human Relations," *Educational Record*, 1930.

16. R. W. Tyler, "Study Center for Behavioral Scientists," *Science,* 1956; also "A Human Campus for the Study of Man," *Architectural Forum,* 1955, and Marianne Marschak, "One Year among the Behavioral Scientists," *Psychiatry,* 1960.

17. Frank Tannenbaum, "University Seminars: Anniversary Report," *Graduate Faculties Newsletter Columbia University,* 1960.

18. *The Josiah Macy, Jr. Foundation 1930–1955,* 1955.

19. The twenty-fifth anniversary volume incorporates discussions of the areas covered by the conferences and includes a bibliography of studies which grew out of the work supported by the Josiah Macy, Jr. Foundation up to 1955.

20. A final expression of the "Macy Conference" form was the World Health Organization Study Group on the Psychobiological Development of the Child (J. M. Tanner and Bärbel Inhelder, eds., *Discussions on Child Development,* 1957–60), under the chairmanship of Frank Fremont-Smith, who had continued and developed the style of conferences inaugurated by Lawrence K. Frank.

NOTES TO CHAPTER 15

1. Margaret Mead, "Values for Urban Living," *Annals of the American Academy of Political and Social Science,* 1957.

2. Margaret Mead, "The Menninger Foundation: A Center of Innovation," *Menninger Quarterly,* 1961.

3. *Science Center New York,* n.d.

4. C. H. Waddington, *The Nature of Life,* 1962.

5. H. B. D. Kettlewell, "Recognition of Appropriate Backgrounds by the Pale and Black Phases of Lepidoptera," *Nature,* 1955.

6. *Bulletin of the University of Cincinnati Graduate Training Program in Psychiatry 1961.*

7. Philip E. Mosely, "The Peasant Family: The Zadruga, or Communal Joint Family in the Balkans and Its Recent Evolution," in *The Cultural Approach to History,* 1940.

8. Evelyn S. Stewart, "The Merrill–Palmer Institute: Deep Probe in the Science of Living," *Michigan Yearbook 1961.*

9. Margaret Mead and Rhoda Metraux, "Town and Gown: A General Statement," 1962.

10. Allan R. Holmberg, "Participant Observation in the Field," *Human Organization,* 1955; William F. Whyte and Allan R. Holmberg, "Human Relations of U.S. Enterprise in Latin America, IV. From Paternalism to Democracy: The Cornell–Peru Project," *Human Organization,* 1956.

11. Alvin Wolfe, "Minerals and Power: Anthropology in a New Vein," 1961.

12. Margaret Mead, "The Social Sciences in the College of Liberal Arts and Sciences," in *The College of Liberal Arts and Sciences—Its Role in the 1960's* [1961].

13. Joseph Alsop and Stewart Alsop, *We Accuse!* 1954; Charles P. Curtis, *The Oppenheimer Case,* 1955; Lewis M. Strauss, *Men and Decisions,* 1962, pp. 267–95.

14. Margaret Mead, "Brushes of Comets' Hair," *Menninger Quarterly,* 1962.

15. *Science Center New York,* n.d.

NOTES TO CHAPTER 16

1. First published as "Dead Star," *Poetry, 35* (1930), 306–07; republished as "Ripeness Is All," in *An Anthropologist at Work: Writings of Ruth Benedict,* by Margaret Mead, 1959, pp. 85–86.

2. Reo F. Fortune, *Omaha Secret Societies,* 1932, p. 55.

3. This phrase, from Shakespeare's *Henry IV,* Part 1, was used by Marjorie H. Nicolson in her Centennial address at Wilson College, "On Behalf of the Humanities" (*Wilson College Bulletin,* 1940), in discussing the worldwide responsibilities of Americans in working toward the future.

4. Margaret Mead, "Towards More Vivid Utopias," *Science,* 1957.

5. Margaret Mead, "Closing the Gap between the Scientists and the Others," *Daedalus,* 1959.

6. Edith Cobb, "The Ecology of Imagination in Childhood," *Daedalus,* 1959; Erik H. Erikson, *Childhood and Society,* 1950; also, Erikson, "Growth and Crises of the 'Healthy Personality,'" in *Symposium on the Healthy Personality,* 1950; Erikson, "On the Sense of Inner Identity," in *Clinical and Theoretical Papers, Austen Riggs Center,* 1954; Erikson, in *Discussions on Child Development,* 1958, passim; Erikson, "The Nature of Clinical Evidence," *Daedalus,* 1958; Erikson, *Young Man Luther,* 1958; Anna Freud, *The Ego and Mechanisms of Defense,* 1946; Anna Freud and D. T. Burlingham, *War and Children,* 1943; Arnold Gesell and Frances Ilg, *Infant and Child in the Culture of Today,* 1943; Melanie Klein, *The Psycho-Analysis of Children,* 1932; also, Klein, *Contributions to Psycho-Analysis, 1921–1945,* 1948; Margaret Lowenfeld, ed., *On the Psychology of Children,* n.d.; also, Lowenfeld, *Play in Childhood,* 1935; Lowenfeld, "The World Pictures of Children: A Method of Recording and Studying Them," *British Journal of Medical Psychology,* 1939; Lowenfeld, *The Lowenfeld Mosaic Test,* 1954; Lowenfeld, *Poleidoblocs,* n.d.; Lois B. Murphy and collaborators, *The Widening World of Childhood,* 1962; Jean Piaget, *Language and Thought of the Child,* 1926; also, Piaget, *Play, Dreams, and Imitation in Childhood,* 1951; Piaget and Bärbel Inhelder, *The Child's Conception of Space,* 1956; Inhelder and Piaget, *The Growth of Logical Thinking from Childhood to Adolescence,* 1958; Lev Semenovich Vygotsky, *Thought and Language,* 1962.

7. Otto Fenichel, *The Psychoanalytic Theory of Neurosis,* 1945.

8. G. E. Hutchinson, "Homage to Santa Rosalia, or Why Are There So Many Kinds of Animals?" *American Naturalist,* 1959.

9. Lowenfeld, "The World Pictures of Children," 1939.

10. Cobb, "The Ecology of Imagination in Childhood," 1959.

NOTES TO APPENDIX A

1. Reprinted from *Anthropological Linguistics,* 1961.

2. Julian S. Huxley, "Evolution, Cultural and Biological," in *Current Anthropology,* 1956, p. 10.

3. George G. Simpson, "The History of Life," in *The Evolution of Life, 1. Evolution after Darwin,* 1960, p. 153.

4. Marshall D. Sahlins and Elman R. Service, eds., *Evolution and Culture,* 1960.

5. Ibid., pp. 18–19.

6. Simpson, "The History of Life," p. 165.

7. Alfred E. Emerson, "The Evolution of Adaptation in Population Systems," in *The Evolution of Life, 1. Evolution after Darwin,* 1960, p. 314.

8. The term "idioverse" was borrowed from the psychologist, Saul Rosenzweig, who used it differently. The "idioverse–multiverse" model of culture was introduced by Theodore Schwartz in an unpublished paper presented to The New York Academy of Sciences, Anthropology Section, in 1958. Later a slightly more complicated form of this model was presented in Margaret Mead and Theodore Schwartz, "The Cult as a Condensed Social Process," in *Group Processes,* 1960.

9. For a presentation of the Logon unit, see Donald M. MacKay, "The Nomenclature of Information Theory," in *Cybernetics,* 1952.

10. See Allen H. Barton, "The Concept of Property–Space in Social Research," in *The Language of Social Research,* 1955; for an explanation of the cosine model of correlation refer to Solomon Diamond, *Information and Error,* 1959, pp. 206–31.

11. For causal chain concept, though "vector" is not used, refer to H. M. Blalock, Jr., "Correlation Analysis and Causal Inference," *American Anthropologist,* 1960.

12. Sahlins and Service, eds., *Evolution and Culture,* pp. 93–122.

13. Allen H. Barton, "The Concept of Property–Space in Social Research."

14. Margaret Mead, "Cultural Discontinuities and Personality Transformation," *Journal of Social Issues,* 1954; Mead, "Manus Restudied: An Interim Report," *Transactions of The New York Academy of Sciences,* 1954; Mead, "Energy Changes under Conditions of Culture Change," *Sociometry and the Science of Man,* 1955; Mead, *New Lives for Old,* 1956; Mead, "Cultural Determinants of Behavior," in *Behavior and Evolution,* 1958; Mead and Schwartz, "The Cult as a Condensed Social Process," 1960; Theodore Schwartz, "The Paliau Movement in the Admiralty Islands, 1946–1954," 1962.

NOTES TO APPENDIX C

1. Margaret Mead, "Vicissitudes of the Study of the Total Communication Process," in *Approaches to Semiotics*, 1964.

2. D. O. Hebb, *The Organization of Behavior*, 1949.

3. Julian H. Steward, *Theory of Culture Change*, 1955.

4. Melford E. Spiro, "Culture and Personality, the Natural History of a False Dichotomy," *Psychiatry*, 1951.

5. Otto Fenichel, *The Psychoanalytic Theory of Neurosis*, 1945.

6. Loren C. Eiseley, *Darwin's Century*, 1958.

7. David Rapaport, ed., *Organization and Pathology of Thought*, 1951.

8. Gardner Murphy, *Personality: A Biosocial Approach to Origins and Structure*, 1947.

9. John P. Scott, *Animal Behavior*, 1958.

10. Mary Capes, ed., *Communication or Conflict: Conferences: Their Nature, Dynamics and Planning*, 1960.

11. *The Josiah Macy, Jr. Foundation, 1930–1955: A Review of Activities*, 1955.

12. Heinz von Foerster, ed., *Cybernetics*, 1950–56.

13. Lloyd Jeffress, ed., *Cerebral Mechanisms in Behavior*, 1951.

14. See Appendix B for brief descriptions of the Pacific field trips, and for publications on each of them.

15. The idea of living models was developed in a series of conferences planned by the late Robert K. Lamb in 1951, and held under the auspices of the Society for Applied Anthropology in preparation for the Tenth Annual Meeting of the Society in September 1951.

References

ABEL, THEODORE, "The Element of Decision in the Pattern of War," *American Sociological Review,* 6:6 (1941), 853–59.

ABRAMSON, HAROLD A., ED., *Problems of Consciousness,* 5 vols., New York, Josiah Macy, Jr. Foundation, 1951–55.

AITKEN, M. J., *Physics and Archaeology,* New York, Interscience, 1961.

ALCOCK, NORMAN Z., *The Bridge of Reason,* Toronto, Canadian Peace Research Institute, 1961 (pamphlet).

ALLEN, GEORGE C., *Japan's Economic Recovery,* London and New York, Oxford University Press, 1958.

———, *A Short Economic History of Modern Japan 1867–1937,* 2d ed. with Supplement Chapter on Economic Recovery and Expansion 1945–1960, London, Allen and Unwin, 1962.

ALSOP, JOSEPH, AND STEWART ALSOP, *We Accuse! The Story of the Miscarriage of American Justice in the Case of J. Robert Oppenheimer,* New York, Simon and Schuster, 1954.

ALTMANN, MARGARET, "The Role of Juvenile Elk and Moose in the Social Dynamics of Their Species," *Zoologica, 45,* Pt. 1 (1960), 35–39.

AMERICAN ASSOCIATION FOR THE ADVANCEMENT OF SCIENCE, *Directory of Officers and Activities for 1962,* Washington, 1962.

ANGELL, JAMES R., "The Yale Institute of Human Relations," *Educational Record, 11*:1 (1930), 3–11.

ARENSBERG, CONRAD M., "Report on a Developing Community, Poston, Arizona," *Applied Anthropology,* 2:1 (1942), 1–21.

———, "Behavior and Organization: Industrial Studies," in *Social Psychology at the Crossroads,* John H. Rohrer and Muzafer Sherif, eds., New York, Harper, 1951, pp. 324–52.

ARIÈS, PHILLIPE, *Centuries of Childhood: A Social History of Family Life,* trans. Robert Baldick, New York, Knopf, 1962.

ASHBY, ERIC, *Scientist in Russia,* Penguin A186, Harmondsworth, Middlesex, Penguin Books, 1947.

ASIMOV, ISAAC, *The Naked Sun,* Bantam A1731, New York, Bantam Books, 1958.

BAKER, G. W., AND D. W. CHAPMAN, EDS., *Man and Society in Disaster,* New York, Basic Books, 1962.

BALINT, MICHAEL, *Thrills and Regressions,* London, Hogarth, 1959.

BANTON, MICHAEL, ED., *Darwinism and the Study of Society: A Centenary Symposium, Conference held at the University of Edinburgh, 8–10 April, 1959,* London, Tavistock, and Chicago, Quadrangle Books, 1961.

BARLOW, ERASMUS DARWIN, "The Dangers of Health," *The Listener, 41*:1430 (1956), 265–67.

BARNETT, S. A., ED., *A Century of Darwin,* Cambridge, Harvard University Press, 1958.

BARTON, ALLEN H., "The Concept of Property–Space in Social Research," in *The Language of Social Research,* Paul F. Lazarsfeld and Morris Rosenberg, eds., Glencoe, Ill., Free Press, 1955, pp. 40–53.

BATES, MARSTON, AND PHILIP S. HUMPHREY, EDS., *Darwin Reader,* New York, Scribner, 1956.

BATESON, BEATRICE, *William Bateson, F. R. S., Naturalist: His Essays and Addresses,* Cambridge, Cambridge University Press, 1928.

BATESON, GREGORY, *Naven,* Cambridge, Cambridge University Press, 1936; 2d ed. 1958, Stanford, Stanford University Press.

———, "Social Planning and the Concept of Deutero Learning," in *Science, Philosophy, and Religion, Second Symposium,* Lyman Bryson and Louis Finkelstein, eds., New York, Conference on Science, Philosophy, and Religion, 1942, pp. 81–97.

———, "Cultural and Thematic Analysis of Fictional Films," *Transactions of The New York Academy of Sciences,* Ser. II, *5*:4 (1943), 72–78.

———, "The Science of Decency," *Philosophy of Science, 10*:2 (1943), 140–42.

———, "Pidgin English and Cross-Cultural Communications," *Transactions of The New York Academy of Sciences,* Ser. II, *6*:4 (1944), 137–41.

————, "An Analysis of the Nazi Film *Hitlerjunge Quex*," New York, Institute for Intercultural Studies, 1945 (mimeographed); abridged 1953, in *The Study of Culture at a Distance,* Margaret Mead and Rhoda Metraux, eds., pp. 302–14.

————, "The Pattern of an Armaments Race, I. An Anthropological Approach, II. An Analysis of Nationalism," *Bulletin of the Atomic Scientists,* 2:5–8 (1946), 10–11, 26–28.

————, "Letters: Anthropological Theories," *Science, 129*: 3345 (1959), 294–98.

————, "The Biosocial Integration of Behavior in the Schizophrenic Family," in *Exploring the Base for Family Therapy,* N. Ackerman, F. L. Beatman, and S. N. Sherman, eds., New York, Family Service Association, 1961, pp. 116–22.

————, AND MARGARET MEAD, *Balinese Character: A Photographic Analysis,* Special Publications of The New York Academy of Sciences, II, 1942; reissued 1962.

————, *Childhood Rivalry in Bali and New Guinea,* Character Formation in Different Cultures Series, New York University Film Library, 16 mm., 20 min., sound, 1952.

————, *Karba's First Years,* Character Formation in Different Cultures Series, New York University Film Library, 16 mm., 20 min., sound, 1952.

BAVELAS, ALEX, "Communication Patterns in Task-Oriented Groups," in *The Policy Sciences,* Daniel Lerner and Harold D. Lasswell, eds., Stanford, Stanford University Press, 1951, pp. 193–202.

————, "Group Size, Interaction, and Structural Environment," in *Group Processes,* Transactions of the Fourth Conference 1957, ed. Bertram Schaffner, 1959, pp. 133–79.

BAWDEN, FREDERICK C., AND OTHERS, EDS., *Symposium on Evolution: Held at Duquesne University, April 4, 1959, in Commemoration of the Centenary of Charles Darwin's The Origin of Species,* Pittsburgh, Duquesne University, 1959.

BEADLE, GEORGE W., "Uniqueness of Man," *Science, 125*:3236 (1957), 9–11.

BELO, JANE, "Balinese Paintings," n.d. (manuscript).

BENDER, LAURETTA, AND J. ALLISON MONTAGUE, "Psychotherapy through Art in a Negro Child," *College Art Journal*, 7:1 (1947), 12–16.

BENEDICT, RUTH, "The Vision in Plains Culture," *American Anthropologist*, 24:1 (1922), 1–23; reprinted 1959, in Margaret Mead, *An Anthropologist at Work*, pp. 18–35.

———, "Psychological Types in the Cultures of the Southwest," in *Proceedings of the Twenty-third International Congress of Americanists, New York, September 1928*, New York, 1930, pp. 572–81.

———, "Dead Star," *Poetry*, 35:6 (1930), 306–07; reprinted 1959, as "Ripeness Is All," in Margaret Mead, *An Anthropologist at Work*, pp. 85–86.

———, *Tales of the Cochiti Indians*, Smithsonian Institution, Bureau of American Ethnology, Bulletin 98, Washington, 1931.

———, *Patterns of Culture*, Boston, Houghton Mifflin, 1934; reprinted 1961, SE8, Boston, Houghton Mifflin.

———, *Zuni Mythology*, 2 vols., Columbia University Contributions to Anthropology, 21, New York, Columbia University Press, 1935.

———, "A Note on Chinese Culture and Personality," Washington, 1943 (mimeographed).

———, *The Chrysanthemum and the Sword*, Boston, Houghton Mifflin, 1946.

———, "Rumanian Culture and Behavior," New York, Institute for Intercultural Studies, 1946 (mimeographed).

———, *Thai Culture and Behavior*, an unpublished War Time Study Dated September 1943, Data Paper No. 4, Southeast Asia Program, Dept. of Far Eastern Studies, Cornell University, 1952.

———, *Race: Science and Politics*, Compass C42, New York, Viking, 1959.

BENET, FRANCISCO, "Explosive Markets: The Berber Highlands," in *Trade and Market in the Early Empires*, Karl Polanyi, Conrad M. Arensberg, and Harry W. Pearson, eds., Glencoe, Ill., Free Press, 1957, pp. 188–217.

BERGSLAND, KNUT, AND HANS VOGT, "On the Validity of

Glottochronology," *Current Anthropology, 3*:2 (1962), 115–53.

BERNDT, R. M., "A Cargo Movement in the East Central Highlands of New Guinea," *Oceania, 23*:1, 2, 3 (1952–53), 40–65, 137–58, 202–34.

——, "Reaction to Contact in the Eastern Highlands of New Guinea," *Oceania, 24*:3, 4 (1954), 190–228, 255–75.

BETTELHEIM, BRUNO, "Feral Children and Autistic Children," *American Journal of Sociology, 64*:5 (1959), 455–67.

——, "Rejoinder" [to Margaret Mead], *American Journal of Sociology, 65*:1 (1959), 76.

BIDNEY, DAVID, *Theoretical Anthropology*, New York, Columbia University Press, 1953.

Biological Effects of Atomic Radiation, The: Summary Reports from a Study by The National Academy of Sciences, Washington, National Academy of Sciences–National Research Council, 1956.

BIRDWHISTELL, RAY L., "Family Structure and Social Mobility," *Transactions of The New York Academy of Sciences*, Ser. II, *21*:2 (1958), 136–45.

——, "Contribution of Linguistic–Kinesic Studies to the Understanding of Schizophrenia," in *Schizophrenia: An Integrated Approach*, ed. Alfred Auerback, New York, Ronald, 1959, pp. 99–123.

——, "An Approach to Communication," *Family Process, 1*:2 (1962), 194–201.

——, "The Kinesic Level in the Investigation of the Emotions," in *Expression of the Emotions in Man*, ed. Peter H. Knapp, 1963, pp. 123–39.

BLALOCK, H. M., JR., "Correlational Analysis and Causal Inference," *American Anthropologist, 62*:4 (1960), 624–31.

BLAUVELT, HELEN, "Dynamics of the Mother–Newborn Relationship in Goats," in *Group Processes*, Transactions of the First Conference 1954, ed. Bertram Schaffner, 1955, pp. 221–58.

——, "Neonate–Mother Relationship in Goat and Man," in *Group Processes*, Transactions of the Second Conference, 1955, ed. Bertram Schaffner, 1956, pp. 94–140.

BOAS, FRANZ, "The Central Eskimo," *Sixth Annual Report of the Bureau of American Ethnology, 1884–1885,* Washington, 1888, 399–669.

———, "The Eskimo of Baffin Land and Hudson Bay," *Bulletin of The American Museum of Natural History, 15,* Pt. 1, New York, 1901, 1–370.

———, "Decorative Designs of Alaskan Needle-Cases: A Study in the History of Conventional Designs," *Proceedings of the U. S. National Museum, 34,* Washington, 1908, 321–44.

———, *Kwakiutl Tales,* Columbia University Contributions to Anthropology, 2, New York, Columbia University Press, 1910.

———, *The Mind of Primitive Man,* New York, Macmillan, 1911; rev. ed. 1938, New York, Macmillan.

———, *Primitive Art,* Instituttet for Sammenlignende Kulturforskning Serie B, Skrifter VIII, Oslo, Aschehong, 1927; reprinted 1955, T25, New York, Dover.

———, *Anthropology and Modern Life,* New York, Norton, 1928.

———, *Bella Bella Texts,* Columbia University Contributions to Anthropology, 5, New York, Columbia University Press, 1928.

BOHANNAN, PAUL, "Letters: Anthropological Theories," *Science, 129*:3345 (1959), 292–94.

BOOMKAMP, J. H. HOOYKASS–VAN LEEUWEN, *Ritual Purification of a Balinese Temple,* Amsterdam, North-Holland, 1960.

BOORSTIN, DANIEL J., *The Image or What Happened to the American Dream,* New York, Atheneum, 1962.

BOULDING, KENNETH E., "Where Are We Going if Anywhere? A Look at Past-Civilization," in *Major Issues in Modern Society,* special issue, ed. Robert J. Smith, *Human Organization, 21*:2 (1962), 162–67.

BOVILL, E. W., *The Golden Trade of the Moors,* London, Oxford University Press, 1958.

BOWDICH, T. EDWARD, *Mission from Cape Coast Castle to Ashantee,* London, Murray, 1819.

BOWEN, R. N. C., *The Exploration of Time,* London, Newnes, 1958.

BRADFORD, JOHN, *Ancient Landscapes: Studies in Field Archaeology,* London, Bell, 1957.

BRICKNER, RICHARD M., "Telencephalization of Survival Characteristics," in *The Frontal Lobes,* Proceedings of the Association for Research in Nervous and Mental Disease, 27 Baltimore, Williams and Wilkins, 1948, pp. 658–88.

BROCK, J. F., AND M. AUTRET, *Kwashiorkor in Africa,* Food and Agriculture Organization of the United Nations, FAO Nutritional Studies, 8, Rome, 1952, pp. 1–78.

BROOKS, JOHN N., *The Fate of the Edsel and Other Business Adventures,* New York, Harper and Rowe, 1963.

BROWN, A. R., 1913, *see* Radcliffe-Brown, A. R.

BROWN, HARRISON, *The Challenge of Man's Future,* New York, Viking, 1954.

———, JAMES BONNER, AND JOHN WEIR, *The Next Hundred Years,* New York, Viking, 1957.

———, AND E. K. FEDEROV, "Too Many People in the World," *Saturday Review, 45*:7 (1962), 16–20, 86.

BROWN, MURIEL W., *With Focus on Family Living,* Vocational Bulletin 249, Washington, U.S. Government Printing Office, Division of Public Documents, 1953.

BUCK, PETER H., *see* HIROA, TE RANGI.

BUETTNER–JANUSCH, JOHN, "Boas and Mason: Particularism versus Generalization," *American Anthropologist, 59*:2 (1957), 318–24.

Bulletin of the University of Cincinnati Graduate Training Program in Psychiatry 1961.

BUNZEL, RUTH, *Explorations in Chinese Culture,* New York, Columbia University Research in Contemporary Cultures, 1950 (dittoed).

BURGESS, ANNE, AND R. F. A. DEAN, EDS., *Malnutrition and Food Habits: Report of an International and Interprofessional Conference,* London, Tavistock, 1962.

CAMUS, ALBERT, *The Stranger,* trans. Stuart Gilbert, New York, Knopf, 1946.

CAPES, MARY, ED., *Communication or Conflict: Conferences: Their Nature, Dynamics and Planning*, London, Tavistock, 1960.

CARPENTER, C. R., "A Field Study of the Behavior and Social Relations of the Howling Monkeys *(Alouatta palliata)*," *Comparative Psychology Monographs, 10*:2, Ser. 48 (1934), 1–168.

CARPENTER, EDMUND, "Eskimo Space Concepts," *Explorations, 5* (1955), 131–45.

CARROLUP SETTLEMENT WESTERN AUSTRALIA, "Aboriginal Children's Art," *Times Educational Supplement* 1857, Dec. 1, 1950, 917–29.

CARSON, RACHEL, *The Sea around Us*, New York, Oxford University Press, 1950.

CARSTAIRS, G. MORRIS, *The Twice-Born*, London, Hogarth, 1957.

CAUDILL, WILLIAM, *The Psychiatric Hospital as a Small Society*, Cambridge, Harvard University Press, 1958.

"Centennial, April 1959," *Proceedings of the American Philosophical Society, 103*:5 (1959), 609–44, 716–25.

CHANDLER, TERTIUS, "Duplicate Inventions," *American Anthropologist, 62*:3 (1960), 495–98.

CHAPPLE, ELIOT D., "Personality Differences as Described by Invariant Properties of Individuals in Interaction," *Proceedings of The National Academy of Sciences, 26*:1 (1940), 10–16.

———, "The Interaction Chronograph: Its Evaluation and Present Applications," *Personnel, 25*:4 (1949), 295–307.

———, AND C. M. ARENSBERG, "Measuring Human Reactions: An Introduction to the Study of the Interaction of Individuals," *Genetic Psychology Monographs, 22*:1 (1940), 3–147.

———, AND LEONARD R. SAYLES, *The Measure of Management*, New York, Macmillan, 1961.

CHILDE, V. GORDON, *Man Makes Himself*, London, Watts, 1936; reprinted 1951, Mentor M64, New York, New American Library.

CHINNERY, E. W. P., AND A. C. HADDON, "Five New Religious Cults in British New Guinea," *Hibbert Journal, 15*:3 (1917), 448–63.

CHRISTMAN, RUTH C., ED., *Soviet Science,* Washington, American Association for the Advancement of Science, 1952.

CLARK, GRAHAME, *World Prehistory,* Cambridge, Cambridge University Press, 1962.

CLARKE, ARTHUR C., *Childhood's End,* Ballantine K398, New York, Ballantine, 1953.

COBB, EDITH, "The Ecology of Imagination in Childhood," *Daedalus* (Summer 1959), 537–48.

CODRINGTON, R. H., *The Melanesians: Studies in Their Anthropology and Folklore,* Oxford, Clarendon Press, 1891.

COHEN, JEROME B., *Japan's Postwar Economy,* Bloomington, Indiana University Press, 1958.

COLLINGWOOD, R. G., *The Idea of History,* Oxford, Clarendon Press, 1946.

COLLINS, HENRY B., "The Origin and Antiquity of the Eskimo," *Smithsonian Institution Annual Report for 1950,* Washington, 1951, 423–67.

———, "Radiocarbon Dating in the Arctic," *American Antiquity, 18*:3 (1953), 197–203.

———, "Archeological Work in Arctic Canada," *Smithsonian Institution Annual Report for 1956,* Washington, 1957, 507–28.

COMFORT, A., "Sexual Selection in Man—A Comment," *American Naturalist, 93*:873 (1959), 389–91.

COUSINS, NORMAN, *Modern Man Is Obsolete,* New York, Viking Press, 1945.

CREEL, GEORGE, *Rebel at Large,* New York, Putnam, 1947.

CURTIS, CHARLES P., *The Oppenheimer Case,* New York, Simon and Schuster, 1955.

DARLING, F. FRAZER, *A Herd of Red Deer,* London, Oxford University Press, 1937.

DARWIN, CHARLES, *The Origin of Species,* reprint of first edition 1859, New York, Philosophical Library, 1951.

———, *Expression of the Emotions in Man and Animals,* New York, Philosophical Library, 1955.

DARWIN, CHARLES GALTON, "Address: The Physical Universe," in *Man's Contracting World in an Expanding Universe,* ed. Ben H. Bagdikian, Providence, R. I., Brown University, 1960, pp. 21–41.

"DARWIN–WALLACE CENTENARY," *Journal of the Linnean Society of London, Zoology, 44*:295 (1958), 1–152.

DAVIES, CHARLES, *The Metric System,* New York and Chicago, A. S. Barnes, 1871.

DEUTSCH, FELIX, "Sample: An Experiment with Associative Anamnesis," in *Expression of the Emotions in Man,* ed. Peter H. Knapp, 1963, pp. 69–76.

DEWEY, JOHN, *The School and Society,* Chicago, University of Chicago Press, 1900; reprinted 1956, Phoenix P3, *The Child and the Curriculum and The School and Society,* Chicago, University of Chicago Press.

DIAMOND, SOLOMON, *Information and Error,* New York, Basic Books, 1959.

DICHTER, ERNEST, *The Strategy of Desire,* Garden City, N.Y., Doubleday, 1960.

DILLON, WILTON S., "Giving, Receiving and Repaying: An Examination of the Ideas of Marcel Mauss in the Context of International Technical Assistance," unpublished Ph.D. Thesis, Teachers College, Columbia University, 1961.

DOBZHANSKY, THEODOSIUS, "Eugenics in New Guinea," *Science, 132*:3419 (1960), 77.

———, AND JOSEPH B. BIRDSELL, "On Methods of Evolutionary Biology and Anthropology," *American Scientist, 45*:5 (1957), 381–400.

DOLLARD, JOHN, AND OTHERS, *Frustration and Aggression,* New Haven, Yale University Press, 1939.

———, AND N. E. MILLER, *Personality and Psychotherapy,* New York, McGraw-Hill, 1950.

DORSEY, GEORGE, *Why We Behave Like Human Beings,* New York, Harper, 1926.

DORSEY, J. O., "Omaha Sociology," *Third Annual Report of the Bureau of American Ethnology, 1881–1882,* Washington, 1884, 205–370.

DOSTOYEVSKY, FYODOR, *The Brothers Karamazov,* trans. Constance Garnett, New York, Random House, 1950.

DUBOIS, RACHEL, *Get Together Americans,* New York, Harper, 1943.

DUGGAR, BENJAMIN M., ED., *Biological Effects of Radiation,* 2 vols., New York, McGraw-Hill, 1936.

EATON, JOSEPH W., AND ALBERT J. MAYER, *Man's Capacity to Reproduce: The Demography of a Unique Population,* Glencoe, Ill., Free Press, 1954.

———, AND ROBERT J. WEIL, *Culture and Mental Disorders: A Comparative Study of the Hutterites and Other Populations,* Glencoe, Ill., Free Press, 1955.

EHRENWALD, JAN, "The Return of Quetzalcoatl and Doctrinal Compliance: A Case Study of Cortes and Montezuma," *American Journal of Psychotherapy, 14*:2 (1960), 308–21.

EISELEY, LOREN C., *The Immense Journey,* Modern Library P47, New York, Random House, 1957.

———, *Darwin's Century: Evolution and the Men Who Discovered It,* Garden City, N. Y., Doubleday Anchor Books, 1958.

ELKIN, A. P., *The Australian Aborigines,* 3d ed., Sydney, Angus and Robertson, 1954.

EMBREE, EDWIN R., AND JULIA WAXMAN, *Investment in People: The Story of the Julius Rosenwald Fund,* New York, Harper, 1949.

EMERSON, ALFRED E., "The Evolution of Adaptation in Population Systems," in *Evolution after Darwin, 1, The Evolution of Life,* ed. Sol Tax, 1960, pp. 307–48.

ENGELS, FREDERICK, *The Origin of the Family, Private Property and the State,* trans. Ernest Untermann, Chicago, Kerr, 1902.

ERIKSON, ERIK H., "Hitler's Imagery and German Youth," *Psychiatry, 5*:4 (1942), 475–93.

———, *Childhood and Society,* New York, Norton, 1950.

———, "Growth and Crises of the 'Healthy Personality,'" in *Symposium on the Healthy Personality,* Second Supplement to the Transactions of the Fourth Conference on Infancy and Childhood, ed. Milton J. E. Senn, New York, Josiah Macy, Jr. Foundation, 1950, pp. 91–146.

ERIKSON, ERIK H., "On the Sense of Inner Identity," in *Clinical and Theoretical Papers, Austen Riggs Center, 1*, ed. Robert Knight, New York, International Universities Press, 1954, pp. 351–64.

———, "The First Psychoanalyst," *Yale Review, 46*:1 (1956), 40–62.

———, in *Discussions on Child Development, Third Meeting, 1955*, J. M. Tanner and Bärbel Inhelder, eds., 1958.

———, "The Nature of Clinical Evidence," *Daedalus* (Fall 1958), 65–84.

———, *Young Man Luther*, New York, Norton, 1958.

ERNST, MORRIS L., AND DAVID LOTH, *The People Know Best: The Ballots vs. the Polls*, Washington, Public Affairs Press, 1949.

ESSAI, BRIAN, *Papua and New Guinea*, Melbourne, Oxford University Press, 1961.

EWERS, JOHN C., *The Horse in Blackfoot Indian Culture*, Smithsonian Institution, Bureau of American Ethnology, Bulletin 159, Washington, 1955.

FENICHEL, OTTO, *The Psychoanalytic Theory of Neurosis*, New York, Norton, 1945.

FINK, RUTH, "The Changing Status and Cultural Identity of Western Australian Aborigines," unpublished Ph.D. Thesis, Columbia University, 1960.

FISHER, JAMES, AND R. A. HINDE, "The Opening of Milk Bottles by Birds," *British Birds, 42*:11 (1949), 347–57.

FLETCHER, ALICE C., AND FRANCIS LA FLESCHE, "The Omaha Tribe," *Twenty-seventh Annual Report of the Bureau of American Ethnology, 1905–1906*, Washington, 1911, 15–672.

FOERSTAL, LENORA, *see* SCHWARTZ, LENORA.

FOERSTER, HEINZ VON, ED., *Cybernetics*, 5 vols., New York, Josiah Macy, Jr. Foundation, 1950–56.

FORTUNE, REO F., *Arapesh*, Publications of the American Ethnological Society, 19, New York, Augustin, 1932.

———, *Omaha Secret Societies*, Columbia University Contributions to Anthropology, 14, New York, Columbia University Press, 1932.

———, *Sorcerers of Dobu*, New York, Dutton, 1932.

————, *Manus Religion,* Philadelphia, American Philosophical Society, 1935.

FRANK, LAWRENCE K., "Cultural Coercion and Individual Distortion," *Psychiatry,* 2:1 (1939), 11–27.

————, *Society as the Patient,* New Brunswick, N. J., Rutgers University Press, 1948.

————, AND OTHERS, "Teleological Mechanisms," *Annals of The New York Academy of Sciences, 50,* Art. 4 (1948), 187–278.

FREEMAN, WILLIAM F., "Decimal Inch Urged as Basic Measure," *The New York Times,* June 9, 1963.

FREUCHEN, PETER, *Eskimo,* trans. A. P. Maerker-Branden and E. Branden, New York, Grosset and Dunlap, 1931.

————, AND FINN SALOMONSEN, *The Arctic Year,* New York, Putnam, 1958.

FREUD, ANNA, *The Ego and the Mechanisms of Defense,* trans. Cecil Baines, New York, International Universities Press, 1946.

————, AND D. T. BURLINGHAM, *War and Children,* New York, Medical War Books, 1943.

FREUD, S., *Totem and Taboo,* trans. A. A. Brill, New York, Moffat, Yard, 1918.

————, *Civilization and Its Discontents,* trans. Joan Riviere, London, Hogarth, 1930; reissued 1958, Anchor A130, Garden City, N. Y., Doubleday.

FRIED, MORTON H., *Fabric of Chinese Society,* New York, Praeger, 1953.

FRISCH, JOHN E., "Research on Primate Behavior in Japan," *American Anthropologist, 61:*4 (1959), 584–96.

FROMM, ERICH, *Escape from Freedom,* New York, Farrar and Rinehart, 1941.

Funk and Wagnalls Standard Dictionary of Folklore, Mythology and Legend, 2 vols., Maria Leach and Jerome Fried, eds., New York, Funk and Wagnalls, 1949–50.

GAJDUSEK, D. CARLETON, "Kuru: An Appraisal of Five Years of Investigation," *Eugenics Quarterly, 9:*1 (1962), 69–74 (see also bibliography).

GEIRINGER, KARL, *The Bach Family*, New York, Oxford University Press, 1954.

"Germany after the War, Round Table—1945," *American Journal of Orthopsychiatry, 15*:3 (1945), 381–441.

GESELL, ARNOLD, *Wolf Child and Human Child*, New York, Harper, 1941.

———, AND FRANCES ILG, *Infant and Child in the Culture of Today*, New York, Harper, 1943.

GLUECK, SHELDON, AND ELEANOR GLUECK, *Family Environment and Delinquency*, Boston, Houghton Mifflin, 1962.

GOLDSCHMIDT, WALTER, ED., *The Anthropology of Franz Boas*, Memoirs of the American Anthropological Association, 89, 1959.

GORER, GEOFFREY, *Himalayan Village*, London, Michael Joseph, 1938.

———, *Burmese Personality*, New York, Institute for Intercultural Studies, 1943 (mimeographed).

———, "Themes in Japanese Culture," *Transactions of The New York Academy of Sciences*, Ser. II, 5:5 (1943), 106–24.

———, *The American People*, New York, Norton, 1948.

———, AND JOHN RICKMAN, *The People of Great Russia*, New York, Chanticleer Press, 1950; reprinted 1962, N112, New York, Norton.

GRANT, MADISON, *The Passing of the Great Race: Or the Racial Basis of European History*, New York, Scribner, 1918; 4th rev. ed. 1936, New York, Scribner.

GRAY, CHARLES E., "An Analysis of Graeco–Roman Development: The Epicyclical Evolution of Graeco–Roman Civilization," *American Anthropologist, 60*:1 (1958), 13–31.

GREENE, JOHN C., *The Death of Adam: Evolution and Its Impact on Western Thought*, Ames, Iowa State University Press, 1959.

GRINNELL, G. B., *The Cheyenne Indians*, 2 vols., New Haven, Yale University Press, 1923.

GROVES, LESLIE R., *Now It Can Be Told: The Story of the Manhattan Project*, New York, Harper, 1962.

GUIART, JEAN, "Forerunners of Melanesian Nationalism," *Oceania, 22*:2 (1951), 81–90.

————, "The Co-operative Called 'The Malekula Native Company,' a Borderline Type of Cargo Cult," *South Pacific, 6*:6 (1952), 429–32.

————, "John Frum Movement in Tanna," *Oceania, 22*:3 (1952), 165–75.

GUNTHER, MAVIS, "Instinct and the Nursing Couple," *Lancet, 268*:6864 (1955), 575–78.

HADDON, A. C., *Evolution in Art,* London, Scott, 1895.

HAECKEL, ERNST, *The Evolution of Man: A Popular Scientific Study,* trans. Joseph McCabe from the 5th ed., New York, Putnam, 1910.

HALL, ROBERT A., JR., *Hands Off Pidgin English,* Sydney, Pacific Publications, 1955.

————, "Colonial Policy and Neo-Melanesian," *Anthropological Linguistics, 1*:3 (1959), 22–27.

HAMILTON, AUGUSTUS, *The Art Workmanship of the Maori Race in New Zealand,* Dunedin, New Zealand Institute, 1896.

HANDY, E. S. C., AND W. C. HANDY, "Samoan House Building, Cooking and Tatooing," *Bernice P. Bishop Museum Bulletin, 15,* Honolulu, 1924, 1–26.

HANSEN, DAVID E., "Letters: Anthropological Theories," *Science, 129*:3345 (1959), 298.

HARING, DOUGLAS G., ED., *Japan's Prospect,* Cambridge, Harvard University Press, 1946.

HARRIS, ZELLIG S., *Methods in Structural Linguistics,* Chicago, University of Chicago Press, 1951.

HAUSER, PHILIP M., *Population Perspectives,* New Brunswick, N. J., Rutgers University Press, 1960.

————, AND OTIS D. DUNCAN, EDS., *The Study of Population,* Chicago, University of Chicago Press, 1959.

HAYES, CATHY, *The Ape in Our House,* New York, Harper, 1951.

HEBB, D. O., *The Organization of Behavior,* New York, Wiley, 1949.

HENDRIX, GERTRUDE, "Learning by Discovery," *Mathematics Teacher, 54*:5 (1961), 290–99.

HERSEY, JOHN, *Hiroshima,* New York, Knopf, 1946.

HERSEY, JOHN, *The Child Buyer,* New York, Knopf, 1960.

HERSKOVITS, MELVILLE J., *Life in a Haitian Valley,* New York, Knopf, 1937.

———, *The Myth of the Negro Past,* New York, Harper, 1941.

HILGARD, E. R., *Theories of Learning,* New York, Appleton–Century, 1956.

HILLABY, JOHN, "Astronauts Get Blessing of Pope," *The New York Times,* Sept. 21, 1956, 27.

HINDE, R. A., AND JAMES FISHER, "Further Observations on the Opening of Milk Bottles by Birds," *British Birds, 44*:12 (1951), 393–96.

HINDS, WILLIAM A., *American Communities,* Corinth AE10, New York, Corinth, 1961.

HIROA, TE RANGI [PETER H. BUCK], "Samoan Material Culture," *Bernice P. Bishop Museum Bulletin, 75,* Honolulu, 1930, 1–724.

HOAGLAND, HUDSON, AND RALPH W. BURHOE, ISSUE EDS., "Evolution and Man's Progress," *Daedalus* (Summer 1961), 411–610.

HOGBIN, H. IAN, *Transformation Scene,* London, Routledge and Kegan Paul, 1951.

———, *Social Change,* London, Watts, 1958.

HOLM, G., "Ethnological Sketch of the Angmagsalik Eskimo," in *The Ammassalik Eskimo: Contributions to the Ethnology of the East Greenland Natives,* Part 1, ed. William Thalbitzer, Copenhagen, Bianco Luno, 1914, pp. 1–147.

HOLMBERG, ALLAN R., *Nomads of the Long Bow,* Publications of the Institute of Social Anthropology, Smithsonian Institution, Monograph 10, Washington, 1951.

———, "Participant Observation in the Field," *Human Organization, 14*:1 (1955), 23–25.

HOOTON, EARNEST A., *Up from the Ape,* New York, Macmillan, 1947.

HOWELL, F. CLARK, "European and Northwest African Middle Pleistocene Hominids," *Current Anthropology, 1*:3 (1960), 195–232.

HOYLE, FRED, *The Black Cloud,* Signet D2202, New York, New American Library, 1959.

"Human Campus for the Study of Man, A," *Architectural Forum, 102*:1 (1955), 130–34.

HUTCHINSON, G. E., "The Importance of Ornithology," in *The Itinerant Ivory Tower*, New Haven, Yale University Press, 1953, pp. 54–64.

———, "Homage to Santa Rosalia, or Why Are There so Many Kinds of Animals?" *American Naturalist, 93*:870 (1959), 143–59; reprinted 1962, in *The Enchanted Voyage*, New Haven, Yale University Press, pp. 110–29.

———, "A Speculative Consideration of Certain Possible Forms of Sexual Selection in Man," *American Naturalist, 93*:869 (1959), 81–91.

HUXLEY, ALDOUS L., *Brave New World*, and *Brave New World Revisited*, New York, Harper Modern Classics, 1960.

HUXLEY, JULIAN S., "Evolution, Cultural and Biological," in *Current Anthropology*, ed. William L. Thomas, Jr., 1956, pp. 3–25.

———, "Introduction," in *The Phenomenon of Man*, by Pierre Teilhard de Chardin, 1959, pp. 11–28.

———, "The Humanist Frame," pp. 13–48, in *The Humanist Frame*, ed. Julian S. Huxley, New York, Harper, 1962.

HUXLEY, THOMAS H., AND JULIAN S. HUXLEY, *Touchstone for Ethics*, New York, Harper, 1947.

HYMES, D. H., "Lexicostatistics So Far," *Current Anthropology, 1*:1 (1960), 3–44.

IMANISHI, KINJI, "Social Organization of Subhuman Primates in Their Natural Habitat," *Current Anthropology, 1*:5–6 (1960), 393–407.

INHELDER, BÄRBEL, AND JEAN PIAGET, *The Growth of Logical Thinking from Childhood to Adolescence*, trans. Anne Parsons and Stanley Milgram, New York, Basic Books, 1958.

INTERNATIONAL PREPARATORY COMMISSION, *Mental Health and World Citizenship: A Statement Prepared for the International Congress on Mental Health, London, 1948*, London, World Federation for Mental Health, 1948 (see also *Mental Health*, 1961).

ITANI, JUNICHIRO, "On the Acquisition and Propagation of a

New Food Habit in the Natural Group of the Japanese Monkey at Takasaki-Yama," *Primates, 1*:2 (1958), 84–98.

JACO, GARTLEY E., ED., *Patients, Physicians and Illness,* Glencoe, Ill., Free Press, 1958.

JEFFRESS, LLOYD, ED., *Cerebral Mechanisms in Behavior: The Hixon Symposium, 1948,* New York, Wiley, 1951.

JELLIFFE, D. B., "Culture, Social Change and Infant Feeding: Current Trends in Tropical Regions," *American Journal of Clinical Nutrition, 10*:1 (1962), 19–45.

Josiah Macy, Jr. Foundation, The, A Review of Activities, 1930–1955, New York, Josiah Macy, Jr. Foundation, 1955.

JOUANNEAU, L. C., ED., *Discussions du Code civil dans le conseil d'Etat,* 3 vols., Paris, 1805–08.

KARDINER, ABRAM, *The Individual and His Society,* New York, Columbia University Press, 1939.

KEESING, FELIX M., *Culture Change,* Stanford, Stanford University Press, 1953.

———, AND MARIE M. KEESING, *Elite Communities in Samoa: A Study in Leadership,* Stanford Anthropological Series, 3, Stanford University Press, 1956.

KELLOGG, WINTHROP N., *Porpoises and Sonar,* Chicago, University of Chicago Press, 1961.

———, AND L. A. KELLOGG, *The Ape and the Child,* New York, McGraw-Hill, 1933.

KETTLEWELL, H. B. D., "Recognition of Appropriate Backgrounds by the Pale and Black Phases of Lepidoptera," *Nature, 175*: 4465 (1955), 943–44.

KEYNES, JOHN M., *Treatise on Money,* New York, Harcourt, Brace, 1930.

KIDD, DUDLEY, *Savage Childhood: A Study of Kafir Children,* London, Black, 1906.

KIERAN, JOHN, *A Natural History of New York City,* Boston, Houghton Mifflin, 1959.

KIMBALL, SOLON T., "Communication Modalities as a Function of Social Relationships," *Transactions of The New York Academy of Sciences,* Ser. II, 25:4 (1963), 459–68.

KISER, CLYDE V., ED., *Research in Family Planning,* Princeton, Princeton University Press, 1962.

KLEIN, MELANIE, *The Psycho-Analysis of Children,* London, Hogarth, 1932.

———, *Contributions to Psycho-Analysis, 1921–1945,* London, Hogarth, 1948.

KLOPFER, PETER H., "An Experiment on Empathic Learning in Ducks," *American Naturalist, 91*:856 (1957), 61–63.

KNAPP, PETER H., ED., *Expression of the Emotions in Man,* New York, International Universities Press, 1963.

KOESTLER, ARTHUR, *Reflections on Hanging,* New York, Macmillan, 1957.

KROEBER, A. L., "The Superorganic," *American Anthropologist, 19*:2 (1917), 162–213; reprinted 1952, in *The Nature of Culture,* Chicago, University of Chicago Press, 1952, pp. 22–52.

———, *Configurations of Culture Growth,* Berkeley and Los Angeles, University of California Press, 1944.

———, *The Nature of Culture,* Chicago, University of Chicago Press, 1952.

———, ED., *Anthropology Today,* Chicago, University of Chicago Press, 1953.

———, "The Place of Boas in Anthropology," *American Anthropologist, 58*:1 (1956), 151–59.

———, "Gray's Epicyclical Evolution," *American Anthropologist, 60*:1 (1958), 31–38.

———, "Comment on: Tertius Chandler's Note," *American Anthropologist, 62*:3 (1960), 498.

———, *A Roster of Civilizations and Culture,* Chicago, Aldine, 1962.

LABARRE, WESTON, *The Human Animal,* Chicago, University of Chicago Press, 1954.

LANDES, RUTH, *The Ojibwa Woman,* Columbia University Contributions to Anthropology, 31, New York, Columbia University Press, 1938.

LANDSBERGER, HENRY A., *Hawthorne Revisited,* Ithaca, N. Y., Cornell University Press, 1958.

LAURENCE, WILLIAM L., "You May Live Forever," *Look, 17*:6 (1953), 29–31.

LAWRENCE, P., "Cargo Cults and Religious Beliefs among the

Garia," *International Archives of Anthropology,* 47:1 (1954), 1–20.

———, "The Madang District Cargo Cult," *South Pacific,* 8:1 (1955), 6–13.

LEAKEY, L. S. B., "Recent Discoveries at Olduvai Gorge, Tanganyika," *Nature, 181*:4616 (1958), 1099–1103.

———, "The Origin of the Genus Homo," in *Evolution after Darwin, 2, The Evolution of Man,* ed. Sol Tax, 1960, pp. 17–32

———, "Exploring 1,750,000 Years into Man's Past," *National Geographic, 120*:4 (1961), 564–89.

———, AND CLARK HOWELL, "The Discovery by L. S. B. Leakey of *Zinjanthropus boisei,*" *Current Anthropology, 1*:1 (1960), 76–77.

LEEDS, ANTHONY, AND ROBERT HARRISON, "Values and State of Knowledge in the Determination of Cultural Cycles—A Test of the Kroeber–Gray Hypothesis," paper presented at the Annual Meeting of the American Association for the Advancement of Science, Dec. 1960.

LEES, ROBERT B., "The Basis of Glottochronology," *Language, 29*:2, Pt. 1 (1953), 113–57.

LEHMAN, FREDERICK, "Some Anthropological Parameters of Civilization: The Ecology and Evolution of India's High Culture," 2 vols., unpublished Ph.D. Thesis, Columbia University, 1959.

LEHRMAN, D. S., "A Critique of Konrad Lorenz's Theory of Instinctive Behavior," *Quarterly Review of Biology, 28*:4 (1953), 337–63.

LEITES, NATHAN, "Trends in Affectlessness," *American Imago, 4*:2 (1947), 89–112.

———, AND ELSA BERNAUT, *Ritual of Liquidation,* Glencoe, Ill., Free Press, 1954.

LEWIS, OSCAR, *The Effects of White Contact upon Blackfoot Culture, with Special Reference to the Role of the Fur Trade,* Monographs of the American Ethnological Society, 6, Locust Valley, N. Y., Augustin, 1942.

LI CHIEN-NUNG, *The Political History of China, 1840–1928,*

trans. and ed. Ssu-yu Teng and Jeremy Ingalls, Princeton, Van Nostrand, 1956.

LIBBY, WILLARD F., *Radiocarbon Dating*, 2d ed., Chicago, University of Chicago Press, 1955.

LIFTON, ROBERT J., "Chinese Communist Thought Reform," in *Group Processes*, Transactions of the Third Conference 1956, ed. Bertram Schaffner, 1957, pp. 219–312.

——, *Thought Reform and the Psychology of Totalism*, New York, Norton, 1961.

LILLY, JOHN C., *Man and Dolphin*, Garden City, N. Y., Doubleday, 1961.

LIPPITT, RONALD, "The Psychodrama in Leadership Training," *Sociometry, 6*:3 (1943), 286–92.

LIVINGSTONE, FRANK B., GEORGE COWGILL, AND F. CLARK HOWELL, "More on Middle Pleistocene Hominids," *Current Anthropology, 2*:2 (1961), 117–20.

LOCRÉ, J. G., ED., *Procès-verbaux du conseil d'État, contenant la discussion du projet de Code civil*, 5 vols., Paris, Impr. de la République, 1803–04.

LOMAX, ALAN, "Folk Song Style," *American Anthropologist, 61*:6 (1959), 927–54.

——, "Song Structure and Social Structure," *Ethnology, 1*:4 (1962), 425–51.

LORENZ, KONRAD Z., "The Comparative Method in Studying Innate Behavior Patterns," in *Physiological Mechanisms in Animal Behavior*, J. F. Danielli and R. Brown, eds., Cambridge, Cambridge University Press, 1950, pp. 221–68.

——, "Morphology and Behavior Patterns in Closely Allied Species," in *Group Processes*, Transactions of the First Conference 1954, ed. Bertram Schaffner, 1955, pp. 168–220.

——, "Comparative Behaviorology," in *Discussions on Child Development, First Meeting, 1953*, J. M. Tanner and Bärbel Inhelder, eds., 1956, pp. 108–31.

——, "The Role of Aggression in Group Formation," in *Group Processes*, Transactions of the Fourth Conference 1957, ed. Bertram Schaffner, 1959, pp. 181–252.

LORIMER, FRANK, AND FREDERICK OSBORN, *Dynamics of Popula-*

tion: Social and Biological Significance of Changing Birth Rates in the United States, New York, Macmillan, 1934.

LOWENFELD, MARGARET, *Play in Childhood,* London, Gollancz, 1935.

————, "The World Pictures of Children: A Method of Recording and Studying Them," *British Journal of Medical Psychology, 18,* Pt. 1 (1939), 68–101.

————, *The Lowenfeld Mosaic Test,* London, Newman Neame, 1954.

————, ED., *On the Psychology of Children,* London, Institute of Child Development, n.d.

————, *Poleidoblocs,* London, Institute for Child Psychology, n.d. (pamphlet).

LOWIE, ROBERT H., *Culture and Ethnology,* New York, McMurtrie, 1917.

————, *An Introduction to Cultural Anthropology,* New York, Farrar and Rinehart, 1934; rev. ed. 1940, New York, Farrar and Rinehart.

————, *History of Ethnological Theory,* New York, Rinehart, 1937.

————, *Indians of the Plains,* The American Museum of Natural History Anthropological Handbook, 1, New York, McGraw-Hill, 1954.

————, "Boas Once More," *American Anthropologist, 58:*1 (1956), 159–64.

————, "Reminiscences of Anthropological Currents in America Half a Century Ago," *American Anthropologist, 58:*6 (1956), 995–1016.

LUSZKI, MARGARET B., *Interdisciplinary Team Research: Methods and Problems,* National Training Laboratories, Research Training Series, 3, New York, New York University Press, 1958.

McCLELLAND, DAVID C., *The Achieving Society,* Princeton, Van Nostrand, 1961.

————, "Business Drive and National Achievement," *Harvard Business Review, 40:*4 (1962), 99–112.

McCOLLUM, ELMER V., "Stanley Rossiter Benedict 1884–1936," *National Academy of Sciences Biographical Memoirs 27,* Washington, 1952, 155–77.

MacKay, Donald M., "The Nomenclature of Information Theory," in *Cybernetics,* Transactions of the Eighth Conference 1951, ed. Heinz von Foerster, 1952, pp. 222–23.

MacLeod, William C., "Certain Mortuary Aspects of Northwest Coast Culture," *American Anthropologist, 27*:1 (1925), 122–48.

———, *The American Indian Frontier,* New York, Knopf, 1928.

———, "On the Southeast Asiatic Origins of American Culture," *American Anthropologist, 31*:3 (1929), 554–60. ⋅

———, "The Nature, Origin, and Linkages of the Rite of Hookswinging: With Special Reference to North America," *Anthropos, 29* (1934), 1–38.

McLuhan, Herbert M., *The Gutenberg Galaxy: The Making of Typographic Man,* Toronto, University of Toronto Press, 1962.

McPhee, Colin, "Children and Music in Bali," *Djawa, 18*:6 (1938), 1–15; reprinted 1955, in *Childhood in Contemporary Cultures,* Margaret Mead and Martha Wolfenstein, eds., pp. 70–94.

———, *A House in Bali,* New York, Day, 1946.

McQuown, Norman A., and others, *A Natural History of an Interview,* n.d. (manuscript).

Maher, Robert F., *New Men of Papua,* Madison, University of Wisconsin Press, 1961.

Mandelbaum, David G., "Wolf-Child Histories from India," *Journal of Social Psychology, 17:* first half (1943), 25–44.

Marett, Robert R., *The Threshold of Religion,* 4th ed., London, Methuen, 1929.

Marschak, Marianne, "One Year among the Behavioral Scientists," *Psychiatry, 23*:3 (1960), 303–09.

Marshall, A. J., *Bower-Birds,* Oxford, Clarendon Press, 1954.

Masserman, Jules H., "Anxiety and the Art of Healing," in *Current Psychiatric Therapies, 1,* ed. Jules H. Masserman, New York, Grune and Stratton, 1961, pp. 216–38.

Matarazzo, Joseph D., George Saslow, and Ruth G. Matarazzo, "The Interaction Chronograph as an Instrument for Objective Measurement of Interaction Patterns during Interviews," *Journal of Psychology, 41:* first half (1956), 347–67.

MEAD, MARGARET, *Coming of Age in Samoa,* New York, Morrow, 1928; reprinted 1949, Mentor MP418, New York, New American Library.

————, *Growing Up in New Guinea,* New York, Morrow, 1930; reprinted 1953, Mentor MD255, New York, New American Library.

————, "Social Organization of Manua," *Bernice P. Bishop Museum Bulletin, 76,* Honolulu, 1930, 1–218.

————, "Talk-Boy," *Asia, 31*:3 (1931), 144–51.

————, *The Changing Culture of an Indian Tribe,* New York, Columbia University Press, 1932.

————, *Sex and Temperament in Three Primitive Societies,* New York, Morrow, 1935; reprinted 1950, Mentor MP370, New York, New American Library.

————, "Woman: Position in Society: Primitive," in *Encyclopedia of Social Sciences,* Edwin R. A. Seligman and Alvin Johnson, eds., *15,* 1935, 439–42.

————, ED., *Cooperation and Competition among Primitive Peoples,* New York, McGraw-Hill, 1937; rev. ed. 1961, BP123, Boston, Beacon.

————, "The Mountain Arapesh, I. An Importing Culture," *Anthropological Papers of The American Museum of Natural History, 36,* Pt. 3, New York, 1938, 139–349.

————, "The Mountain Arapesh, II. Supernaturalism," *Anthropological Papers of The American Museum of Natural History, 37,* Pt. 3, New York, 1940, 317–451.

————, "The Comparative Study of Culture and the Purposive Cultivation of Democratic Values," in *Science, Philosophy, and Religion, Second Symposium,* Lyman Bryson and Louis Finkelstein, eds., New York, Conference on Science, Philosophy and Religion, 1942, pp. 56–69.

————, "Our Educational Emphases in Primitive Perspective," *American Journal of Sociology, 48*:6 (1943), 633–39.

————, "Personality, the Cultural Approach to," in *Encyclopedia of Psychology,* ed. P. L. Harriman, New York, Philosophical Library, 1946, pp. 477–88.

————, "Professional Problems of Education in Dependent Countries," *Journal of Negro Education, 40*:3 (1946), 346–57.

————, *Male and Female,* New York, Morrow, 1949; reprinted 1955, Mentor MP369, New York, New American Library.

————, "The Mountain Arapesh, V. The Record of Unabelin with Rorschach Analyses," *Anthropological Papers of The American Museum of Natural History, 41,* Pt. 3, New York, 1949, 285–390.

————, "The Comparative Study of Culture and the Purposive Cultivation of Democratic Values, 1941–1949," in *Perspectives on a Troubled Decade: Science, Philosophy, and Religion 1939–1949, Tenth Symposium,* Lyman Bryson, Louis Finkelstein, and R. A. MacIver, eds., New York, Harper, 1950, pp. 87–108.

————, *The School in American Culture,* Cambridge, Harvard University Press, 1951.

————, *Soviet Attitudes toward Authority,* New York, McGraw-Hill, 1951; reissued 1955, New York, Morrow.

————, "The Study of National Character," in *The Policy Sciences,* Daniel Lerner and Harold D. Lasswell, eds., Stanford, Stanford University Press, 1951, pp. 70–85.

————, "What Makes the Soviet Character?" *Natural History, 60:*7 (1951), 296–303, 336.

————, "Review: *Methods in Structural Linguistics,* by Zellig S. Harris," *International Journal of American Linguistics, 18:*4 (1952), 257–60.

————, ED., *Cultural Patterns and Technical Change,* Paris, Unesco, 1953; reprinted 1955, Mentor MD134, New York, New American Library.

————, "National Character," in *Anthropology Today,* ed. A. L. Kroeber, 1953, pp. 642–67.

————, "Recommendations for the Organization of Group Research," in *The Study of Culture at a Distance,* Margaret Mead and Rhoda Metraux, eds., 1953, pp. 451–53.

————, "Cultural Discontinuities and Personality Transformation," *Journal of Social Issues,* Suppl. Ser., no. 8 (1954), 3–16.

————, "Manus Restudied: An Interim Report," *Transactions of The New York Academy of Sciences,* Ser. II, *16:*8 (1954), 426–32.

MEAD, MARGARET, "Research on Primitive Children," in *Manual of Child Psychology*, 2d ed., ed. Leonard Carmichael, New York, Wiley, 1954, pp. 735–80.

———, "The Swaddling Hypothesis: Its Reception," *American Anthropologist*, *56*:3 (1954), 395–409.

———, "Children and Ritual in Bali," in *Childhood in Contemporary Cultures*, Margaret Mead and Martha Wolfenstein, eds., 1955, pp. 40–51.

———, "Energy Changes under Conditions of Culture Change," *Sociometry and the Science of Man*, *18*:4 (1955), 201–11.

———, "The Implications of Insight—II," in *Childhood in Contemporary Cultures*, Margaret Mead and Martha Wolfenstein, eds., 1955, pp. 449–61.

———, *New Lives for Old: Cultural Transformation—Manus, 1928–1953*, New York, Morrow, 1956; reprinted 1961, Mentor MT324, New York, New American Library.

———, "Towards More Vivid Utopias," *Science*, *126*:3280 (1957), 957–61.

———, "Values for Urban Living," *Annals of the American Academy of Political and Social Science*, *314* (1957), 10–14.

———, "Cultural Determinants of Behavior," in *Behavior and Evolution*, Anne Roe and George G. Simpson, eds., 1958, pp. 480–503.

———, "The Group as the Unit of Social Evolution," *Man*, *63*, Art. 233 (1958), 178.

———, *An Anthropologist at Work: Writings of Ruth Benedict*, Boston, Houghton Mifflin, 1959.

———, "Apprenticeship under Boas," in *The Anthropology of Franz Boas*, ed. Walter Goldschmidt, Memoirs of the American Anthropological Association, 89, 1959, pp. 29–45.

———, "Closing the Gap between the Scientists and the Others," *Daedalus* (Winter 1959), 139–46.

———, "Cultural Factors in Community-Education Programs," in *Community Education*, ed. Nelson B. Henry, Chicago, Chicago University Press, 1959, pp. 66–96.

———, "Feral Children and Autistic Children," *American Journal of Sociology*, *65*:1 (1959), 75.

———, "Weaver of the Border," in *In the Company of Man*,

ed. Joseph B. Casagrande, New York, Harper, 1960, pp. 175–210.

———, "Cultural Determinants of Sexual Behavior," in *Sex and Internal Secretions,* 2 vols., 3d ed., ed. W. C. Young, Baltimore, Williams and Wilkins, 1961, *2,* pp. 1433–79.

———, "The Menninger Foundation: A Center of Innovation," *Menninger Quarterly, 15*:1 (1961), 1–5.

———, "The Social Sciences in the College of Liberal Arts and Sciences," in *The College of Liberal Arts and Sciences —Its Role in the 1960's,* Minneapolis, Minnesota, Lutheran Brotherhood Insurance Society [1961], pp. 11–15.

———, "Brushes of Comets' Hair," *Menninger Quarterly, 16*:2 (1962), 1–5.

———, "Anthropology and the Camera," in *The Encyclopedia of Photography, 1,* ed. Willard D. Morgan, New York, Greystone, 1963, pp. 166–84.

———, *Moeurs et sexualité en Océanie,* trans. Georges Chevassus, Paris, Plon, 1963.

———, "Patterns of Worldwide Cultural Change in the 1960's," in *Science, Technology, and Development: United States Papers Prepared for the United Nations Conference on the Application of Science and Technology for the Benefit of Less Developed Areas, 7, Social Problems of Development and Urbanization,* Washington [1963]. pp. 1–15.

———, "Some General Considerations," in *Expression of the Emotions in Man,* ed. Peter H. Knapp, 1963, pp. 318–27.

———, "*Totem and Taboo* Reconsidered with Respect," *Bulletin of the Menninger Clinic, 27*:4 (1963), 185–99.

———, "Vicissitudes of the Study of the Total Communication Process," in *Approaches to Semiotics,* T. E. Sebeok, A. S. Hayes, and M. C. Bateson, eds., The Hague, Mouton, 1964.

———, AND RUTH BUNZEL, EDS., *The Golden Age of American Anthropology,* New York, Braziller, 1960.

———, AND FRANCES C. MACGREGOR, *Growth and Culture,* New York, Putnam, 1951.

———, AND RHODA METRAUX, EDS., *The Study of Culture at a Distance,* Chicago, University of Chicago Press, 1953.

———, "Town and Gown: A General Statement," unpublished report prepared for Regional Plan Association, Program on Urban Research and Education, 1962.

MEAD, MARGARET, AND OTHERS, "Man in Space: A Tool and Program for the Study of Social Change," *Annals of The New York Academy of Sciences, 72,* Art. 4 (1958), 165–214.

———, AND THEODORE SCHWARTZ, "The Cult as a Condensed Social Process," in *Group Processes,* Transactions of the Fifth Conference 1958, ed. Bertram Schaffner, 1960, pp. 85–187.

———, AND MARTHA WOLFENSTEIN, EDS., *Childhood in Contemporary Cultures,* Chicago, University of Chicago Press, 1955; reprinted 1963, Phoenix P124, University of Chicago Press.

MEADE, EDWARD S., *Story of Gold,* New York, Appleton, 1908.

"Measures and Weights," *Encyclopaedia Britannica, 15,* 1956, 138–42.

MEDAWAR, P. B., *The Future of Man,* New York, Basic Books, 1960.

MEGGERS, BETTY J., ED., *Evolution and Anthropology,* Washington, Anthropological Society of Washington, 1959.

MENNINGER, KARL, *Love against Hate,* New York, Harcourt, Brace, 1942.

Mental Health in International Perspective: A Review made in 1961 by an International and Interprofessional Study Group, London, World Federation for Mental Health, 1961.

METRAUX, RHODA, "Parents and Children: An Analysis of Contemporary German Child-Care and Youth Guidance Literature," in *Childhood in Contemporary Cultures,* Margaret Mead and Martha Wolfenstein, eds., 1955, pp. 204–25.

———, "A Portrait of the Family in German Juvenile Fiction," in *Childhood in Contemporary Cultures,* Margaret Mead and Martha Wolfenstein, eds., 1955, pp. 253–76.

———, "Effects of Cultural Anticipation and Attitudes toward Aging," in *The Neurologic and Psychiatric Aspects of the Disorders of Aging,* Proceedings of the Association for Research in Nervous and Mental Disease, *35,* Baltimore, Williams and Wilkins, 1956, pp. 248–51.

————, "Immigrants and Natives in the Space Age," paper presented at the 40th Annual Meeting of the American Orthopsychiatric Association, March 1963.

MINER, HORACE, *St. Denis: A French–Canadian Parish,* Publications in Anthropology, Ethnological Series, Chicago, University of Chicago Press, 1939.

MISHKIN, BERNARD, *Rank and Warfare among the Plains Indians,* Monographs of the American Ethnological Society, 3, Locust Valley, N. Y., Augustin, 1940.

MIXTER, RUSSELL L., ED., *Evolution and Christian Thought Today,* Grand Rapids, Mich., Eerdmans, 1959.

MOCK, JAMES R., AND CEDRIC LARSON, *Words That Won the War: The Story of the Committee on Public Information 1917–1919,* Princeton, Princeton University Press, 1939.

MOONEY, JAMES, "The Ghost-Dance Religion and the Sioux Outbreak of 1890," *Fourteenth Annual Report of the Bureau of American Ethnology, 1892–1893,* Washington, 1896, 641–1136

"More on Lexicostatistics," *Current Anthropology, 1*:4 (1960), 338–45.

MORGAN, LEWIS H., *Ancient Society,* New York, Holt, 1877.

MORGENBESSER, SIDNEY, "Role and Status of Anthropological Theories," *Science, 128*:3319 (1958), 285–88.

————, "Letters: Anthropological Theories," *Science, 129*: 3345 (1959), 298, 347–48.

MOSELY, PHILIP E., "The Peasant Family: The Zadruga," in *The Cultural Approach to History,* ed. Caroline F. Ware, New York, Columbia University Press, 1940, pp. 95–108.

MOSTELLER, FREDERICK, AND OTHERS, *The Pre-election Polls of 1948: Report to the Committee on Analysis of Pre-election Polls and Forecasts,* New York, Social Science Research Council Bulletin, 60, 1949.

MULLER, HERMANN J., "The Guidance of Human Evolution," in *Evolution after Darwin, 2, The Evolution of Man,* ed. Sol Tax, 1960, pp. 423–62.

————, "Should We Weaken or Strengthen Our Genetic Heritage," in "Evolution and Man's Progress," *Daedalus* (Summer 1961), 432–50.

Murdock, George P., *Social Structure*, New York, Macmillan, 1949.

Murphy, Gardner, *Personality: A Biosocial Approach to Origins and Structure*, New York, Harper, 1947.

——, *Human Potentialities*, New York, Basic Books, 1958.

Murphy, Lois B., and collaborators, *The Widening World of Childhood: Paths toward Mastery*, New York, Basic Books, 1962.

Murray, H. A., and others, *Explorations in Personality*, London and New York, Oxford University Press, 1938.

Myrdal, Gunnar, *An American Dilemma*, New York, Harper, 1944; reprinted 1962, New York, Harper and Row.

——, *The International Economy*, New York, Harper, 1956.

——, *Rich Lands and Poor*, New York, Harper, 1957.

——, *Beyond the Welfare State*, New Haven, Yale University Press, 1960.

Needham, Joseph, *Science and Civilization in China*, 2, Cambridge, Cambridge University Press, 1956.

Nicolson, Marjorie H., "On Behalf of the Humanities," in "Toward an Honorable World," *Wilson College Bulletin*, 3:4 (1940), 11–19.

——, *Science and Imagination*, Ithaca, N. Y., Cornell University Press, 1956.

——, *Voyages to the Moon*, New York, Macmillan, 1960.

Noble, G. K., and H. T. Bradley, "The Mating Behavior of Lizards: Its Bearing on the Theory of Sexual Selection," *Annals of The New York Academy of Sciences*, 35, Art. 2 (1933), 25–100.

Nuffield House, Musgrave Park Hospital, Belfast: The Case History of a New Hospital Building, London, Nuffield Foundation Division for Architectural Studies, 1962.

Ogburn, William F., *Social Change with Respect to Culture and Original Nature*, New York, Huebsch, 1922.

——, "The Wolf Boy of Agra," *American Journal of Sociology*, 64:5 (1959), 449–54.

——, and Dorothy Thomas, "Are Inventions Inevitable," *Political Science Quarterly*, 37:1 (1922), 83–98.

OGDEN, JEAN, AND JESS OGDEN, *Small Communities in Action*, New York, Harper, 1947.

OLIVER, CHAD, *Shadows in the Sun*, Ballantine B91, New York, Ballantine Books, 1954.

OLIVER, DOUGLAS L., *The Pacific Islands*, Cambridge, Harvard University Press, 1952; reprinted 1961, Anchor N14, Garden City, N. Y., Doubleday.

"Origin of Species, The—A Centennial Symposium," *Australian Journal of Science, 22*:1 (1959), 8–49.

OSBORN, FAIRFIELD, *The Limits of the Earth*, Boston, Little, Brown, 1953.

PARSONS, ELSIE C., "Nativity Myth at Laguna and Zuni," *Journal of American Folk-Lore, 31*:120 (1918), 256–63.

———, "Pueblo-Indian Folk-Tales, probably of Spanish Provenience," *Journal of American Folk-Lore, 31*:120 (1918), 216–55.

———, "Spanish Elements in the Kachina Cult of the Pueblos," in *Proceedings of the Twenty-third International Congress of Americanists, New York, September 1928*, New York, 1930, pp. 582–603.

PARSONS, TALCOTT, "The Problem of Controlled Institutional Change: An Essay on Applied Social Science," *Psychiatry, 8*:1 (1945), 79–101.

PEARL, RAYMOND, *The Biology of Population Growth*, New York, Knopf, 1925.

PELL, CHARLES E., *The Law of Births and Deaths*, London, Fisher Unwin, 1921.

PETTIT, WALTER, *Case Studies in Community Organization*, New York and London, Century, 1928.

PIAGET, JEAN, *Language and Thought of the Child*, trans. Marjorie Warden, New York, Harcourt, Brace, 1926.

———, *Play, Dreams, and Imitation in Childhood*, trans. C. Gattegno and E. M. Hodgson, New York, Norton, 1951.

———, AND BÄRBEL INHELDER, *The Child's Conception of Space*, trans. F. J. Langdon and J. L. Lunzer, London, Routledge and Kegan Paul, 1956.

PITT–RIVERS, GEORGE H. L. F., *The Clash of Culture and the Contact of Races*, London, Routledge, 1927.

RABI, I. I., in "Symposium: The Physical Universe," in *Man's Contracting World in an Expanding Universe,* ed. Ben H. Bagdikian, Providence, R. I., Brown University, 1960, pp. 51–55.

[RADCLIFFE-]BROWN, A. R., "Three Tribes of Western Australia," *Journal of the Royal Anthropological Institute, 43* (1913), 143–94.

RADCLIFFE-BROWN, A. R., *The Andaman Islanders: A Study in Social Anthropology,* Cambridge, Cambridge University Press, 1922.

RADIN, PAUL, "The Winnebago Tribe," *Thirty-Seventh Annual Report of the Bureau of American Ethnology, 1915–1916,* Washington, 1923, 33–560.

RAPAPORT, DAVID, "Technological Growth and the Psychology of Man," *Psychiatry, 10*:3 (1947), 253–59.

————, ED., *Organization and Pathology of Thought: Selected Sources,* New York, Columbia University Press, 1951.

RAY, VERNE F., "Review of *Franz Boas: The Science of Man in the Making,* by Melville L. Herskovits," *American Anthropologist, 57*:1 (1955), 138–40.

————, "Rejoinder," *American Anthropologist, 58*:1 (1956), 164–70.

REED, KENNETH E., "Leadership and Consensus in a New Guinea Society," *American Anthropologist, 61*:3 (1959), 425–36.

REPORT OF THE COMMITTEE ON FOOD HABITS, "Manual for the Study of Food Habits," *National Research Council Bulletin, 111,* Washington, 1945; reprinted 1962.

REPORT OF THE SECOND BOWLING GREEN CONFERENCE, *The Education of Teachers: New Perspectives,* Washington, National Educational Association of the United States, 1958.

RICHARDSON, LEWIS F., *Arms and Insecurity,* Nicolas Rashevsky and Ernesto Trucco, eds., Pittsburgh, Boxwood Press, and Chicago, Quadrangle Books, 1960.

————, *Statistics of Deadly Quarrels,* Quincy Wright and C. C. Linau, eds., Pittsburgh, Boxwood Press, and Chicago, Quadrangle Books, 1960.

RICHTER, C. P., "The Self-selection of Diets," in *Essays in Biology in Honor of Herbert M. Evans,* Berkeley, University of California Press, 1943, pp. 499–605.

ROBINSON, JAMES H., *The Mind in the Making,* New York, Harper, 1921.

ROE, ANNE, "The Psychology of the Scientist: A Definite Personality Pattern, Encompassing a Wide Range of Traits, Characterizes the Creative Scientist," *Science, 134*:3477 (1961), 456–59.

———, AND GEORGE G. SIMPSON, EDS., *Behavior and Evolution,* New Haven, Yale University Press, 1958.

ROETHLISBERGER, F. J., AND W. J. DICKSON, *Management and the Worker,* Cambridge, Harvard University Press, 1939.

RÓHEIM, GÉZA, *The Riddle of the Sphinx,* London, Hogarth, 1934.

RUESCH, JURGEN, AND GREGORY BATESON, *Communication: The Social Matrix of Psychiatry,* New York, Norton, 1951.

RUSSELL, BERTRAND, *Has Man a Future?* New York, Simon and Schuster, 1962.

SAHLINS, MARSHALL D., AND ELMAN R. SERVICE, EDS., *Evolution and Culture,* Ann Arbor, University of Michigan Press, 1960.

SAMUEL, A. L., "Some Moral and Technical Consequences of Automation—A Refutation," *Science, 132*:3429 (1960), 741–42.

SARGENT, WILLIAM, *The Battle for the Mind,* Garden City, N. Y., Doubleday, 1957.

SASLOW, GEORGE, AND JOSEPH D. MATARAZZO, "A Technique for Studying Changes in Interview Behavior," in *Research in Psychotherapy,* Eli A. Rubinstein and Morris B. Parloff, eds., Washington, American Psychological Association, Division of Clinical Psychology, 1959, pp. 125–59.

SCHAFFNER, BERTRAM, ED., *Group Processes,* 5 vols., New York, Josiah Macy, Jr. Foundation, 1955–60.

Schools and Community Organization, The, Education and National Defense Series, Pamphlet 5, Washington, U.S. Office of Education, Federal Security Agency, 1944.

SCHWARTZ, LENORA SHARGO (Lenora Foerstal), "Cultural

Influence in Perception," unpublished Master's Essay, Stella Elkins Tyler School of Fine Arts of Temple University, 1959.

SCHWARTZ, THEODORE, "The Paliau Movement in the Admiralty Islands, 1946–1954," *Anthropological Papers of The American Museum of Natural History, 49,* Pt. 2, New York, 1962, 207–422.

————, AND MARGARET MEAD, "Micro- and Macro-cultural Models for Cultural Evolution," *Anthropological Linguistics, 3*:1 (1961), 1–7.

Science Center New York, n.d. (pamphlet).

"SCIENCE AND HUMAN SURVIVAL," *Science, 134*:3496 (1961), 2080–83.

SCOTT, HOWARD, *Technocracy: Science versus Chaos,* New York, Technocracy, 1933 (pamphlet).

SCOTT, JOHN P., *Animal Behavior,* Chicago, University of Chicago Press, 1958.

SEARS, PAUL B., "The Processes of Environmental Change by Man," in *Man's Role in Changing the Face of the Earth,* William L. Thomas, Jr., and others, eds., 1956, pp. 471–84.

SECOY, FRANK, *Changing Military Patterns on the Great Plains,* Monograph of the American Ethnological Society, 21, Locust Valley, N. Y., Augustin, 1953.

SELIGMAN, EDWIN R. A., *The Economic Interpretation of History,* New York, Columbia University Press, 1902; reissued 1961, 2d ed. rev., New York, Columbia University Press.

SEWARD, G. H., "Studies in the Reproductive Activities of the Guinea Pig, II. The Role of Hunger in Filial Behavior," *Journal of Comparative Psychology, 29*:1 (1940), 25–41.

SHAPIRO, HARRY L., *The Heritage of the Bounty,* rev. ed., Anchor N23, Garden City, N. Y., Doubleday, 1962.

SHAPLEY, HARLOW, "Man's Fourth Adjustment," *American Scholar, 25*:4 (1956), 453–57.

SHARP, ANDREW, *Ancient Voyagers in the Pacific,* Polynesian Society Memoir, 12, Wellington, New Zealand, Polynesian Society, 1956.

SIMONDS, PAUL E., "The Japan Monkey Center," *Current Anthropology, 3*:3 (1962), 303–05.

SIMPSON, GEORGE G., *The Major Features of Evolution,* Columbia Biological Series, 17, New York, Columbia University Press, 1953.

——, "The History of Life," in *Evolution after Darwin,* *1, The Evolution of Life,* ed. Sol Tax, 1960, pp. 117–80.

SINGH, J. A. L., AND R. M. Zingg, *Wolf Children and Feral Man,* New York, Harper, 1942.

SINNOTT, EDMUND W., L. C. DUNN, AND T. DOBZHANSKY, *Principles of Genetics,* 4th ed., New York, McGraw-Hill, 1950.

SKINNER, B. F., *Walden Two,* New York, Macmillan, 1948.

——, *Science and Human Behavior,* New York, Macmillan, 1953.

——, "The Science of Learning and the Art of Teaching," in *Programmed Learning: Theory and Research,* Wendell I. Smith and J. W. Moore, eds., Princeton, Van Nostrand, 1962, pp. 18–33.

SLADEN, WILLIAM J. L., "Social Structure among Penguins," in *Group Processes,* Transactions of the Second Conference 1955, ed. Bertram Schaffner, 1956, pp. 29–93.

SLEEPER, RAYMOND S., "The Technological Conflict," *Air University Quarterly Review, 14*:1, 2 (1962–63), 6–18.

SNOW, C. P., *Science and Government,* Mentor MP444, New York, New American Library, 1962.

SODDY, KENNETH, ED., *Mental Health and Infant Development,* 2 vols., New York, Basic Books, 1955.

SPENCER, ROBERT F., "Culture Process and Intellectual Current: Durkheim and Ataturk," *American Anthropologist, 60*:4 (1958), 640–57.

SPENGLER, OSWALD, *The Decline of the West,* trans. Charles F. Atkinson, New York, Knopf, 1932.

SPICER, EDWARD H., ED., *Human Problems in Technological Change: A Casebook,* New York, Russell Sage Foundation, 1952.

SPIRO, MELFORD E., "Culture and Personality: The Natural History of a False Dichotomy," *Psychiatry, 14*:1 (1951), 19–46.

——, *Kibbutz: Venture into Utopia,* Cambridge, Harvard University Press, 1956.

SPIRO, MELFORD E., *Children of the Kibbutz,* Cambridge, Harvard University Press, 1958.

STERN, BERNARD J., *Lewis Henry Morgan: Social Evolutionist,* Chicago, University of Chicago Press, 1931.

STEVENSON, ROBERT LOUIS, *A Child's Garden of Verses,* Baltimore, Penguin, 1948.

STEWARD, JULIAN H., "The Economic and Social Basis of Primitive Tribes," in *Essays in Anthropology Presented to A. L. Kroeber,* Berkeley, University of California Press, 1936, pp. 331–49.

———, ED., *Handbook of South American Indians,* 7 vols., Smithsonian Institution, Bureau of American Ethnology, Bulletin 143, Washington, 1946–59.

———, *Theory of Culture Change,* Urbana, University of Illinois Press, 1955.

———, AND OTHERS, *The People of Puerto Rico,* Urbana, University of Illinois Press, 1956.

STEWART, EVELYN S., "The Merrill–Palmer Institute—Deep Probe in the Science of Living," *Michigan Yearbook 1961, 3* (1961), 110–14, 206–07.

STOETZEL, J., *Jeunesse sans chrysanthème ni sabre,* Paris, Plon-Unesco, 1954.

STOVER, CARL F., ED., "The Encyclopaedia Britannica Conference on the Technological Order," *Technology and Culture, 3*:4 (1962), 380–658.

STRAUSS, LEWIS L., *Men and Decisions,* Garden City, N. Y., Doubleday, 1962.

SUGGS, ROBERT C., "The Archaeology of Nuku Hiva, Marquesas Islands, French Polynesia," unpublished Ph.D. Thesis, Columbia University, 1959.

———, *The Island Civilizations of Polynesia,* Mentor MD304, New York, New American Library, 1960.

———, "Sexual Customs of the Marquesas," n.d. (manuscript).

SURFACE, FRANK M., AND RAYMOND L. BLAND, *American Food in the World War and Reconstruction Period: Operations of the Organizations under the Direction of Herbert Hoover, 1914 to 1924,* Stanford, Stanford University Press, 1931.

SWADESH, MORRIS, "Lexicostatistic Dating of Prehistoric Ethnic Contacts," *Proceedings American Philosophical Society, 96* (1952), 452–63.

———, "Towards Greater Accuracy in Lexicostatistic Dating," *International Journal of American Linguistics,* 21:2 (1955), 121–37.

TANNENBAUM, FRANK, "Men and His Institutions," in *Miscelania de estudios dedicados a Fernando Ortiz, por sus discipulos, colegos y amigos,* 3 vols., Havana, 1955–57, *3,* pp. 1411–16.

———, "University Seminars: Anniversary Report," *Graduate Faculties Newsletter Columbia University,* May 1960, 1–5.

TANNER, J. M., "Growth and Constitution," in *Anthropology Today,* ed. A. L. Kroeber, 1953, pp. 750–70.

———, AND BÄRBEL INHELDER, EDS., *Discussions on Child Development,* 4 vols., New York, International Universities Press, 1957–60.

TARDE, G., *The Laws of Imitation,* trans. Elsie Parsons, New York, Holt, 1903.

TAX, SOL, ED., *Evolution after Darwin,* 3 vols., Chicago, University of Chicago Press, 1960.

———, AND OTHERS, EDS., *An Appraisal of Anthropology Today,* Chicago, University of Chicago Press, 1953.

TAYLOR, EDMOND, *The Fall of the Dynasties,* Garden City, N. Y., Doubleday, 1963.

TEILHARD DE CHARDIN, PIERRE, *The Phenomenon of Man,* trans. Bernard Wall, New York, Harper, 1959.

———, *The Divine Milieu,* trans. Bernard Wall, New York, Harper, 1960.

THOMAS, ELIZABETH M., *The Harmless People,* New York, Knopf, 1959.

THOMAS, WILLIAM L., JR., ED., *Current Anthropology,* Chicago, University of Chicago Press, 1956.

———, AND OTHERS, EDS., *Man's Role in Changing the Face of the Earth,* Chicago, University of Chicago Press, 1956.

THOMPSON, WILLIAM R., "Social Behavior," in *Behavior and*

Evolution, Anne Roe and George G. Simpson, eds., 1958, pp. 291–310.

THOMPSON, W. S., AND P. K. WHELPTON, *Population Trends in the United States*, New York, McGraw-Hill, 1933.

THORPE, WILLIAM H., *Learning and Instinct in Animals*, 2d ed., Cambridge, Harvard University Press, 1963.

TINBERGEN, N., *The Study of Instinct*, Oxford, Clarendon Press, 1951.

TINDALE, NORMAN B., "First Australian," *Pacific Discovery*, *9*:5 (1956), 6–13.

————, "Culture Succession in South Eastern Australia from Late Pleistocene to the Present," *Records of the South Australian Museum*, *13*:1 (1957), 1–49.

TOYNBEE, ARNOLD J., *The Study of History*, 2 vols., abridged by D. C. Sommervell, New York, Oxford University Press, 1947, 1957.

TRUMBULL, ROBERT, "Peking Opens a New Drive to Limit Population," *The New York Times*, June 16, 1963.

TYLER, R. W., "Study Center for Behaviorial Scientists," *Science*, *123*:3193 (1956), 405–08.

U.S. OFFICE OF STRATEGIC SERVICES ASSESSMENT STAFF, *Assessment of Men: Selection of Personnel for the Office of Strategic Services*, New York, Rinehart, 1950.

"Urbanization and Standard Language: A Symposium Presented at the 1958 Meetings of the American Anthropological Association," *Anthropological Linguistics*, *1*:3 (1959), 1–41.

VERCORS, *You Shall Know Them*, trans. Rita Barisse, Boston, Little, Brown, 1953.

VYGOTSKY, L. S., *Thought and Language*, ed. and trans. Eugenia Hanfmann and Gertrude Vakai, New York, Wiley and M.I.T. Press, 1962.

WADDINGTON, C. H., "The Biological Effects of Bomb Tests," *New Statesman and Nation*, *54* (June 8, 1957), 725–28.

————, *The Strategy of the Genes*, New York, Macmillan, 1957.

————, "Evolutionary Systems—Animal and Human," *Nature*, *183*:4676 (1959), 1634–38.

———, *The Ethical Animal,* New York, Atheneum, 1961.

———, "The Human Animal," in *The Humanist Frame,* ed. Julian S. Huxley, 1961, pp. 65–80.

———, "The Human Evolutionary System," in *Darwinism and the Study of Society,* ed. Michael Banton, 1961, pp. 63–81.

———, *The Nature of Life,* New York, Atheneum, 1962.

———, AND OTHERS, *Science and Ethics,* London, Allen and Unwin, 1942.

WAGLEY, CHARLES, *Amazon Town: A Study of Man in the Tropics,* New York, Macmillan, 1953.

WALLACE, ANTHONY F. C., "Handsome Lake and the Great Revival in the West," *American Quarterly, 4*:2 (1952), 149–65.

———, "Revitalization Movements," *American Anthropologist, 58*:2 (1956), 264:81.

WALTER, W. GREY, *The Living Brain,* New York, Norton, 1953.

———, *The Curve of the Snowflake,* New York, Norton, 1956.

WAX, MURRAY, "The Limitations of Boas' Anthropology," *American Anthropologist, 58*:1 (1956), 63–74.

WEDGWOOD, CAMILLA H., "Notes on the Marshall Islands," *Oceania, 13*:1 (1942), 1–23.

WEINRICH, URIEL, *Languages in Contact: Findings and Problems,* Publications of the Linguistic Circle of New York, 1, New York, Linguistic Circle of New York, 1953.

WELLS, H. G., *Joan and Peter: The Story of an Education,* New York, Macmillan, 1935.

WELTFISH, GENE, *The Origin of Art,* Indianapolis, Bobbs Merrill, 1953.

WELTY, JOEL C., *The Life of Birds,* New York, Knopf, 1963.

WESTERMARCK, EDWARD, *The History of Human Marriage,* 3 vols., 5th rev. ed., London, Macmillan, 1921.

WHITE, LESLIE A., "Energy and Evolution in Culture," *American Anthropologist, 45*:3 (1943), 335–56.

———, "The Concept of Culture," *American Anthropologist, 61*:2 (1959), 227–51.

WHITE, LESLIE A., *The Evolution of Culture,* New York, Mc-Graw-Hill, 1959.

WHITE, LYNN JR., "Tibet, India, and Malaya as Sources of Western Medieval Technology," *American Historical Review, 65*:3 (1960), 515–26.

———, *Medieval Technology and Social Change,* Oxford, Clarendon Press, 1962.

WHITE, WILLIAM ALLEN, *Objectives of the Committee to Defend America by Aiding the Allies,* New York, July 1940 (pamphlet).

WHITEHEAD, T. N., *The Industrial Worker,* Cambridge, Harvard University Press, 1938.

WHYTE, L. L., "Developmental Selection in Mutation," *Science, 132*:3440 (1960), 1692–94.

WHYTE, WILLIAM F., AND ALLAN R. HOLMBERG, "Human Relations of U.S. Enterprise in Latin America, IV. From Paternalism to Democracy: The Cornell–Peru Project," *Human Organization, 15*:3 (1956), 15–18.

WIENER, NORBERT, *Cybernetics,* New York, Wiley, 1948; 2d ed. 1961, New York, M.I.T. Press.

———, *The Human Use of Human Beings,* Boston, Houghton Mifflin, 1950; 2d rev. ed. 1954, Anchor A34, Garden City, N. Y., Doubleday.

———, "Some Moral and Technical Consequences of Automation," *Science, 131*:3410 (1960), 1355–58.

WILLEY, GORDON R., "The Early Great Styles and the Rise of the Pre-Columbian Civilizations," *American Anthropologist, 64*:1 (1962), 1–14.

WILLIAMS, C. A. S., *Outlines of Chinese Symbolism and Art Motives,* 3d ed., Shanghai, Kelly and Walsh, 1941.

WILLIAMS, F. E., "The Vailala Madness and the Destruction of Native Ceremonies in the Gulf Division," *Papuan Anthropology Report, 4,* Port Moresby, 1923, 1–72.

———, *Orokaiva Magic,* London, Oxford University Press, 1928.

———, "The Vailala Madness in Retrospect," in *Essays Presented to C. G. Seligman,* E. E. Evans-Pritchard and others, eds., London, Kegan Paul, 1934, pp. 369–79.

WILLIAMS, HENRY S., "Nest-Building—New Style," *Natural History, 34*:5 (1934), 431–46.

WILLIAMS, MOYRA, *Horse Psychology,* London, Methuen, 1956.

WILSON, THURLOW R., "Randomness of the Distribution of Social Organization Forms: A Note on Murdock's Social Structure," *American Anthropologist, 54*:1 (1952), 134-38.

WISSLER, CLARK, *Man and Culture,* New York, Crowell, 1923.

WITTFOGEL, KARL A., *Oriental Despotism,* New Haven, Yale University Press, 1957.

WOLFE, ALVIN, "Minerals and Power: Anthropology in a New Vein," paper presented at the Twenty-first Annual Meeting of the Society for Applied Anthropology, Kansas City, Mo., May 1961.

WOLFE, BERTRAM D., *Three Who Made a Revolution,* New York, Dial, 1948.

WOLFENSTEIN, MARTHA, "Fun Morality: An Analysis of Recent American Child-Training Literature," in *Childhood in Contemporary Cultures,* Margaret Mead and Martha Wolfenstein, eds., 1955, pp. 168–78.

———, *Disaster: A Psychological Essay,* Glencoe, Ill., Free Press, 1957.

Worldmark Encyclopedia of the Nations, The, New York, Harper, 1960.

WORSLEY, PETER, *The Trumpet Shall Sound,* London, MacGibbon and Kee, 1958.

WRIGHT, ESMOND, "Making History," *The Listener, 68*:1755 (1962), 803–04.

WURM, S. A., "The Changing Linguistic Picture of New Guinea," *Oceania, 31*:2 (1960), 121–36.

———, AND D. C. LAYCOCK, "The Question of Language and Dialect in New Guinea," *Oceania, 32*:2 (1961), 128–43.

WYNDHAM, JOHN, *The Midwich Cuckoos,* New York, Ballantine Books, 1957.

ZANDER, ALVIN F., AND RONALD LIPPITT, "Reality Practice as Educational Method," *Sociometry, 7*:2 (1944), 129–51.

Index of Sources*

* Excluded from this index are the bibliographical portions of Appendix B and the Fijian firewalking references in Appendix C.